STRUCTURING INTERNATIONAL PARTNERSHIP PROGRAMS:

How to Design and Draft for Sustainability, Efficiency, and Development Impact

A BOOK FOR BUILDERS

— Complete with Annotated Charter —

Andrea E. Stumpf

STRUCTURED
PARTNERSHIPS

To my daughter, my ultimate partner, for whom
my love knows no bounds or balance.

FOREWORD

In today's world, the scale and complexity of development problems call for collaboration across actors. That includes governments, civil society, the private sector, and international development agencies, positioned collectively at the center of cross-sectoral solutions. The limitations of single-sector, single-actor approaches are more evident than ever. It takes strong cooperation and broad coordination to address the technical, political, multidisciplinary, globally-interdependent challenges we face today.

Effective and sustainable collaboration across actors and sectors takes capacity, resources, and political will. It also takes the right institutional arrangements. If a partnership program is well-structured, many things happen: actors leverage their comparative advantages, partners build higher levels of trust, participants learn from doing to improve their efforts and foster innovation, potential turns into practical effect, resources turn into development impact, and ultimately the whole becomes greater than the sum of its parts. It is trite but true for those who have seen it in action.

This *Book for Builders* points the way. It encourages space for everyone to contribute—in my experience, every organization has something to contribute, whether resources, technical expertise, political legitimacy, access to stakeholders and beneficiaries, or more. In fact, partnership should never be about money. If the right meeting of ideas exists, and is sustained in the right institutional arrangements, money will follow. This book recognizes that the business of partnering is not a sum of transactional events, but a living, evolving package of interactions and interrelationships. It promotes understanding of the structural landscape as a path to informed decisions and solid foundations. And it asks partners to be thoughtful, intentional, and mindful, to find their balance and maximize their partnering potential.

A first step, perhaps less intuitive for partners who are sector experts, is recognizing the value of partnership expertise. I can say that from running a secretariat. Staff who face both inward and outward, as part of their organizations while also serving their partnership programs, need a special skillset. But expertise can also clarify who has what roles and responsibilities, how obligations and expectations are memorialized and aligned, and which trade-offs can be harnessed to build critical mass and consensus. Amateurish, volunteeristic approaches are bound to fall short.

Andrea Stumpf presents this partnership structuring as a practice area, and I think she is right. I have seen her practice her craft, as the bridge between legal and business aspects. There is tremendous value in this kind of structural awareness and expertise. This *Book for Builders* is a much-appreciated building block for the kind of collaboration this world needs.

Roby Senderowitsch
Practice Manager,
Governance Global Practice, Europe and Central Asia—West
World Bank

ACKNOWLEDGMENTS

As you page through this book, you will understand why my primary thanks go to my graphic designer, Joe Bernier. Joe has been the perfect partner for me, with my distinct aesthetic sensibilities. No matter what I sent him, all my layout files, cue cards, chicken scratch, PowerPoints, mark-ups, scans, questions, and suggestions, he took them in stride and made them work on the two-page spread. He didn't even flinch when I suggested eighty Mondrian-style pages and then sent him files upon files of mock-ups. As this is a *Book for Builders*, maybe it is fitting that building each page was half the fun. I could not have asked for a more capable, responsive, patient, even-keeled, tireless collaborator.

My thanks also go to my family, starting with my mother. She has no cause to scrutinize international partnership programs, but nonetheless read her way through this book. I have benefited from her diligence and attention to detail all my life, but hearing her list of items, chapter by chapter, was another level altogether. Between her and Lauri Scherer, my wonderfully personable and positive copy editor, I am especially grateful for the guardrails they brought to my creative impulses.

Lauri and Joe have been with me throughout this whole journey, from my *Primer for Partners* to this *Book for Builders*. Although I encourage others to write their own books, I also tell them you need a great team—like the one I have had. Both books in this series reflect Lauri's and Joe's terrific support over several years. For all the talk of partnerships, I am truly thankful for this one.

My daughter, too, gets my immense thanks. Having weathered the *Primer* with me, she also actively supported and reassuringly humored my constant attentions to "book two," occasionally commenting on my obsession with structured pancakes, but always giving me more than enough room to indulge my passion. Once she agreed to be my illustrator again, there was no stopping this book. It gives me great joy to have my daughter contribute her own brand of creativity to this project, as we give her Männlein their international debut.

Looking back at my greatest inspiration for this practice area, I again want to give credit with deep gratitude to my favorite manager and mentor, Tom Duvall, who hired me into the World Bank and was my Chief Counsel for many years. He created an expansive space in the Legal Department for business teams to realize their partnering ambitions, a space in which his staff flourished, as did the partnerships. Omri Sender, a former World Bank colleague and international law expert, also merits special mention for his ever-ready support and encouraging feedback.

These days I also give thanks to my clients, who not only champion international partnering, but also strive to partner sustainably, efficiently, inclusively, and impactfully. The privilege of working with Hermann Amecke, Inga Beie, Martina Gaus, Björn Gillsäter, Avnish Gungadardoss, Irina Hotz, Mustafa Hussain, Olivier Lavinal, Clare Narrod, Augustina Nikolova, Nicole Pflock, Dan Pimlott, Keir Prince, and many others has kept me inspired and persuaded, more than ever, that international partnering can benefit from more informed, more thoughtful, and more intentional structuring. Together we understand that effective international partnering *and* structuring are imperative for the achievement of our global and local goals.

PREFACE

Never say never. All through law school I had sworn not to go into corporate practice, since I was public sector–bound, and then—as life happens—I found myself in the Paris and New York offices of a U.S. law firm assigned to global securities offerings and mergers and acquisitions. After avoiding any and all law school classes about stocks and shareholders, duties and disclosure, representations, indemnifications, and corporate anything, I got a mild case of panic. Then some good soul handed me the newly minted *Model Stock Purchase Agreement with Commentary*, a 400-page tome published by the American Bar Association (ABA). I read page after page and the blinders fell off. Suddenly I saw the meanings behind the words, and the reasons behind the clauses. I could read a stock purchase agreement and know where I was in the deal. From there it was but a short step to the negotiating table, where my fresh confidence of perspective and range of understanding let me thrust and parry. I saw options and alternatives—crucially, I could find solutions, not just problems—in what had previously been an impenetrable black box.

This book is offered in the same spirit. Whether you are interested in a specific topic (look at the table of contents and index to find your subject area) or a broad understanding (follow the logic from front to back), I hope this exploratory guide provides the same kind of insights that opened doors for me. Unlike the ABA guide, which was the product of some thirty senior lawyers over nine years, this book offers but one practitioner's voice from one transactional career. I offer this guide as a starting point to prove that the topic is worthy of a community of practice. Perhaps with time, as "structured partnerships" in the international arena become a recognized practice area with acknowledged experts, this resource can broaden into a collective sense of what works and how.

This is the second book in a series of two: first *A Primer for Partners* (2019) and now *A Book for Builders*. These two books are meant to be read side-by-side, and this second book amply cross-refers to the first. You can use the *Primer* to understand the fundamental components within which the design and drafting dynamics explained in this book occur. You can use this book to think about the different ways to create and maintain the edifice for the benefit of all partners and their beneficiaries.

Book one explains how structure works. Partners are the owners and occupants; they need to understand their options, make informed decisions, and then live their partnerships. Book two explains how structure happens. Builders—like lawyers, accountants, policy drivers, and risk managers—are the architects and construction crew. They need to decide what goes where, how it fits together, where to fasten the nuts and bolts, where to put the windows and doors. This book pitches a solid floor (the charter) and a secure roof (the governing body) to make room for all the design details in between. This is about turning the house into a home for all those who live and breathe their international partnerships.

International partnership programs are wonderful constructs in the international arena. We owe it to each other and the world to make the most of them.

Andrea E. Stumpf
December 2020

TABLE OF CONTENTS

—— Complete with Annotated Charter ——

SEVEN LISTS OF ELEVEN

PRIMER FOR PARTNERS OVERVIEW

*Designing International Partnership Programs—A Primer for Partners:
How to Structure for Sustainability, Efficiency, and Development Impact*

PART ONE: MAIN FOUNDATIONS

In this Part, we review basic types and core elements of international partnership programs, a particularly popular form of structured partnership for international collaborations.

Chapter 1: Ten Take-Aways
Every writer has a point of view, so this is full disclosure—here are ten one-liners that carry throughout the pages of this book.

Chapter 2: Like Rock, Like Water
It takes stability to have flexibility, and it takes both to have sustainable, effective, and impactful international partnership programs.

Chapter 3: Typology
In locating international partnership programs on the spectrum of structured partnerships, we pay special attention to one-stop-shops and international platforms.

Chapter 4: International Partnership Programs
Deconstructing international partnership programs, we identify six main "collectives": decision making, funding, support, activities, knowledge, and brand.

Chapter 5: Governing Bodies
Taking the first collective, we consider informal governing bodies—as distinguished from formal, corporate bodies—from both institutional (partner) and individual (representative) perspectives.

Chapter 6: Secretariats
Here we shine a light, with great appreciation, on the essential and wide-ranging secretariat support functions that hold international partnership programs together.

Chapter 7: Trust Funds
Not all partnership programs have them, but when they do, it helps to understand trust funds as accounts in relation to donors, recipients, roles, money flows, and the mechanics that make them so popular.

PART TWO: BUSINESS CONSIDERATIONS

In this Part, we pick up aspects to help partners—as organizations and individuals—make business decisions.

Chapter 1: Ten Tried and True Tips
Clear, clean, modular, flexible, comprehensive, balanced, contextual, ready, aware, and simple—these are watchwords for designing international partnership programs.

Chapter 2: Structure
Different ways of seeing structure make for more informed choices: upstream/downstream, bilateral/multilateral, contractual/structural, follow the power/follow the money, and more.

Chapter 3: Trade-Offs
Trade-offs abound. Examples like the horizontal buy-in spectrum, the central harmonization spectrum, and the vertical continuity spectrum reveal how structural choices can manage and maximize trade-offs.

Chapter 4: Risk and Review
How partners see and assess partnering opportunities and risks, from start to finish, affects the stability and effectiveness of their engagement in international partnership programs.

Chapter 5: Partners and People
We come as partners—institutions structurally and people operationally—and convene and collectivize organically. Remembering this can help us manage our partnering dynamics.

PART THREE: KEY ELABORATIONS

In this Part, we take some deeper dives on select topics that can make a big difference.

Chapter 1: Partnering Internationally
Benefits of partnering in the international arena are best preserved if they are better appreciated, including in terms of what law applies and how that affects governing bodies.

Chapter 2: Decision Making
Here we explore the virtues of consensus decision making and the benefits of no objection decision making, breaking each mode down and showing exactly how it works.

Chapter 3: Supporting Entities
In full recognition of the central supporting entity role, we unpack what that means for partners, including the supporting entities themselves.

Chapter 4: Custodial Effect
In this chapter, we highlight the unacknowledged role of the partnership program "custodian," which usually attaches to the legal entity function and fills in as needed.

Chapter 5: Synergistic Conflicts
By taking a closer look at "conflicts of interest" in partnership programs, we discover inherent and intentional features that are in fact valuable partnership synergies.

Chapter 6: Trustee Types
From full trustees to limited trustees, and modular combinations and downstream variations, different options let partners position trustees to fit partnership program purposes.

Chapter 7: Use of Funds
This chapter gives us a chance to consider fund use not just as a trust fund matter but more broadly from partnership program perspectives.

Chapter 8: Fund Use Responsibility
As a corollary to fund use, here we look at different kinds of responsibility: implementation responsibility, two kinds of fiduciary responsibility, and collective oversight responsibility.

BOOK FOR BUILDERS OVERVIEW

Structuring International Partnership Programs—A Book for Builders:
How to Design and Draft for Sustainability, Efficiency, and Development Impact

PART ONE: INTERNATIONAL PARTNERING

In this Part One, we get the lay of the land of international partnership programs, with an introduction to key elements and characteristics, followed by a catalogue of ways they interrelate, all in the interest of framing structure and design decisions and drafting.

Chapter 1: Eleven Take-Aways
Every writer has a point of view, so this is full disclosure—here are eleven themes that carry throughout the pages of this book.

Chapter 2: Context
To start, we review the key elements of our subject: being international, being structural, and doing that through partnership programs and trust funds.

Chapter 3: Dynamics
Within this landscape, we consider four key dynamics about international partnership programs: They are everywhere and nowhere, contextual, organic, and a practice area.

Chapter 4: Balance
After introducing the "like rock, like water" stability and flexibility of international partnership programs in the *Primer*, we widen the scope to see that, ultimately, it's all in the balance.

Chapter 5: Dualities
Everywhere we look, we can find dualities at play, all of which factor into partnership program balance.

PART TWO: CHARTEROGRAPHY

In this Part Two, we zero in on charters, the key document that creates, defines, and sustains international partnership programs, first with some context and then a prototype, followed by a systematic unpacking, clause-by-clause, that brings all the concepts in the *Primer for Partners* and this *Book for Builders* to bear and makes them meaningful.

Chapter 1: Constitutive Documents
Charters and similar documents that establish partnership programs and are owned by the collective have many virtues. We consider what these documents are, why they are useful, and how they work.

Chapter 2: The Prototype Charter for International Partnership Programs with Trust Funds
Given the many variables and variations of international partnership programs, it is challenging to create a "model" charter that is anything more than a placeholder. But this prototype charter gives us a useful starting point to layer in specifics.

Chapter 3: The Clause-by-Clause Guide for the Annotated Charter
To give the choices around charter drafting some structure, this short guide explains how each clause is put through three filters: first with an explanation of its relevance, then with drafting variations to address common cases, and finally with questions that partners may want to consider.

Chapter 4: The Annotated Charter Featuring Clause-by-Clause Analysis
Clause-by-clause, we tackle the prototype charter from front to back, unpacking key points for legal drafters and decision makers to consider when formulating their own partnership program manifestos.

PART THREE: INTENTIONAL LAWYERING

In this Part Three, we study, we study words, documents, and deliberations from a practitioner's perspective: being dexterous while holding the pen, bringing coherence and comfort through careful alignment, and creating closure by making it all come together—plus a closing shout-out to those who make it happen.

Chapter 1: Deft Drafting
Whether a lawyer or someone else is putting the partnership program to paper, a sense of articulation as architecture, along with some sly ways to work with words, can make for a steady hand.

Chapter 2: Agile Alignment
Part of the art lies in aligning adopted documents and signed agreements. This chapter presents a step-by-step guide on how to mesh the charter with contribution agreements.

Chapter 3: Practical Packaging
Moving from words to documents to negotiations, we build a holistic approach to establishment documents, treating them as a package.

Chapter 4: A Taxonomy of Trust Fund Agreements
Recognizing the importance of international trust funds as drivers and definers of partnership programs, we delve into fund flow agreements from upstream to downstream and beyond.

Coda: The Role of the Lawyer
Hail to the lawyers! We cannot leave the subject without recognizing the unsung heroes that orchestrate and integrate, from business plans to memorialized programs, from disparate views to common understandings, from concepts to closure, and thereafter for ongoing support.

KEY TERMS

For ease of reference, here are brief descriptions of frequently used terms that are more fully described throughout this book:

CUES

>@ see "more at" a cross-referenced chapter or section

BfB *Book for Builders* (this book)

PfP *Primer for Partners* (the other book)

ABBREVIATIONS

AKA also known as

COI conflict(s) of interest

CSO civil society organization

IFI international financial institution

M&E monitoring and evaluation

MDB multilateral development bank

NGO nongovernmental organization

ODA official development aid

P&I privileges and immunities

TAC technical advisory committee

TOR terms of reference

UN United Nations

STRUCTURES

Coordination partnerships: A type of international partnership program whose partners convene through an informal governing body for coordination and light collaboration, primarily to share knowledge and experience, without dedicated pooled funding and with separate downstream implementation outside the partnership program; AKA learning platforms.

Dedicated entity partnerships: Legal personality partnerships that consist of new entities under domestic law that are created to convene and implement the partnerships, often mobilizing major funding; with no reliance on existing legal functions, these are not partnership programs; AKA, for example, international institutions under the Swiss Host State Act.

Embedded partnerships: Partnerships with all partnering inputs provided upfront and actual implementation delegated to a supporting entity; with no shared governance, these are not partnership programs.

International partnership programs: Partnership programs with mostly international partners, like national governments and international organizations, that engage and convene in the international arena.

International platforms: A type of international partnership program with a strong informal governing body that convenes around a trust fund with a limited trustee, usually with multiple downstream fiduciaries.

One-stop-shops: A type of international partnership program for which the supporting entity plays multiple roles, including as full trustee for a dedicated trust fund.

Partnership programs: Structured partnerships that are not legally incorporated entities and instead feature shared governance through informal governing bodies, rely on existing supporting entities, and may have dedicated funding sources, like trust funds.

Structured partnerships: Partnership arrangements by which partners participate through collective terms and mechanisms that include the use of structure to define and delineate roles and responsibilities.

Trust-funded partnership programs: Partnership programs that are supported by one or more dedicated trust funds.

Umbrella arrangements: A type of international partnership program that links multiple funding vehicles and programs through a common, overarching informal governing body.

COMPONENTS AND ROLES

Contributions: Funds flowing to trust funds from donors, including paid cash contributions and to-be-paid contributions receivable.

Donors: Contributors of funds to trust funds under terms agreed with trustees; AKA development partners.

TWO-TIER RECIPIENTS

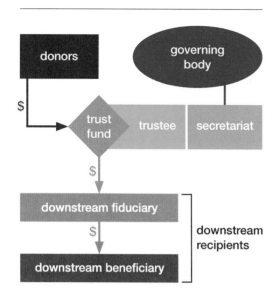

Downstream beneficiaries: Recipients that directly receive funds from either trustees or downstream fiduciaries for fund use, usually under supervision; AKA grantees, beneficiary recipients (including beneficiary countries).

Downstream fiduciaries: Downstream recipients that directly receive both funds and fiduciary responsibility from trustees; or, by continuity of function, full trustees that keep downstream responsibility; AKA fiduciary entities, fiduciary recipients, implementation support agencies.

Downstream recipients: Recipients of funds disbursed from trust funds either directly from trustees (as downstream fiduciaries or downstream beneficiaries) or subsequently from downstream fiduciaries (as downstream beneficiaries) under agreed terms.

Full trustees: Trustees that have fiduciary responsibilities (including supervision) for any use of funds from their trust funds, including by their direct downstream beneficiaries, potentially along with other roles, like secretariat-type functions.

Governing bodies: Shared governance, either decision-making or advisory, through informal bodies with agreed participants, roles, and responsibilities; AKA governing councils, steering committees, advisory committees (preferably not "boards").

Grants: Funds flowing from trustees or downstream fiduciaries to downstream beneficiaries.

Implementers: Entities with implementation responsibilities, including some trustees and downstream recipients.

Inhouse secretariats: Secretariats that are part of supporting entities; AKA embedded secretariats.

Limited trustees: Trustees that have fiduciary responsibilities for funds in their trust funds only as long as they hold the funds, up to the point of transfer to downstream fiduciaries; AKA pass-through trustees, fiscal agents.

Members: Decision-making participants in governing bodies of international partnership programs.

Multi-donor trust funds: Trust funds that receive contributions from more than one donor.

Observers: Non-decision-making participants in governing bodies of international partnership programs.

SUPPORTING ENTITY

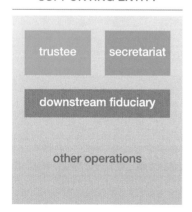

Secretariats: Administrative units, usually in supporting entities, that have agreed partnership program roles and responsibilities, particularly vis-à-vis informal governing bodies; AKA coordination units, focal points, management units, program teams, inhouse secretariats, embedded secretariats.

Supporting entities: Existing international organizations, like MDBs or in the UN, that provide support to partnership programs in addition to their regular operations, including as secretariats, trustees, and downstream fiduciaries.

Trustees: Administrators and financial managers of trust funds, including full trustees and limited trustees, that manage funds on behalf of donors and are part of supporting entities; AKA fiduciary entities.

Trust funds: Accounts managed by trustees on terms agreed with donors that support international partnership programs and are usually operated by international organizations outside of domestic laws.

CHARACTERISTICS

Downstream: The part of partnership programs that involves activities and results, which in the case of trust funds includes trustee disbursements and implementation, often by downstream recipients.

Formal: Governed by domestic statutory frameworks and jurisprudence, as with incorporated legal entities established under domestic law.

Informal: Not governed by domestic statutory frameworks and jurisprudence, as with international partnership programs, which are not incorporated.

Modular: Consisting of discretely identifiable structural components, usually based on designated roles and responsibilities, that can be fit together in different ways within a partnership program.

Upstream: The part of partnership programs that includes donor contributions and shared governance, potentially including fund allocation decisions by governing bodies.

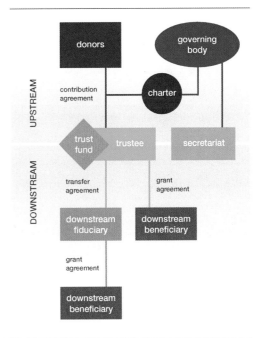

A Second Look at Some Labels

On the question of who's who, it is good to say what you mean. Some cases in point:

"Founding partners": This is a label that creeps into many a charter, but is often best avoided for three reasons. First, why make such a bold distinction between classes of partners? This defies the spirit of the collective from day one. Second, are founding partners forever? Their status is relevant in the beginning, but less so over time. It is quite possible that a founding partner later wants out, so then what? And third, what does it actually mean? When the label is used, it usually remains unclear whether founding status has any implications, like carrying greater or lesser responsibility. Rather than memorialize an ambiguous term, think about using this label only if it is a distinct category with defined status and terms.

"Development partners": This is a euphemism for donors of official development aid (ODA), which refers to so-called developed countries using their taxpayer funds to help so-called developing countries. In this book, we simply say "donors" when thinking of trust funds, although "contributors" could be used more generically. The genesis of this euphemism hints at a discomfort about money. The power of the purse can be wielded with great effect, but not necessarily in (ahem) polite, diplomatic company. More overtly, however, this label reflects a deliberate intent of development financiers to be viewed as partners on par with other partners, as serious collaborators and constructive content providers, not just money buckets. Supporting entities have the same cross to bear. Rather than being relegated merely to funding or service roles, both donors and supporting entities usually want to be known as partners. The problem with claiming development partners as a header for donors is that they are hardly the only development partners. Without taking away any of the good intent, this book refers directly to donors and leaves room for every participant to be a development partner.

"Implementing entities": This is often used downstream to describe fiduciary recipients—the mid-level—of international platforms. (>@ PfP: Trust Funds—Recipients—Fiduciary Recipients) That is unfortunate, misleading, and confusing. Fiduciary recipients may do some implementing, and in many cases, like United Nations entities, that may be their only *modus operandi*. However, many fiduciary recipients limit their own implementation to only what is necessary, with a clear preference for implementation by their downstream recipients. Over the years, this on-granting approach has become synonymous with country ownership and capacity building. As a result, the real implementation often happens one level below, making the term "implementing entity" an oversimplifying misnomer for fiduciary recipients. In this book, the more precise terms "fiduciary recipient" and "downstream recipient" seek to overcome poor labeling and point to more modular implementation structures.

DOCUMENTS

Charters: Baseline establishment documents adopted by informal governing bodies that set forth agreed terms defining roles, responsibilities, governance, and other essential partnership aspects.

Constitutive documents: Baseline establishment documents, such as charters and fund flow agreements, that set forth agreed terms for structured partnerships.

Contribution agreements: Fund flow agreements between donors and trustees for trust fund contributions.

Fund flow agreements: Agreements with trustees to accompany either the receipt of funds into, or disbursement of funds out of, trust funds, including contribution agreements, grant agreements, and transfer agreements.

Grant agreements: Fund flow agreements between downstream beneficiaries and full trustees or downstream fiduciaries for trust fund disbursements.

Transfer agreements: Fund flow agreements between downstream fiduciaries and limited trustees for trust fund disbursements.

Codes of conduct: Itemization of expected and encouraged behavior by partners regarding partnership program activities, usually approved by governing bodies as partnership-wide frameworks.

Framework agreements: Bilateral agreements that frame donor-trustee relationships at a higher level than the subsequent contribution agreements that they govern.

Holding agreements: Bilateral agreements that enable donors to commit their contributions to trustees prior to establishment of the trust funds for which those contributions are intended.

Operations manuals: Detailed compilations of procedures, standards, requirements, responsibilities, expectations, relationships, and other operational aspects governing activity implementation.

Rules of procedure: Rules agreed by governing bodies to govern the conduct of their business during and between meetings, including in relation to their secretariats.

LEGAL TERMS

Accountability gap: The lack of privity a donor has with respect to fiduciary terms, including recourse, governing its funds when a limited trustee enters into a transfer agreement that passes both funds and fiduciary responsibility to a downstream fiduciary.

Adopted: A governing body decides to approve a document for itself, as with a charter adopted by consensus.

Binding: Reflecting the intent of the parties (signatories) to an agreement that agreed terms are committed to and enforceable against each other.

Incorporation by reference: When an agreement refers to another document or set of agreed terms for the purpose of bringing the document or those terms into their agreement as part of its totality, as when a charter is incorporated by reference into contribution agreements.

Prevalence: For the case when terms in one agreement conflict with terms in another, a clear ranking as to which terms take precedence over the other terms, usually specified on an agreement level.

Privity: Being a party to an agreement, normally as a direct signatory of the agreement.

Privileges and immunities: Legal protections like organizational immunity (no search or seizure of property or assets), staff immunity (no judicial process against individual staff), and archival immunity (no access to documents and records) that sovereigns grant each other or specific entities.

Signed: Two (or more) signatory entities provide signatures through their respective, duly authorized representatives, as with a bilaterally signed contribution agreement.

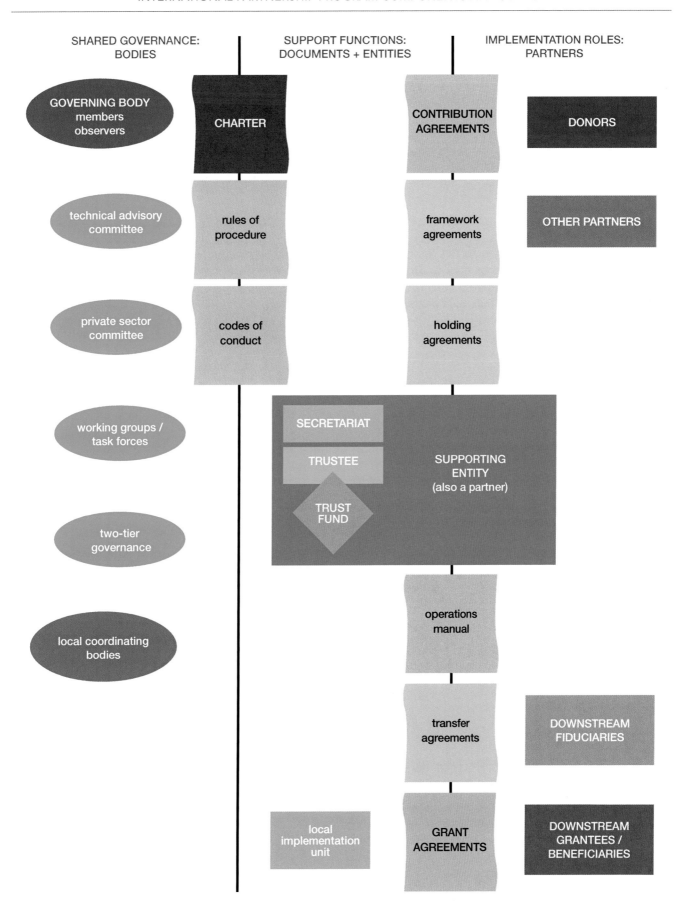

INTRODUCTION

You're an expert in your field—be it climate smart agriculture, extractive industries transparency, reproductive health, sustainable fisheries, internally displaced persons—and you know your stuff. As the team lead, you also know you need to convene and collaborate to implement and advocate, to make a difference. And therein lies the rub. For all your expertise, none of it directly pertains to structuring and designing the partnership platform that is essential to achieving results.

What's worse than lacking the expertise you need? Being the purported expert that you turn to. Say you're the lawyer being asked to structure, draft, and negotiate this partnership platform—you're the expert, you do deals, you paper transactions— but this is one topic you never learned in law school, have no experience with, and no resources to boot. But you do have a policy environment to contend with, and maybe some standard forms, most of which apply by analogy, along with specific requirements and expectations of other partners, not to mention the inevitable urgency to meet impending deadlines.

This is not a happy situation, for anyone—not the sector-expert team, nor the professional lawyer, nor the other partners, or, most critically, the intended beneficiaries. And yet, lack of structuring and design know-how is what usually happens.

So let this book empower you. Let it lift the curtain, open the window, and shine a light on the elements and angles of what it means to partner internationally. Indeed, let's just take this topic outdoors, where we can focus on international partnership programs as a favorite, hybrid modality that uses existing legal and operational infrastructure, while adding bespoke governance, programming, and branding to come up with effective partnering platforms. And let's see what amazing role charters can play.

You need not be an expert to understand a few fundamentals about international partnership programs. And yet, some basic understanding can help you consider alternatives, make informed choices, and create fit-for-purpose arrangements that are sustainable, efficient, and impactful. It's about being collective and contextual. It's about knowing your goals, knowing your roles, and keeping it simple. And, like rock, like water, it's all in the balance.

Welcome to the wide and wonderful world of international partnership programs and international trust funds. As a partner, but especially as a practitioner, you *can* get your arms around the topic, be a resource for your business and professional peers, and navigate the synergies and dualities that make this area both an art and a science—a practice area where your understanding and ideas matter.

How Best to Read This Book

For a smooth ride to a sustained, efficient, and impactful destination, please follow these guideposts:

1 *Nothing in this guide is gospel.*

Whatever your circumstances, this guide is meant to give you principles, placeholders, and pointers. Read about proposed approaches, potential pitfalls, and accompanying commentary, and check them against the reality of your own circumstances.

2 *Use this guide to get the gist.*

This book goes out on a limb to take positions and suggest good practices, but only as starting points to get you going. You are your own architect and can leverage the creative space in the international arena to your advantage.

3 *Look up your specific topic.*

This book intentionally breaks material out into lots of topics and subtopics. It tries to treat each topic comprehensively—apologies in advance for any overlaps—with ample cross-referencing (look for >@). Zero in on what you need.

4 *Read for common threads.*

Many of the issues covered here are crosscutting and correlated. The themes speak to each other, and undergird, layer, complement, and circle back. Wherever you start to read, let the concepts carry you.

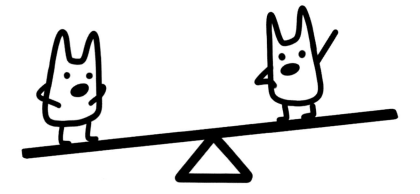

PART 1

INTERNATIONAL PARTNERING

Being International Partners

In this Part One, we get the lay of the land of international partnership programs, with an introduction to key elements and characteristics, followed by a catalogue of ways they interrelate, all in the interest of framing structure and design decisions and drafting.

Chapter 1: Eleven Take-Aways

Every writer has a point of view, so this is full disclosure—here are eleven themes that carry throughout the pages of this book.

Chapter 2: Context

To start, we review the key elements of our subject: being international, being structural, and doing that through partnership programs and trust funds.

Chapter 3: Dynamics

Within this landscape, we consider four key dynamics about international partnership programs: They are everywhere and nowhere, contextual, organic, and a practice area.

Chapter 4: Balance

After introducing the "like rock, like water" stability and flexibility of international partnership programs in the *Primer*, we widen the scope to see that, ultimately, it's all in the balance.

Chapter 5: Dualities

Everywhere we look, we can find dualities at play, all of which factor into partnership program balance.

IT'S ALL IN
THE
BALANCE

1 ELEVEN TAKE-AWAYS

1   Partnering needs balance to achieve sustainability, efficiency, and impact.

2   International partnership programs rely on the written word to exist and operate.

3   Adopted documents, like charters, reflect and empower the collective.

4   Charters embody stability and flexibility, with room to adapt and adjust over time.

5   Fit-to-context structures create synergies, leverage dualities, and foster inclusion.

6   For every approach, there are alternatives, variations, and permutations.

7   Due diligence and risk assessments belong to each individual partner.

8   Lawyers are there to bridge common vision and common ground to common documents.

9   Trust funds feed into partnership programs, not the other way around.

10   Adopted documents and signed agreements should align and work in tandem.

11   The future lies in global public goods. We need international partnership programs to get us there!

2 CONTEXT

Here we are, in the international arena. And here we go, talking about structure and design. We are focused on international partnership programs, along with their favorite supporting cast, international trust funds. Each of these four dimensions deserves some explanation.

The International Angle

Picture yourself in a furnished room. Somebody spent a lot of time on the interior design: positioning a couch, chair, and coffee table set, matching upholstery to the rug, putting just the right trinkets on the mantle, and arranging bright lights to reach every corner. It is a well-defined, well-honed, well-settled space. Welcome to corporate structures.

Now let's step outside, into the international arena. We can get on the swing, climb a tree, or put out the picnic blanket. We may have to deal with a few bugs and a chance of rain, but if we light up the citronella and open up the umbrella, we can invite our friends and enjoy the space. Everyone can come as they please—no need to take off your shoes—and bring their own dishes for a multicultural, multifunctional potluck with food to spare.

This book focuses on the international arena for three reasons. First, it is a creative space with fewer externally imposed rules and requirements than a domestically incorporated partnership entity. Second, it is an institutional space where the partners can be themselves, where partnerships are made up of independent legal entities, even as they convene their individual representatives. And third, it is a neglected space. When it comes to structure and design, this absence of attention garners even more creativity, but can also result in unnecessary pitfalls, tensions, costs, and churn.

That is not to say the international arena is just a wide-open field under an endless sky. Each partner wears its hat and brings its baggage, especially the supporting and fiduciary entities. And there are certainly rules of decorum: no boom boxes, no cigarettes, no trash left behind. But if you're looking for some fresh air and a chance to try some new dishes, the international arena is as good a place to pitch a tent as any. (>@ PfP: Partnering Internationally)

What does it take to be international? The status attaches to nature of the partners, either as "nations" or as derived from nations. If you are a sovereign country (a nation) or an organization created by sovereign countries (an inter-nation organization), and you interact with others of the same, your status puts you in the *inter-nation*(al) arena. For countries, this typically means engagement through ministries or agencies representing the government. For international organizations, the most common are the major multilaterals, like multilateral development banks and UN agencies, of whom many countries are the governing members and shareholders. International partners are a closed circle, and yet, there are few limitations on who can partner with international partners in international space.

INTERNATIONAL ARENA

■ international partnership program

◆ international trust fund

The Structural Angle

What is it about structure and design? When everyone is focused on the challenge and impact, why focus on the framing and filler? There are lots of reasons, but the main one is that we can do better.

Because international space is outdoors (among sovereigns and their multilateral organizations), not indoors (within nationally framed entities), international structure is as-defined, not pre-defined. Granted, domestic corporations can also do a lot of their own defining and detailing. However, as a matter of degree, if you do not encase your partnership in a corporate entity, you open up space for partners to build their own structures and define their own rules and relationships. (>@ PfP: Governing Bodies—Characteristics)

In international partnership programs, those rules and relationships tend to include the following structural elements:

- Partners convene informally, not formally.
- Partners sit on governing bodies as entities, not individuals.
- Roles and responsibilities are allocated among entities.
- Fiduciary responsibilities are contractually defined.
- Contractual elements intermingle with structural elements.
- Vertical fund flows intersect with horizontal peer partners.
- Supporting entities become partner custodians.
- Privileges and immunities frame partner dispositions.
- Branding creates umbrella exposure.
- Consensus embraces inclusive voice.
- Partners define themselves to define their partnerships.
- Partners stack, share, parse, and package for balance.
- Complexity accrues if you don't keep it simple.

Oversimplifying to make the point:

International structure is as-defined;

national structure is pre-defined.

STRUCTURAL DIVISION OF LABOR

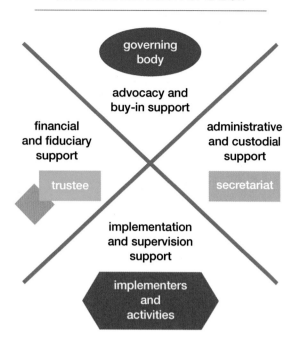

These are characteristic aspects that offer extra benefits to, but also require extra managing by, international partners. It is no free picnic, but there is room for good practice.

Who knew that the international arena is structurally speaking so special? Most international partners simply walk the park, without recognizing the clear paths that mark the way and the noble trees that lend their canopies. Partners may instead give in to bushwhacking temptations, snagging brambles or stepping into quicksand, if they fail to find the balanced and simple road ahead. Or they may dig themselves into a hole if they force standardized approaches, rather than build into the landscape, like a fit-for-purpose Frank Lloyd Wright Fallingwater.

Structure is a matter of perspective. It's there if you see it. Actually, it is always there, but seeing is appreciating—and shaping and sustaining. Once you become aware of structural aspects, you can become aware of structural options. And once you see the landscape, with the forest and the trees, you can make choices that are informed, contextual, and coherent.

As you become a true believer in the benefits of inclusive collaboration and the synergies of international partnership, being an international structuralist becomes a calling.

Partnership is the lens of this book, as the focal point, frame of reference, and magnifying scope.

The Partnership Programs and Trust Funds Angle

There are hundreds, if not thousands, of international partnership programs dispersed across the international community. Development actors are forever under pressure to show they are making a difference. Ideas for more innovation, scale, and impact abound. If you can get a few partners on board and convince a supporting entity that it has a key role to play, then depositing money in an international trust fund that involves shared governance—an international partnership program—can be a relatively easy place to park your latest collaboration.

It works. Over and over again, these international arrangements validate themselves with enough shared engagement, risk-reducing delegation, and evidence-based results that partners cook up more ideas, collect more funds, and structure more partnership programs and trust funds. Varied and versatile, the potential for coordination and collaboration is immense. There is something for everyone.

THE INTERNATIONAL PARTNERSHIP
PROGRAM AT ITS MOST BASIC

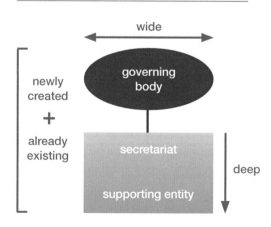

The beauty of international partnership programs lies in their combination of the old and the new. As defined here, international partnership programs have two necessary ingredients: a governing body (new) and a supporting entity (old). This makes them a hybrid—neither all in, nor all out—and able to go deep and wide at the same time. (>@ PfP: Typology—The Broader Landscape of Partnership Programs)

Being in the international arena, these partnership programs operate according to rules the partners define for themselves, largely driven by requirements of the supporting entities. To start, partners choose themselves and declare themselves a partnership, chicken and egg. (>@ BfB: Constitutive Documents—How the Charter Happens) When the supporting entity also steps up as a partner, as it typically does in this international context, these platforms become especially effective and synergistic.

The partnership program/trust fund combination is particularly powerful in the international arena. There is no partnership platform without funding, even if partners individually pay their own way. When partners go further, however, and collectivize their funding in a dedicated pool, and then use it to undertake partnership-branded activities, the platform becomes a means of both convening and implementing, as it operates around important upstream/downstream feedback loops. (>@ PfP: Structure—Collectivizing) International trust-funded partnership programs are hugely popular, vertically integrated, horizontally led mini-businesses without the trappings of corporate settings. What's not to love?

It is not possible to set up an international trust-funded partnership program without undertaking a structure-and-design exercise—whether the partners realize that is what they are doing or not. In fact, the incredible variety of arrangements (>@ the next two pages) is the first clue that international partnership programs and their trust funds are products of structure and design. And yet, for all that variety, and the innumerable business choices that go with it, there are common strands and consistent themes that come through again and again. It is these contours that make such a rich area for study and refinement. By leveraging these discernible elements and angles, international partners can maximize their potential for sustainability, efficiency, and impact.

THE INTERNATIONAL PARTNERSHIP
PROGRAM WITH A TRUST FUND

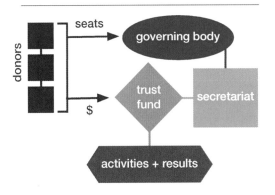

It's the partnership program chicken and egg:
Partners designate themselves partners to declare themselves a partnership.

Partnerships vs. Trust Funds

Here is my bias: Partnerships come first; trust funds come second. In this book, international partnership programs are the focal point and frame of reference. That is a deliberate reframing. It is a rejoinder to those who say it's all about the money, baby. When international trust funds come into the picture, all eyes seem to fixate on the funds, even when they are supporting partnership. As a result, partnership aspects, like shared governance, centralized support, lessons learned, branding, and other collectives, tend to get short shrift.

Correct the neglect;
get more balance.

Why would partners be less important than their funds, why would funding vehicles drive the program more than the partnership? To which I say, if we can add a greater understanding of partnership elements, we can correct the neglect and find more balance.

The Variety Is Endless

TWO-TIER GLOBAL-COUNTRY STRUCTURE EXAMPLE

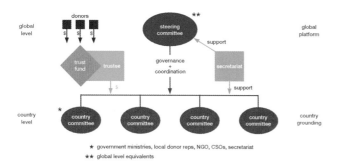

* government ministries, local donor reps, NGO, CSOs, secretariat
** global level equivalents

UPSTREAM / DOWNSTREAM VIEW

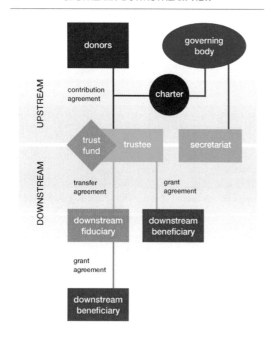

MULTI-DONOR, MULTI-FIDUCIARY

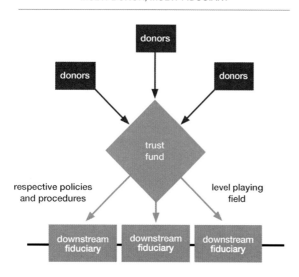

CLASSIC ONE-STOP-SHOP

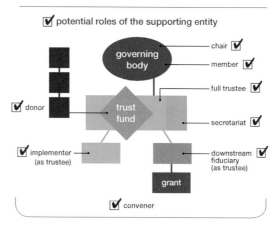

TWO-TIER RECIPIENTS

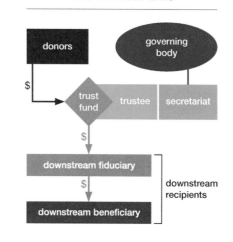

DIRECT AND INDIRECT SUPERVISION

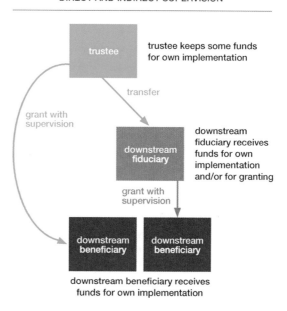

COORDINATION PARTNERSHIPS

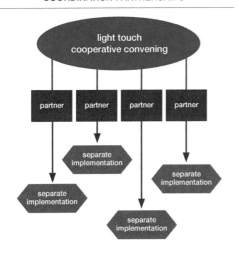

CLASSIC INTERNATIONAL PLATFORM

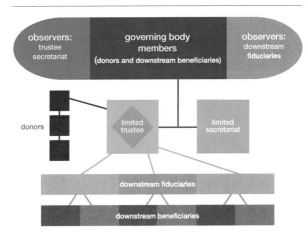

UMBRELLA ARRANGEMENTS

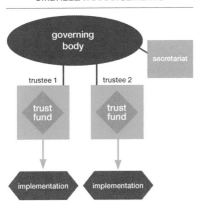

LIGHT SHARED GOVERNANCE

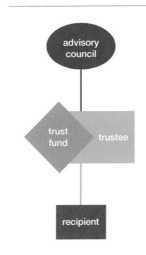

SINGLE-COUNTRY TRUST FUND

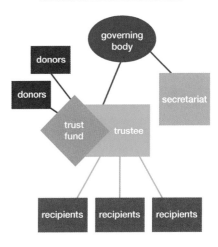

All of these diagrams are taken from the *Primer for Partners*.

WITH PASS-THROUGH CHANNEL

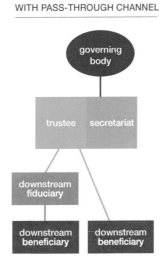

EXPERT TAC ADDITION

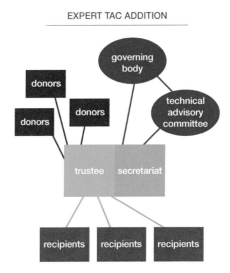

International Partnership Programs

There are two basic ways to understand international partnership programs: in terms of hybrid structure and in terms of agreed collectives.

Hybrid Structure

STRUCTURED PARTNERSHIP INFRASTRUCTURE

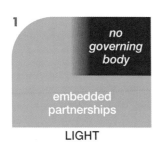

International partnership programs are what I call "hybrid" structures. (>@ PfP: Typology—The Even Broader Landscape of Structured Partnerships) They are neither fully embedded in existing organizations, nor fully separated into stand-alone, dedicated, legal entities. They take the best of both by operating through existing organizational infrastructure, but with new, dedicated governance. One part is embedded, one part is appended, and the relative proportions span the gamut from more supporting entity control to more governing body control. (>@ PfP: International Partnership Programs—Shared Decision Making) The specific placement of a particular partnership program on this spectrum is a product of negotiations and agreement among the partners and depends on the circumstances. As noted throughout this book and my *Primer for Partners*, the challenge—and reward—is to develop a fit-for-purpose structure that is sustainable, efficient, and impactful.

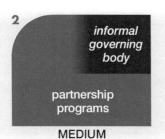

International partnership programs (#2) are the hybrid of

- **existing infrastructure (the supporting entity) and**
- **new governance (the informal governing body).**

Agreed Collectives

International partnership programs are about partnering through various "collectives." (>@ PfP: International Partnership Programs) Partners can collect themselves in any number of ways, sometimes more, sometimes less. Most collectives have structural dimensions. They start when partners identify common ground, enough to pool resources or intentions, and deliberately agree to operate on a unified basis. Collectives without some degree of shared commitment, whether informal or contractual, tend to unravel, so one of the key collectives is a statement of the collective intent. This is where charters come in—at the center of this book. Agreements are said to reflect a meeting of the minds, but charters reflect a meeting of the minds and expectations. They can be as aspirational as legal, as voluntary as committed. (>@ BfB: Constitutive Documents—What to Watch For—Legal Status) There is no contradiction in recognizing the layered complementary and synergistic ways that international partnership programs tend to work.

Collectives around which international partners converge and convene are features or actions they take to reach common goals and collaborative results. In the *Primer for Partners*, we consider six classic collectives of international partnership programs, of which all or some can be used, in addition to which many others can be created. As a refresher, here on the next page are the six in brief.

International partnership programs are great in part because their partners can define and own their collectives. To paraphrase Spiderman, this opportunity is also a responsibility: the chance to craft collectives that suit the partners and maximize results, while also being clear with each other and justifying the resources needed to collectivize for those results. Unpacking this opportunity and this responsibility are two reasons for this *Book for Builders*.

Introducing
charterography
in Part Two.

Six Classic Collectives—Use Some or All (and Others)

1. Shared decisions. From upfront establishment choices to ongoing engagement, international partnership programs are products of collective decisions. Shared decision making can range from high-level strategic direction and oversight to down-in-the-weeds micromanaging of day-to-day implementation, but it occurs as shared governance in a governing body that represents the partners. This governing body is the "new" part that gets added to "old" existing entity support, which creates the new-old hybrid defined as an international partnership program.

2. Central support. Most international partnership programs need a centralizing force that holds the collectives together over time, as the glue, the gatekeeper, the legal status, the custodian. The tasks can range from administrative to substantive, but usually benefit from dedicated individuals in both senses of the word—assigned to the position and amped up to make it work. Although calling it a "secretariat" may sound bureaucratic and clinical, this collective can be the heart and soul of the partnership program.

3. Pooled funding. No international partnership program ever survived without financial resources. Sometimes a shoestring is enough, but the more it takes on downstream implementation, the more it needs resources. When international partners join their efforts, they instinctively think about pooling their funds. Enter international trust funds, a hugely popular development modality. Trust funds are not just a major driver of partnership programs; they are often the raison d'etre, even to the point of overshadowing the partnering they came from.

4. Coordinated activities. Partners need not use partnership programs to implement new activities and achieve more results. They can simply use these platforms to coordinate their own respective activities. Or they can do both, create and coordinate. Either way, the coordination function, among partners and beyond, has huge value, even if partners practice this collectivizing without using those words. The annual work plan and the agreed results framework are two common, powerful, operationalized collectives, together serving ex ante planning and ex post reporting.

5. Combined knowledge. The feedback loops that partnership programs can generate are often the least acknowledged, and least leveraged, benefits of convening internationally. It takes a more patient, deliberative style—not only driven to disburse and implement—to collect information, take stock, analyze honestly, and adjust conscientiously. But the potential for collectives around information and experience—like shared perspectives, lessons learned, avoiding reinventing the wheel, and creating multiplier effects—can be immense.

6. One brand. All for one, and one for all, nothing says it like the brand. An international partnership program that wants to be more than a wallflower or just a flash in the pan will typically pick an easy-to-articulate name or catchy acronym to message and advocate around. And voilà, the brand gives partners the most encompassing collective of all. Under a common header, all partners are exposed to all branded activities, for better or worse. As long as it remains the former, all partners are happy to get credit for associating with all branded achievements.

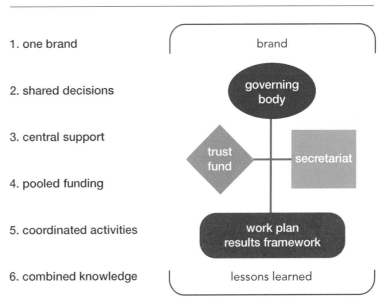

THE SIX MAIN "COLLECTIVES" OF
INTERNATIONAL PARTNERSHIP PROGRAMS

1. one brand

2. shared decisions

3. central support

4. pooled funding

5. coordinated activities

6. combined knowledge

brand

governing body

trust fund

secretariat

work plan results framework

lessons learned

Five facets:

1. donors
2. trustees
3. supporting entities
4. decision making
5. implementation

International Trust Funds

There are a number of ways to understand international trust funds, which are often used to channel funds to and from international partnership programs. We can compare-and-contrast them across five separate dimensions: donors, trustees, supporting entities, decision making, and implementation.

1. Single-donor vs. Multi-donor Trust Funds

There are single-donor trust funds (SDTFs) and multi-donor trust funds (MDTFs). These labels consider the trust fund at the point of fund entry and reflect how many donors contribute to the trust fund account. Certain things happen when more than one donor contributes, which is why the distinction is made. Specifically, a single-donor trust fund aligns the specific account with the individual contributing entity. That one-to-one relationship can give the single donor unique control over trust fund scope, clean visibility of fund use, and exclusive credit for results. For sure, few donors are averse to such benefits, which are diluted with multi-donor trust funds.

The main problem with single-donor trust funds is their lack of scalability. Few trustees want to open a new trust fund every time a donor whistles, especially if each one requires a new set of negotiated terms. Unchecked trust fund proliferation can end up more complex and costly than the sum of its parts.

The other problem with single-donor trust funds is that they are not collectives. They do not pool funds to create a larger whole. Beyond missing economies of scale, they do not bring donors together collaboratively to join forces. Although it is possible to create partnership programs that combine two, twelve, or any number of SDTFs under an overarching governance structure and within a single brand, that stops short of the full potential of collectivization.

Multi-donor trust funds, by contrast, commingle funds, whether into one main account at the point of entry or into a series of initial entry points (so-called windows). This account architecture is part of what donors and the trustee negotiate, based on what the trustee is willing to offer. (>@ PfP: Trustee Types— Modular Combinations) Multi-donor trust funds embed the commitment to collectively engage directly into the funding vehicle, and many other collective elements can flow from there. MDTFs are therefore at the center of many international partnership programs whose broad purpose is to combine resources for effective results.

A downside of commingled pools is that donors lose the ability to directly track their individual funds. They can no longer physically tie their specific dollars to a specific use. As a result, MDTFs can be challenging for donors that insist on financial tracking or want to contribute restricted funds, often for unavoidable, internal budget reasons. And yet, the trustee usually prefers a fully fungible, commingled pool that not only funds specific, on-the-ground activities (with "restricted" funds), but also pays for a broader scope of activities, including core support, like trustee and secretariat budgets (out of "unrestricted funds"). This see-saw has been the nub of many a trust fund negotiation, where the trustee may seek the largest aggregation of funds and the least restrictions on fund use, while donors push to restrict and earmark to meet their requirements. Fortunately, there are ways to reconcile these views and keep the see-saw in balance. (>@ PfP: Trade-Offs—The Central Harmonization Spectrum)

SINGLE-DONOR
TRUST FUND

one donor

tracked

bilateral
donor + trustee

MULTI-DONOR
TRUST FUND

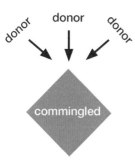

donor   donor   donor

commingled

multilateral
donors + trustee

2. Full vs. Limited Trustees

As reflected in the two major paradigms that were introduced in the *Primer for Partners* and that flow throughout this book—one-stop-shops and international platforms (>@ PfP: Typology—Introducing Two Mighty Oaks)—there are two main kinds of trustees: "full" and "limited." Neither term quite captures the nuances, but as a general matter:

- *Trustee-plus fiduciary.* One-stop-shops feature trustees that provide a full package of support, covering multiple roles, where trustee, secretariat, supervision, implementation, and other support roles flow together. It is a highly integrated, deliberately synergized model (>@ PfP: Synergistic Conflicts) that puts the donor's full faith and credit into one pair of trusted hands. The full trustee is a kind of trustee-plus variant. (>@ PfP: Trustee Types—One-Stop-Shops, Full Trustees)

- *Trustee-minus fiduciary.* International platforms do the opposite and feature trustees that limit their fiduciary support, while also clearly delineating themselves from other roles. Instead of one trustee with multiple roles, this is, from a fiduciary perspective, one trustee handing off to multiple other fiduciaries (possibly including to its own entity) in separate, delineated fiduciary roles. The limited trustee is a kind of trustee-minus variant. (>@ PfP: Trustee Types—International Platforms, Limited Trustees)

Both types of trustees have their pros and cons, and the choice of trustee type depends—no surprise—on the context. What matters is what donors need and want and what trustees can and will offer, including with respect to each partner's policy environment, strategic intentions, and overall goals. On the one hand, donors are designed to give money, but seek "value for money" in return, hoping to do more with less. And on the other hand, trustees are usually happy to take the money and augment their work programs, but are also mindful of the diligence and care it takes to be a fiduciary—or at least they should be.

Lots of business choices: trustee-plus, trustee-minus, trustee-secretariat, trustee≠secretariat, and more.

3. Trustees vs. Secretariats

How the trustee and secretariat are positioned vis-à-vis the partners and each other are business decisions to be made by the partners. As a general matter, however, the trustee is within the trustee entity and the secretariat is within the supporting entity, and that distinction is meaningful even if those two are the same entity. For anyone willing to get into the weeds, referring to the trustee entity as a "supporting entity" is somewhat of a misnomer (even though I occasionally elide the distinction to streamline the sentences in this book). How the trustee provides support to the trust fund is crucially different from how secretariat functions tend to provide support. (>@ PfP: Supporting Entities—Baselines)

Critical to this distinction is for whom the entity operates, and to whom and how it is accountable. In the case of the trustee, it is invariably a contractual, arm's-length relationship through the trustee entity—this is in the nature of fund flow agreements. In the case of the secretariat, however, it is typically an informally structured relationship through one of the partners as the supporting entity, not merely an outsourced, contracted relationship. Partners, especially donors, actually like to bring the secretariat closer, rather than keeping their delegated distance. This is all fine as long as partners recognize the difference and manage the dynamics. Otherwise it can get messy.

As lawyers will appreciate, it comes down to risk profiles. The trustee is contractually bound, operating as trustee in its own right as a principal, legally for itself and not on behalf of the partners. Trustees that operate within international financial institutions, like multilateral development banks, are easily viewed as having deep pockets, even though trust fund liability is not meant to be personal (institutional), but rather limited to the funds in the specific trust fund. Nevertheless, a trustee acting in its principal capacity carries a direct liability profile in case of its own misuse or negligence, including when supervising someone else's use. If the trustee agreed to supervise, but was negligent in this supervision, or otherwise failed to follow its own rules, this can pinch the pocket in the form of refunds. Trustee entities have to take this exposure to heart. Fiduciary obligations are not performance guarantees, but they are serious business. (>@ BfB: Dualities—Informal and Formal)

By contrast, secretariat functions operate on a different plane. Precisely because donors like to have close relationships with their supporting entities, to both exert more influence and get more responsiveness, they favor structures that are not merely contractual. In the international arena, both are possible at the same time—having your cake and eating it, too. The trustee accepts legal commitments and liability, while the secretariat layers on custodial care. (>@ PfP: Custodial Effect) Whether in one-stop-shops or international platforms, you can find this interlacing of arm's-length obligations and arms-embracing relations.

Many international trust funds do not recognize this distinction, much less articulate the difference. And yet, it plays out in practice. In cases where the trustee entity and the secretariat entity are one and the same, that entity has to take measures to protect itself. This is where we can again see why our two mighty oaks are so prominent, the two ends of the forest that help define all the rest (>@ PfP: Typology—Introducing Two Mighty Oaks):

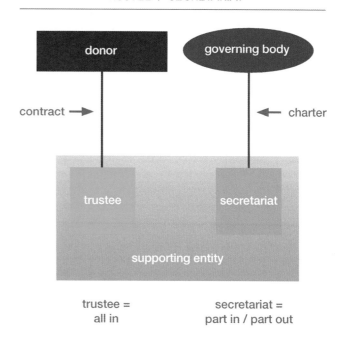

TRUSTEE ≠ SECRETARIAT

trustee = all in

secretariat = part in / part out

- *Full-package one-stop-shops.* When trustee and secretariat functions are part of a complete package, often so interlinked that they are not even separately identified (for example, globally referred to as "administrator" functions), the supporting entity sets itself up for tension. This soup-to-nuts modality practically forces the supporting entity to err on the side of caution, to demand more control and influence, to cede less to the donors and other partners. Shared governance may be reduced and within tight bounds. Secretariat-type support, like branding, advocacy, stakeholder events, and other activities that cater to the partnership program beyond fiduciary obligations, may be strong, but on supporting entity terms. The secretariat is never free of the trustee's legal shadow, since the contractual and structural support can never be fully separated. If donors and other partners want full support and do not mind a supporting entity-centric model, this fits the bill.

- *Modular, limit-defined international platforms.* The same thing happens in international platforms, but with a different outcome. The supporting entity positions itself first and foremost in protective mode (or if not, positions itself for trouble). Rather than provide all-encompassing support with full-exposure risk, however, it provides "limited" and clearly delineated support, with limitations that affect both trustee and secretariat functions. The limited trustee is a circumscribed fiduciary, whose trust fund obligations rest on negatives as much as positives. This in turn results in a limited secretariat, whose functions are equally circumscribed to avoid becoming a backdoor trustee. (>@ PfP: Trustee Types—International Platforms, Limited Trustees) Once again, the secretariat is not free of the trustee's legal shadow. Limitations on the trustee prescribe limitations on the secretariat. In cases where such limitations do not carry over, other issues and tensions are likely to arise.

This is where international partnership programs often fall short: They fail to identify trustee (contractual) functions separately from secretariat (structural) functions. (>@ PfP: Structure—Connecting Fund Flows and Decision Flows; BfB: Dualities—Structure and Contract) They fail to appreciate the inward-looking demands of the trustee role and the outward-looking dynamics of the secretariat role. As a result, they fail to recognize the specific risks and manage each appropriately, whether as combo or modular roles. Why do many partnership programs experience tensions between donors and their supporting entities? When the relationships are different in nature and degree—trustee and secretariat—you have to appreciate the underlying reasons for those differences to balance the relations.

4. Pre-agreed vs. Programmatic Allocations

A fourth way to categorize trust funds is by the fund allocation process. Deciding to whom funds go and for what is an important part of trust fund governance, a part that is often opened up to shared governance with the donors and perhaps other partners. Certainly, for the donors, it is their money, so they often want to have a say and may feel entitled. Then again, if the point is to delegate responsibility to the trustee (or other downstream fiduciary), continued input or instructions may not be called for and could be viewed by the trustee qua implementer as inefficient and unwelcome micromanaging. The negotiated result ideally finds the partners' sweet spot between donor control and influence vs. trustee leeway and follow-through.

There are, in effect, two general ways to handle decision making around the use of funds:

- *Upfront and delegated.* In cases where there is early clarity about what a trust fund will finance—for example, when the money is for support of a well-cooked project either in total or blended in with other funding—the trustee and donors can choose to agree on all essential terms upfront, at the point of establishment, and delegate the rest to the trustee. Project-based trust funds have their place and can be especially suited for cofinancing and other piggybacking on already planned operations. The scope of these trust funds is usually narrow, limited to a single project or defined activity, output, investment, or deliverable. Once contribution agreements are signed, the trust fund is established, and funds are received by the trustee, then donors can step back and stay hands-off. They can fully leverage the trustee entity by leaving downstream operations in trusted hands.

This kind of one-off trust fund falls outside the definition of partnership program, missing both the shared governance and programmatic approach. However, for every project-based trust fund, it is worth asking whether a programmatic trust fund could have provided the financing more efficiently through economies of scale, more effectively as part of a broader plan, or more strategically with room to determine priority needs over time.

- *Iterative and ongoing.* This is what it means to be a programmatic trust fund: Partners know broadly what the funds are for at the start, but make specific fund allocation decisions over time. They initially agree on a plan, both as to the kinds of activities and the process for decision making, but approve specific activities, with agreed levels of detail, subsequently. Things like multi-tranche funding, work plans and budgets, and results frameworks let the initial scope stay broad, with the idea that approved projects and activities are kept within the scope and matched to available funds as they come in.

This phased approach to trust funds, being program-based not project-based, is logically the kind of trust fund that supports partnership *programs*. This programmatic approach emphasizes the framework at inception, while enabling a multi-year time frame that leaves room for accumulating donor contributions, governing body decision making, downstream coordination, evolving work plans, pilots and lessons learned, responsive engagement, and other elements that give priority to partnership.

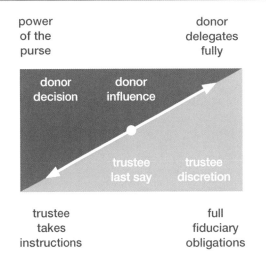

DONOR-TRUSTEE SPAN ON FUNDING DECISIONS

power of the purse — donor delegates fully

donor decision / donor influence

trustee last say / trustee discretion

trustee takes instructions — full fiduciary obligations

EMBEDDED PROJECTS VS. PARTNERSHIP PROGRAMS

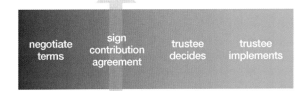

donor hand-off

negotiate terms — sign contribution agreement — trustee decides — trustee implements

embedded trust-funded project

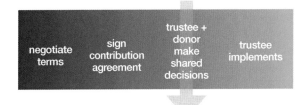

negotiate terms — sign contribution agreement — trustee + donor make shared decisions — trustee implements

donor hand-off

trust-funded partnership program

5. Fiduciary vs. Recipient Execution

A fifth way to slice trust funds is to look at who does the implementing. Implementation of programs, work plans, projects, and other activities is a matter of fund use. (>@ PfP: Use of Funds) Donors care that funds are used properly, and trustees are given that duty of care. As fiduciaries, classic internatonal trustees undertake one of three implementation modalities: (1) their own implementation (inhouse fiduciary execution); (2) someone else's implementation (transferred fiduciary execution); or (3) someone else's supervised implementation (recipient execution with fiduciary supervision). More specifically:

1. *Inhouse fiduciary execution.* If agreed with the donors, the trustee can implement—and by extension, if part of the same legal entity, the secretariat can also implement. This means the funds stay at home, where the trust fund resides. Fiduciary functions attach to the legal entity, so that any part of the same entity, including a secretariat function or downstream implementing function, can implement through internal (inhouse) transfers. Inhouse fiduciary execution usually applies to the fiduciary entity as a whole, since the legal entity is the contracting party, regardless of which part of the entity has internal responsibility for implementation.

2. *Transferred fiduciary execution.* Fiduciary execution can drop down, at arm's length, to another entity a level below the trustee. Rather than have the trustee entity implement, the trustee can transfer funds to a second fiduciary entity, if agreed with the donors. To avoid overlapping fiduciaries—indeed, one overlapping the other is a bad idea (>@ PfP: Use of Funds—Role of the Fiduciary)—the original trustee steps back seamlessly as the second fiduciary steps forward. This kind of fiduciary execution (sometimes called a "transfer out") is not performed by the original trustee, but by a so-called implementing entity or implementation support entity. Readers familiar with international platforms will recognize this horizontal inclusion of multiple downstream fiduciaries as one of that modality's hallmarks. (>@ PfP: Typology—Introducing Two Mighty Oaks—International Platforms)

THREE TRUST FUND IMPLEMENTATION MODES

inhouse fiduciary execution — trustee / secretariat / downstream fiduciary / supporting entity → implementation

transferred fiduciary execution — limited trustee → transfer of fiduciary responsibility → downstream fiduciary → implementation

supervised recipient execution — full trustee → supervised recipient → implementation

3. *Supervised recipient execution.* Funds can also be transferred (granted) to non-fiduciaries, in which case the grantmaking fiduciary (the original trustee or downstream fiduciary) typically stays engaged in the form of monitoring and supervision. For example, when a government ministry of a developing country gets a grant and uses the funds for an agreed project, that recipient usually does not meet the financial management and other donor standards needed to qualify as a fiduciary. (>@ PfP: Trust Funds—Recipients) No problem; the trust fund is designed to layer on a qualified fiduciary that will keep track of how funds are used and whether progress is being made. The key is that any fund use is always under the overview and purview of an entity that the donors trust.

Some trust funds are designated fiduciary-execution funds and others recipient-execution funds, but most are hybrids, combining the two. Partnership programs often find their strength in combining downstream modalities. To add to the variety, consultants, firms, and other experts can also be procured, but that does not change the overall fiduciary or implementation responsibility. (>@ PfP: Fund Use Responsibility—Implementation Responsibility—Procurement vs. Grantmaking)

--●--

The Supervising Fiduciary

When trust fund supervision happens in a development context, it is not just about proper fund use; it is also about progress on objectives. A supervising fiduciary considers whether the recipient is acting with diligence, while also asking if development objectives are being achieved, addressing problems as they arise, identifying key risks and mitigation strategies, reporting regularly on progress, and preparing completion reports at the end. Donors want to know how it is going, with confidence that it is all being handled.

--●--

Conclusion

Location, location, location—it does make a difference. By positioning partnership initiatives in the international arena, partners have the freedom, and responsibility, to structure and design their engagements to be sustainable, efficient, and impactful.

Partnering is natural, but must be intentional. For all the effort involved, international partners have no business partnering unless they can make the whole greater than the sum of its parts. To do this, they must come together primed to contribute the best they have to offer (their comparative advantages) and motivated to leverage their collective efforts (synergies). They must build for balance. Time and again, international partners have found a winning formula when combining existing, robust operating frameworks with new, dedicated governance mechanisms.

These international partnership programs hold great potential for impact, both among partners and on the ground. But they deserve care in their making and maintaining. Each partnership program is different and deserves to be contextual, as the product of innumerable business decisions, both at inception and over time, that the partners can collectively own and steer. To make the most of their partnering, these partners need architects and builders who know their craft, understand the landscape, and carry their toolbox of fitting words, clear clauses, and packaged documents.

A world without partnering is impossible to imagine. A world without collective engagement defies reality. A world without combined efforts to create global public goods and improve the greater good denies humanity. We need to be the best international partners we can be.

International partners; intentional partnering.

3 DYNAMICS

International partnership programs are:

1. everywhere and nowhere
2. contextual
3. organic
4. a practice area

Four dynamics about international partnership programs are noteworthy. They are everywhere and nowhere. They are contextual. They are organic. And they are a practice area.

Let me explain.

First, they are everywhere and nowhere.

As the world converges, what used to be local interests become global interests. Responsibilities that belong to local and national governments increasingly rely on international cooperation and collaboration. Particularly in international development, challenges invariably call upon multiple development actors, from donor countries to beneficiary countries, from multilateral organizations to sector-specific entities, to operate in tandem. Many issues are already cross-border in nature—like climate effects, contagious diseases, trade and markets, refugees and migrant flows—and require cross-coordination in response. Even local projects in one country can benefit from experiences of local projects in other countries. It is hard to imagine a single donor or lone agency tackling a development problem without engaging others. International partnering is everywhere.

And yet, "partnering" as anything more than an approach can be is hard to pin down. The term itself means many different things to many different partners, with little specificity. Particularly when it comes to international partnership programs and their trust funds, partnering can be more mantra than thing, more assumption than direction, more event than structure. It is in the air, in the engagement, everyone talks about it—but what are they saying? And what are they actually doing?

Perhaps you work in a major development institution. Chances are that partnering is the sine qua non of your institution's existence, the lifeblood of its engagement, and a complement to its comparative advantages. But when it comes to partnering as an institutional element, chances are you have:

- No business line for partnering
- No business process for partnering
- No business guidance for partnering
- No data on partnership engagements
- No cataloguing of partnership engagements
- No reporting about partnership engagements
- No staff recognition for partnering
- No typology for partnering
- Not even vocabulary for partnering

Am I right? (I'd like to be wrong.)

On the last two points, my *Primer for Partners* was written in part to offer typologies and vocabulary to an otherwise unmarked international partnering landscape. There was no way to write a primer without basic types and terms. Lacking a ready roadmap, I had to come up with a number of labels, like *supporting entity*, *one-stop-shop*, *umbrella arrangement*, *dedicated entity partnership*, and many more. When it comes to the nuts and bolts of partnering, which is to say, the structural components and design features, there is much the international community has failed to articulate—and accordingly also fails to fully understand, appreciate, negotiate, and decide. How can we partner internationally based on collective understandings, or negotiate fit-for-purpose structures, or make deliberate design decisions, without even a common language? I am inclined to put it this way: It isn't a thing until you name it. It isn't good practice until you work it.

All over the place and no place.

It's not a thing until you name it.

It's not good practice till you work it.

Second, they are contextual.

Our goal:

To leverage comparative advantages and create synergies to achieve more and do better, with less and faster.

Accommodate at inception; adapt over time.

What is the point of partnering if the whole is not greater than the sum of the parts? Each partner is making its own trade-offs in deciding whether to go unilaterally, bilaterally, or multilaterally; there are always pros and cons. However, the balance of consideration depends on how well the participants partner together. In the jargon of the day, donors look for value-for-money, and partners look for evidence-based results. In my own terms, can the international partners leverage their comparative advantages and create synergies to achieve more and do better, with less and faster? Can they partner sustainably, efficiently, and impactfully?

The answer is always contextual. If the partnership program is not fit to match the circumstances, it cannot be fit-for-purpose, which means it cannot possibly maximize its potential and magnify its resources and reach. You only have to look at the many constellations and configurations of partnership programs that have already aligned, no two alike, and not one the same as it was a year ago, to realize that contextualizing is an imperative. (>@ BfB: Context—The Variety Is Endless) Partnership programs that do not last are ones that do not accommodate at inception or adapt over time. Partners need room to define the form of their partnership program, and must not let forms define them.

This should be a no-brainer, but it is harder to do than one might think. Even while being passionate about finding the right fit, there are some limits to contextuality:

- *It's not all à la carte.* Being contextual does not mean partners can take everything à la carte, each partner for itself. Partnering takes some discipline, compromise, and concessions. Part of maximizing the whole is creating the common denominators that bring partners together. It is not just about accommodating outside interests, but also finding convergence. A partnership program that is all contour and no center likely has too much context and too little cohesion. (>@ BfB: Dualities—Harmonization and Individuation)

- *It's not full carte blanche.* Being contextual also does not mean partners can have full carte blanche on whatever they want. Particularly when it comes to the role of the supporting entity, a degree of standardization and regularization necessarily applies. That entity is probably supporting not one, but many partnership arrangements, and the equation needs to be manageable and scalable. That is no contradiction. The supporting entity is part of the context that needs accommodating. All partners should understand what the supporting entity context consists of and confirm their acceptance, eyes wide open. (>@ PfP: Custodial Effect—Eyes Wide Open)

Clearly, relevant points of context can pull and stretch in different directions and even conflict. Being contextual is accordingly an exercise in recognition and negotiation, with all components in view, outlines traced and bottom lines drawn. Hopefully, including with the help of lawyers (>@ BfB: Coda—The Role of the Lawyer), the picture comes together from a full palette. It is more than connect-the-dots or color-between-the-lines. Multi-party, multi-interest, multi-setting partnering is multidimensional, like designing and drafting in chiaroscuro.

Full vs. Limited Trustee Choices

Here is a context question: You want a trust fund, but should the trustee be full or limited? The choice depends on the context. What do the partners want? Whom do they have? How will they engage? This is all about fit-for-purpose.

- Option One: Do the partners want a delegated, centralized, soup-to-nuts hand-off? Does the partnership program have a strong trustee/supporting entity that wants primary responsibility (and control)? Does that entity have the expertise, reach, policies, track record, and like-mindedness to do what it takes? (>@ PfP: Typology—Introducing Two Mighty Oaks—One-Stop-Shops) *Go for the full trustee.*

- Option Two: Do the partners want an inclusive, diversified, multi-fiduciary platform? Do they have multiple, peer-to-peer actors that want to collectivize their convening more than their implementing? Will a strong governing body have the heft, expertise, bandwidth, buy-in, and like-mindedness to do what it takes? (>@ PfP: Typology—Introducing Two Mighty Oaks—International Platforms) *Go for the limited trustee.*

Even these two dimensions are not binary in practice, however, and the calculus can take more factors into account. There are full trustees that can hand over a portion of the funds in limited trustee mode. There are limited trustees that hand over the funds for implementation in full trustee-type (full fiduciary) mode. How the fiduciaries mix, match, and stack depends on what trustee entities are willing to set up and where partners are willing to end up. It is—or should be—a deliberate combination of institutional, multilateral, political, procedural, relational, even circumstantial aspects that converge to define the relevant context and inform the pending business decisions.

Being contextual also means being comprehensive. The trust fund should not obscure the partnership. The upstream should be aware of and connected to the downstream. Every partner needs to see their part within the whole package and feel settled within the whole framework. Builders, in particular, like lawyers and policy keepers, cannot afford to construct in the abstract, but need to build from and to the whole.

It is a balancing act, to be sure, but the next time you are simply handed a standard form or recited a policy requirement, it is worth making sure it fits the context. Maybe it is the wrong form or requirement given the circumstances. Maybe it unduly restricts the options given the actual scope for alternatives. Maybe it exacerbates the risks. Or maybe it even risks undermining sustainability, efficiency, or impact to the point where partnering becomes less than the sum of its parts. Legally, operationally, politically, and practically, fit-for-purpose partnership programs fit their context.

> Fit-for-purpose to fit the context legally, operationally, politically, and practically.

Some Not-Quite-Random Examples of Contextual Considerations

There are thousands of contextual inputs and thousands of related decisions. Here is a sampling.

- **Supporting Entity.** The access to information policy calls for public disclosure unless exceptions apply. Partners decide to characterize governing body business as deliberative with no public disclosure, but agree to publish minutes of proceedings.

- **Trustee.** The trustee needs to have the last say to manage its reputational risk and follow policies. The governing body approves an annual work plan, but leaves specific project decisions to the trustee.

- **Secretariat.** Secretariat staff are subject to a headcount limit under supporting entity policies. Partners acknowledge supporting entity limitations, but also get supporting entity agreement to add seconded staff.

- **Donors.** Taxpayer funds must be accounted for and productively spent in a transparent manner. The governing body agrees on a results framework and discusses progress reports that track this framework, all of which informs the publicly disseminated annual report.

- **Funding.** Donors want to earmark to specific projects. The trustee allows soft preferencing, while donors approve annual work plans and receive progress reports that reflect those preferences.

- **Decision Making.** NGOs are bringing their views and asking for direct seats at the table. The governing body agrees to add one NGO seat and coordinates with a representative group of NGOs for them to designate representation on a rotating basis.

- **Beneficiaries.** Countries want to follow their priorities, use their systems, and become self-sufficient. Several country representatives are included as decision makers on the governing body, and the governing body allocates a block of funding for technical assistance.

- **Risks.** The setting is low capacity, security-challenged, extra costly, and risk-prone. The governing body adopts a risk matrix that identifies high risk aspects and risk mitigation strategies, against which project proposals are reviewed.

- **Participation.** Partners want to divide implementation among multiple downstream fiduciaries. A limited trustee arrangement is set up to enable each downstream fiduciary to take full responsibility and follow its own operating rules.

- **Negotiations.** Parties are willing to convene in a full plenary session to close out last issues. Draft establishment documents are circulated in advance, discussed at the speak-now-or-forever-hold-your-peace plenary, followed by circulation of final documents for no-objection approval.

- **Constituencies.** Thirty donors are contributing to the trust fund. To manage the number of members on the governing body, participation is based on a smaller number of regional constituencies, where each constituency sets up its own rules of representation.

- **Private Sector.** For-profit companies show interest in joining the partnership program. To allow for open access, without favoring individual companies, a representative trade association agrees to designate a company representative on an annual basis to sit on the governing body.

- **Documents.** Donors want governance terms to be part of their contribution agreements with the trustee. However, other non-donor partners also want to agree to the governance terms for the whole partnership. All partners decide to adopt a partnership-wide charter that includes the governance terms, which is then incorporated by reference into the contribution agreements.

Third, they are organic.

To repeat a phrase, and this is a clue: No two are alike, and not one is the same as it was. That could be snowflakes, but the point here—and one I love to make—is that partnership programs are organic. Partners are people, and personalities permeate partnership programs, as governing body representatives, supporting entity staff, and ultimate beneficiaries. Nine times out of ten, a troubled partnership program can trace at least some of its woes to the wrong person in the wrong place. Partnership programs are also a matter of perception, a very human, potentially fickle act, which may, for example, determine whether donors want to keep putting in or recipients feel like they are being helped out.

This book about structure is not about two-by-fours and toggle bolts. We are not balancing beams. It is instead a reminder that the roots of partnering lie in the individuals who find a common spark—in the hallway, over coffee, at a conference, under whatever propitious circumstances—and then rally others to their cause. Partnerships do not spawn widgets, but grow cumulatively through ideas and experiences, connections and associations, sometimes by happenstance, but usually directed and driven.

Like anything organic, partnership programs are in a constant state of flux. Even the sturdiest sequoia is still growing. If the partners become too sedentary, or the partnership structure becomes too rigid, the partnership program will get stuck, and time will pass it by. Without continuous germination and regeneration, an international partnership program will decompose and deteriorate.

That is why charters—the subject of much of this book—should be living, breathing documents. (>@ PfP: Like Rock, Like Water—Like Water) As the partners evolve, and the partnership matures, and the partnership program adjusts, so its constitutive terms should, too. Owned by the partners, amendable by the governing body, the charter can be malleable to changing circumstances and shifting contexts. It offers a framework for partners to maintain internal cohesion and balance over time, while making progress on their objectives.

The key is to anticipate change. Partners can use structure and design to embed stability and enable flexibility from the start. Then, when change is needed, the path is there. This is the notion behind "like rock, like water." An international partnership program that is strong in its foundation with flexibility for transformation can keep its balance and be more sustainable, efficient, and impactful over time.

Like rock, like water:

Embed stability, enable flexibility, keep the balance.

The German *Rettungsgasse*

Anyone who drives the German autobahn has a heightened awareness of speed and discipline. You can't push the limits of acceleration without clear rules of the road. (No passing on the right!)

In this context, Germans have the perfect example of "like rock, like water": the *Rettungsgasse (ret'-ungs-gah-suh)*, or rescue lane. Here is how it goes: When traffic backs up behind an accident, drivers do not just stand there. They gently shift to the outer lane and shoulder, all of them, left to left and right to right, creating an open corridor down the center. When the ambulance comes rushing to help, it speeds right through—wide open all the way to the accident scene where it can get right to business. If you have ever seen a fire truck honking at the back of a mile of cars or a tow truck trying to get through, a pit in your stomach thinking of those who might be injured and knowing the blockage will take forever to clear, you know this is not trivial. The *Rettungsgasse* is nothing short of amazing.

But here is why it matters: It does not happen by itself. It is pre-planned, pre-engineered. When everyone is primed, then at the crucial moment, everyone knows what to do and kicks into action. You cannot simply instigate a *Rettungsgasse* right when the accident happens. It has to be pre-arranged beforehand. The German autobahn is a wonder of speed, discipline, and preparation.

Preparation that is both structure and design. First, the highway has to be built wide enough for outward shifts to leave a full lane in between. Somebody made sure the structure was fit-for-purpose for more than one scenario. Second, drivers need to know the drill. Through training, signage, publicity, and experience, rules become collectively owned, efficiently applied, and effective. "Like rock, like water"—**combining solid and flexible aspects** when structuring and designing international partnership programs—works the same way.

Fourth, they are a practice area.

How are you going to choose between a one-stop-shop and an international platform if you do not know the difference between a full trustee and a limited trustee? Or how can you appreciate secretariat staff if you do not recognize them first and foremost as employees of the supporting entity? And what are the chances of having a living, breathing partnership program if you do not have living, breathing documents? How are you going to understand your choices if you do not know you have options?

Structured Partnerships

If you are like many international partners, you rely on extensive sector expertise, intense policy parameters, and expansive relationships, but may still feel something missing. Who is there to explain structural mechanisms or lay out design features? Probably not the policy people, who are busy shoehorning bespoke relationships into mainstreamed operations. Probably not the lawyer, who may be considered a last obstacle before the finish line. Maybe you are lucky enough to get good, business-minded legal support from the start, but even then, a contextual understanding of international structure and design is not guaranteed. The obstacle may not be the lawyer, but everyone's lack of awareness and understanding.

International partnership program set-ups are not intuitive, but can be logical and ordered. They will in any case be structured and designed, if only by default, whether partners realize it or not. But there is too much money, time, and effort in play, and too much at stake, including lives and our planet, to partner internationally by default. And there is too much room for greater sustainability, efficiency, and impact to ignore the potential. This includes better positioning of comparative advantages, better coordination of collectives, better choices around trade-offs, better modulation of risks, better engineering of documents, and better balance across the board.

You do your level best … but something is still missing.

If by "practice area" we mean a knowledge base that arises from experience and expertise, then I offer you my *Primer for Partners* and this *Book for Builders* and rest my case. I offer my *Primer* to empower partners because understanding is within reach. And I offer this book to fortify builders because these baseline understandings can power your practice. The point is to build your own practice area, develop your own fundamentals, and craft your own techniques based on your institutional and operational priorities and imperatives. My books are here to jump-start your work with terminology, typology, handles, concepts, visuals (try out the *Primer* tip sheet that follows this chapter), and even a first draft (try out the prototype charter in the middle of this book). If these pages resonate with you, that is a promising start.

The goal is not just to build international partnership programs, but also to build the practice around them. As you develop your own structuring and design experience and expertise, you, too, will come to see this as a practice area and others will learn to appreciate it that way. At the end of the day, this much may be true: It won't become a practice area until we treat it as one.

To make it a practice area, we have to treat it as one.

What Do I Mean by "Practice Area"?

A practice area is an area that benefits from experience and expertise. Experience and expertise become relevant when issues repeat and themes recur, when there is potential for lessons to be learned and good practice to evolve. There is no need to establish set standards or invoke formal certifications to recognize that an area can benefit from practice, practice, practice, rather than just one-off, ad hoc, or even absent treatment. Can experience and expertise make a difference in structuring and designing international partnership programs? An emphatic yes!

The Lawyer Practitioner

Who is most likely to make the structuring of international partnership programs a practice area? To answer, let's give the lawyers a cameo. (>@ BfB: Coda—The Role of the Lawyer) Lawyers and legal staff are usually well-equipped to be at the crux of partnership program establishment. They can help promote the good (a sound partnership with strong impact) and avoid the bad (a failed partnership with reputational risks). Presumably everyone involved is looking out for issues, including reputational exposure, but lawyers typically have both a scope and a lens that gives them a broader and more penetrating view than most. This is amplified when lawyers are given a "clearance" role, a term that is often applied expansively as a sign-off on all aspects of the proposed plan. Arguably this is expecting too much, even for lawyers who are especially close to their business counterparts. But many a team leader has learned (sometimes the hard way) how good it can be for lawyers to assume that responsibility, or at least share the load.

On the one hand, it is difficult to separate business from legal—in partnership program matters, virtually all legal topics have business aspects. Accordingly, it is also difficult for lawyers to distance themselves from overall responsibility when they are asked to clear a partnership program document or a fund flow agreement. On the other hand, some aspects are truly legal in nature, or ones where lawyers have special expertise or insights. For these, lawyers and business counterparts can interact to assure comprehensive coverage, to make sure all key aspects are surfaced and managed. Here is a short list of potential partnership program matters within a lawyer's portfolio for her or his partnering organization:

Legal Aspect	Practical Consequences
Institutional mandate	Does the partnership program engagement fit within the purposes of the partner organization, including under the terms of its own constitutive documents?
Internal approvals	Does partnership program engagement involve internal approvals or other procedures or requirements, initially and over time; are they understood and being sought?
Applicable rules	Is there a clear understanding of the operating framework and applicable rules for partnership program activities (like safeguards, fiduciary controls); are they up to standard?
Privileges and immunities	If the partner organization has any P&I, are they preserved in the partnership program's establishment documents, like the adopted charter?
Applicable law	In the international arena, do any bodies of law or "rules of the organization" apply or have relevance, including for signed agreements and adopted documents; is silence a safe(r) approach?
Responsibility vs. control	Does a partnership organization that provides administrative or other support (secretariat, trustee) have mismatched responsibility for activities it does not fully control or influence?
Indirect liability	Has the partner organization's exposure by association to the actions of other participants, and the related potential for indirect liability, been assessed; how can it be managed?
Reputational risk	Have reputational risk through association, failure to meet expectations, lack of transparency, and other factors been due diligenced; are adequate mitigations and procedures in place?
Board representation	For representatives on a partnership program governing body, is staff sitting in an institutional capacity; is the role clear to staff; does it carry any potential liabilities?
Private sector participants	Since private sector entities are bound by business interests, are safeguards in place to make sure engagements are not (ab)used for competitive advantage or profit motives?
Intellectual property (IP)	Who has rights to use and distribute materials produced on behalf of the partnership program or financed by donor funding; are these intended for the public domain?
Document disclosure	To promote transparency as part of good governance, how much disclosure are partners willing to allow for partnership program materials, including agreements and meeting minutes?
Governance structures	Are roles and responsibilities of governing components (governing body, secretariat, trustee, etc.) comprehensive and clear; are relationships among them clarified and well-considered?
Governance documents	Do documents that paper the agreed terms of the partnership program reflect good practice by creating a strong foundation with efficient flexibility?

Conclusion

Sustainability, efficiency, and impact—and like rock, like water, all in the balance—by now you have seen enough of these phrases to make them mantras. All well and good, but these are characteristics that come from a cause. The baseline premise for everything in this book is in fact two-fold. The first point is collective engagement, and the second is results. This entire discussion of international structure and design rests on these two pillars, the twin objectives of working together and making a difference. Lest we lose sight of why any of this matters, the bottom line is collective action for the common good.

It's about using collective action for the common good.

But here is the other bottom line: Collective action to achieve results and have impact necessarily takes structure and design. The moment collective forces are convened or collective resources are combined, it becomes an exercise in structure, an exposition of design. There are many convening options for international partners, but one of them deserves more attention: international partnership programs, often paired with international trust funds. If you want to know more about how to build these versatile hybrids, taking the best of existing organizations and adding the best of new partner-specific elements, read on.

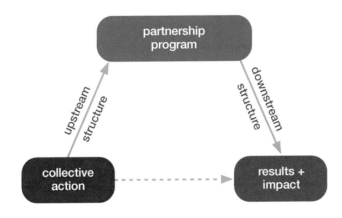

A *Primer for Partners* Tip Sheet

An Excerpted Selection

THE PARTNERSHIP HAT TRICK

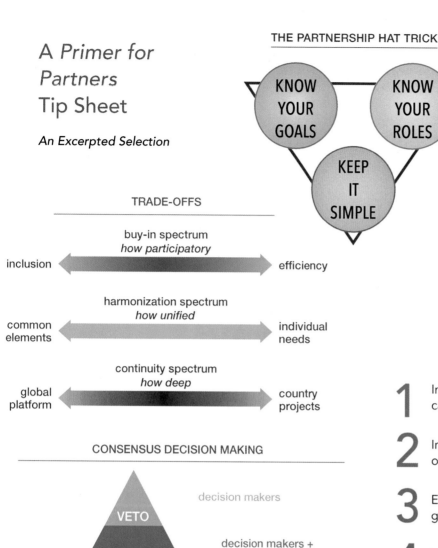

KNOW YOUR GOALS

KNOW YOUR ROLES

KEEP IT SIMPLE

TRADE-OFFS

buy-in spectrum
how participatory

inclusion ⟷ efficiency

harmonization spectrum
how unified

common elements ⟷ individual needs

continuity spectrum
how deep

global platform ⟷ country projects

CONSENSUS DECISION MAKING

VETO — decision makers

VOICE — decision makers + active observers

PRESENCE — everyone in the room

CONFLICTS OF INTEREST

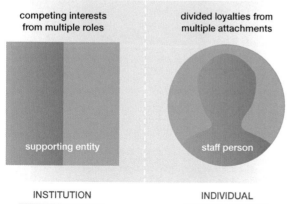

competing interests from multiple roles

divided loyalties from multiple attachments

supporting entity

staff person

INSTITUTION

INDIVIDUAL

Be clear.
Be clean.
Be modular.
Be flexible.
Be comprehensive.
Be balanced.
Be contextual.
Be ready.
Be (a)ware.
Keep it simple.

---

1 International partnership program design can be contextual and fit-for-purpose.

2 International partnership programs are organic, about people more than funds.

3 Effective partnership programs need good, like-minded partners.

4 International partners have a stunning number of business choices.

5 Clarity and modularity promote stability and flexibility.

6 Informed trade-offs and leveraged synergies are reinforcing.

7 Money talks; donors drive for results with the power of the purse.

8 Supporting entities join as partners and bring their policies and risk profiles.

9 International partnership programs are in the hybrid sweet spot.

10 Best to keep it simple; it will get complex enough.

THE DIVERSITY SWEET SPOT

LESS DIVERSITY ⟵——————⟶ MORE DIVERSITY

poor buy-in   promising prospects   poor consensus

INTERNATIONAL PARTNERSHIP PROGRAM

the trust fund,
it's just a funding vehicle . . .

NO OBJECTION DECISION MAKING

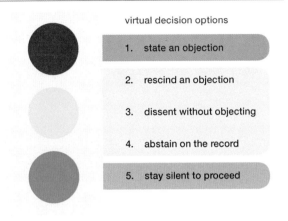

virtual decision options

1. state an objection
2. rescind an objection
3. dissent without objecting
4. abstain on the record
5. stay silent to proceed

LIVING, BREATHING FRAMEWORK

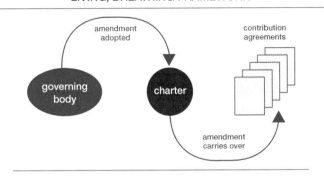

amendment adopted

governing body   charter

contribution agreements

amendment carries over

ROCK & WATER STRUCTURE

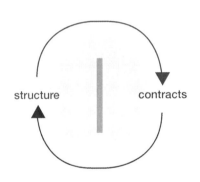

structure   contracts

FOUR CORNERS OF THE CONTRIBUTION AGREEMENT

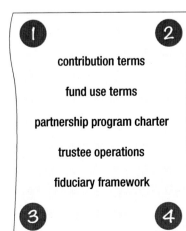

1   2

contribution terms

fund use terms

partnership program charter

trustee operations

fiduciary framework

3   4

1. **SPACE:** International partners convening and operating in the international arena benefit from a creative, informal, and modular space for collaboration.

2. **OPPORTUNITY:** Collectivized structures—like governing bodies, secretariats, and trust funds—increase opportunities for coordination, harmonization, and synergies.

3. **RESPONSIBILITY:** Collective input for shaping and decision making does not result in collective responsibility for implementation, but channels responsibility where it best belongs.

4. **COMPARATIVE ADVANTAGE:** Clean and clear allocation of roles and responsibilities enables partners to contribute in accordance with their comparative advantages.

5. **EXISTING ENTITY:** Partners that rely on existing supporting entities can lean on well-tuned operations, robust fiduciary frameworks, and proven track records.

6. **DEDICATION:** Supporting entities chosen from among partners are especially dedicated to making things happen, with all-encompassing support.

7. **SYNERGY:** Partners can comfortably and transparently perform multiple roles, both upstream and downstream, thereby leveraging structure and reinforcing synergies.

8. **LEVERAGE:** Shared governance through governing bodies allows partners to leverage each other's views and experience for greater buy-in and richer lessons learned.

9. **INCENTIVES:** Governing body engagement can create incentives for partners to keep participating and supporting, along with the collective ability to make changes over time.

10. **IMPACT:** Feedback loops that channel upstream, downstream, and back again enable partnership programs to grow, mature, and become more effective with greater impact.

4 BALANCE

It's all in the balance.

Pushing the envelope and angling for more have their place, but sustainability lies in the balance. For international partnership programs that want to provide long-term support (the hallmark of development work), or even for humanitarian platforms that want to keep short-term support always on tap, having a balanced structure is crucial to providing support for the duration.

International partnership programs are tiered and layered, modular and multimodal, in ways that need a solid foundation and even keel. They are replete with connections and delineations, separations and linkages, that require positioning and poise. The more they are centralized, the more they can rely on their own strong core. The more they are decentralized, they more they need to find their critical mass. The more diversified, the more they will want to map interconnected roles and responsibilities. The more inclusive, the more they benefit from creating cohesion.

It is hard to talk about structuring and designing partnership programs without reverting to ideas and images of balance. This book is filled with references to how something is positioned in the broader landscape or how partnership elements are placed in relation to each other. This book is also a study in ramifications. "If you do this, then consider the consequences and also do this." Or, "you can do this, but then be mindful of that." These are all balancing exercises.

Nature lives in the balance. It takes the cacophony of the universe and creates order—enough order to live (more or less) sustained lives. It brings routine and rhythm into a constantly changing, evolving world. And yet, life survives only if it adapts, staying both reactive and proactive to ever changing circumstances. Each life has to find its own sustainable equilibrium—of food, activity, sleep, or whatever it needs for sustenance. It has to keep the balance.

Like life, like partnership programs. How I love pointing out that partnership programs are organic. (>@ BfB: Dynamics—It's Organic) They have life cycles. (>@ PfP: Risk and Review—At the Front End) They are made of and by people. (>@ PfP: Partners and People) Partners have to stay interested and engaged. Programs have to stay effective and impactful. Feedback loops have to reinforce and re-energize, and, as needed, lead to replenishment and revision. Partners and their partnership programs have to stay on their toes and avoid churn to stay afloat.

The idea of staying afloat in the sea of change leads me back to my other theme: *like rock, like water.* This is the leitmotiv of my *Primer for Partners*, the companion to this book. (>@ PfP: Like Rock, Like Water) Taking this ancient wisdom to heart, the ability to join stability with flexibility is where this study of international partnership programs began. Positioning the *Primer's* dual quest for stability and flexibility now in this book as a matter of balance is a natural (organic) extension.

In the *Primer*, I describe how classic elements of partnership programs—signed agreements coupled with adopted documents, partnerships embodied in governing bodies, centralized support from secretariat functions, and pooled funds managed by fiduciary functions—can leverage stability and flexibility to create sustainability, efficiency, and impact. The *Primer* is one end-to-end discourse about the concepts, terms, tools, tips, and images that maximize stability and manage flexibility. Now, in this *Book for Builders*, we can take this a step further to better appreciate balance as the alpha and omega, the principle that underlies and overarches all. If stability and flexibility are seen in that prism, we can re-evaluate the dimensions and dynamics of partnership programs and revisit the tools and techniques we have to enhance balance.

The charter is one of those tools. Leveraging adopted documents is one of those techniques. If a charter is positioned squarely and forthrightly at the center of the partnership program, where it garners full buy-in, it can both shape and respond to partner ambitions and expectations. It can articulate ways to straddle the gaps, even the inputs and influence, set baselines and limits, anticipate tensions, prevent challenges, pre-agree remedies, position accountability, and so much more—all in a few pages, all in the name of keeping the balance.

As a document that simultaneously describes, creates, and unifies a partnership around its program, the charter can become a source of structural stability. As a document that is owned by the governing body, ideally adopted by consensus (>@ PfP: Decision Making), it can become an efficient avenue for flexibility. It would not be saying too much to name balance for partners and their partnership as the goal of the charter. And it would not be going too far to say a successful charter lies in the balance.

What does this mean in practice? Before we get too lofty and abstract, let's break it down with some concrete examples. We can tease out the specific pivots and placements in the partnership program balancing act in many different ways. Here are a number of common ones that traverse these pages, ones you will encounter in your own partnerships over and over again.

A successful charter balances stability and flexibility.

In the balance:

1. finding the sweet spot
2. creating critical mass
3. securing stability
4. strengthening the core
5. leveling the field
6. preserving consensus
7. managing trade-offs

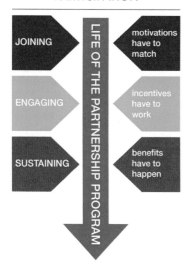

Finding the Sweet Spot

International partnership programs are voluntary. They have to work for everyone who participates—or they won't participate. They have to offer something for everyone who joins, engages, and sustains that participation. To put it another way:

a) Only those who have **motivations** to partner will seek to become partners.
b) Only those who have **incentives** to participate will get involved as partners.
c) Only those who realize the **benefits** of partnering will stay on as partners.

Each of these factors matters, and one leads to another. Partnership program interest starts with motivations, is galvanized by incentives, and becomes sustained over time through actual benefits.

Interestingly, all partners need not have the same motivations, incentives, and benefits. In fact, they often do not. A deliberately "apolitical" multilateral (with express political prohibitions in its articles) will have a different set of interests than a sovereign donor using taxpayer money with its national interest in mind. Those interests are in turn different from a private company that runs a business with a duty to maximize shareholder value. And yet, all can come together as partners in a common platform with a common goal.

Where these disparate interests converge is the sweet spot—a place where partners with divergent starting points can find common ground, where disparate profiles can come together around common goals.

Transparency is a core value of most international partnership programs. In that spirit, partners also do well to transparently acknowledge and appreciate their different starting points. This forms a basis of mutual respect among partners. It allows for an honest testing of compatibility and—in the interest of maintaining consensus—like-mindedness. (>@ PfP: Partners and People—Choosing Partners) It also occurs within limits. Each partner can acknowledge and accommodate the interests of the other partners only as long as this does not undermine its own interests.

And therein lies the balance. Putting this to the test early on, including through development of a partnership-wide charter that articulates this common ground on common terms, is an important confirmation of the partnership program's sweet spot. It is worth confirming from the start that the sweet spot is broad enough and deep enough to firmly ground the partnering effort over time.

THE PARTNERING SWEET SPOT

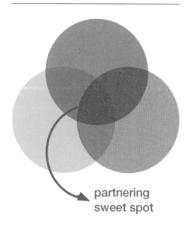

partnering
sweet spot

Venn Diagrams

We use Venn diagrams to depict relationships. Each partner is a set of interests and abilities that positions itself in relation to other partners and their interests and abilities. In partnering, Venn diagrams let us map out these overlaps for welcome confirmation of:

• Common interests that represent like-mindedness
• Agreed terms that represent collectives

These pages are full of references to like-mindedness and synergies as drivers of partnership, what makes them cohere and what makes them worthwhile. And these pages highlight the importance of finding common denominators and agreeing on common elements to create structural overlaps, which make up the partnership program. The sweet spot is but the starting point for engagement. Once we have that, partnership programs are all about plotting relationships, establishing connections, and finding intersections. Just like Venn diagrams.

Creating Critical Mass

Physics was never my strong suit in school, but I have since found that principles of mass and gravity are highly relevant to partnership programs. Picture the configuration of an atom, with protons and neutrons at the center and electrons drawn in, but still spinning around. It is about locating the core, with enough internal cohesion to keep the partnership connected. You can join together in a looser network with lighter bonding, or you can create a nucleus, become structured, and join together as a partnership.

The process of establishing a partnership program includes the accretion of *critical mass*—enough participation to become operational and achieve results. For example, you do not need all donors to be on board before launching, but you do want a critical mass, enough key donors, and enough funds to justify the effort and ensure some success. Even one champion donor may be enough critical mass to proceed. What constitutes critical mass is relative to what is proposed and projected. (>@ PfP: Typology—One-Stop-Shops vs. International Platforms)

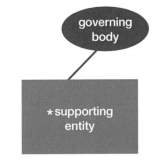

one-stop-shops:
in the supporting entity

In this sense, critical mass becomes a source of balance. If you have critical mass, whether in funding, or buy-in, or operational support, you can hoist your flag and then raise it over time. Or another image: Critical mass gives you the ballast needed to keep the boat afloat, with room for more funds, partners, and activities to come on board even after you have set sail.

A related concept is *center of gravity*. It is helpful to locate the partnership program's center of gravity, both to recognize how it shapes the rest and to manage its effects. If the supporting entity is the center of gravity, that can provide a solid foundation for everyone, especially if donors and other partners intend to give the supporting entity the dominant role. If they don't, perhaps they want to shift the center of gravity to the governing body, where they have more of a say. This they can do by rearranging roles and responsibilities, giving more to the governing body and less to the supporting entity.

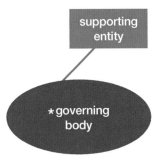

international platforms:
in the governing body

Partners can ask themselves: Does the center of gravity lie more in the trust fund (power of the purse) or the secretariat (power of the supporting entity) or an inclusive governing body (power of the collective)? Shifts in one or the other direction have a tremendous effect on the nature and culture of operations in ways that may be more intrinsic than intentional, but still reflect business decisions—or omissions. A partnership program can be deliberate about its center of gravity. It can choose to be "country-led" and then position content and processes around country participation. It can choose to be "evidence-based" and then position content and processes around results, evaluations, lessons learned, and other back-end functions. Partners that locate their center of gravity and build structures and procedures around it are building better balance.

DONOR-TRUSTEE DYNAMICS

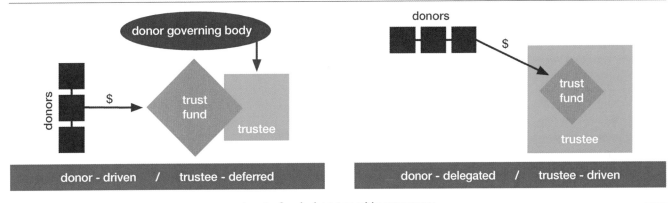

trust - funded partnership programs

Securing Stability

Partners can find balance in their sweet spot, their critical mass, and their center of gravity, but those alone are not enough. They need to build on it. They need to add enough infrastructure to create stability. The scale of operations or the amount of complexity that partners can afford is inversely related to the degree of stability that they bring to bear. The more ambitious a partnership program wants to be, the more it pays to invest in stability. It all adds up to balance.

What creates this kind of stability? A firm foundation, with buttressing in the wings, a bunch of glue, some structural pillars, a wide roof to protect from the elements, and even a lightning rod to subdue the storm surge are among the features that come to mind. It is, of course, possible to do some patching over time—put some caulking in the cracks or sand over the blemishes—but both the New Testament and the Three Little Piggies tell us that building a house on mere sand or with straw can have crippling consequences.

Firm Foundations

For that firm foundation, it is generally better to anticipate the load and lay the brick-and-block foundation from the start. We have already highlighted the *charter* as a tool to reinforce common ground as the basis of the venture. We can also focus on the **supporting entity** as a foundational piece for international partnership programs. It works both ways:

- A partnership program that is deeply embedded in a supporting entity through crucial secretariat and trustee operations will have a solid footing within a robust operating environment, potentially with P&I.

- A supporting entity that is deeply embedded in the partnership program, where it participates as an integrated partner (>@ PfP: International Partnership Programs—Central Support), will offer a full panoply of resources as part of the support package, making for an even stronger foundation.

But even here, balancing is in order. A supporting entity that overly absorbs a partnership program can undermine the other partners, while a partnership program that tries to override a supporting entity can end up in a resource-draining tug-of-war (>@ PfP: Supporting Entities—Baselines). While the specific point of balance will differ from case to case, depending on how much partners want to collectively determine or conveniently defer, finding the right balance with the supporting entity can make or break a partnership program.

Buttresses

Stability is not just bottom-up; it comes in many different forms. The dimensions of a partnership program are not just vertical, but also horizontal. When we look horizontally, we can see additional opportunities for increased stability, like these:

- **More inclusive participation.** The governing body may already be sized up to the max, and yet there are other partners worthy of inclusion. What to do? In the *Primer for Partners*, I list ten "workarounds" to manage the numbers, including constituencies, additional bodies, and stakeholder events. (>@ PfP: Trade-Offs—The Horizontal Buy-In Spectrum) When this supplemental participation adds up to more buy-in, increased advocacy, and better lessons learned, this can provide reinforcement and buttress stability.

- **Greater technical expertise.** The seated partner representatives may be perfect for the governing body, but may not represent all the expertise available. It is worth thinking about ways to crowd in expertise, including to share the load, especially when partners are willing to provide additional staff support as in-kind contributions. (>@ PfP: Partners and People—Crowding In Expertise) This could come in the form of ad hoc working groups or task forces. It could be collected in an available roster of experts. It could even become a standing technical advisory committee with specific support functions. More expertise can converge into more robust programming and implementation, all of it buttressing.

- **Better diversified implementation.** Partnership programs vary widely in their implementation constellations. Very commonly, it is one trust fund with one and the same implementation channel. But it can also be one trust fund with multiple channels, or multiple trust funds each with its own channel, or multiple funding sources with even more channels. The point is that partnership programs can bring in multiple implementing modalities. The ability to leverage the comparative advantages of different implementers—to engage in more projects or tougher environments, like fragility and conflict zones—is another form of buttressing. More fit-for-purpose implementation can build broader, but still balanced, operations.

We could go on with examples: Partners love "lean" secretariats, but it is better not to trim the fat to the point of being unfit. The glue provided by secretariat functions— around the brand, for advocacy, to support governing body input, and so much more—is essential for stability. Similarly, a governing body that carefully balances like-mindedness with inclusion may better weather criticism from outside by co-opting some of it within, a delicate but potentially effective calculation. (>@ PfP: Trade-Offs—The Horizontal Buy-In Spectrum—Inclusion vs. Efficiency) Or a governing body chair that is perceived as fair and practices good outreach can be an individual source of stability that quickly grounds the sparks when lightning flies.

Bottom line, if partners think about where their sensitivities and vulnerabilities lie, there are a hundred and more ways they can leverage structure to build stability.

FIRM BOTTOM AND FANNED BUTTRESSES

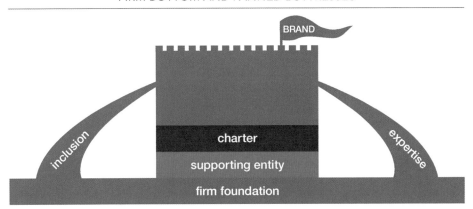

"Neutral" or "Independent" Chairs

The capability and credibility of the chair of the governing body can have a major bearing on the stability of a partnership program. Personality is a factor (>@ BfB: The Annotated Charter—Governing Body—Governing Body Chair), but how the position is structured can also play a role. In this respect, partnership programs, particularly some international platforms, occasionally decide to have "neutral" or "independent" chairs. They like the idea that the chair is not overly aligned with any of the partners. This is a management, rather than partnership, approach to the function. It is modular with intentional separation, rather than synergistically integrated.

Even so, these arrangements are often more conceptually than factually neutral or independent. For example, one of the decision-making members of the governing body can fill the chair position with a second, non-decision-making representative, while keeping its decision-making representative. Or the supporting entity that already seats trustee and secretariat representatives can add a senior level, non-decision-making chair to the mix. This works if all partners, including the supporting entity, believe the "neutral" chair can, in good faith, fairly and constructively represent the interests of the partnership program as a whole over those of her own institution (hopefully never to directly conflict). Neither scenario assures complete neutrality, but can at least free all member and observer representatives to focus on their respective roles, while the neutral chair focuses on chairing.

This kind of "neutrality" relies on performance and perception, rather than bringing someone in from the outside. It is the rare international partnership program that truly engages an "independent" chair from beyond the partnership ranks. It sounds good in theory, but is challenging to implement. The move risks creating a third-wheel dynamic that interferes with partnership synergies and complicates partnership engagement. If an outsider chair is engaged as a check-and-balance against the supporting entity or other dominant partners, query why the balance is off to begin with. Tipping the balance with an arm's-length chair could well exacerbate, rather than alleviate, off-kilter relations. Fixing the partnership by weakening the partnership may not be the best answer.

Strengthening the Core

Taking a closer look, the essence of partnership program structure lies in connections and delineations. (>@ BfB: Dualities— Connections and Delineations) As one might expect, balance lies in the strength of these connections and the clarity of these delineations. By teasing out the links that make up the web of relationships and responsibilities, partners can consider gaps and overlaps, thereby fortifying their partnership landscape.

Some of these linkages are more important than others. We can highlight a few of the important ones:

- The secretariat-trustee axis (>@ PfP: Secretariats—Embedded, Inhouse Secretariats—Benefits) is a particularly potent, structural beam, especially if both functions reside in the same supporting entity. Even if the trustee entity and secretariat supporting entity are different, how well these two functions play together has ramifications for balance across the partnership program.

- How well the secretariat supports the governing body, and how well that support is recognized as distinct from trustee functions (>@ PfP: Secretariats—Lessons Learned), also factors into how well the partnership program sustains partner interest and program operations.

- As one of our perennial topics, how well we set up the fit between the partnership program and the supporting entity is crucial. A disconnect between the supporting entity's mandate and strategies and the overall partnership program could prove fatal to operations. (>@ PfP: Supporting Entities—Nuclear Option)

- From a document point of view, how well constitutive documents and signed agreements are aligned with each other and with other partnership documents—strategies, work plans, results frameworks, operations manuals— determines the framework's durability. (>@ BfB: Agile Alignment)

- Even from one partnership program to the next, how well they align is worth some attention. We can look for ways to make partnering initiatives more complementary than competitive on the international scene.

Everywhere there are relationships that need to stay in equilibrium for partnership programs to thrive and survive.

There is a way to avoid tipping over or going under: *incrementalism.* It is perfectly okay to start small and grow over time. It is possible to build bit-by-bit, rather than launch with a big bang. It can work great to start on a shoestring or with a narrow scope and then plan to add on. Do any of the following apply?

- Is a set of partners ready to constitute the governing body, signaling a start while still crowding in funding and more participants?

- Can a champion donor provide seed funding to get a secretariat going before launching a dedicated, multi-donor trust fund?

- Can a pilot project proceed to generate results and then persuade others to scale up?

That may be enough to go for it.

In this regard, incrementalism dovetails with innovation. A tried-and-true structure can suit a classic partnership program, of which there are plenty. But some partners want to stretch their resources into new modalities, or push the envelope into riskier arrangements, or depart from established business lines, or color outside the lines of existing policies and procedures. For them, the path will likely be more challenging. Institutional support, donor contributions, and partner buy-in may not be forthcoming without proofs of concepts, beta runs, and pilot projects—but that could perhaps still happen step-by-step, incrementally.

Growing by Phasing

Here, by way of example, is a scenario about growth and maturity, about being accretive:

The Outcomes-Funded Approach Partnership Program (known as O-FAPP) wants to pilot new approaches to get greater, results-driven impact and realizes it will need to adjust and expand over time. From a life cycle perspective, the partners envision three phases: (1) a founding phase with a core group focused on a single sector that supports local efforts in a select group of beneficiary countries; (2) a consolidating phase with an expanded group of partners based on one or two successful modalities in more countries; and (3) a scale-up phase, with expanded funding for a multi-pronged leveraging of the partnership program's technical expertise and fiduciary framework into more sectors.

1 *Phase 1* starts with a light touch by the partners. Initially, downstream implementation is influenced by the partnership, but undertaken by some of the partners outside of the partnership. The main Phase 1 partnership element is a governing body with secretariat support, as defined in a simple charter. Partners develop a common strategy and results framework, coordinate implementation efforts, and share reports on progress. After collecting data and commissioning an independent evaluation, all positive, Phase 1 partners decide to promote a Phase 2 platform and engage additional partners.

2 *Phase 2* wins over some key donors and adds a trust fund with contribution agreements that point to the existing but revised charter. Dedicated funding also supports direct developing country participation alongside donors and implementing partners. Phase 2 continues for several years, leading up to another independent evaluation. The assessment is again positive.

3 *Phase 3* is kicked off with a replenishment event under revised charter terms that broaden activities based on lessons learned during Phase 2.

All throughout, the same supporting entity provides critical continuity, starting with secretariat-type support and then expanding into management of dedicated funds from champion donors that are persuaded by Phase 1 results. The light governance terms agreed for the Phase 1 charter are replaced by a more comprehensive charter in Phase 2, with an eye to further changes going into Phase 3. The dedicated trust fund is carefully aligned with existing partnership documents. For Phase 3, the supporting entity and partners agree to establish several new, sector-specific trust funds, both to avoid legacy issues under Phase 2 terms and allow donor earmarking by sector. All trust funds are positioned under the purview of the single governing body and apply the charter terms, as revised over time, through their contribution agreements.

This staged but seamless step-by-step approach is well-considered from the start through aligned documents that accommodate governing body decision making. This puts the ownership where it belongs, in the hands of the partners, and lets those partners define the structure, not the other way around. (>@ BfB: Agile Alignment)

In general, when planning partnership programs, consider phasing. It is better to build from the core than start by reaching for the sky. If the wings are too long, they may crack. But if the body is strong, with a clear center of gravity or enough critical mass, partners can add sound and sturdy appendages. The load should not overwhelm the load-bearing beams. If a partnership program grows too fast or becomes overextended, it may be time to pause and consolidate.

Once again, it is in the balance. Partners do not need to sell themselves short or be underambitious. They can be simultaneously prudent and opportunistic. But remember, when you anchor your rope on the mountainside, make sure the link is strong and secure before climbing on to higher heights.

Leveling the Field

Try playing on an uneven field, and you are apt to trip and lose your balance. We use the "level field" in talk of partnership programs as a euphemism for fairness. Even so, partnership programs rarely refer to "fairness" in their ranks. International partners are usually in diplomacy, not morality, mode. (>@ PfP: Trust Funds—Trust). Development partnerships are all about cooperation and support, but good will and magnanimity are largely assumed, and decorum does not like to point fingers. And yet, the pressure points are there, including when partners want or expect to get their due. Whether partner relations or partnership benefits are "fair" and balanced—whether the playing field is level—merits some attention.

There are readily apparent scenarios where fairness comes into play. It is then up to partners to decide whether and how to balance the interests.

While fairness may be in the eye of the beholder, fairness in partnership programs can become a collective value with partnership implications. We have three examples on the next page—equal recognition of voice, equal opportunity to engage, and equal access to funding—that show how partners may need to actively balance. Where the allocation of partnership resources, like influence, participation, and funds, become measures of fairness, partnership programs may need to invoke structure to even things out. Sustained participation will then turn on whether partners believe they are being treated fairly, whatever that means for each of them individually, in ways that the collective structuring can help drive.

Preserving Consensus

Apropos fairness, it is appropriate to appreciate consensus. Consensus as a decision-making modality is a model of equality. It gives due recognition to every decision-making voice, and therein lies a form of fairness. Of course, how fair ultimately depends on who is included as decision makers—essentially, who are the decision-making members of the governing body—but requiring consensus within that body is eminently more equalizing and inclusive than the fractional voting alternative. (>@ PfP: Decision Making—Voting)

Voting, as compared to consensus, allows divisional decision making. Whatever the fraction required, whether plurality (more than other positions), majority (more than half) or supermajority (like two-thirds or three-quarters), decisions made by vote can be made without getting everyone to agree. Consensus decision making, by contrast, results in a decision only if no one—not a single decision-maker—objects. To put it another way, consensus gives each voice a veto. You can't get more equal than that.

Some partners are challenged by the prospect that any individual partner could single-handedly hold up progress. They may have nightmares of being paralyzed, sabotaged, and stymied, all because of one outlier. And yes, at the margin, that is possible. I have come across a single partnership program among hundreds where a particularly ill-disposed, ill-willed partner put the entire partnership program into abeyance for over a year. But that is truly what that was: an outlier.

We can always be transparent about the fact that international partnership programs work only if all partners cooperate. There is no forcing or enforcing behavior; this is largely a voluntary engagement, often on a handshake. (>@ PfP: Trust Funds—Trust) Without beating around the bush, this requires a shared dedication among like-minded partners and a willingness to be good citizens. (>@ PfP: Partners and People—Being a Good Partner) Partners can select each other carefully and demand a constructive commitment to a common goal as the price of participating.

Against that backdrop, it is immensely reassuring for each partner to know its opinions and positions are valued. A donor, stacked with millions, has as much heft as a country government, whose future is at stake. A supporting entity, with soup-to-nuts exposure, can rest easy on its risk profile without pulling a special trump card in terms of influence. Regardless of contribution, impact, exposure, or other variables, consensus says that unless everyone is on board, no one is on board.

There is one thing to be said about preserving consensus: It's worth it. The counterfactual experience of partners that proceed despite objections, or plow ahead despite dissenting blocks, is disruption and dissolution. It is almost always worth the extra effort to find the sweet spot, manage concerns and contrarians, and tuck and nip the package until it fits everyone as a whole. Remember, too, that consensus is not unanimity. It needs just enough buy-in to overcome any objection. Abstentions and dissents on the record are all okay if they do not block the decision. (>@ PfP: Decision Making—Consensus)

Where the essence of partnership hits the road, in the governing body where the partners convene, deciding by consensus levels the playing field. And keeping consensus keeps the balance.

Smoothing Out the Field—Three Examples

Donor-recipient dynamics. In the vertical hierarchy of fund flows, donors are on top, recipients on the bottom. (>@ PfP: Structure—Bridging Action and Results—Upstream/Downstream) This is the power of the purse, and it takes deliberate effort to even the scale. A first marker in that regard was the 2005 Paris Declaration, which memorialized the intention of development partners to strike a different balance. In particular, it sought to give developing countries—the recipients of aid—a place at the table. Even in the structure of the Paris Declaration, where each constituency put forward its commitments, there was a signal that we are all in this together, a tenor of equality. (>@ BfB: Dualities—Verticals and Horizontals) Some may worry that bringing grant recipients into decision making poses a conflict of interest, but in fact, it represents the essence of development partnership. (>@ PfP: Synergistic Conflicts) How else to ensure that a beneficiary benefits but to ask the beneficiary? More fundamentally, development work has shifted from a top-down colonial model to more of a partners-on-a-par egalitarian model. As a result, international partnership programs have come a long way in leveling the playing field between haves (Part 1 countries) and have nots (Part 2 countries). Examples abound where fund flow hierarchies are tempered by peer-to-peer partnering. (>@ PfP: Trust Funds—Recipients—Beneficiary Recipients)

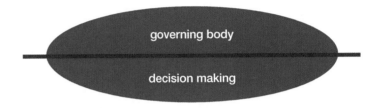

Private sector participation. Sovereigns and multilaterals often talk about partnering with the private sector. However, bringing private companies into international partnership programs as direct partners can be challenging. (>@ PfP: Partners and People—Engaging the Private Sector) For-profit companies with business motives are not inherently bad partners, since there is plenty of room for a sweet spot of converging interests, but that competitive backdrop does complicate matters. There is something less than palatable when a specific company has entrée to a partnership program, but when its direct competitors do not, especially if that entrée bestows good visibility and do-gooder publicity. Instead, the rule to follow—to level the playing field—is open access. If partners open the door to the private sector, they need to open it come one, come all, rather than selectively relying on an invitation-only approach. Only that way is it—or is it at least perceived to be—fair. And although this kind of open access could wreak havoc with the numbers, that can be surmounted through various techniques. (>@ PfP: Trade-Offs—The Horizontal Buy-In Spectrum—Workarounds)

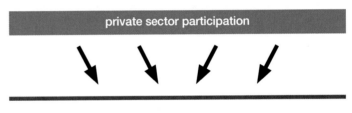

Downstream fiduciaries. In partnership programs with multiple downstream fiduciaries, as is typical of international platforms, the fiduciaries are usually motivated to participate by the prospect of funds flowing their way. These fiduciaries are not commercial competitors, as in the case of private sector companies, but may nonetheless "compete" for funds. Trust fund disbursements come from a finite pool, and fund flows are usually based on case-by-case decisions, rather than pre-agreed or guaranteed amounts. As a result, even just the perception of bias in how those funds are allocated can rankle prospective recipients. If, for example, the downstream operations of the trustee entity have an inside track over other downstream fiduciaries, that would normally not be okay. This is one reason limited trustees and their accompanying limited secretariats are "limited," and why they are usually scrupulous about staying within their bounds—coordinating and facilitating, without favoring specific proposals. (>@ PfP: Typology—International Platforms) They deal with administrative and compliance aspects, but leave substantive and decision-making aspects to the governing body.

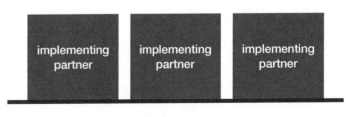

Managing Trade-Offs

Let's look at one more example of balance, one that follows the entire life cycle from conception to completion and permeates every partnership program's day-to-day: trade-offs. (>@ PfP: Trade-Offs) Managing trade-offs is a matter of maintenance. It is part of making things work. I subscribe to the view that women can't have it all (see the Slaughter-Sandberg debate), and the same can be said of partnership programs. That is life, and life is not nirvana. The best we can do is be mindful of priorities and conscientious about resources. We can come to grips with finite funds, short attention spans, capacity constraints, and absorption limits. We can recognize when competing goals or conflicting interests need reconciling into manageable arrangements.

This is typically what managers do, and often the orchestrating, sequencing, juggling, and even triaging is left to the secretariat head and staff. But in partnership programs, this need not be secretariat-only or implementation-only work. The partners themselves have a collective role to play, if they care to step up. They can be either iterative decision makers or upfront framers:

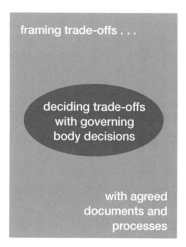

COLLECTIVE TRADE-OFFS

framing trade-offs . . .

deciding trade-offs with governing body decisions

with agreed documents and processes

- *Deciding trade-offs.* Depending on how micromanaging the governing body wants to be, versus how much it delegates to trustee, secretariat, and other functions, or depending on where the partners want to put the critical mass of decision making (>@ PfP: International Partnership Programs—Shared Decision Making), partners can decide how much the governing body gets to decide. This is usually reflected in the roles and responsibilities enumerated in the charter or equivalent document. More point-for-point decision making by the governing body means more collective management of trade-offs.

- *Framing trade-offs.* If the governing body sets the stage, it need not act in the play. By framing the terms of engagement upfront, it can comfortably stay hands-off later. A partnership-adopted charter is such a framework document. For example, if the charter includes objectives, that sets priorities. It can include selection criteria for allocating funds, annual work plan processes for keeping a strategic focus, or technical review steps for bringing in the right amount of expertise. A meta-results framework is another framing tool, as an overarching blueprint for monitoring progress, as a way to shape and steer all partnership program activities. Whether mandatory or just guidance, these collectively agreed terms can frame the scope within which trade-offs are made.

The management of trade-offs is political, operational, strategic, and substantive. A partnership program where the views of all partners are actively reflected can stay vibrant by embracing trade-offs as collectives. Placing every decision before the governing body is usually too much; decisions about day-to-day operations is what secretariats, trustees, and other fiduciaries are for. But framing is usually essential. Setting priorities and parameters for subsequent decision making can be an effective way to temper extremes, avoid bias, set baselines, keep to priorities, and generally hold to account in a way that speaks to every partner's intentions and expectations.

Giving collective voice to partnership program trade-offs is a way to promote balance. If the contours are established from the start, it can keep the partnership program within bounds. If, with all hands on deck, the currents are channeled and sails are trimmed, it is easier to keep an even keel, while still sailing far and fast.

Conclusion

With aspects to balance wherever you look in partnership programs, there is also a constant chance of getting off kilter. The many ways to create balance also reflect the many ways balance can be undone. And yet, partners usually participate with the collective in mind, believing the whole can be greater than the sum of its parts. That bodes well for being measured, moderate, and mindful of others, all forces for balance. Partners may intuit the sensitivity and agility it takes to both keep steady and go with the flow—like rock, like water—so as to stay in the balance.

As with any journey, however, the better one knows the terrain, the easier the path and the quicker the journey. Partners that have a good sense of the landscape do a better job of navigating their trek and reaching their goals.

Among the dynamics that sway international partnership programs are forces that push and pull, planes that stretch up and out, flows that go up and down. Finding equilibrium is also a matter of finding the many points of balance within many different dimensions. Where partners place themselves are by-and-large business decisions—whether deliberate or by default—that turn on structure and design. Without understanding the dimensions, however, it is mighty hard to find that even keel. So in the name of balance, we would also do well to consider how to spot and leverage the many dualities— which we do next.

Be measured, moderate, and mindful of others.

5 DUALITIES

In pairs:

1. connections and delineations
2. upstream and downstream
3. verticals and horizontals
4. structure and contract
5. informal and formal
6. multilateral and bilateral
7. inward and outward
8. conflicts and synergies
9. stability and flexibility
10. standardization and customization
11. harmonization and individuation

This and that, to and fro, yin and yang, you and me: The world is full of dualities. Naturally, that includes international partnership programs. Partnership program structure is all about relationships, and that is exactly what a duality is, how one thing relates to another. Being multidimensional, and often quite complex, international partnership programs embody many layered and intertwined relationships that can sometimes make for a pretty swirly spaghetti graphic. However, for purposes of getting a handle on the topic, we need something more graspable than spaghetti strands, so let's start by breaking it down into pairs.

Once you start looking for dual relationships in international partnership programs, you notice they are all over the place. I have eleven here, right off the bat. If you read the *Context* and *Balance* chapters, you will recognize most of them. It is hard to describe the fundamentals of international partnership programs without seeing the pairings. As you work your way through this list, I hope you sense the richness of the landscape, the potential for options and alternatives, and the value of this practice area as an inspiration for improvement.

Connections and Delineations

Classically, there are two kinds of lawyers: litigators and dealmakers. They are quite different, so when someone decides to go to law school, it is a good idea to know which path they prefer. Having gone to law school to keep my options open, I did not, but fortunately ended up on the right path for me. Nothing against litigators, but they usually get to deal with situations where parties oppose each other. They engage in the ex post, the aftermath, the land of dispute and controversy. Dealmakers, on the other hand, get to deal with parties as they seek to come together. They engage in the ex ante, the land of potential and promise. Clearly oversimplified, but in the one you are creating and defining relationships, and in the other, you are mending and managing them. It is obvious that one has a bearing on the other. If you create and define well upfront, the need to mend and manage over time is lessened. I like being at the front and friendly end, where I can stay mindful of the back end.

The practice of structuring and designing international partnership programs and their trust funds fits in the category of dealmaking. It is not commercial in the for-profit sense, but akin to setting up a business. It is transactional, with the usual rhythms and orchestrations—concepts, due diligence, term sheets, negotiations, documentation—that ultimately, hopefully, culminate in closure.

In all of this, the key element is **relationships**. It is all about how the parties relate to each other. Who has what rights or obligations—and is one party's right another party's obligation? Who has what roles, what responsibilities? Is there a hierarchy—are some giving and others receiving instructions? Who has a veto, a last say, a right of consent? Who delegates, who defers? Where are the exposure points—operationally, who depends on whom? Reputationally, is everyone exposed to everyone else?

Which brings me to the first duality: connecting and delineating. The act of defining relationships has both elements to it. On the one hand, parties (partners) are being connected. On the other hand, they are being separated. It makes sense; you cannot connect things that are already melded. You have to separate to connect. You have to delineate to define relationships.

International partnership programs are at their modular best with clean and clear connections and delineations. (>@ PfP: Ten Tried and True Tips— Be Modular) They are constructions built by and of partners—they are constructing themselves. Each partner is a building block. Sometimes they connect, as in a governing body, and sometimes they disconnect, as in separate implementation streams, but always, the linkages are important.

When partners come to me with a new partnership in the making, I instinctively start by drawing a diagram. We map the components and draw the lines. (>@ PfP: Structure—Whiteboarding) We follow the power, we follow the money. We can see how one partner appears in multiple places, filling multiple roles. We can see who is on the horizontal, who is on the vertical, often on both. We can see the links we are embedding and the synergies we are leveraging. And sometimes we see how complex it is getting—that spaghetti graphic—and think about ways to simplify.

This connecting-delineating duality is a powerful dynamic in constructs that are, by structure and design, meant to be self-reinforcing. Without delineations, you have a morass. But for every delineation, you want a connection to ensure a critical mass, to get the center to hold.

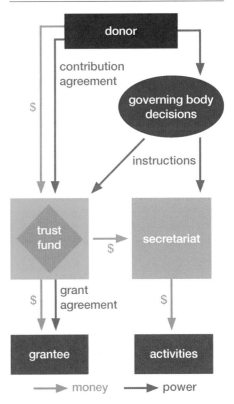

donor money and power go together

ON THE HORIZONTAL,
ON THE VERTICAL

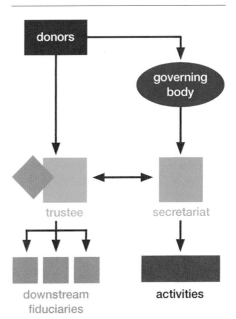

power and money verticals

governance, administration,
implementation horizontals

Upstream and Downstream

Another duality that plays into these dynamics reflects a view of the world more than an actual topology. International partners regularly refer to upstream and downstream realms. It just rolls off the tongue. But what does this division refer to? What line is being drawn—and where?

Given the prevalence of international trust funds, one might say this has a funding connotation, and that makes sense. Fund flows are perceived as a vertical hierarchy from donor to trustee to recipient. However, this worldview has more facets than just fund flows, in the same way international partnership programs are about more than the money. We can consider a number of upstream/downstream variants:

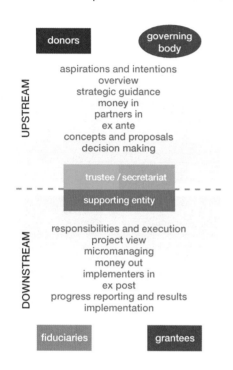

- Upstream money coming in (contributions from donors) and downstream money going out (distributions to recipients)
- Upstream decision making (governing bodies) and downstream implementation (implementation partners)
- Upstream ex ante (concepts and proposals) and downstream ex post (projects and results)
- Upstream partner aspirations and intentions (multilateral) and downstream responsibilities and execution (bilateral)
- Upstream high-level overview (strategic guidance) and downstream micromanaging (project decisions)

And so on. These stratifications fit individual partnership programs to varying degrees, but it is interesting to think about where that line lies between up and down. Does it have the same location in all cases or vary depending on the scenario?

Clearly, where you stand determines what you see. I submit that this international up/down distinction almost always takes a particular point of view: that of the supporting entity. When scoping international partnership programs, one of the most obvious and common positions from which to look is the operative center, the locus of financial and administrative support. This basically means viewing the world with supporting entity-centric eyes. And if you think about the importance of the supporting entity in the scope of the partnership program, that rings true.

Of course, framing the partnership program from that angle skews the view, as would any vantage point. However, seeing things from a supporting entity perspective is not bad, for several reasons:

- You have the best view, wider and deeper, of the entire partnership program.
- You start from the core, where things come together, to see what holds and how well.
- You connect directly to the primary policy environment and risk profile undergirding the whole.
- You tap into the supporting entity's role as driver, custodian, and glue of the partnership program.

Other partners may resent that the supporting entity puts itself so prominently into this central position. However, chances are that the partners themselves put the supporting entity there, by relying on it for any number of functions and activities that a partnership program needs and that accrue to the supporting entity by both design and default. (>@ PfP: Custodial Effect) How much the center of gravity lies with the supporting entity is variable, sometimes negotiable, and depends on both what partners explicitly agree and what they collectively decide not to do themselves. More often than not, partners implicitly leave center stage to the partner that otherwise holds the bag.

Identifying the upstream and downstream can orient you when considering international partnership program structure and design. It makes sense to build from the crux of the engagement. In virtually all cases, there will be administrative support functions: of the governing body, for branding, for any of the partnership dimensions. That will be the ongoing source of continuity, a steady towline as it were, even as other partners engage on and off. Moreover, if there is an active trust fund, this includes a financial support function, a fiduciary center. Seeing both of these support roles as central hubs from which the partnership program emanates, and into which the partnership program connects, lets you organize the lines and show the relationships. This up and down is in any case a useful starting point. From there we can think about what's in and out, over and under, in international space and on the ground, and sometimes all around.

Verticals and Horizontals

When we are talking about upstream and downstream, we are also talking about verticals and horizontals. The up and down spheres are juxtaposed in a vertical hierarchy that is divided by a horizontal plane. If you identify the vertical and horizontal planes, you can think about integration within each plane and across both planes. That again means connections, with opportunities for leveraged synergies. How do the vertical elements relate to each other? How do the horizontal elements interact? How do the two planes intersect? Let's take a closer look, starting with our two mighty oaks (>@ PfP: Typology—Introducing Two Mighty Oaks):

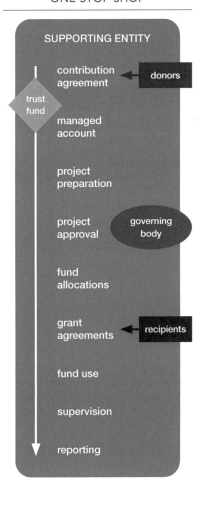

- *The vertically-integrated one-stop-shop.* At one end of the dense forest of possibilities, we have the one-stop-shop, the comprehensive "package" version where the supporting entity offers a full suite of services, while also stepping up as a partner. (>@ PfP: International Partnership Programs—Central Support) It is the drop-and-go option, where donors and other partners make their contributions and hand off basically all responsibility. It is the supporting entity bear hug, where partners might at times feel smothered, but mostly rest easy, knowing they can rely on someone else to get things done.

  The dominant feature of the one-stop-shop is the vertically-continuous, unbroken chain of fiduciary responsibility, following the funds from contribution to final use. Although the one-stop-shop also aggregates related functions into its ambit—governing body support, secretariat and custodial support, implementation and supervision support, evaluation support—one-stop-shops are built around international trust funds. With this focus on fund flows, from upstream to downstream, one-stop-shops vertically integrate all elements off of this central spine, like a pagoda's noble *shinbashira*, which serves as a structural pillar of the overall partnership program.

- *The horizontally-spread international platform.* If one-stop-shops are the temple of the supporting entity, at the altar of the trust fund, then international platforms put the emphasis on the congregation. The trust fund is still central to its operations, and funds are still funneled in and out of a commingled pool, but in a more polytheistic, more diversified way. This happens both upstream and downstream. Upstream, the governing body has an expanded role when trustee and secretariat roles are more limited; this is the first collective plurality. Downstream, the fiduciary role is dispersed across multiple downstream partners, each with full standing in its own right; this is the second collective plurality.

International platforms are less packaged than parsed, leaving room for more diverse participation, while also calling for more partnership and coordination. They get more input from more players, emphasizing the collective, rather than relying on a single, channeled, delegated effort. In other words, the international platform fans out. Managing these dynamics of inclusion becomes an exercise in maintaining level playing fields, particularly vis-à-vis downstream fiduciaries. (>@ BfB: Balance—Leveling the Field) Operating across the platform takes reach and balance across horizontal planes.

HORIZONTAL SPREAD: INTERNATIONAL PLATFORM

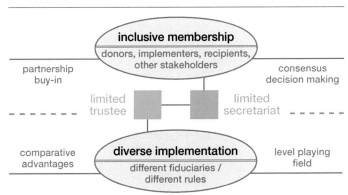

Now let's consider two other important horizontals, ones that come up a lot in these pages:

- **The horizontal, post-to-post secretariat-trustee axis.** Of all the synergies in the partnership program pantheon, the interlocking handclasp of the secretariat and trustee is one of the most powerful. It is especially powerful when both roles are handled by the same entity, sometimes so interlocking, they are not separately named. (>@ PfP: Secretariats—Embedded, Inhouse Secretariats) Both roles pivot between the upstream and downstream, functioning from within the horizontal, administrative plane that lies between inputs and outputs, while supporting fund flows and decision flows. This axis connects shared governance and fiduciary obligations. It meshes external partner and internal supporting entity dynamics. It becomes the core around which trust-funded partnership programs cohere. At the epicenter, this axis is a reinforcing girder in both one-stop-shops and international platforms.

If you think about a car, axles transfer power and torque from engine to wheels. They sustain the full weight of the car, plus any passengers and load. They withstand acceleration and deceleration, hills and valleys, bumps and potholes. This is the secretariat-trustee axis at its well-tuned best: enabling a smooth drive, keeping everyone on board, and absorbing shocks along the way.

SECRETARIAT-TRUSTEE AXIS

partnership governance and brand

financial focus   partnership focus

administrative plane — **trustee** - - - **secretariat** — same or different supporting entity

contractually bound   structurally engaged

activities and results

- **The horizontal, peer-to-peer governing body.** In important ways, the governing body is the antidote to the trust fund. When all eyes follow the money, partnership perspectives are trained on the hierarchy of fund flows. From this vantage point, donors are up, recipients are down, developed countries (haves) are on top, and developing countries (have nots) are on the bottom. That has a practical effect, as fund flow terms are dictated by their source, and a symbolic effect. When you are at the bottom of the food chain, you may not feel like much of a partner, with others determining your priorities and deciding your fate. This asymmetry helped precipitate the internationally resonant Paris Declaration in 2005, which sought to reset the relationships and give developing countries more partnership voice. That spirit lives on.

An inclusive governing body puts partners as peers, in a shared venue where topics are discussed, issues are deliberated, and decisions are made. It is not always easy to fairly and effectively combine the views of benefactors and beneficiaries, but it has a purpose. (>@ BfB: Balance—Leveling the Field) Partnership programs can even position horizontal governance at both global and country levels. (>@ PfP: Trade-Offs—The Vertical Continuity Spectrum—Global-to-Country) A second line of country-specific, often government-led, platforms can coordinate locally, closer to the actual implementation. There are many variations on the theme. The main point is that leapfrogging beneficiaries into shared governance is a way to flip from vertical to horizontal, thereby reinforcing partnership synergies. (>@ PfP: Synergistic Conflicts—Seeing and Seeking Synergies—Upstream/Downstream Synergies)

PEER-TO-PEER, ON A PAR

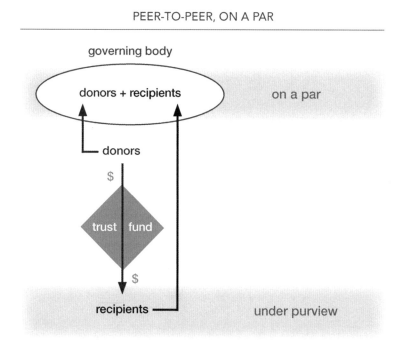

governing body

donors + recipients   on a par

donors

$

trust fund

$

recipients   under purview

In addition to flipping funding verticals into governing horizontals, inclusion is strengthened by two other verticals:

- *Vertically-connected global-country linkages.* Mentioning two-tier governance brings up the topic of global-country linkages. Most international partnership programs operate on both global and country planes and seek the right balance. This can involve trade-offs among finite resources—money, attention, secretariat staff, publicity. In fact, though, global-country linkages do more to amplify each other than compete. The stronger the global presence, the greater the means for local engagement. The stronger the country engagement, the greater the basis for global support. The feedback loops between global and local efforts can galvanize advocacy, mobilize resources, enrich knowledge, generate lessons learned, and generally fortify the partnership program. Far from zero sum, global-country linkages have lots of positive sum potential. (>@PfP: Trade-Offs—The Vertical Continuity Spectrum—Feedback Loops)

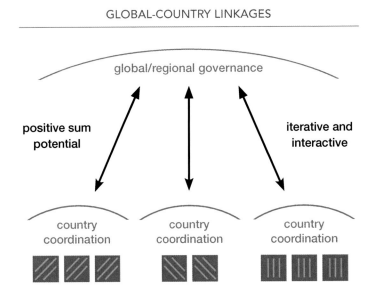

GLOBAL-COUNTRY LINKAGES

- *Vertically-integrated developing country voice.* Horizontal inclusion through the governing body means vertical integration of developing country voice. The overall partnership program is fertile ground to layer in fund recipients and beneficiaries as partners. This shift is not necessarily easy or intuitive. It upends the vertical (hierarchical) flow of funds and enforces the horizontal (partnering) approach of partnership programs. But partnership programs attuned to the countries they serve can make this shift. The result may not fully level the playing field—by definition, donors are givers and developing countries are receivers—but the balance of interests and power can be deliberately and structurally adjusted. For example, if developing country representatives sit at the same table with the same decision-making status as donors, and decision making is based on consensus, then voilà— everyone has an equal veto, everyone's voice has equal heft, and everyone's buy-in is an equal prerequisite.

For international partnership programs that take partnering seriously, an inclusive approach prefers horizontals to verticals. But with partnership programs that incorporate dedicated funding vehicles, like trust funds, there will inevitably be important verticals. These dualities are at play whether partners realize it or not. The trick is to recognize them, so they can be organized and fortified in ways that lend greater balance and lead to more sustainability, efficiency, and impact.

COUNTRY-BASED PARTNERSHIP PROGRAM

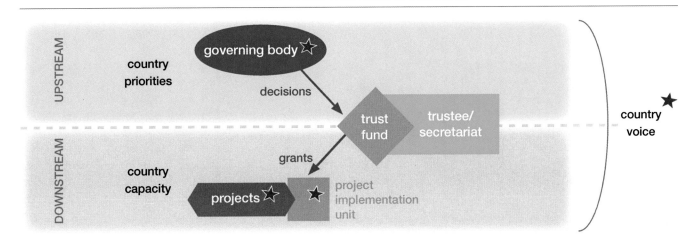

Structure and Contract

One of the main reasons international partnership programs become the neglected stepchild of international trust funds is that fund flow agreements for trust funds are more of a thing than are partnership structures. If a donor wants to contribute funds, or a recipient wants to receive funds, the partners have to memorialize the relationship. You simply do not hand over funds, especially taxpayer funds, without specifying their terms of use, or at least clarifying prohibited uses. That means you need a contract, and that in turn usually means you need a lawyer. In most organizations, there are also standard forms, specified approaches, required clauses, and prescribed procedures that go with the package. In other words, trust fund relationships trigger a whole host of mandatory steps that take up most of the attention.

Not so with partnership programs. When international partners want to convene, with or without commingling their funds, they are often at a loss as to how exactly to paper their relationships. Or maybe they do not take that part very seriously or even realize there is something to define. If trust funds are involved, with all attention drawn to the obligatory fund flow agreements, partners may drop a few lines about shared governance or secretariat support, but more likely think they are already covered or even overlook the partnering aspects altogether. And if trust funds are not involved, the neglect can be even greater. Partnership-only efforts tend to be more about doing than memorializing. If no institutional process is triggered, structuring aspects may not be written up at all. Partners are much more apt to define and write up the substance around which they partner than the structure through which they partner.

How curious is that? There is perhaps only so much oxygen in the room, but you would still think partners would attend to themselves. And yet, money tends to drive the matter, and partners are closure-minded, preferring to get on with it. Why complicate things with more details, more deliberations, more delay?

One reason to look beyond contracts is that they are formal to create and rigid over time. In the international arena, where binding, enforceable terms are not deemed as essential (>@ PfP: Partnering Internationally), putting the partnership emphasis on funding vehicles and tying partnership terms to fund flow agreements can be unnecessarily limiting and confusing. The partnership program itself—the subject of this book—is not just a footnote. To the contrary, it should be front and center as the impetus, justification, and framework for the commingled fund flows, not the other way around.

So let's consider again how structure fits in. For international partnership programs, most partnership elements are embodied in structure, not contracts. More often than not, partnering relationships—who is where on what—exhibit themselves through governing bodies, assigned roles, delegated responsibilities, and just plain individuals (like the chair), plans (like the work plan), and communications (like the website).

Empirically, we know that structural elements (other than the money buckets) typically do not get papered the way fund flows do. There is, for example, little instinct to clarify which activities are under the partnership program umbrella—which ones are branded—or even whether everyone has to agree about that. Hardly anyone thinks of getting the partners to regulate the partnership program's website; the supporting entity can take care of that. Similarly, there is no imperative to spell out the relationship of the secretariat to the international partnership program. Indeed, there is no imperative to even spell out that secretariat functions are being provided by one of the partners. It is only when the partners prevail upon the supporting entity to hire more individuals to staff the secretariat, and the supporting entity declines because of its internal hiring freeze, that the structure, and the partnering relationships in that structure, become acutely visible. At which point, they can also become tricky.

A WEB OF RELATIONSHIPS

combining structural and contractual links

fund flows

signed contracts

funders

recipients

knowledge community (sharing lessons learned)

partnership program

target beneficiaries (impact, results)

governing body

secretariat

governance / administration

adopted documents

The point is not only that both structural and contractual elements are key to defining partnership programs, but also that these two aspects entail some pretty wonderful synergies—if you tap into them. Let's start by putting fund flows and partnership relationships side-by-side. In the international arena, both have in common that they are **as defined** by the parties/partners. However, that definition takes different forms. As a general rule, when it comes to international, trust-funded partnership programs, fund flows follow contractual lines, and partnership relationships follow structural lines. (>@ PfP: Structure)

Partly because of this difference, the way terms are memorialized can also be different. Instead of using **signed contracts** for structural terms, as with fund flows, partners can agree on written terms in **adopted documents**. What does this mean?

- In the signed case, two or more signatory parties sign on the dotted line. These signatures tend to signify commitments to abide by the terms. Each **signature is an individual act** and a legal representation that the signatory individual is duly authorized by her or his entity to step up to the stated agreement terms.

- In the adopted case, two or more and usually multiple partners adopt through a decision point. Adoption occurs at a meeting or virtually, whatever the agreed procedures, and usually reflects approval by the deciders. **Adoption is a collective act** and an operational step that indicates the will of the deciding body.

In the international development arena, especially when partnership programs revolve around trust funds, relationships can be either structural or contractual, and these partnership programs invariably combine both elements. Designing this type of coordinated governance involves working out the interplay of structural and contractual elements. The goal is not only making sure the structure and contracts are in synch with each other, but also leveraging the placement of structural and contractual components for greater efficiency and effectiveness. (>@ PfP: Like Rock, Like Water) Both elements can be leveraged by shifting between structural and contractual solutions to reach desired outcomes.

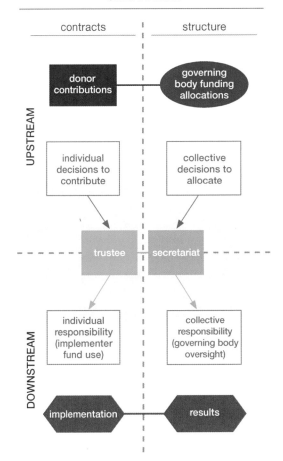

SIDE-BY-SIDE

Fund flows follow contractual lines.

Partner relations follow structural lines.

SIGNING VS. ADOPTING

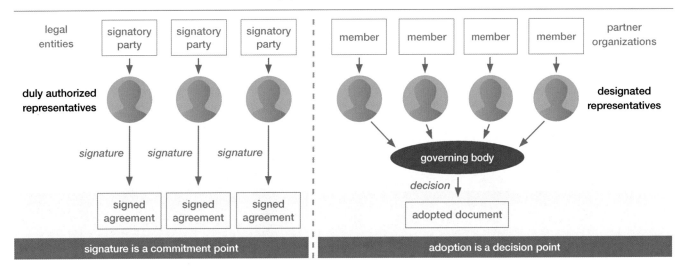

Informal and Formal

This structural/contractual difference in international partnership programs is also reflected in the informal/formal status of the elements. On the one hand, contribution agreements and grant agreements are signed by duly authorized representatives with intended legal status, usually binding by design and thus more rigid or "formal." That is in the nature of fund flows and fiduciary obligations. On the other hand, structural elements tend to be "informal," like an informal governing body and informal secretariat support, that commonly arise without signatures. (>@ PfP: Governing Bodies—Characteristics—Informal vs. Formal)

This kind of partnership program informality reflects engagement through partners—of the partners—as when they voluntarily sit on governing bodies and carry their own costs, or when supporting entities contribute as partners more than hired service providers. This informality can also be more responsive to partners—by the partners—as when members of a governing body adopt charter amendments that keep the partnership program fit-for-purpose in changing contexts. These de facto, not de jure, structures can be more fluid and participatory because they are not trapped in contractual formalities.

This structurally based informality of the partnership program governing body and its supporting secretariat are compounded—indeed enabled—by the unincorporated informality that abounds in the international arena. (>@ PfP: Partnering Internationally) Informality is doubled in this case, reflecting the absence of both formal contracts and formal incorporation. More often than not, these structurally positioned elements are neither the product of signed, enforceable relationships, nor are they created in accordance with domestic, statutory regimes.

Both kinds of informality bring distinct advantages to international partnership programs. The like rock, like water paradigm (>@ PfP: Like Rock, Like Water) reflects the way that formal contractual relationships can interplay with informally constituted, but still legitimate and representative, governing bodies. This interplay gets increased latitude through the sui generis nature of international partnership programs that arise in the relatively open and unprescribed way the international arena operates. (>@ PfP: Typology—The Broader Landscape of Partnership Programs)

Within this permissive scope, international partners will want to find ways for the formal/informal dynamics to come together when creating and operating international partnership programs. For the sake of cohesion and a stronger center, fund flows and partnership relationships need to be integrated and aligned. Signed agreements and adopted documents need to speak and connect to each other. Contract terms and meeting decisions need to relate to each other. Fund flows need to occur within the scope of partner relations, and partner relations need to be embedded into fund flow terms. For the architect of the overall edifice, it helps to keep this mix of formal and informal elements in mind.

FORMAL VS. INFORMAL

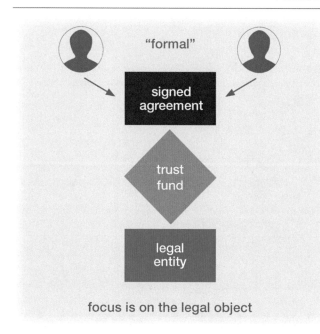

focus is on the legal object

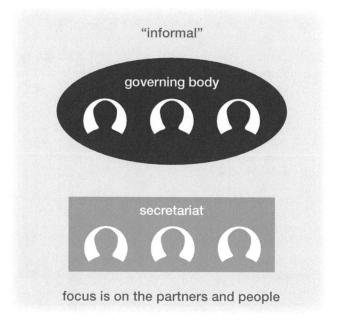

focus is on the partners and people

No Performance Guarantee

We have already said that international trust funds do not offer performance guarantees. (>@ BfB: Context—International Trust Funds) This is a case in point where the informal/formal difference can be seen. Contribution agreements are usually considered firm commitments, but the trustee is not offering results-for-hire. Instead, these agreements have a lighter contractual touch that swings toward the informal. For good reason.

It is in the nature of development work that results are not simply bought by aid donors. We all hope for specific results—we target them in a results framework, we mark them with key indicators to be measured, and we track them through progress reports—but there is no refund if results are not achieved, no remedy for lack of impact, only the ability to shift course and try anew. Particularly in the case of grants to beneficiary governments and other local actors, the outcomes and impacts of development aid are often more aspirational than deliverable. Development grants intentionally fund low capacity settings, rely on local engagement, and leave room for risk—and that translates into room for governing bodies to make decisions and for the trustee to monitor and supervise, both without direct responsibility for delivery. (>@ PfP: Fund Use Responsibility)

It is possible to see these international trust fund arrangements as sui generis responses to the vagaries and challenges of development work. They position responsibilities delicately, more informally than formally, allowing for margins of error, lessons learned, and incremental approaches, as all participants seek to responsibly achieve their goals and make change happen.

International informality: beyond signed contracts and statutory incorporation.

Formal Incorporation vs. Informal Creation

The use of "formal" and "informal" here is somewhat loose and can also be used to describe a crucial legal difference in the international arena. There is (as yet) no international government, no universally legitimized force that creates and imposes the rule of law, no global Leviathan that reigns over its worldwide subjects. We are a world of nation-states, each of which has sovereign jurisdiction over its citizens, each of which regulates private business structures within its legal, statutory purview. You can, as an individual or together with your partners, incorporate a Delaware corporation or a Swiss association, but you cannot establish a "world" foundation, not with incorporated status.

Nevertheless, in the international arena, states amongst themselves can come up with all sorts of configurations, with various forms of legal status. The "formal" version of international governance is multilateral and treaty-based. Groups of countries can formally agree to terms (for example, articles of agreement) that establish a legal entity of which they are the members and shareholders. This is the model of international financial institutions, including multilateral development banks, as well as United Nations agencies. Groups of countries can also form an international organization, where governance is delegated to a governing body that is more inclusive, rather than just made up of themselves.

By contrast, we have the "informal"—and more common—version of international configurations, the non-treaty arrangements. An act of international partnering through signed or adopted arrangements that do not create treaty-level obligations is an informal act by default. If international partners do not ascribe treaty status, there is nothing else that imposes formality. Informality thus reflects the ability of international partners to set their own terms, typically also avoiding recourse to their respective national courts. Granted, this more freewheeling, nonstick-Teflon approach is under scrutiny and even attack (including a recent U.S. Supreme Court decision that held international organizations do not have absolute immunity under the U.S. International Organizations Immunity Act). But even with an increasing specter of legal liability (>@ BfB: The Annotated Charter—Privileges and Immunities), international partners have an amazingly wide scope for configuring their partnering relationships and defining their respective roles and responsibilities beyond what the formalities of national, statutory environments tend to allow.

Multilateral and Bilateral

When looking at international partnership programs, one of the elements that makes the structure/contract duality so pronounced is the combination of the parties. The natural expectation is that all partners are on board for all terms—that would be a pretty basic definition of partnership. But dare I tell you that it's actually more complex than that? Of course!

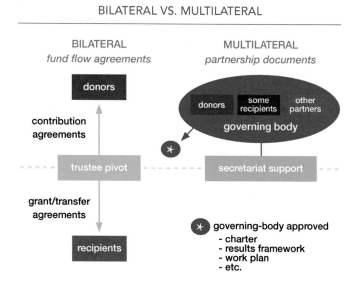

BILATERAL VS. MULTILATERAL

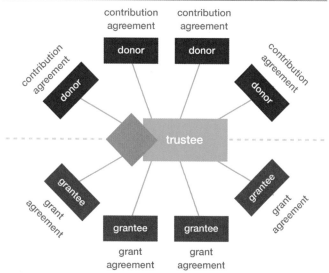

TRUSTEE HUB AND SPOKES

Adopted documents are by their nature multi-party. Adoption takes place as a collective act by a convened body. What makes adopted documents so powerful is that they represent the will of the group in one stroke—one decision point. Adopted means approved, and that carries expectations (essentially commitments) that everyone will act accordingly. (>@ PfP: Partners and People—Being a Good Partner) Once approved, the adoption becomes immediately effective, unless it is specifically attached to a later time or condition. Group-approved documents may take some time to put into place. For international partnership programs, that usually means a group process culminating in consensus (>@ PfP: Decision Making), which is a higher bar than individual or fractional approvals. However, the heft of having a consensus-adopted, group-approved document is usually worth the effort. When it comes to these voluntary platforms, you want everyone on board.

Signed contracts, by contrast, tend to be bilateral. There is no problem making contracts multi-party, but vis-à-vis individual fund flows, the nature of the transaction usually favors one-on-one relationships, negotiated and signed separately. That gives just enough room for customization, where available (less with commingling; see the box below). It also accommodates different timing for different agreements. Not everyone has to be ready to commit all at once. Instead, signed contracts (agreements) for contributions can be entered into on a rolling basis.

Bilateral agreements are the norm for international trust funds. Whether pointing upstream to donors (contribution agreements) or downstream to recipients (grant agreements), the trustee is the pivot. (>@ PfP: Trust Funds—Accounts) For a multi-donor trust fund, donors all give to, and recipients all receive from, one and the same trustee for one and the same trust fund—even as every agreement, like spokes on a wheel, is separate and bilateral.

Commingling and Common Terms

With respect to commingled funds, the bilateral approach to agreements is more form than substance. That is because all upstream bilateral agreements for pooled contributions are mostly replicas of each other, and all downstream bilateral agreements for fund distributions flow from the same terms. Commingled funds have to be on common terms. There is no way to treat separate dollars differently out of a common pool; whatever terms apply to one dollar apply to all. In this way, even though multi-donor trust funds are usually patterned on bilateral contracting arrangements, they have a multilateral basis. (>@ BfB: A Taxonomy of Trust Fund Agreements—Upstream Agreements)

Multilateral/Bilateral Opportunities

This multilateral/bilateral duality in partnership programs makes for some curious dynamics, but also creates some opportunities. For example:

- Secretariats tend to operate multilaterally, since they support the governing body and partnership program writ large. By contrast, trustees tend to operate bilaterally, since they engage each donor and recipient individually when contracting rights and obligations. To a degree, this frees the trustee to pursue its own interests as the fiduciary counterpart, thereby facilitating a more protective, institutional posture. Meanwhile, the secretariat is always caught in the partnership paradigm, since that is its scope of activity and very reason for being. (>@ PfP: Trustee Types—Trustee Entity; Secretariats—Inhouse Secretariat Roles)

- When partners participate in governing bodies, they are, generally speaking, more attuned to each other and see themselves as partners. By contrast, when partners enter into legally binding, signed agreements, they are more attuned to their individual interests, especially in bilateral contexts where they can negotiate separately, rather than collectively. The trustee has to set guardrails, with help from the secretariat, to ensure that bilateral terms do not overly diffuse or undermine multilateral partnership terms.

- Where partners have baseline requirements, bilateral agreements provide a natural, formal avenue for positioning rights or setting limits. It is telling that rights of consent and termination are carved out by the trustee—a backstop that also serves other roles of the same entity— in its formal, bilateral relationships. This is partly because multilateral documents, like charters, are ill-suited for specific secretariat or other protections, since that is where the supporting entity positions itself as a partner among peers, not a specific support role with extra risk exposure. In the same vein, the supporting entity's ability to match its responsibilities with control (>@ PfP: Supporting Entities—Risk Profile) is typically safeguarded through consensus decision making (everyone has a veto), as opposed to a special, supporting entity-only veto.

Combining these two modalities—and thinking about which aspects fit better into which mode—can make for a stronger foundational structure, effectively reinforcing each other. The specific nature of each partner, each joining institutionally, can be preserved, while the collective nature of the partnership program can be enhanced, with neither one threatening or undermining the other. This is a conscious balance that can be struck by the partners: being bilateral enough to fortify rights and obligations where needed, and multilateral enough to emphasize common efforts and goals where desired.

> You need a balance of both: bilateral enough to fortify rights and obligations, and multilateral enough to emphasize common efforts and goals.

As it happens, much of this balancing act occurs naturally and inadvertently. However, without room for both individual protections and collective engagements, partnership programs may tilt out of whack. This happens when partner institutions cannot sufficiently be themselves to enable their participation or partnering aspects cannot garner enough common ground to cohere as a partnership.

> You need a balance of both: partners that are enough themselves to participate as partners, and partnering with enough common ground to cohere as a partnership.

The one partner that has to be a particularly active player in this calculus is the supporting entity, melding its bilaterally signed relationships with its multilaterally agreed relationships. Whether the supporting entity does this well has a huge impact on the long-term health of the partnership program. In addition, the more other partners can understand and appreciate this duality, the more all partners can actively position their requirements, interests, and common goals in overall support of the partnership program.

Inward and Outward

Another duality common to international partnership programs is the inward-and-outward facing dynamic of participation. For partners (entities) and their representatives (individuals), commitments run both inward within the partnering organization and outward toward the partnership. All partners presumably have the interests of both their own institutions and the partnership program in mind when they make decisions: Will approving this project be good for both our own organization and the partnership program (including reputationally)? Will undertaking a midterm review at this point meet our internal requirements, while also benefiting the partnership program? A conscientious, good citizen partner keeps the partnership program interests in mind alongside its own. (>@ PfP: Partners and People— Being a Good Partner)

Normally this inward-outward duality is hardly apparent because both home base and partnership interests perfectly align. Activities that could harm a specific partner's interests are likely to harm the partnership program overall. A rushed, poorly conceived, half-baked project proposal is apt to be rejected, or invited to be resubmitted when improved, because it won't look or do good when it fails. This overlap of inward-outward interests fortifies the partnership platform.

Occasionally, however, the inward-outward duality can lead to friction. A specific partner may require a midterm partnership program evaluation for internal purposes, but other partners may think it is premature and apt to make the partnership program look bad, rather than allowing a few more projects to develop and produce tangible results. How the specific partner reconciles these two competing interests has to do with how that partner manages this internal-external dynamic. Can it find a compromise? Can it put the partnership program's interests first? Which pull will win the tug-of-war?

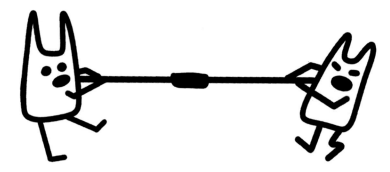

More acute examples arise from more acute scenarios. I recall a partnership program that faced allegations of fraud and corruption. Traditional donor partners were rattled because that meant their taxpayer funds, provided as development aid, would have been misused and gone to waste. The beneficiary recipient, the user of those funds and also a partner, was naturally also rattled. Everyone agreed to keep the matter confidential until the facts were sorted out. However, traditional donor partners also wanted to suspend all future fund disbursements pending the results of a review, along with some prescribed organizational reforms. The beneficiary recipient warned that this would undermine its operations, potentially beyond the point of recovery. But the traditional partners, in coordination with the trustee, held the funds anyhow, even at the risk of tanking the partnership program. Their own interests (and reputational exposure) trumped the well-being of the partnership program when those interests were no longer aligned.

Every institutional partner has to deal with this duality to a degree, but supporting entities feel it the most. That is because they have the most exposure to the partnership program, along with the most potential fault lines. With embedded functions like trustee and secretariat, supporting entity obligations run inward as part of the institution and outward as part of the partnership across a huge gamut of activities. A supporting entity always has to hope that its own interests will stay aligned with those of the partnership program, and it usually keeps a last say to make sure it does. (>@ PfP: Supporting Entities)

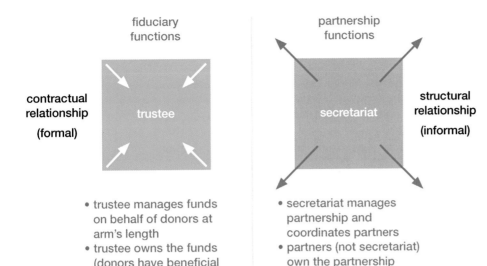

fiduciary functions

partnership functions

contractual relationship (formal)

trustee

secretariat

structural relationship (informal)

- trustee manages funds on behalf of donors at arm's length
- trustee owns the funds (donors have beneficial interests)

- secretariat manages partnership and coordinates partners
- partners (not secretariat) own the partnership program

both trustee and secretariat are embedded in their supporting entity(ies), subject to internal management rules

Even so, there is a nuanced difference in the inward-outward balance for the trustee as compared to the secretariat, putting the secretariat in the hot seat. The trustee, like the other partners, is operating in its own right, for itself, specifically as a contracted party. It agrees to hold funds in trust on behalf of donors, but its actual obligations are only as legally stated within the four corners of the contribution agreement. (>@ PfP: Use of Funds—Four Corners of the Agreement) Contrast that with the secretariat, which sets itself up as broad support for the partnership program, with functions that stretch from being the legal entity to staff, center point, custodian, and more (>@ PfP: Secretariats—Inhouse Secretariat Roles), all on behalf of the partnership program (to be clear, not individual partners, but the partnership program as a whole). The secretariat functions, whether part of a named secretariat or merged with the trustee, are at such high risk of tension that one of the secretariat's unstated roles is to undertake active, preventive, and proactive efforts to manage any whisper of misalignment. As the secretariat knows better than anyone, the success of the partnership program rests on a strong alignment of interests.

In fact, secretariat staff know this best because they live it day-to-day. Not only is there a duality at the institutional level, but also at the staff level—their burden of "dual loyalty." (>@ PfP: Supporting Entities—Duality and Balance) Most civil servants, including international civil servants who work for the multilateral organizations that are frequently tapped as supporting entities, owe their duty of loyalty to their employer. And yet, partners expect secretariat staff, who are only in the picture because of the partnership program, to be "loyal" to the partnership program. It behooves the partners to understand this complexity from the start, so the dynamics can be transparent and manageable, with no surprises.

And what is the upshot of this duality? Secretariat staff owe their first loyalty to their institution and managers, with a secondary responsibility to the partnership program. To put it succinctly, they are subordinate to their managers and accountable to the partners. Under the best of circumstances, any issues are kept minimal or manageable because everyone works to keep them aligned. (>@ PfP: Secretariats)

REPORTING UP AND OUT

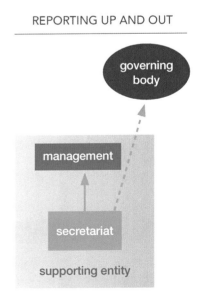

governing body

management

secretariat

supporting entity

Conflicts and Synergies

Having just addressed the inward-outward duality of interests and dual loyalties, this might be a good time to address conflicts of interest (COI) in general. The way to do this in the context of international partnership programs is to recognize when conflicts are synergies. This involves more than simply seeing the positive instead of the negative, or the glass half full rather than half empty. It is about the very essence of partnership.

I have a whole chapter on "synergistic conflicts" in my *Primer for Partners* (>@ PfP: Synergistic Conflicts) to make the case, but suffice to say here that international partners intuit the synergies in partnership programs, enough to be undeterred by the legalistic parsing of conflicts. There are clearly conflicts of interest to be avoided, but the kind to be tolerated, or even embraced, are the "conflicts" that are more about cooperation, coordination, and collaboration.

We have already seen two classic examples in the previous dualities. The first one is that of "conflicted" secretariat staff, who face both inward and outward. But it is really the opposite; they combine the best of both worlds. Partners are usually happy to leave human resources to the supporting entity, while benefiting from well-managed support. The fact that secretariat staff stay loyal to their organization while serving the partnership program is not a fatal contradiction. There is no subterranean bias or unfair advantage. Instead, this duality can be transparently disclosed, widely understood, and clearly appreciated.

The second classic example is developing country voice. From a hierarchical, fund-flows point of view, that developing country is a recipient at the bottom of a chain of agreements, conditions, and obligations. (>@ Trust Funds—Recipients) And yet, it is also a partner in determining what the funds are to be used for—setting country priorities, engaging local stakeholders, building capacity, and owning implementation—which also justifies being on horizontal footing with the other partners. If the "conflicts" view prevails, recipients would never be part of deciding the terms of the funds they receive because they would be deemed conflicted. I have seen that happen. But how can that make sense in a development context? Country recipients *are* the context, and their funding should be fit-for-*their*-purpose.

This also plays out on an intra-institutional scale, where whole business lines are at stake. Let's take one-stop-shops, which combine many different roles within a single supporting entity. (>@ PfP: Typology—Introducing Two Mighty Oaks—One-Stop-Shops) Is that entity conflicted by all its roles? From a development perspective, the answer should be a resounding no—one-stop-shops are more synergistic than "conflicted." In fact, partners love the end-to-end package of support that the full trustee, secretariat, and rest of the supporting entity provide. Ultimately, all these roles and synergies are part of the same supporting entity, converging under the same senior management, making it harder to see conflicts when it is all one and the same institution. Conflicted with itself?

For that matter, I have never seen a donor express concerns about being "conflicted" as a shareholder of the same multilateral development bank that is managing its trust fund contributions. Far from a conflict, this is considered good business—as if to say "we established and funded this multilateral precisely so it could carry out this downstream development role for us." Being simultaneously donors and board members is apparently a legitimate synergy inasmuch as it is not questioned.

The conflict-synergy duality is worth mentioning primarily to correct the record. The next time someone refers to a prohibitive conflict of interest in an international partnership program setting, make sure it is not in fact a synergy, where the synergy may even be the point of it all.

SYNERGISTIC RELATIONSHIPS

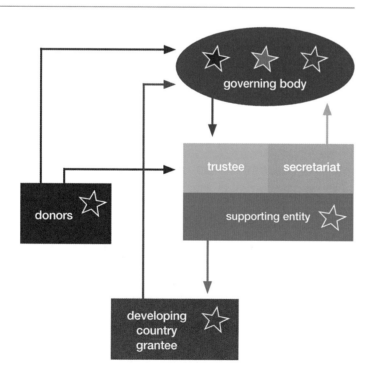

Contributing to the Fund You Manage

Each situation is unique, but in general, there is no "conflicts" reason to prohibit the combination of trustee and donor roles in the same entity. While the trustee is safeguarding other donors' funds, it can safeguard its own as part of the commingled pool. That said, it is good practice—as with any case of multiple supporting entity roles—to be transparent with other partners about the overlap. The trustee entity should disclose and manage its dual role as donor and trustee.

Beyond disclosing, what is there to manage? Here are a few dynamics:

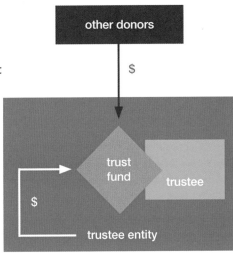

- Trustee entities are commonly supporting entities with a host of additional roles, like member and chair of the governing body, secretariat, downstream implementer (what we here call one-stop-shops). If the trustee/supporting entity also contributes its own cash to the trust fund, being a donor adds one more layer to an already multi-faceted arrangement.

- Other partners appreciate this full-package approach, where trust in the trustee includes confidence that the trustee/supporting entity can maximize synergies and manage conflicts. Sometimes that means separating out roles into different business units, even though they ultimately all report to the same upper management. There is no need, however, to go to the extreme with impermeable information barriers. They end up defeating any synergies and can be pretty unworkable within the culture of multilateral organizations. More important is articulating clearly what the different roles are and how they relate to each other, the trust fund, and the overall partnership program.

- Upsides include the weighted value of the trustee/supporting entity's contribution—not all dollars are equal. Having the trustee entity also care for its own funds is a confidence booster for all partners. Even a small amount provided as catalytic funding can send a loud signal. Suddenly the trustee/supporting entity has skin in the game, which gives other donors a greater comfort level. And there is greater funding efficiency in commingling even the trustee entity's funds, in particular when they are unpreferenced, unrestricted, and fully available for core support.

- Downsides include expectations of more. Rather than focus on its comparative advantage as fiduciary, partners may come to see the trustee as a donor. The partnership program may think it is long-term entitled, or it may become overly reliant, especially if the funds are needed for core support that others are not providing. The added donor role also undermines the arm's-length relationship between the trustee and the other donors. It instead magnifies the fiduciary and legal risks of the trustee entity with direct exposure to the whole commingled pool, not just its fiduciary management of the pool.

- Is the trustee entity giving to itself? Not really, although from a practical perspective, the contribution does not leave the trustee entity when it enters the trust fund. The trust fund is an inhouse account. However, from legal and accounting perspectives, the funds change their status. The trustee entity retains legal ownership of the funds, but they go from being part of its own assets to assets held in a pool where each contributor retains only a beneficial interest in its pro rata contribution. (>@ BfB: The Annotated Charter—Funding Sources) The contribution agreement likely says something like this:

    The funds deposited in the Trust Fund shall be kept separate and apart from the funds of the Trustee Entity. The Trustee Entity, in its capacity as trustee, has legal title to the funds deposited in the Trust Fund.

In sum, when combining trustee and donor roles within one entity, the nub is not so much about conflicts of interest as understanding that this adds partnership program complexity, while increasing partner confidence. It adds trustee entity exposure, while increasing trust fund efficiency. These are all things to manage and balance.

Stability and Flexibility (Like Rock, Like Water)

Like rock, like water, the theme of my *Primer for Partners*, is a tale of stability and flexibility. (>@ PfP: Like Rock, Like Water) It is not about texture (hard and soft), but movement and flow. Rocks center in their gravity; they are grounded. Water shapeshifts to hug the context; it is malleable. But also, rocks delineate, and water connects. Rocks are parched without water, and water is aimless without rocks. Rocks and water together, that is a symphony of modularity and modulation, the organic essence of a healthy, holistic, balanced partnership program.

Let's consider a rock-and-water example to see how things can both stay stable and move:

A symphony of modularity and modulation.

> The Migration Movement Partnership Program starts with three founding groups—donor countries, beneficiary countries, and implementing partners—all represented on the governing body. To define participation and manage the numbers, the initial partners decide on some eligibility rules at the start:
>
> - *Donors.* Up to four donors can participate in the governing body regardless of the amounts they each contribute to the dedicated trust fund. If more than four donors contribute, all donors form a constituency and decide amongst themselves (with the help of the chair and secretariat, if needed) how to apportion representation among four seats, whether by rotation, size of contribution, seniority, or many other variations. (>@ PfP: Trade-Offs—The Horizontal Buy-In Spectrum—Workarounds) All donors are represented as decision makers, either directly with seats or indirectly through others with seats. (>@ BfB: The Annotated Charter—Amendments) Prospective donors may participate as observers.
> - *Beneficiary Countries.* Up to four beneficiary countries eligible for new grants are chosen annually by donors. The annual slate of beneficiary countries is invited to participate as decision makers in the governing body for that year. Countries with ongoing grants are also invited to participate in the governing body at any time as observers. The dedicated trust fund pays for the participation of beneficiary countries.
> - *Implementing Partners.* Four implementing partners (international fiduciary organizations) are designated from the start and may participate in the governing body as observers, except that they have decision making status with respect to charter amendments or other decisions that directly affect their interests.
> - *Chair.* The governing body is chaired by the supporting entity, who also participates as a decision-making member, including for the secretariat and trustee functions.

Now suppose one year into the partnership program, the partners want to add two relevant international agencies as decision makers to the governing body. Governing body terms, including composition, are defined in the charter, and the contribution agreements incorporate the charter by reference. The secretariat prepares an amendment to the charter, working with the supporting entity's legal department. The governing body approves the amendment by consensus at its next meeting (or virtually by no objection). As soon as the decision is taken, the chair sums up the decision for the minutes, the amendment takes effect under the charter, but additionally vis-à-vis all contribution agreements under their existing terms, which include the carry-over clause. (>@ BfB: Agile Alignment—Step-by-Step Alignment for Trust-Funded Partnership Programs, #7)

Done; representatives of the two agencies can participate as decision makers, including at that very meeting (as opposed to a drawn-out signing exercise with each and every donor). (>@ ibid., #6)

That is rock, a solid set of pre-agreed rules and processes, and water, an easy and immediate way to make a change across the relevant partnership and trust fund documents. (>@ BfB: Dynamics— It's Organic)

Adding Donors to Governing Bodies

Membership in governing bodies is seldom static, whether at the entity (partner) or individual (representative) level. One of the most common modulating features is the ability of donors to join governing bodies as and when they contribute to a partnership program's dedicated trust fund. This is a great resource mobilization tool, typically baked in from the start. Early donors know that other donors will join—their contribution agreements usually say as much—and yet, rarely do those original donors have a say in whether and what new donors are added.

Is that surprising, when their reputations could potentially be affected by association with unsavory characters? Not really, not if the trustee has established internal due diligence procedures that these donors trust. And especially not if these donors are members of the entity that houses the trustee. And even less so if the trustee entity itself is a partner, which is usually how international trustees perceive themselves. In that case, the trustee has as much interest in avoiding tainted associations as anyone. This adds up to a triple-decker latch system, more than safe enough for everyone to rely on.

International partnership programs may need a lot of water. That is normal. Internally, externally, things are constantly changing, and yet, things can stay stable. That is ideal. Even if it all turns out differently than envisioned or planned, the flexibility of moving through charter amendments that directly affect contribution agreements can still be there.

It is so much easier if partners anticipate change from the start. Part of making it easy is attitude, but the other part is the toolbox. With good guidance and deliberate drafting, partners can lean on use of a charter, governing body decision making, supporting entity continuity, donor champions, document adaptability, and a range of tools to build flexibility into the structure.

Standardization and Customization

Within the relative freedom of the international arena (>@ PfP: Governing Bodies—Characteristics), each partnership program is basically as defined by the partners. For partnership programs that feature collaborative governance and dedicated funding around a specific development topic, the details of the initiative can consist of a huge number of variables to be decided by the partners. For lawyers, this means "as negotiated" and results in a structured solution that plays out within a multiplicity of functions and cascading tiers of relationships, primarily around fund flows and decision-making processes. Partners may think that each partnership program is essentially green field, but they will also discover that their push for customization and innovation needs to balance with the pull for standardization and regularization.

Let's put it all in context—and by that I mean put partnership programs in their contexts. When water flows and rocks divide, a partnership program operates in the situation it is in, including its goals, challenges, participants, beneficiaries, politics, and risks. But the list is longer. Context for international partnership programs also includes their institutional settings—the "old" part of this hybrid model (>@ PfP: Secretariats—Options), which primarily means the operating frameworks of their supporting and fiduciary entities. As we have been saying, being contextual is the way to be fit-for-purpose, and being fit-for-purpose is the way to be sustainable, efficient, and impactful. To do that, international partnership programs have to fit into standardizing contexts, while also adapting to customizing contexts. On the one hand, when partners structure and design their partnership programs with context in mind, this points toward a high degree of customization. On the other hand, keeping context in mind, partners have to work within the frameworks of their supporting entities (not having a supporting entity is often not a viable choice).

Partners also need to structure and design with prudence in mind. As a business matter, every customized element comes at a cost, costly to set up and operate. Customized elements that end up outside of existing control systems or standard operating procedures can be especially costly and risky. While some amount of customization is necessary, being bespoke needs taming and framing to be efficient and effective. This is the perennial duality between customization and standardization.

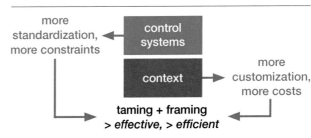

STANDARDIZATION VS. CUSTOMIZATION

Tame and frame your customization.

The Organics of Contexts

Being contextual is a balancing act. Whether maneuvering between the rock and hard place of Scylla and Charybdis, or managing the currents of the Southern Ocean, or any lesser pulls and pressures, partnership programs have a lot of context to accommodate. Being multilateral and multilayered, they are susceptible to little ripples becoming big rip tides. Every partner has to balance its own participation, which then needs balancing across the partnership, with new stimuli on hand every day. The life of a partnership program need not be volatile, but for sure, it is contextually prone. This means two things:

1. Contextualizing is not a series of adaptations in isolation, but rather the product of many trade-offs, some iterated in response to others. (>@ PfP: Trade-Offs)
2. Any effort to standardize or customize cannot be static, but needs room to shift and straddle over time.

Bottom line: Being fit-for-purpose is not a product of any specific point in time or any particular point of reference, but an ongoing response to the aggregate, in the aggregate. It is ongoing organic.

To stay fit-for-purpose, be ongoing organic.

Helpful or not, standardization takes some of the variability out of the equation. It can be helpful when partners do not need to start from scratch and become overwhelmed by an almost infinite number of variables, but rather work from established policy parameters or tried-and-true business models. It can be helpful when standard approaches leverage existing IT and other business platforms for risk control, data aggregation, systematized management overviews, widely understood terminology, and clear avenues for waivers and damage control. The key is to standardize in the right places on the right things, where doing so is more helpful than harmful, where it does not dogmatically restrict or undercut the benefits of partnering. (>@ PfP: Risk and Review—Institutional Factors)

We can see this especially in trust-funded partnership programs, where, as so often, the trustee ends up driving much of the behavior. The degree of standardization vs. customization of partnership elements may turn on the kind of trustee package the supporting entity is willing to support:

- Some supporting entities find their safe zone by leaning on their regular, non-trust fund operations. They accordingly draw the trustee and other support inward, where there is more control and uniformity of approach. They standardize the variability into a tighter, more concentric package. The end effect is something like a **one-stop-shop** that goes light on shared governance.

- Other supporting entities have no problem with trustee support that is more stand-alone. They do not push to mainstream or leverage the trustee with other operations; they may not even have other operations. They standardize from a more narrow base. The end effect can look like an **international platform** that points outward more than inward, often with more bells and whistles and, crucially, open to more shared governance.

Standardization in trust fund settings is inevitable, and it will invariably bump up against partnership dynamics. Trustees are perpetually seeking to balance between giving donors what they want and keeping the lid on donors' special requests. (>@ PfP: Trust Funds—Contributions) Sometimes the power of the purse decides (money talks), but mostly the donor-trustee tug-of-war makes for almost entertaining theatre. Every time the trustee undertakes an all-out standardization exercise to rally donor consensus, with great effort, it may succeed for at least a brief moment, until some other special request comes along and it all starts anew. But even donors, who tend to be most cost-conscious of all, appreciate not only the economies of scale in collectivizing funds, but also in standardizing terms across the trust fund portfolio. If they step back from their special requests, they, too, can recognize that off-the-shelf agreement terms and minimized negotiations reduce costs upfront, while light governance and minimized extra requirements reduce costs over time.

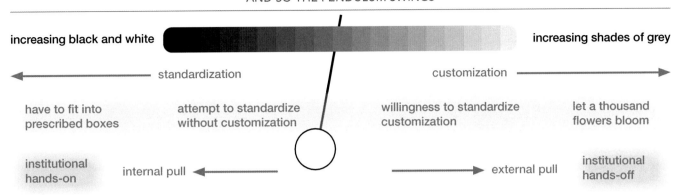

increasing black and white   increasing shades of grey

←———————————— standardization   customization ——————————→

| have to fit into prescribed boxes | attempt to standardize without customization | willingness to standardize customization | let a thousand flowers bloom |

institutional hands-on   internal pull ←————   ————→ external pull   institutional hands-off

But here is a conundrum: As long as there are partnership programs, partnership dynamics will not cease. Partners will drive variability. Partnerships revolve around people, while trust funds turn on cash. It is much easier to put the latter in a box than the former. And so the pendulum swings. The trick is to standardize where necessary and feasible, but customize where the context counts, where you want that custom fit. And that takes some overall understanding and mindful negotiating.

An organization's culture may also tip in one direction or the other. In some institutions, customization is a dirty word in light of pressures to standardize. It is a sure bet that the larger the institution—the more bureaucratic and top down, and the more tightly wound and policy oriented—the less tolerant of customized structure and design it will be. In other entities, however, like start-ups, standardization is the dirty word amidst the drive to innovate and extrapolate. And yet, environments that are weak on control systems, untethered to management machinery, or blissfully unconstrained by policies are probably also less stable, less mature, and more vulnerable to disruptive externalities. Whether buttoned up or freestyle by nature, there is room for both standardization and customization, with balance.

Standardize where necessary and feasible; customize where context counts.

Balance of this kind takes effort to find and work to maintain. The starting point can be a high-level policy environment or conceptual outline that sets outside limits, ultimate goals, and broad parameters, coupled with a guiding framework that shapes the business approach without constraining the business. Even better is when this guidance is regularly updated, expanded, and improved to reflect experience and lessons learned, through a reinforcing, internal feedback loop. In addition, for every rule, there can be a process for waiving that rule. Not that waivers need be welcome—they should remain the exception—but there will be unanticipated scenarios for which a little leeway can make or break the plan. Managers are there to be reasonable and resourceful, and they should ideally have the whole toolkit—rock and water—in hand.

THE ROCK-AND-WATER FEEDBACK LOOP

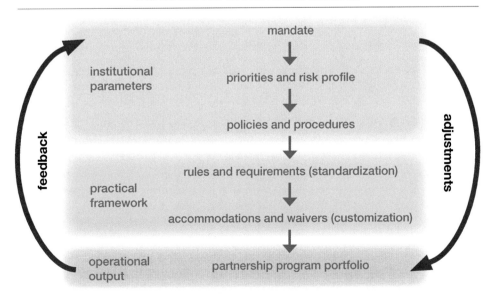

Recommended: The Standardized Customization of Governing Bodies

Organizations that have well-developed trust fund policies have been known to extend those policies into partnership program governance. This can warp opportunities to convene into mere funding appendages. And yet, these "trust fund" governing bodies exist for the partners as much as the funds. Their roles could potentially go far beyond fund allocations and money affairs, instead of being undercut by narrower trust fund perspectives.

To put it more concretely, say an organization tries to standardize trust fund governance to limited participation (only donors), limited application (only high level), and limited effect (only advisory). The justification may be that the trustee needs to keep complete control in relation to its complete fiduciary responsibility. That view may have its place, but ignores the potential of such governing bodies to bring in the voices of other key stakeholders, to coordinate activities and initiatives across diverse partners, and to learn from greater sharing of experiences in a widened feedback loop with expanded multiplier effects—all of which can happen without ceding control. Even if a governing body is set up in the context of a trust fund, it need not—it arguably should not—be restricted to narrow trust fund purposes when it has dimensions that go beyond the trustees, donors, and specific funding vehicle.

Bluntly put, standardizing along trust fund dimensions can bastardize partnership dimensions. But rather than shoehorn shared governance into a fixed formula of trustee and donors only, for example, the governing body can embrace larger partnering objectives without risking fiduciary responsibilities. This calls for opening to standing participation by targeted beneficiaries, other international players, other expert organizations, and other key stakeholders. This then points to a charter document, rather than just a series of bilateral agreements. (>@ BfB: Constitutive Documents)

This degree of partnership-driven customization, going beyond mere trust fund-driven standardization, can be considered healthy and within bounds. It is a *standardized governance approach* that accepts some amount of governing body customization in order to promote partnership potential.

A standardized approach can make customized governing bodies a standard feature.

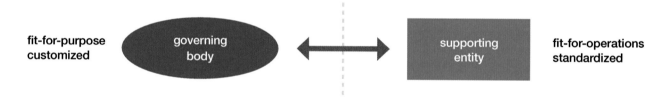

| fit-for-purpose customized | governing body | ⟷ | supporting entity | fit-for-operations standardized |

A customized trust-funded partnership program needs a robust, standardized back office.

Recommended: The Non-Negotiability of Back Office Operations

At the same time that partnership elements justify some customization, like the composition of the governing body, some trust fund aspects call for mostly standardization. On the one hand, international partnership program configurations and their shared governance arrangements resist the cookie cutter approach. But on the other hand, back office operations of the supporting entities resist negotiation. This is true in spades for the trustee, whose back office relies heavily on automated systems with built-in controls that deal with fund flows, investment income, currency exchange, accounting treatment, fund availability, basis of commitment, donor reporting, audits, and more, down to the penny—all tied to contractual obligations. With a lot of moving parts and large volumes of cash, there is little room for error, and adding deviations or manual procedures may be asking for trouble. So while shared governance should fit the context and amplify partnership potential, as articulated in an agreed charter, standard terms for trustee operations in contribution agreements should be considered basically non-negotiable.

Harmonization and Individuation

When it comes to international partnership programs, the same standardization/customization tension that supporting entities feel in their support roles also arises in the harmonization/individuation dynamic that partners feel in their partnering. The central issue is how much should be the same and how much can afford to be different, in the one case across a partnership program portfolio and in the other case across partners. Just as when a supporting entity lines up its partnering activities and boxes them into standard approaches to make them more manageable, partners can line themselves up and expand on their collectives to become more coherent and—well, more partnered.

This is a common denominator dynamic, where the denominator can be as high as every member of the partnership and everyone gets their specific fraction. Or it can be as low as one, where everyone is unified into one commingled pool of unrestricted funds, or everyone sits on the governing body, or everyone agrees to the same terms for recourse and remedies. (>@ PfP: Fund Use Responsibility—Transferred (No) Responsibility— Managing the Accountability Gap) It can also be somewhere in between, with some commonality, but also some differentiation, as when donors contribute to a single, commingled, multi-donor trust fund, but may state their preferences for specific fund use. (>@ PfP: Trade-Offs—The Central Harmonization Spectrum—Unrestricted vs. Restricted Funds) Let's play out this example:

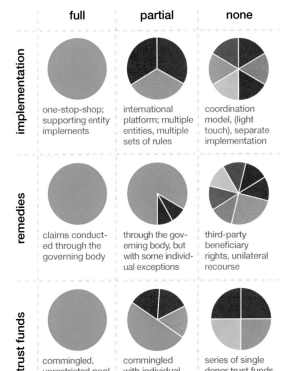

DEGREES OF COLLECTIVES

	full	partial	none
implementation	one-stop-shop; supporting entity implements	international platform; multiple entities, multiple sets of rules	coordination model, (light touch), separate implementation
remedies	claims conducted through the governing body	through the governing body, but with some individual exceptions	third-party beneficiary rights, unilateral recourse
trust funds	commingled, unrestricted pool of funds	commingled with individual preferencing of some funds	series of single donor trust funds within overall program

- *Overall harmonization.* All donors contribute unrestricted funds to a common pool. No donor can specify what its particular funds are to be used for because all fund use is subject to collective decision making. An individual donor's funds can finance only what everyone agrees to finance. All funds are available for any aspects within the broadest defined scope, allowing deployment of funds to be more strategic, more adaptable to priorities and context, and more responsive to needs.

- *Light-touch individuation.* Even in contributing to the common pool, a donor may be allowed to express its intentions or "preference" that all or some of its particular funds be used for a specific purpose. This specificity can track broad geographic or sector categories—for example, funds tagged for Africa or climate change—that satisfy donor requirements without overly undercutting the purpose of pooling funds. The goal is a trust fund that maximizes the benefits of commingling, while offering just enough individuation to maximize resource mobilization.

To be sure, in this particular combination of harmonization and individuation, the trustee is not promising to honor the preference, especially if that decision belongs to the governing body. And yet, in the amicable, like-minded world that international trust funds tend to be, everyone is put on notice in a way that is likely to be respected. The contribution agreement language can look something like this:

> *The Donor has expressed its preference that the Contribution be used to finance [describe preference]. It is understood that the Trustee (i) cannot ensure that the Contribution will be used for such preference, and (ii) will not have any obligation to the Donor if such preference cannot be achieved.*

A decision to commingle funds in a trust fund drives a high degree of harmonization—that is the point. With partnership programs overall, however, the many choices around harmonization and individuation can be more differentiated and discretionary. The going-in position is individuation (each individual partner), which makes the whole partnering exercise one of determining the degree of harmonization. This is where we refer to collectives—what and how much to collectivize— and recognize that many aspects are ripe for collectivization across a wide spectrum of convergence. (>@ PfP: International Partnership Programs—Collectivizing)

Cover Agreements (Individuation) and Common Annexes (Harmonization)

Staying on the trust fund theme, multi-donor trust funds epitomize the combination of harmonization and individuation. This is especially visible in their contribution agreements, which have to mesh the harmonized with the individualized. A common practice is to separate common terms that govern the commingled funds into annexes. These annexes are then replicated verbatim across all donors, while the cover agreement takes up the specific contribution and donor details. (>@ BfB: A Taxonomy of Trust Fund Agreements—Upstream Agreements—Contribution Agreements for Multi-Donor Trust Funds)

What goes into the cover agreement vs. the annexes? As a rule of thumb, here is the litmus test to apply when donors ask to customize their individual contribution agreements for a commingled fund:

- YES, customizable: anything having to do with (1) contribution specifics (e.g., amount, currency, payment schedule), or (2) legal status of the donor (which specific entity) or agreement (e.g., agreement or arrangement). These aspects go into the cover agreement.
- NO, not customizable: anything having to do with (1) the commingled pool of funds (e.g., allocation, use, reporting), (2) trustee operations, and (3) shared governance. These aspects belong in the annexed common terms across all donors.

The amount of individuation a partnership program can tolerate tends to correlate to the amount of common ground it forges. More commonality—including an all-encompassing association with a partnership program brand (>@ PfP: International Partnership Programs—One Brand)—allows for more distinctions and divisions without falling apart. For example, extra effort put into drawing the partners together upstream in terms of governance and coordination can give more room for divergent (and even unbranded) implementation downstream. If the partnership program's only ambition is to convene and coordinate upstream, that may well be enough. (>@ PfP: Typology—The Broader Landscape of Partnership Programs—Coordination Partnerships)

In this sense, a variant of individuation is modularity. Not everything needs to be done together or undertaken through one and the same vehicle. Collectivizing can also happen through coordination, where some parts converge and others diverge. On the upstream/downstream plane, we have a good, familiar example of the variety around convergence and divergence: full trustees vs. limited trustees. (>@ PfP: Trustee Types) The full trustee is full-on convergence, whereas the limited trustee is a modulated combination of convergence and divergence that centralizes upstream and decentralizes downstream. Both full trustees and limited trustees serve as the collective upstream conduit for commingling donor funds, but then their assignments change at the point of downstream disbursement. The full trustee remains the full fiduciary down to the end use of funds, but the limited trustee diversifies into multiple fiduciaries as funds are disbursed. Or if complete segregation is preferable, partners also have the umbrella arrangement option (>@ PfP: Typology—The Broader Landscape of Partnership Programs—Umbrella Arrangements), where multiple trust funds, each with a different fiduciary, fit under a single governing body. Different trustee modalities fit different contexts. There is room to vary between what is harmonized and what is individualized, including through modular coordination of structural elements.

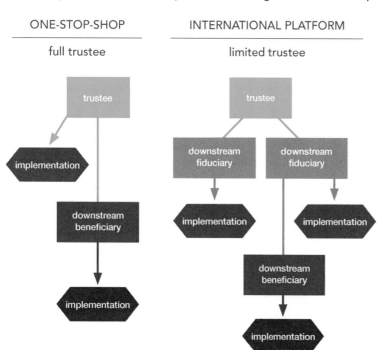

ONE-STOP-SHOP — full trustee

INTERNATIONAL PLATFORM — limited trustee

Let's take another example, one that goes with governance: consensus decision making. When a governing body uses consensus decision making, it gives veto power to each decision maker. This veto represents powerful individuation within equally powerful harmonization for collective decisions. But consensus also involves a degree of nuancing that protects partners from pitting their yes's against no's—they can abstain, or they can dissent on the record without objecting. These shades of engagement enable a balancing of interests that works to bring partners closer together. It allows for convergence in the midst of divergence (and vice versa as well). (>@ PfP: Decision Making)

Harmonizing is not just about the partnership program itself, but also what the partners can do with their activities. Here are a few classic ways that international partnership programs can "harmonize" their environments for the good of all:

- Require donors to follow uniform reporting requirements, going easy on the recipient
- Require recipients to follow uniform data submission formats, allowing apples-to-apples comparisons
- Engage partners to develop international standards, setting the bar higher
- Engage partners to develop a knowledge platform to collect wisdom, turning experience into learning

The more common ground, the stronger the partnership, the more effective the partnership program, that is usually the trajectory. To get there, however, international partnership programs may need some political heft for some real concessions and compromise. It may take considerable convergence to end up with a robust common platform on common terms, where customization does not defeat collectivization.

Harmonization is derived from "harmony" for a reason. It is more harmonious to sing from common sheet music, be it an agreed template for proposal submissions or a common results framework that focuses all efforts. In partnerships, the key is for these common approaches to arise from the collective, as aspects that are commonly approved or accepted. This usually happens through the governing body, where individual entities harmonize their views on the basis of consensus decisions. And this is usually reinforced by the secretariat and trustee, which can troubleshoot for efficiencies, gaps, and overlaps. With collective buy-in and dedicated staffing, the sum of the individual parts can be transformed into an individuated but harmonized whole, all the while striking the right balance.

Conclusion

From navigating like rock, like water, to keeping it all in the balance, to managing dualities, there is clearly a theme going on here. A vibrant international partnership program is an adventure, never a dull day, but it should be a pleasure. And it should be effective. Partners that see themselves in relation to the whole, not just from a trust fund perspective or within a hierarchy, can understand their options and make informed choices about their partnering. Partnership programs that both perform and pivot over time, enough to stay fit, fresh, and relevant, can be both grounded and regenerative.

Illuminated by all these dynamics, a deeper understanding of structure and design can help build and bolster partnership documentation. That is what we will turn to next.

2

CHARTEROGRAPHY

Documenting International Partnerships

In this Part Two, we zero in on charters, the key document that creates, defines, and sustains international partnership programs, first with some context and then a prototype, followed by a systematic unpacking, clause-by-clause, that brings all the concepts in the *Primer for Partners* and this *Book for Builders* to bear and makes them meaningful.

Chapter 1: Constitutive Documents

Charters and similar documents that establish partnership programs and are owned by the collective have many virtues. We consider what these documents are, why they are useful, and how they work.

Chapter 2: The Prototype Charter

Given the many variables and variations of international partnership programs, it is challenging to create a "model" charter that is anything more than a placeholder. Even so, this prototype charter gives us a useful starting point to layer in specifics.

Chapter 3: The Clause-by-Clause Guide

To give the choices around charter drafting some structure, this short guide explains how each clause is put through three filters: first with an explanation of its relevance, then with drafting variations to address common cases, and finally with business questions that partners may want to consider.

Chapter 4: The Annotated Charter

Clause-by-clause, we tackle the prototype charter from front to back, unpacking key points for legal drafters and decision makers to consider when formulating their own partnership program manifestos.

IT'S ALL IN
THE
BASICS

We have:

- *philately* and *sigillography* for stamps and seals
- *vexillology* and *ethnography* for flags and cultures
- *etymology* and *epistemology* for words and wisdom
- *epigraphy* and *diplomatics* for inscriptions and records
- *onomastics* and *numismatics* for names and money
- *paleography* and *codicology* for texts and books
- *topography* and *cartography* for terrain and maps

and now, introducing:

charterography for constitutive documents of international partnership programs.

1 CONSTITUTIVE DOCUMENTS

Somewhere, somehow, there should be a set of common, partnership-wide terms that frames the partnership program, that articulates the common ground. Why are we here? What are we each, collectively and independently, responsible for, and what not? Who makes decisions, on what and how? These are some of the questions partnership program participants should naturally ask themselves. It is prudent for partners to answer these questions in ways that everyone grasps and agrees, to set common understandings and expectations.

Constitutive documents of international partnership programs, also known as establishment documents or foundational documents, are the governing documents around which partners convene, documents that effectively create or "establish" these partnership programs. As part of launching a partnership initiative, these primary documents collectivize the identifying intentions and agreements of the partners.

The centerpiece of these establishment documents is often called a *charter*, but can appear under many other headers as well, like governance terms, terms of reference, partnership framework, governing instrument, constitution, and compendium. The point is that the existence of the partnership program arises from the documents the partners create. These documents are called constitutive because they do just that. They constitute the coming together (*con*) and setting up (*statuere*), from the Latin etymology.

Constitutive documents like charters take effect in different ways, but a favored way is by adoption. International partnership programs can readily take this step because by definition they have some form of governing body, which can do the adopting. *Adopting* a document to give it effect is in contrast to *signing* it. One is a group activity; the other is an individual activity. One produces a multilateral product; the other is usually bilateral. One happens as an *informal (non-corporate) decision point* based on participation; the other is a *formal (contractual) commitment* based on due representation. One is not considered inherently binding or legally enforceable; for the other, being so is often the point. (>@ BfB: Agile Alignment—Constituting Trust-Funded Partnership Programs)

This is not to claim that charters are the only way to memorialize partnership programs. As a common alternative, unifying documents often take the form of common annexes to contribution agreements (>@ ibid., #2), instead of stand-alone partnership terms. By the same token, adoption is not the only way to give effect to constitutive documents. They can be signed, rather than adopted, as in the case of contribution agreements. If the trust fund is central to the partnership, and partners are not familiar with alternatives, relying only on contribution agreements may be a logical way to proceed. But a separate charter is an alternative worth thinking about. And adoption has its advantages, too. (>@ PfP: Like Rock, Like Water)

What's So Great About Charters

So what's so great about charters? They are my go-to modality for memorializing and establishing international partnership programs, as a legal tool, but they are also my insurance policy that partners understand each other, as a business tool. Even when other documents are in play, like contribution agreements—more on those ahead—it still usually makes sense to capture the partnership elements, which largely means the structural elements, in an adopted constitutive document that belongs to the partners through the governing body. But the biggest advantage is the ability of charters to be organic, just as international partnership programs themselves are organic. (>@ BfB: Dynamics—It's Organic) Charters can be positioned as living, breathing documents, subject to change as things evolve over time. (>@ PfP: Like Rock, Like Water) They can even integrate seamlessly with contribution agreements to enable flexibility in the midst of stability. (>@ BfB: Agile Alignment)

Charters are *so* great that they are the point of this book. Not only is *Charterography*, all of this Part II, on charters, but all of Part I builds to this Part II, and all of Part III is about implementing this Part II. So here we are at the crux of the matter, presenting the sample charter and then taking up each individual clause for systematic study through three angles: drafting variations, background explanations, and business considerations.

Before going into the specifics, however, let's consider more closely what charters are—what purpose they serve, how they work in practice, what they typically contain, when their use is recommended, and what to watch for.

Charter drilldown:
1. what's so great about them
2. what purpose they serve
3. how they come into being
4. whom they belong to
5. what they contain
6. when they are recommended
7. what to watch for

constitutive

↓

con + statuere

↓

charter

Annotated pages:
1. original clause
2. explanations
3. variations
4. considerations

What's a Charter Good For?

Here's a short list of ten attributes, plus a bonus eleventh, though we could surely come up with more:

1. CONFIRMING LIKE-MINDEDNESS. In articulating common ground, partners can be reassured that they have a constructive basis for consensus decision making.

2. PROMOTING OWNERSHIP. By developing terms together, partners become part of the process and bring their issues and imprimatur into the end result.

3. SURFACING DIFFERENCES. Through combined inputs, partners reveal where they have differing views and can work to align perspectives.

4. DEFINING CONTOURS. In articulating the scope in terms of content and reach, what and who is "in," the charter can establish visible and agreed perimeters.

5. EVIDENCING INCLUSION. For every entity that is considered a decision-making insider, being part of adopting and amending the charter means having a voice in the partnership.

6. PROMOTING ADVOCACY. In plain English, with clear and effective messaging, partners can concisely express their key goals and objectives under a shared brand.

7. EASING AMENDABILITY. As a collective document subject to governing body decision making, the charter allows changes to be efficient and immediate.

8. MANAGING CONFLICTS. When partners allocate roles and responsibilities in a comprehensive roadmap of who does what, they disclose and validate dynamics.

9. CREATING ACCOUNTABILITY. If everyone knows who is responsible for what in relation to each other, expectations and reliance rise, along with the level of accountability.

10. GIVING COMFORT. Neither too legalistic nor too loose, a document adopted by an informal governing body, with entities beholden to themselves, lets partners slot into a comfort zone.

11. BEING BRIEF. Partners that value brevity can say only as much or as little as they want. Keep it simple, keep it short.

Amendability

Constitutive documents have an agreement quality in that partners agree on their terms, although typically through adoption without formal signatures. Once adopted through collective decision making—through a governing body—these documents can also be amended in the same straightforward way, without major signing exercises. The beauty of partnership programs is their ability to leverage the governing body for change, and to let the governing body own the partnership and program enough to modify essentials over time. This malleability is built directly into the charter. As the partnership program changes over time, a properly structured constitutive document can readily adapt to these changes through governing body decisions. (>@ PfP: Like Rock, Like Water)

Organic partnerships need dynamic documents.

Contribution Agreements as Constitutive Documents

For better or worse, trust-funded partnership programs are habitually constituted through the trust fund more than the partnership. Upstream, funds come into the trust fund after a donor and the trustee agree on terms. A bilateral contribution agreement is signed by both parties. This is then repeated with all the donors to a multi-donor trust fund, in a series of bilateral agreements, all feeding into the same pool of funds. Naturally, the common pool takes common terms, so all bilateral agreements contain a series of clauses that are identical across all donors to the same trust fund.

It is, of course, possible to capture all common trust fund terms in one joint agreement signed by the trustee with all donors together, rather than have a series of bilateral agreements, donor by donor. This would ensure that all donor terms are completely aligned, since all parties would be signing one and the same document. However, the timing and logistics of such a signing jamboree can be daunting, even if signed by counterpart (meaning everyone can sign a physically separate page). Moreover, the parties still need to accommodate a series of donor-specific terms (like contribution amounts and payment dates), which donors like to see in the same place as the rest of the agreed terms. This results in a strong tendency toward bilateral agreements that couple contribution specifics with common annexes, rather than multilateral agreements followed by separate, subsequent steps to record donor specifics.

How does this relate to constitutive documents? When trust funds support partnership programs, the first instinct may be to include governance and additional partnership terms in the contribution agreements. This makes sense because contribution agreements should include everything that affects the use of the funds and trustee operations. (>@ BfB: Dualities—Harmonization and Individuation) As explained elsewhere, if there is any collectivized or shared governance, by which donors and possibly others help shape or steer the trust fund, that should appear in the four corners of the contribution agreement. (>@ PfP: Use of Funds—Four Corners of the Agreement)

But there is a catch. What if the partnering goes beyond the trust fund? What if the shared governance includes partners beyond the trustee and the donors? If the only shared governance participants are the donors plus the trustee, the common governance terms can comfortably reside in the contribution agreements, where everyone involved is a contracting party. However, if the shared governance includes others, like beneficiary governments, NGOs, or other international/multilateral organizations, these partners get left out because they are not part of the agreed, signed documents.

What to do to bridge this gap? The solution is a stand-alone, adopted charter—involving all the governing body participants—which can then be brought into the contribution agreements. (>@ BfB: Agile Alignment—Step-by-Step Alignment for Trust-Funded Partnership Programs, #4) The advantages of charters—greater flexibility, visibility, ownership, and more—can be so compelling that even donor/trustee-only situations, where all the partners have signatory status, can benefit from separate charters alongside contribution agreements.

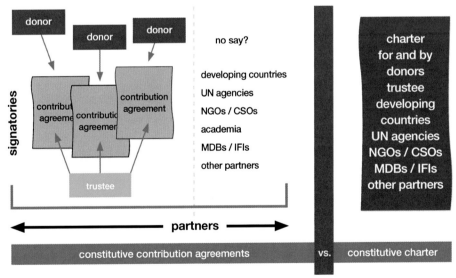

With this backdrop, it is easy to see why charters might end up competing with contribution agreements for establishment status. But that would miss out on the synergies. It is better to see the two in tandem, as complementary, not in competition. When charters constitute the partnership, and contribution agreements contractualize the relationships, they can be mutually reinforcing, like a roof beam welded to a pillar, if the fit is right. (>@ BfB: Agile Alignment—Constituting Trust-Funded Partnership Programs)

Why Have a Charter

To be efficient and sustainable, good practice calls for partners to articulate their basic understandings in a common foundational document, one that reflects all core partners and gets the explicit sign-off from all decision-making partners. This is where a charter-type document, as constituted by the partners, comes in. International partners must first decide how much structure and definition they want, and second, how to memorialize that. There is no widely accepted, internationally sanctioned standard template.

Indeed, the need to be intentionally articulate about partnering is especially pronounced in the international arena. On the one hand, there are no mandatory global corporate requirements or other fixed international rules of establishment for partnership arrangements. Partnership structures cover the spectrum, from informal networks on a rolodex (anyone remember those?) to formally incorporated legal entities. (>@ BfB: Context) There are as many forms of international partnerships as there are ways to paper them. On the other hand, specifically in the case of international partnership programs, establishment is not linked directly to any national statutory framework, but is undertaken by the partners directly. (>@ PfP: Partnering Internationally—Applicable Law) The partner-agreed charter is used as a baseline document to establish the partnership program's existence. It defines the structure and governance, while generally articulating the foundational understandings shared by the partners. Without global or national corporate statutory requirements or other pan-international rules of establishment for international partnership programs, the need to establish their terms of engagement is all the more important.

It turns out that international partnership programs are ideally suited to charter-type arrangements. They feature shared decision making through a governing body, typically along with dedicated funding and dedicated support. (>@ PfP: International Partnership Programs—The Quintessence) They lie in the middle of the spectrum, neither very loose, nor very legal. (>@ PfP: Typology—The Even Broader Landscape of Structured Partnerships) Their virtue lies in applying collective decision making, collective support, and typically collective funding, without becoming separate legal entities, instead relying on existing legal entities—supporting entities—for specific support functions. The collectively-owned, partnership-wide nature of charters makes them a natural for international partnership programs.

What About MOUs?

Partners love MOUs, or so it seems. They are so common that partners may sign them without knowing what the three letters stand for: memorandum of understanding—literally a memo of some thoughts we've shared. Unfortunately, MOUs are a go-to format more by default than deliberation. Their prevalence among international partners is a sign that we lack a well-laid-out, well-manicured partnership landscape in the international arena. They are red flags, conspicuous in the absence of other well-considered, more suitable ways to structure and memorialize international partnerships. (>@ PfP: Like Rock, Like Water—Like Water)

So what really is an MOU? From this lawyer's point of view, pretty much anything and often much of nothing. Half of the time, it is intended to be binding, even though it is labeled a memorandum instead of an agreement. The other half of the time, it is presented as non-binding, even though it may include commitment-type language that raises expectations upon which partners tend to rely. And the rest of the time (yes, that is more than 100% of the time), different partners interpret the MOU in different ways, and may do so differently again depending on future circumstances, so that often there is no clear and real meeting of the minds.

Is it a legal document? Who knows. The name is not much of a clue, since the catch-all label is used to cover everything from formal texts replete with legalese to informal aspirational niceties. And the contents range from press-release-type statements to funding commitments, from intentions, declarations, and exhortations to aspirations and wishful thinking.

MOUs may have their place to send signals or express ideas, and they may help partners articulate their common ground. But they are not designed for structuring or defining partnerships. The best MOUs are probably ones that say little and commit less. If the point is to say more and engage more, there are usually other, better ways to do it.

When partners set out to create their partnership program, the first driver for a constituting document is the desire to set a strong foundation. A strong partnership basis then charts the way forward. This charting—or chartering—sets forth the key elements that make up the partnership program's common ground. Accordingly, constitutive documents are primarily about what is shared: the common vision, shared decision making, pooled funding, centralized support, one brand, and more. (>@ PfP: International Partnership Programs—Collectivizing) With a charter, partners can affirm their partnership program's contours and content:

- **As to contours**, charters help delineate what is in and what is out. (>@ PfP: Typology—Trust-Funded Partnership Programs) By spelling out the contouring scope of the partnership program, the charter has a ringfencing role. This works on several fronts: partners, names, activities, results. The charter becomes a gatekeeper for membership and shapes the umbrella for the brand. It focuses what the partnership program does. That in turn determines what results can be claimed as partnership program achievements, where everyone gets credit for everything done in the partnership program's name.

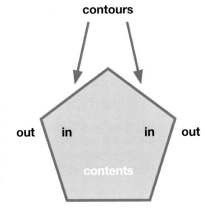

- **As to content**, charters help delineate who works with whom on what. This is structural content, the infrastructure of the partnership program. All partners are first connected through the common venture, then roles and responsibilities are delineated, and then relationships among them reconnect. (>@ PfP: Structure—Taking Context into Account) The charter does all this by taking a collective view of modular elements and a practical view of functional engagements. While some of this can end up in fund flow documents, there is usually more to the partnership program than the workings of the funding vehicle.

In their adopted form, charters usually have a stand-alone quality. They exist on their own terms, separate and apart from other documents. However, they do not operate in isolation. (>@ BfB: Practical Packaging) International partnership programs can have multiple establishment documents, especially if they are supported by trust funds and involve fund flow agreements. Indeed, trust-funded partnership programs are so focused on their trust funds that all the baseline, establishment terms that might otherwise appear in a charter regularly end up subsumed into the donor-driven contribution agreements. When this happens, the trust fund effectively co-opts the partnership. But even then, donors and trustees can still opt for a charter, as a more inclusive, organic, plain English, collectively-owned, and distinctly visible statement of the partnership program.

What About Operations Manuals?

Like MOUs, operations manuals have an identity problem. The name gets used for a variety of scenarios, and you cannot be sure what you are getting by the label alone. Very generally: Partners gravitate toward MOUs to express high level, conceptual principles or parameters for engagement, as going-in positions. By contrast, OMs are used for the back end, to spell out trenches-level, operational requirements, processes, and other details for implementation. In an overstated way, MOUs and OMs are foils, and not just by their lettering.

While MOUs usually do not memorialize fund transfers (you use real agreements for that), operations manuals mostly arise where fund transfers take place. In this sense, operations manuals can have a strong fiduciary quality—prescriptive and prophylactic—as documents that buttress fiduciary supervision. Funds for the activities in question are to be used only in accordance with the operations manual, which can go on for an extenuating number of pages, so everything is crystal clear and all scenarios are addressed.

The lack of discipline around these labels may be okay if the purpose is clear. At the partners' behest, I have drafted "operations manuals" that describe the functioning of the partnership program at the partnership level, rather than the project level. This made some sense in an international platform setting with a lot of mechanics to describe and agree upon. Acting as both a charter-type document and how-to manual, this emphasized the nuts-and-bolts and usefully collected everything anyone needed to know, upstream and downstream, in one place (and fund flow agreements were correspondingly slim).

How the Charter Happens

WE AGREE TO BE WHAT WE ARE.

It's as basic as agreeing and therefore being.

In logic, a tautology is when a conclusion equals the premise. That aptly describes a charter. It is the partnership that the partners say it is. Indeed, partnership programs and their constitutive documents are like the proverbial chicken and egg. Which comes first? One begets the other when partners convene to adopt their governing terms, thereby constituting themselves as a partnership program with the prerogative to adopt those terms. Those wishing to be the ultimate partnership program authority designate themselves as the ultimate authority. In other words, a partnership program is established by establishing itself.

It all may sound complex, but is just a matter of agreeing and therefore being.

Complexity arises not in the process, but in the context and the content. What requires work is developing what the constitutive document says and making it fit the setting. Depending on the set-up, there can be dozens or hundreds of key variables that make up an international partnership program, on the higher side for ones that have more partners, more pieces, more functions, and more features. The charter is looking for that Goldilocks amount of baseline agreement, not too much, not too little, that lets partners join in partnership to launch a program that will sustain them over time.

Ideally, the supporting entity, and more specifically, the secretariat (or the trustee taking on secretariat-type roles), will already be on the case prior to the launch, enough to handle the necessary drafting and coordinating of views around the foundational charter document. Fortunately, this often happens naturally, since the supporting entity partner is frequently also the convener, leveraging its own desire to partner into a platform for collective engagement. Or if not, an initiating partner's first move may be to find that crucial supporting entity.

The supporting entity is in any case the obvious partner to step up to the charter creation role. It will later be the central nexus, clearing house, compliance function, record keeper, and general custodian, with responsibility for keeping the partnership program connected to its core purpose, as articulated in the charter. (>@ PfP: Secretariats—Embedded, Inhouse Secretariats)

A Charter Creation Scenario

Let's spell this out in practice. Here's a scenario, taking it step-by-step:

1. *Initiation.* Imagine a sovereign donor decides through its national budgeting process to allocate a significant sum to address plastics in the oceans. It can channel those funds internally for its own ministries and agencies to act on the problem. Or, because it needs a wider approach, the government can hand out the money piecemeal to lots of others to individually stage activities that address the issue. Or, because this needs a global effort, it can look to international partnering as a way to combine resources, coordinate approaches, scale activities, leverage visibility, share experiences, and amplify impact. Maybe an international partnership is already on it, so these funds can add to an existing effort without further fragmenting the aid architecture. But if not, the donor country can rally others, with a common sense of the issue, to join the cause and create a new platform.

2. *Articulation.* Someone in that group of initial partners will presumably take up a pen and start to spell it all out. It could be the initiating country, which needed that description for internal purposes anyhow. Or if that country can rally the help of a supporting entity (like a multilateral organization, of which it may well be a member), chances are that the supporting entity will put the pen in hand and start drafting on the basis of its internal operations and the support it can offer.

3. *Foundation.* To rally engagement and confirm expectations, the original concept description can become a foundational document for baseline agreement. This requires two things: narrowing the text to establishment-type terms and getting buy-in for the exact wording. This can be a feat of coordination, articulation, iteration, and negotiation. It probably takes one or more lawyers—preferably creative ones that are skilled at converging disparate views onto a shared page and matching policy environments to partnership ambitions.

4. *Ratification.* Once that shared basis is captured in a shared document, the partners are ready to say "I do." The document says who belongs, who has a right to decide, how that decision takes place—and the partners follow those terms. Usually that is the governing body with specified members that agree by consensus and—chicken and egg!—the charter is adopted. One decision point and the deed is done. The partnership program now exists, and the partners are its partners.

Who Owns the Charter

Normally the main governing body "owns" the charter—collective ownership over collective terms. Ownership here means both control and self-identification. The charter is adopted by that body and can be amended by that body; the charter projects what the partners want to be.

What this means practically for the partners depends on the scope of that ownership. Among the elements to be articulated in the charter is who makes decisions about what. That first involves deciding how broadly to cast the partnership net and then deciding who in the membership pool has jurisdiction over what aspects. This includes deciding what is collectively decided and what is delegated to support elements, like the trustee, secretariat, or implementing entities.

In one-stop-shops, the critical mass lies in the full-support supporting entity. (>@ PfP: Typology—One-Stop-Shops vs. International Platforms) The governing body may own the charter, but within narrower decision-making bounds and on more limited terms, and the rest of the decisions are filled in by the supporting entity (primarily in the guise of secretariat, trustee, and implementer).

In international platforms, there is less reliance on the supporting entity and more on the governing body. In these cases, with critical mass in the governing body, ownership of the charter by the governing body reflects overarching ownership of the partnership program. Within that more detailed framework, supporting entity roles are expressly "limited." (>@ ibid.)

Charter ownership is thus a factor of decision making. That is particularly true when charters are not adopted once and forever, but amended over time. Charters are relevant and thrive where partners are active decision makers, where their ongoing imprimatur is part of the partnership program. Where, by contrast, key decision making is efficiently vested in the supporting entity, as in one-stop-shops, there is less emphasis on the governing body and less room or need for a charter. One-stop-shops may even be reluctant to embrace charters because they offer partners too much decision making—at least from the perspective of the supporting entity. Avoiding a charter-like document in such cases is a value-judgment on the partnership, with more stock put directly into implementation and operations.

Decision making in international partnership programs can take various forms. In some cases, the desire to avoid unwieldy decision making can result in two-tier governing bodies (>@ BfB: The Annotated Charter—Members), or the desire for inclusivity can engage broader fora, like stakeholder events (>@ PfP: Structure—Broader Context). These dynamics may also lead partners to segment decision making into constituencies or subgroups (>@ PfP: Governing Bodies—Composition), where some members agree to be represented by other members, or some topics belong to some subgroups. As a result, ownership within a partnership program may be very straightforward, with just one body in one decision-making setting, or it may involve more complex membership terms and partnership bodies through delegation and segmentation, resulting in more modular decision making across the partnership program. How charter adoption and amendment fit into these more varied structures is not prescribed, but is itself part of the decisions to be made.

In the end, whether the originating partners grant purview over the constitutive document to all participants or just a subset, and how and with what import, becomes part of the agreed basis upon which the partnership program governs itself through its constitutive document. (There is that tautology again.)

Charter ownership is a factor of decision making.

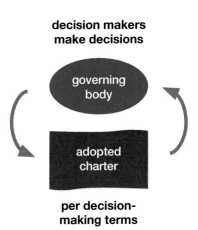

decision makers make decisions

governing body

adopted charter

per decision-making terms

What's in the Charter

There is no hard and fast rule for what constitutes a constitutive document. Each one is different; each one should be suited to its specific circumstances. It is okay to start with a model or template—otherwise I would not be putting one in this book! (>@ BfB: The Prototype Charter)—but only as a broad starting point. The specifics should always be contextualized, and the end result should always reflect deliberations and negotiations. It amazes me how often sponsoring teams ask for a "sample" charter without sharing even the first detail of their planned initiative. It would be professionally irresponsible for me to provide a version without a sense of the context. Instead, I need enough details to make a good choice, or multiple choices, varied as they are, including whether a charter is called for at all.

As a general matter, charters are definitional and cover the essential partnering elements, the *sine qua nons* that make this partnership different from all the others. Broad categories include:

1. mission, purpose, objectives—what it's for and why we're here
2. membership—who's in (and by implication, who's out)
3. bodies—who meets and decides about what and how
4. roles and responsibilities—who's in charge, who's on the hook
5. rights and rules—amendments, disclosure, privileges and immunities, etc.

Charters and other constitutive documents are best kept at a structural level. The charter's essential partnership focus should not become cluttered with day-to-day detail. Instead, charters are typically more about the upstream definition of the partnership program, the shared decision making, the funding environment, the core, plus the linkages and relationships that flow from there—follow the money, follow the power (>@ PfP: Structure—Whiteboarding). They are less about the downstream implementation, which emerges and evolves programmatically and operationally, including as defined in operations manuals (>@ BfB: A Taxonomy of Trust Fund Agreements—Complementary Documents).

Membership usually takes up a big chunk of the charter. Normally the charter identifies the initial partners, at least those comprising the governing body, and indicates how new partners may be added over time. Partnership membership is usually a process of mutual agreement, since all partners effectively agree to be partners with each other.

By nature, international partnership programs are voluntary affairs. A partner that does not agree at the beginning need not join; a partner that does not agree over time can walk—with two major caveats:

- First, if a partner signs a legal agreement that obligates it to perform certain roles, an exit is usually more complicated and hopefully spelled out in the agreement. For example, donors obligate themselves to future payments, and trustees obligate themselves to manage trust fund operations for the life of the fund. The contribution agreements would normally explain whether and how individual donors can get payouts and terminate, while also allowing the trustee to terminate. Admittedly, a unilateral decision by the latter carries major operational implications.

- Second, if a partner contributes to a commingled fund, its ability to withdraw funds is limited to proportional amounts of trust fund balances that have not yet been disbursed or committed. And even then, some of its funds will always remain part of the funds that have been disbursed and committed. In that respect, a complete and total exit for donors from a commingled pool is not quite possible midstream.

There's an annotated sample charter later in this Part Two.

The charter usually also assigns roles and responsibilities and clarifies accountabilities among the different elements, like the governing body, secretariat, and trustee. This is particularly important once funds start to flow, since fiduciary obligations under contribution agreements are affected by and may even depend upon other elements doing their part. For example, a limited trustee needs the governing body to decide about fund allocations and the secretariat to transmit the instructions. A clean and clear charter will have a section on each element that includes a list of principal roles and responsibilities. And in a well-honed charter, each of these sections will reflect the others. If, for example, the governing body approves the annual report prepared by the secretariat, as listed under the governing body's roles, the secretariat list should include that it prepares the annual report for the governing body to approve.

The Prerogative of the Collective

When and how the partners as a collective get to weigh in is the kind of thing that belongs in the charter. The collective can express itself through the governing body, which makes the governing body's description in the charter Exhibit A for the scope of the partners' prerogative. For example:

- Does the negotiated framework reflect the agreed balance of roles and responsibilities?

- Does this include expectations of governing body oversight and strategic purview?

- Does the governing body have subsequent decision rights, such as approving a high level, annual work plan (light touch) or allocating pooled funds on a case-by-case basis (heavy touch)?

- Can the governing body agree to bring other activities into the brand as part of the partnership program portfolio?

Process questions like these impact the substance of the partnership program. They position the nexus between governance, activities, funding, and responsibility under the partnership program umbrella.

Charters need not spell out the specific results frameworks, annual work plans and budgets, or other operational elements that have periodic cycles of review and revision or are subject to funding inflows, progress reports, and other variables over time. Rather than position operational details in a founding charter, these working level aspects can have many other homes, including as:

- part of ongoing partnership proceedings through documents tabled at governing body meetings or shared virtually. This can have various guises, including manuals (an operations manual), codes of conduct (a conflict of interest code), or guidelines (disclosure guidelines).

- delegated into the operational responsibilities of supporting or implementing functions. This can be as simple as cross-referring to "applicable policies and procedures" of the supporting entity or fiduciary recipient (>@ BfB: Deft Drafting—The Art of Writing—Defined Terms), without overlapping itemization in the charter.

- lodged in other supporting documents promulgated by the secretariat. This can take the form of templates, information notes, frequently asked questions (FAQs), and similar products that are posted or distributed after consultations or agreement with the governing body or individual partners.

Overall, there is no fixed rule beyond pragmatism. Sometimes a few partnership elements end up in the operations manual; sometimes the charter broadens into a few operational details. The more interesting question is who has decision making power over what content. All manner of memorializing can be fine if it suits the context, strengthens the foundation, avoids overlap, and efficiently enables change over time. (>@ BfB: The Clause-by-Clause Guide)

As baseline documents, charters should embody both stability and flexibility. (>@ PfP: Like Rock, Like Water) They should promote and preserve balance. (>@ BfB: Balance) The opportunity to provide clear, defining terms from the start sets up the ability to manage those terms and adjust them as necessary over time. Anything that is articulated early on becomes a visible candidate for honing and updating later on.

When the Charter Is Most Useful

Across the full partnership spectrum, there are times when charters and similar constitutive documents are appropriate, and times when they are too much or not needed. The sui generis, hybrid partnership programs addressed here, however—the ones with dedicated governing bodies, dedicated support, and typically also dedicated funding—can always benefit from constitutive documents.

Because international partnership programs basically start from scratch, they are as the partners define them to be. That puts a premium on defining. The very act of placing decision-making responsibility into collective hands calls for a collective document explaining the scope of that act. By engaging a supporting entity, partners also take a consequential step toward collective agreement on roles and responsibilities. And if partners also add funding vehicles, which come with contractual obligations, the clear articulation of roles and responsibilities, and other governance aspects, becomes even more important. In addressing these aspects clearly and collectively, charters become instruments of efficiency and sustainability.

The charter's basic purpose may be seen as memorializing the act of partnering, but its full utility also arises from the following:

- *Adherence to common terms.* Whenever convening partners want to express and confirm their common ground, a constitutive document can provide a clear and disciplined platform for articulating shared goals, harmonized standards, and transparent expectations without corporate formality or legal rigidity.

- *Distribution of powers.* Whenever partners wish to allocate rights and responsibilities to a subset of partners (like constituencies or working groups) or to specific partners (like a supporting entity secretariat or trustee), a constitutive document can usefully delineate roles and place responsibilities.

- *Visible branding.* Whenever partners are communications-conscious with an emphasis on messaging and advocacy, including for their fund-allocating ministries and their taxpaying citizens, a constitutive document can garner buy-in for a foundational vision or mission that all partners can project.

- *Multiple funding vehicles.* Whenever partners want purview over more than one funding vehicle, potentially with broad oversight of activities, a constitutive document can provide clarity and cohesion that links the funding vehicles and related agreements to shared governance and allocated responsibilities.

- *Multiple components.* Whenever partners seek to harmonize downstream approaches for independently executed activities, want a brand name associated with an array of separate endeavors, or are otherwise looking for an overarching umbrella, a constitutive document can link the different elements.

- *Amendability.* Whenever partners anticipate their partnership program will grow and evolve over time (invariably the case), a constitutive document can provide the living, breathing flexibility to make changes efficiently. (Of course, there is ultimate flexibility in having no constitutive document, but that would lose the baby with the bathwater.)

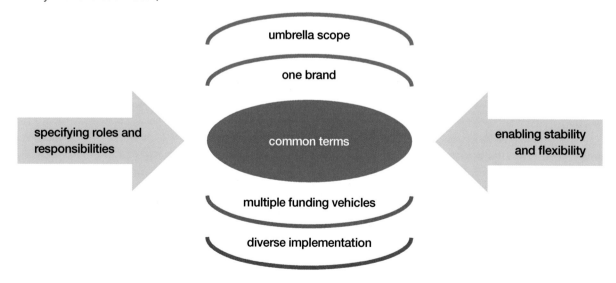

What to Watch For

A heightened awareness on a few interrelated fronts can go a long way toward making more meaningful charters:

Key points:
1. multiple roles
2. embedded, inhouse secretariats
3. signed vs. unsigned
4. legal status
5. document alignment
6. package controls

1. Multiple roles.

Supporting entities, in particular, frequently perform multiple roles in a partnership program, simultaneously serving, for example, as member or even chair of the governing body, secretariat for the partnership program, trustee of one or more funding vehicles, donor, implementer, and supervisor. The potential for multiple roles to scramble lines of responsibility, undercut transparency, and strain partner expectations makes it especially important for everyone to clearly understand the arrangement. Charters and other constitutive documents play a major part in establishing a partnership's accountability framework. Among the choices to be made is whether multiple roles by one and the same partnering entity should be integrated (as in one-stop-shops) or separated (as in international platforms). By transparently framing and delineating which functions carry what responsibilities by whom, partners can readily disclose and manage potential or perceived conflicts of interest into validated synergies. (>@ PfP: Synergistic Conflicts)

2. Embedded, inhouse secretariats.

Supporting entities that house secretariats have some sense of the innumerable ways in which their support is brought to bear. The partnership program's secretariat function puts the supporting entity in the role of "custodian" (>@ PfP: Custodial Effect), including in terms of good governance, recordkeeping, and risk management. This is often lost on other partners, who can be quick to take this expansive level of support for granted. Charters are a starting point for making that level more visible, and it behooves the supporting entity to be explicit about the support it is able and willing to provide. It is, by default, the secretariat's responsibility to make sure proper constitutive documents are in place and up-to-date, usually posted in their most current versions along with other basic partnership documents on the partnership program's website. This special custodial role is key for all participants, no less the supporting entity itself, whose added degree of reputational exposure more than merits close attention to constitutive documents.

3. Signed vs. unsigned.

Charters are adopted, agreements are signed, and both together can populate the partnership program's defining landscape. It is common practice for international partnership programs to have trustee-donor signed agreements for fund flows, in addition to charter-style adopted terms. As described earlier, that is especially relevant for participants beyond the trustee and the donors. In these cases, extra sensitivity is needed for consistent terms between signed and adopted partnership program documents. Despite differences in their legal nature, these documents are more alike than different from business perspectives. An unsigned charter functions like signed agreements as a matter of setting expectations, incurring reliance, and informing risk assessments. Whether they arise from legally enforceable commitments (signed) or consensus-raised expectations (adopted), both modes cause reliance by the partners and add up to the same operative heft. It is polite, practical, and prudent to view adopted, constitutive documents as equivalent to signed, fund flow agreements.

4. Legal status.

To reiterate the point, since charters for international partnership programs are usually adopted rather than signed, partners may view them as convening documents more than committing documents. They may be seen as stakes in the ground to confirm common intentions, but not legal hooks to exact firm commitments. That, however, downplays their importance. Charters are clearly more than letters of intent (LOIs) or memoranda of understanding (MOUs). They put concrete steps into motion that build upon each other. They cause partners to act in reliance on their terms, like when donors provide funding based on promised governance involvement. And they frequently become contractualized when incorporated by reference into binding agreements, like contribution agreements, of which they become an "integral" part. (>@ BfB: Agile Alignment—Step-by-Step Alignment for Trust-Funded Partnership Programs, #4) Indeed, this contractualization is one of the reasons to keep charters short and to the point. (>@ BfB: A Taxonomy of Trust Fund Agreements—Complementary Documents)

———————————————————————— ● ————————————————————————

Binding Terms?

Charters are normally not considered binding. There are usually no clauses that say they are binding, and usually no signatures to bind. Vis-à-vis sovereigns and international organizations that have privileges and immunities, they usually offer limited, if any, judicial enforceability. Indeed, at least a few of the traditional sovereign donors will not accept explicitly binding terms. But that need not become a problem. In contribution agreements, the trustee can respect this by refraining from clauses that say "this is binding upon the parties," even though everyone expects the trustee to be fully bound, and everyone is relying on the future contributions. Here we see that the difference between binding commitments and relied-upon expectations is paper thin. From a practical perspective, this legal variance will likely never be tested (the trustee is not about to sue the donor to enforce its contributions receivable), and the upshot is the same either way. Against this backdrop, silence can be golden, whether in charters or contribution agreements. No one says it is binding or not, which leaves room for both interpretations across common terms—and yet, everyone knows what is at stake and how to behave. (>@ BfB: Deft Drafting—The Art of Writing—Staying Silent)

———————————————————————— ● ————————————————————————

Charters convene, but can also commit.

———————————————————————— ● ————————————————————————

Signed Charters?

It is possible to sign a charter-type document, instead of adopting it, while still emphasizing ownership by the governing body. Every decision maker could put its name on the dotted line, rather than rely on a collective decision point. If so, partners are not just members of a governing body, but also become parties to formal, shared commitments.

Signature signifies a higher degree of commitment than adoption, typically with more language on breachability, liability, recourse, and remedies. That may be a good fit for some cases. For example, private sector partners may see their comfort zone in contractual relationships, the modality they are used to among themselves. Or a beneficiary government may find it easier to route budget and in-kind support toward shared objectives if it has a signed agreement to point to. There is no one-size-fits-all. Every set of partners will want to think contextually—weighing the benefits of adoption against the benefits of signing—as with every other topic having to do with partnership programs.

Even with signing, however, the benefits of adoption for amendability can still be built in. Initial signatures can make the document effective, but revisions over time can come from governing body decisions. This mixed approach starts with an agreement modality, based on individual signatures for effectiveness, but shifts to a structural modality, based on collective decisions for amendments. As long as the governing body is representative of the signatory parties, a one-time decision process can supplant a more extensive, usually cumbersome multi-party signing process. Language for that could look like this:

> *This [signed] Charter may be amended by Governing Body approval [as described herein] without the need for further written or signed amendments among the Parties.*

———————————————————————— ● ————————————————————————

5. Document alignment.

Partnership program documents, both signed and unsigned, need to fit together. No participants, including especially the trustee and secretariat, can afford to find themselves caught in the middle of conflicting or diverging sets of terms, with the need to manage and mediate parallel universes. Pitfalls can be avoided by aligning documents through cross-references, clarifying which document prevails, and allowing amendments to carry over from one document to another. (>@ BfB: Agile Alignment—Step-by-Step Alignment for Trust-Funded Partnership Programs, #7) From a practical drafting perspective:

- **Conflict.** Directly conflicting terms are to be avoided. Although many institutions have minimal regular clearance processes for unsigned partnership documents, partners should take care not to enter into signed agreements (like contribution agreements) that conflict—or could foreseeably in the future conflict—with other governing documents, like charters. Just because a lawyer carefully inserted a clause saying contribution agreement terms prevail over charter terms is no good reason to allow conflicts to happen.

- **Overlap.** Overlapping terms should also be avoided. Partners should watch for duplicative statements across different documents. Even nuanced differences in wording can cause confusion, if not actual conflict. Every lawyer knows that a conjunction or comma can make for an entirely different meaning. It is usually better to articulate specific terms once and clearly, rather than require adherence to two sets of terms that may or may not align. It is also better to amend once, not twice, to make a change.

It is worth scanning the documents to decide what content is best placed where—mapping content to context—and then adding cross-references where helpful. (>@ ibid., #5)

> Don't even try to manage or mediate parallel universes–best to stay aligned.

> Map content to context and then cross-reference.

●

Channeling the Charter

Diving into the legal weeds, there are two primary ways to bring the charter into the contribution agreements (>@ BfB: Agile Alignment—Step-by-Step Alignment for Trust-Funded Partnership Programs, #4):

- First, the charter can be "incorporated by reference." This incorporation makes the charter an integral part of the agreement, in effect contractualizing the adopted document. The signature that makes the contribution agreement effective essentially carries over to include the charter.

- Second, the charter can be made to "apply" to the trust fund. This phrasing in the contribution agreement is a lighter touch than formally incorporating and contractualizing.

To be sure, there is little practical difference to this legal nuance. At the end of the day, the trustee still knows what to do, and donors still expect the trustee to do it, whether the charter is integrally incorporated or operationally applied. Donors may prefer one or the other for internal reasons, but the same approach should be used across all donors to the same multi-donor trust fund, as a common term affecting trustee operations.

●

6. Package controls.

It takes a comprehensive perspective to view the written underpinnings of a partnership program holistically. Individual parties will presumably make sure they know what they are signing or adopting, but is anyone looking at the whole picture to make sure it all fits together? Does anyone have overarching, or undergirding, responsibility for the whole thing?

- *Overarching (external) controls.* The overarching perspective can come from the governing body, for which the litmus test is true consensus. When a partnership program is being established, the scope of this consensus should reach across all key participants and across all baseline terms, both signed and adopted, including as cross-referenced. What constitutes this "baseline" depends on what partners consider essential to their decisions to partner. And who should be part of this consensus depends on who is considered an insider, who is part of the partnership, which can go beyond the official decision makers. (>@ PfP: Like Rock, Like Water—Like Rock)

- *Undergirding (internal) controls.* Another control function is through the supporting entity, which serves itself and the whole partnership program by taking a more vigilant approach to structure and design. It will in any case want a closer look because of its degree of association and exposure at the crux of the partnership program. This heightened regard can in turn be helpful for all other participants, especially if getting constitutive documents and fund flow agreements seamlessly in place also belong to the supporting entity's roles and responsibilities—which, for the secretariat and trustee, they usually do. (>@ PfP: Custodial Effect)

If both of these external-internal controls are fully functional and working in tandem, then that is the best kind of bear hug, which bodes well for a sustainable partnership program.

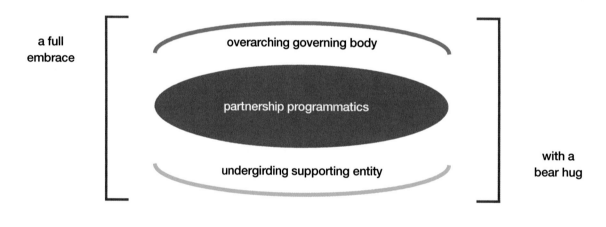

No Charter Needed

Constitutive documents are not needed for *loose networks* that rely on mailing lists, at the far end of the structured partnership spectrum where there is virtually no structure. In these cases, a charter-type document would be more like a mission statement, with little else to write.

The same is true at the other end of the structured partnership spectrum, where we have formalized, statutory structures. There the documents take on a more legal character, in the form of articles of association, by-laws, and the like that establish *legally incorporated entities* under local legal requirements. For these dedicated entity partnerships (>@ PfP: Typology—The Even Broader Landscape of Structured Partnerships), an additional charter would largely duplicate what is already statutorily necessary.

By contrast, international partnership programs expressly distance themselves from domestic legal regimes, instead residing somewhere in the international ether, structurally never really touching down on national ground. (>@ PfP: Partnering Internationally) Being out in international space like this, and having a good amount of (infra)structure to be decided and described, makes a charter-type document relevant in these cases.

Multilateralism vs. Bilateralism

Because charters are documents by the collective about the collectives (>@ PfP: International Partnership Programs), they are the partnership antidote to bilateralism. Bilateralism usually comes about through fund flow agreements—donor to trustee, trustee to recipient—which are, on their face, at odds with collectivizing partnership intentions. Common terms in common annexes are a partial remedy to these piecemealed, bilateral relations, and they are necessary for commingled pools of funds. (>@ PfP: Trust Funds—Accounts) However, the more direct and transparent way to say things in one voice is through one document. What goes in a charter is what brings and holds the partnership program together—the essential terms of the collectivized essence.

> Charters are
> by the collective
> about the collectives.

Conclusion

The central importance of a centralizing document, agreed and owned by all partners, should be obvious, but is all too often overlooked or undervalued. A culture of commonality among partners includes a common expression of purpose and positions, visible to themselves and others.

It need not take much to lay down the roadmap of intentions and expectations. A mere handful of pages can provide the contours and contents of an international partnership program in ways that guide operations and anticipate change. What follows in the next pages is a concrete example to make the topic real. And what follows after that is a host of options and considerations to make a charter fit-for-purpose across a range of circumstances and scenarios.

Read on and be empowered!

2 THE PROTOTYPE CHARTER

for International Partnership Programs with Trust Funds

CHARTER OF
[NAME OF THE PARTNERSHIP PROGRAM]

As adopted on _____, 20__ [and amended on _____, 20__]

NB1: The fourth chapter of this Part 2, The Annotated Charter, presents each clause separately, one-by-one, with detailed explanations and analysis.

NB2: Terms with initial capitalization represent defined terms that are defined within the text, unless a separate glossary is preferred. Short documents tend to have better flow if definitions are in situ.

NB3: You can contact the author at andrea@structuredpartnerships.com for an editable Word version, including Variations.

Part I. Introduction

1. *Background.* [describe history/genesis/context/strategic approach/challenge]

2. *Mission.* [describe mission/vision/goals/intentions/values]

3. *[Principles] [Strategic Objectives].* [list fundamental parameters]

Part II. Scope

4. *Program Objectives.* [provide description]

5. [optional] *[Eligibility] [Participation Requirements].* [specify terms]

6. *Activities.* The Partnership Program focuses on the following activities: _____.

7. [optional] *Funding Sources.* The Partnership Program is supported by a dedicated trust fund (the Trust Fund).

8. [optional] *Funding Requirements.* [insert minimum contributions/waiver process/ etc.]

Part III. Governance

Governance Overview

9. *Governance Overview.* The governance of the Partnership Program is designed to [state objectives]. It consists of

    a) the [governing body];
    b) the [other events/bodies, if any];
    c) the [secretariat]; and
    d) the [trustee].

Governing Body

10. *Governing Body Context.* The Partnership Program is governed by the Governing Body. [describe broad partnership role, plus relationships to other governance elements, as relevant]

11. *Governing Body Decision-Making Members.* The Governing Body comprises the following decision-making members (Members): _____.

12. *Governing Body Member Representation.* Each Member participates in the Governing Body through a standing representative. The names of current Member representatives are notified to the Secretariat at all times, including as names of record for no-objection decision purposes.

13. *Governing Body Non-Decision-Making Observers.* The Governing Body includes the following [active] observers without decision-making participation (Observers): Secretariat Head, Trustee, and _____. Each Observer participates through a standing representative. The names of current Observer representatives are notified to the Secretariat at all times. At the invitation of the [Chair], additional non-decision-making participants may attend specific meetings for specific purposes.

14. *Governing Body Chair.* The Governing Body is chaired by [a senior representative of the supporting entity].

15. *Governing Body Roles and Responsibilities.* The primary roles and responsibilities of the Governing Body are as follows [by way of example, pick and edit as relevant]:

    a) Providing strategic guidance for the Partnership Program;
    a) Overseeing the Partnership Program;
    a) Approving Partnership Program [strategies] [priorities];
    a) Allocating envelopes of funding [to specified fiduciary recipients] for implementation in accordance with [agreed terms];
    a) Approving annual work plans [and indicative budgets] for the Partnership Program, as prepared by the Secretariat, including fully-funded Secretariat and Trustee costs;
    a) Approving funding allocations from the Trust Fund based on funding requests submitted to [and pre-screened by] the Secretariat;
    a) Consider whether other proposed activities financed or undertaken by Members can be part of the Partnership Program based on requests submitted to the Secretariat.

b) Approving a multi-year results framework for the Partnership Program;

c) Approving a risk management strategy for the Partnership Program;

d) Approving an annual work plan for the Partnership Program;

e) Reviewing financial reports prepared by the Trustee;

f) Reviewing progress reports [prepared] [compiled] by the Secretariat;

g) Agreeing on conflict of interest, confidentiality, and transparency [rules] [standards] for the Partnership Program;

h) Supporting resource mobilization efforts for the Partnership Program;

i) Approving the establishment of [working groups] [task forces] based on terms of reference prepared by the Secretariat;

j) Selecting the Chair of the Governing Body based on [recommendations by the Secretariat] [nominations from the Members];

k) Approving new Members and Observers;

l) Adopting and approving amendments to this Charter;

m) Reviewing and evaluating the overall performance of the Partnership Program, including the Governing Body;

n) Guiding monitoring and evaluation arrangements for the Partnership Program; and

o) Commissioning periodic independent evaluations of the Partnership Program.

16. *Governing Body Decision Making.* Decisions of the Governing Body may be made in person at meetings or electronically between meetings. Decisions at meetings are taken on a consensus basis by the Members present. Consensus means a decision is approved if no Member blocks the proposed decision. It need not reflect unanimity. A dissenting Member that does not wish to block a decision may state an objection to be recorded in the meeting minutes. Members may also abstain from the decision. The Chair articulates the consensus view to be recorded in the minutes. Decisions made electronically between meetings are taken on a no-objection basis by Members. No-objection decision processes are handled by the Secretariat.

17. *Governing Body Meetings.* The Governing Body meets at least annually and may meet more frequently. Governing Body meeting locations, dates, and agendas are proposed by the Secretariat and determined by the Chair in consultation with the Members.

Other Bodies

18. [optional] *[Other Bodies—name of body or element].* [provide description]

Secretariat

19. *Secretariat Context.* The Secretariat provides [overall] [administrative] support to the Partnership Program and the Governing Body [and other bodies].

20. *Secretariat Roles and Responsibilities.* The roles and responsibilities of the Secretariat include *[by way of example, pick and edit as relevant]*:

a) *[hands-on]* Providing overall support to the Partnership Program, including carrying out the Partnership Program's annual work plan, managing its day-to-day operations, supporting the Governing Body, and generally facilitating the work of the Partnership Program; [Any matters for decision by the Governing Body are initially directed through the Secretariat for review;]

a) *[hands-off]* Providing administrative and coordination support to the Partnership Program; [The Secretariat does not intend to encroach on the authority and prerogative of the Governing Body, which remains responsible for the substance of its decision making, nor does it intend to overlap with or act counter to the role of the Trustee;]

b) Arranging meetings of the Governing Body, including preparing the agenda and compiling supporting documentation;

c) Maintaining records of Governing Body business, including meeting minutes and no-objection decisions;

d) Participating in the Governing Body as an Observer [through the Secretariat Head or alternate];

e) Preparing annual Partnership Program work plans and indicative budgets for Governing Body review and [approval] [comment];

f) Pre-screening funding proposals for compliance with Partnership Program requirements;

g) Managing the roster of experts for feedback on funding proposals for Governing Body review;

h) Distributing funding proposals for Governing Body review and [decision] [comment];

i) Distributing financial reports for Governing Body review and comment;

j) [Preparing] [Compiling] and distributing progress reports for Governing Body review and comment;

k) [Coordinating implementation of] [Implementing] the annual work plan;

l) Preparing the Partnership Program's annual report for Governing Body [approval] [review];

m) Organizing the annual stakeholders forum in consultation with [the Chair of] the Governing Body;

n) Coordinating and supporting any [standing committees] [working groups] [task forces];

o) Managing the Partnership Program website;

p) [Managing] [Coordinating] relations and communications for the Partnership Program with national authorities, the media, stakeholders, and partner organizations;

q) Facilitating the sharing of data and development of lessons learned from Partnership Program activities;

r) Coordinating with the Trustee as needed to carry out their respective responsibilities;

s) Supporting resource mobilization efforts for the Partnership Program;

t) [Preparing] [Coordinating] background notes and other materials for Governing Body business;

u) Commissioning [periodic] [midterm] reviews and independent evaluations of the Partnership Program, including as requested by the Governing Body; and

v) Presenting to the Governing Body for review and decision any proposed amendments to this Charter.

Trustee

21. [if relevant] *Trustee Context.* The [Trustee entity] acts as the trustee (Trustee) of the Trust Fund. Contributions to the Trust Fund are made under contribution agreements entered into by the Trustee with each donor. Trustee staff operate, and Trust Fund operations are conducted, under [Trustee entity] management in accordance with the [Trustee entity's] applicable policies and procedures.

22. [if relevant] *Trustee Roles and Responsibilities.* The roles and responsibilities of the Trustee are as defined in the contribution agreements entered into by the Trustee with each of the donors to the Trust Fund, consistent with the [Trustee entity's] applicable policies and procedures. The Trustee participates [as an Observer] in the Governing Body and coordinates with the Secretariat as needed to carry out their respective responsibilities.

Monitoring and Evaluation

23. *Monitoring and Evaluation Framework.* The Partnership Program's monitoring and evaluation (M&E) approach is designed to support successful execution of the Partnership Program's [annual work plans] [other plan or strategy] and translate the Partnership Program's [mission] [goals] into tangible results. Periodic, evidence-based assessments are conducted on the extent to which Partnership Program activities, governance, and other aspects have achieved, or are likely to achieve, stated objectives. Donors are [expected] [encouraged] to manage their M&E needs with respect to the Trust Fund and other Partnership Program funding sources collectively through common processes.

Part IV. General

24. *Privileges and Immunities.* Nothing in this Charter is intended to impair or limit, or may be considered a waiver of, any privileges or immunities of any Partnership Program participant under its relevant governing documents or any applicable law, all of which are expressly reserved.

25. *Disclosure.* The Partnership Program seeks to operate in a transparent manner, which includes public disclosure of this Charter. The Secretariat [and Trustee] may disclose Partnership Program [and Trust Fund] information in accordance with [its] [their] policies and procedures on access to information.

26. *Amendments.* This Charter becomes effective upon adoption by a consensus or no-objection decision of the Governing Body. Amendments may be proposed to the Secretariat for Governing Body consideration and approval by consensus or no objection. The Secretariat maintains and distributes the records of any such amendments. Amendments to this Charter are expected to apply directly to the Trust Fund's contribution agreements, as stated therein, without further need to amend such contribution agreements; provided that the amendments are consistent with (i) such contribution agreements and (ii) the [Trustee entity]'s applicable policies and procedures, both of which prevail over this Charter in case of conflict.

3 THE CLAUSE-BY-CLAUSE GUIDE

for the Annotated Charter

It is daunting, if not daring, to present a draft charter for international partnership programs. The one message that surely rings most true in my *Primer for Partners*, and now this book, is that every partnership program is different. Indeed, they must be different if they are to respond to their circumstances and be contextual and fit-for-purpose.

There is some audacity, maybe hubris, in thinking I can share a draft charter with any real value. Certainly the clauses by themselves do little to support the cause. That is why my prototype charter is followed by an annotated charter in the next chapter. The point is not the clauses per se, but the analysis that goes with them. The prototype charter is but a placeholder for unpacking each clause, one-by-one in diligent detail. It is an excuse to beg the question and a license to go for the deep dive.

An intended benefit of this clause-by-clause approach is that you need only look up what is relevant to you. If your supporting entity is chairing the governing body, you may be set on that point, nothing to ask or add. But if you are toying with the idea of minimum contributions or constituency representation to keep from letting the governing body get too large, those are the points you can look up. Even for aspects that are relatively clear, the annotated analysis may still give you ideas, alert you to issues, streamline your drafting, and help with your presentation.

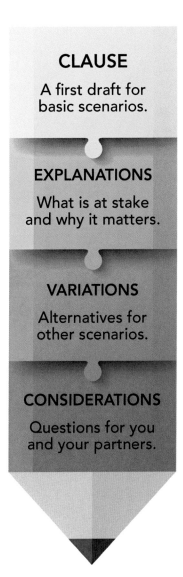

CLAUSE
A first draft for basic scenarios.

EXPLANATIONS
What is at stake and why it matters.

VARIATIONS
Alternatives for other scenarios.

CONSIDERATIONS
Questions for you and your partners.

There is a lot of trustee and trust fund language in the prototype charter. Do not let that mislead you into thinking international trust funds are essential elements of international partnership programs. It is just that so many of them rely on trust funds, and that is also where many of the common issues arise. If your case does not involve this kind of funding vehicle, the drafting suggestions and issue analysis may still give you useful ideas for whatever funding sources you have. Or if collectivized, dedicated, or branded funding is not the point, just read past the trustee/trust fund portions and focus on what fits in your corner.

And of course, the final caveat: Nothing here is gospel. For every suggestion, there are exceptions and distinctions. Please read thoughtfully and judiciously; take in concepts more than clauses. As I say in the *Primer*:

> Whatever your circumstances, this guide is meant to give you principles, placeholders, and pointers. Read about proposed approaches, potential pitfalls, and accompanying commentary, and check them against the reality of your own circumstances.

> You are your own architect and can leverage the creative space in the international arena to your advantage.

Each Prototype Charter clause is examined in four parts in the Annotated Charter:

1. *The Clause.* A first draft for basic scenarios.
2. *Explanations.* What is at stake and why it matters.
3. *Variations.* Alternative wording, depending on circumstances.
4. *Considerations.* Things to ask yourself and other partners.

THE CLAUSE: Step One—Start with a lonely clause in the abstract.

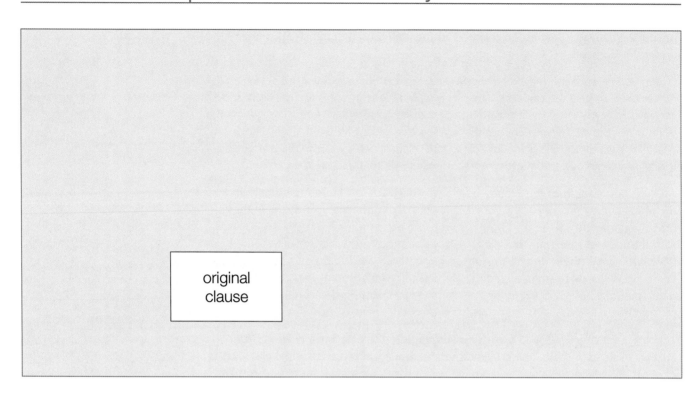

EXPLANATIONS: Step Two—Add some context.

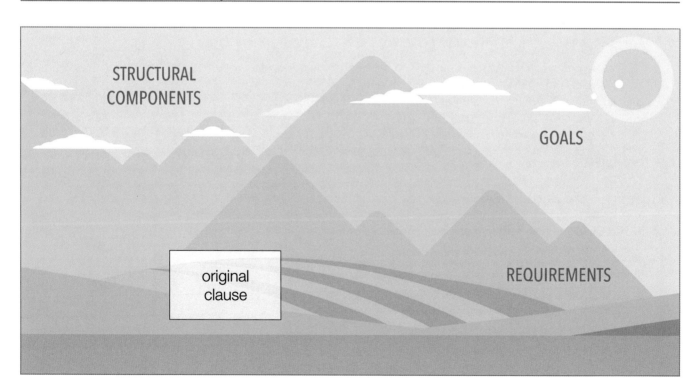

VARIATIONS: Step Three—Consider situational alternatives.

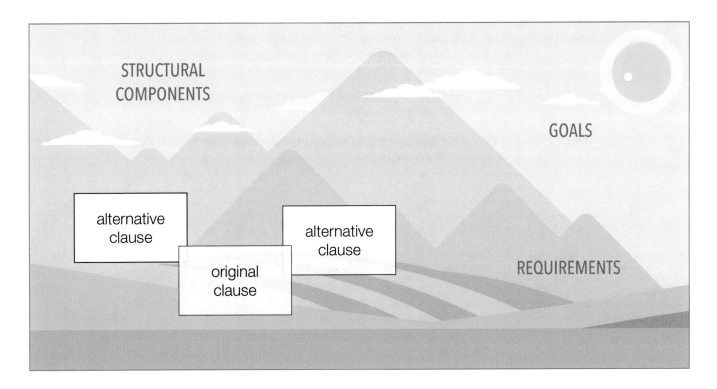

CONSIDERATIONS: Step Four—Engage in iteration and negotiation.

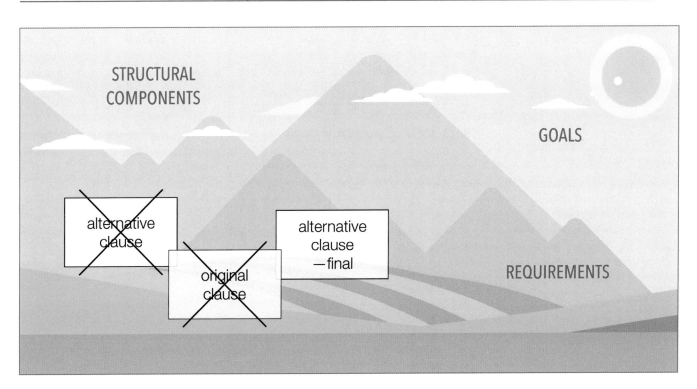

In this way, an idea travels through wording and wordsmithing to become a fit-for-purpose clause. It is a journey of articulation and negotiation, through iteration upon iteration. To achieve this fit-for-purpose goal, partners and their lawyers need room for three D's:

1. **Deliberation.** Partners need to exchange thoughts and develop common positions.

2. **Drafting.** Whoever holds the pen needs to float drafts, get feedback, and hone wording.

3. **Decision.** Partners need to review drafts and converge on approved content and text.

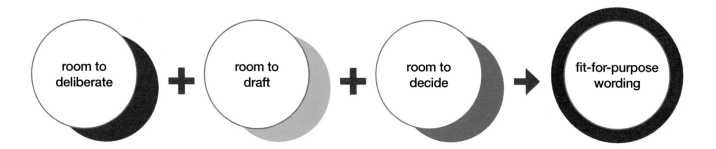

Sometimes lawyers can find themselves doing a tap dance on a balance beam to get things in place. It is hard enough to pull all the many pieces together, and harder if the lawyer is operating from the back row, or even invisible behind the scenes, while business teams are out front, pitching their visions and persuading their partners.

Absolutely crucial is that those business teams recognize legal support as a thing of value. (>@ BfB: Coda —The Role of the Lawyer) This is about more than just words on a page or check-the-box clearances. Putting the charter in place and aligning it with contribution agreements and other establishment documents is not a perfunctory exercise or mere indulgence of bureaucratic whims. Admittedly, some agreements are like that, but not charters—at least not the ones that are owned by the partners and truly serve the partnership program.

What is the value-add that lawyers bring to the exercise? For translating plans to paper, business terms to documents, I like to think of three filters that lawyers use to guide their teams:

1. What's relevant

A lot is relevant, but lawyers can be particularly helpful where teams tend to have blind spots: the internal landscape. Often lawyers have the best panorama to see not only the details of the deal, but also the institutional policies and procedures—and let's be honest, the make-it-or-break-it central unit personalities. The most effective legal support comes when teams, including lawyers, mesh external parameters (partners, politics, and perceptions) with internal parameters (policies, procedures, and people). Who has not suddenly found themselves in a bureaucratic hot spot or gotten caught in institutional sensitivities, wishing they had known enough to manage and maneuver in advance?

2. What's possible

Through the same prism, when obstacles emerge, lawyers can think about options, alternatives, and workarounds. Lawyers who know where the internal barriers and hurdles are, as well as what the partners want and what the documents say, can help navigate the path from concept to closure. Of course, the goal is not subterfuge or deception, far from it. Lawyers can help teams develop above-board, legitimate ways to proceed. That is their job. And with the backing of the legal department, especially one that is business-oriented and closure-minded, teams can benefit from the institutional imprimatur.

3. What's artful

Negotiations can be hard. Indeed, they can come at you from all sides. Sometimes the hardest negotiations are not external, but internal. Either way, much has to fit, converge, align—and even one view can throw that off. Lawyering is not magic, but it can be an art. Choices about what words to use, how to define terms, when to stay silent, how to persuade, when to comfort, and where to draw the line—these all become part of the toolbox through years of practice. But only if you are grounded in a firm and comprehensive understanding of the subject matter. That is what it means to have a *practice* of structuring international partnership programs. If you can see the forest and the trees, while also planting seeds and pruning branches, you can be a master of the trade. Your teams will love you for it.

APPLYING THE LEGAL LENS

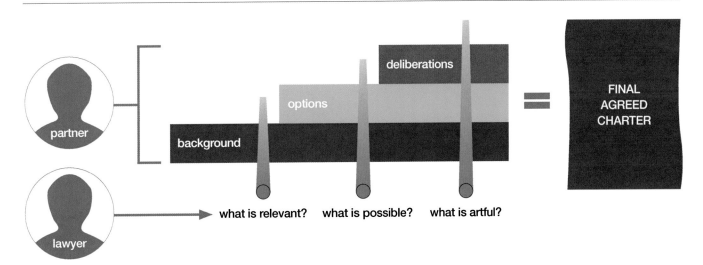

Conclusion

Creating a charter is a process, a journey, one that continues from adoption through the life of the partnership program. As long as the governing body is on board, the secretariat is on base, and the trustee is on the case, the partnership program can be an ongoing organic reflection of the partners. To keep things grounded while staying flexible, it helps to have a sense of the institutional and contextual parameters, along with room for inclusive processes and a multi-faceted lens trained on a variety of perspectives. Now that you have read through the guide to the guide, you can page through the real thing and pick out whatever is relevant to you..

4 THE ANNOTATED CHARTER

Featuring Clause-by-Clause Analysis

OPENING

CHARTER OF [NAME OF THE PARTNERSHIP PROGRAM]

As adopted on _____, 20__ [and amended on _____, 20__]

Part I. Introduction

1. *Background.* [describe history/genesis/context/strategic approach/challenge]

2. *Mission.* [describe mission/vision/goals/intentions/values]

EXPLANATIONS

The introductory part of the Charter is the preamble that sets the stage for what follows. It can also be the calling card for all to see. It is best presented succinctly at the highest level—portraying the essential genesis of the partnership program, how and why it came to be, and what it sets out to do: the quintessence of ambitions that merit its creation. Long tomes about history, development challenges, political discourse, and theories of change can be presented in other documents, potentially referenced here.

Is the partnership program intended to support peacebuilding and recovery, reduce poverty, limit global gas flaring, promote climate smart agriculture, fund outcomes, increase knowledge exchange, build capacity, or some or all of the above? What is the hook that brings the partners together, the gap partners hope to fill, the challenge they want to address?

Ideally kept to no more than a page, the introductory section can be a compelling statement for engagement. It crystallizes what matters and sets the tone for the operative terms to come. It's the partnership program at-a-glance. (>@ BFB: Constitutive Documents—What's in the Charter)

What's on your shingle? It's where you're visible.

VARIATIONS

Names. There is no shortage of variety in partnership program names. If the name is treated as a visible brand, as most are, it helps if it is easy to say, easy to remember, and easy to grasp, whether the full name or the acronym. Some emphasize the partnership (Global Partnership for ***), others emphasize the funding vehicle (*** Multi-Donor Trust Fund), and some do both (*** Multi-Partner Fund). For partnership programs that feature multiple funding vehicles, there is *** Facility or *** Platform. For partnership programs without dedicated funding vehicles, *** Alliance or *** Network could be a good fit. And many more.

VARIATIONS

The Charter's opening description is highly context-specific. The section headers proposed here are just examples. They can be sorted, arranged, mixed, and matched, depending on what is worth highlighting and where partners want to put the emphasis. Each section can be longer, shorter, combined, or separated, in whatever order makes sense and flows. The content and presentation should in any case be consistent with the rest of the Charter and related documents, and also reflect the overall branding and messaging of the partnership program. Here are some examples to give an impression:

Example: *[vision]* The Partnership Program's vision is to reduce poverty and hunger, improve human health and nutrition, and enhance ecosystem resilience through high quality international agricultural research, partnership, and leadership. *[goal]* The Partnership Program's primary goal is to benefit all users of Partnership Program research, including farmers and consumers.

Example: *[vision]* The Partnership Program seeks a world free of Dangerous Disease. *[challenge]* Over thirty million people die of Dangerous Disease every year. With the right vaccinations, that number could plummet. *[genesis] The Partnership Program was launched at the World Summit on Preventing Dangerous Disease.* Partnership Program participants desire to overcome barriers in preventing Dangerous Disease by sharing global best practices and implementing country-specific programs. *[approach]* The Partnership Program facilitates efforts to prevent Dangerous Disease by being a catalyst for policy change, stakeholder facilitation, and project implementation in participating countries.

Example: *[goal/genesis]* The goal of the Partnership Program, established after extensive discussions through the Global Platform, is to increase the capacity of developing countries to produce and use quality statistics for measuring and managing country development results. *[purpose]* The Trust Fund supporting the Partnership Program supports this goal through catalytic financing for country proposals emerging from national partnerships of donors, governments, and other stakeholders. *[approach]* The Trust Fund is being established with an initial pilot phase in a few countries. Once well underway, progress toward achieving results will be assessed prior to expanding to additional countries.

Example: *[mission]* The Partnership Program is a global partnership for urban poverty reduction and promoting the role of cities in sustainable development. *[intention]* Primarily a vehicle for partnership, the Partnership Program seeks to improve the quality and coherence of support to city and national governments in the developing world, as well as its members' own programs. *[approach]* The Partnership Program does not have separate implementation capacity, but works through the capacity of its members and other partners. It promotes new partnerships among local and national governments, slum dwellers, private foundations, the private sector, NGOs, and other partners.

Example: *[values]* In subscribing to the Global Compact, Partnership Program participants are called to promote transparency, clarity, and trust, with careful attention to development effectiveness. Poverty reduction is an integral part of the Partnership Program. *[approach]* The Partnership Program relies on a clear and effective structure of governance and decision making, with broad participation by partner countries and civil society. The Partnership Program also aims to promote mutual learning on what works to improve outcomes. Adaptability is a key characteristic of the Partnership Program.

Example: *[goal]* The Partnership Program provides a global platform for mobilizing additional resources for the Relevant Sector *[approach]* through:
   a) Domestic resources;
   b) Resources from bilateral and multilateral donors at the country level;
   c) Resources from new donors, including private sector companies and foundations; and
   d) Partnership Program trust funds.

Defined Terms

The Introduction can be used to position "defined terms," words that are given specified meanings and then capitalized. Definitions can appear in a separate glossary, but the charter may be easier to follow with terms defined directly in the text, to go with the flow. My own preference is the flow approach, at least for shorter documents, since it also gives the document less of a legal character, something partners tend to appreciate. (>@ BfB: Deft Drafting—The Art of Writing—Defined Terms)

What's in a name?
It's alphabet soup.

CONSIDERATIONS

Is the name brandable? Participants may say the partnership program is about impact on the ground, not making a name for itself. But even so, its name can affect the success of the venture, especially if it rolls off the tongue. The first thing to notice is that nine times out of ten, the name becomes an acronym, adding punch and pop. An artfully chosen combination of words, and a deft shortening, can flip a name into a brand, ready for visibility and marketing. It is alphabet soup out there and not by happenstance. From UNICEF to GAVI to SE4ALL, these clever combinations and truncations are made more memorable, like vanity plates for a cause.

What is the quintessence of the partnership program? The opening salvo, short and sweet, should capture the essence of the partnership program. If done well, the introductory section can serve both internal and external purposes. It tees up an operative document, mapping out the essential, baseline understandings among participants. It can also be an important messaging piece—a compact of sorts, a summary statement of deliberate intentions and determination—with a potential reach well beyond the partners. In anchoring all partners, it can also send a broader message of intentions and impact.

Are the essentials for all participants reflected? Different participants may have different reasons for joining the partnership program, with different points of emphasis. (>@ BfB: Balance—Finding the Sweet Spot) The charter can collect all of those, as a foundational document for everyone, but should not become too diffuse. It is worth striving for an opening that is crisp and coherent.

Fit the Phrase

The words I have chosen here need not be yours. Even with this basic prototype, some words have more baggage than others; some settings have customary expressions, others prefer customized ones. Here are a few alternatives to get you thinking about your choice of words:

Charter—too formal? Try *governance terms, governing document, compendium, compact* (but avoid MOU). (>@ BfB: Constitutive Documents—How the Charter Happens)

Partnership Program—too unwieldy? Try *facility, platform, partnership, coordination mechanism* (okay, also unwieldy).

Secretariat—too pompous? A partnership program secretariat is usually not meant to be a grand institution, so you can downplay the label with *coordination unit, management unit, focal point, partnership office, support center*, or even absorb the role into the trustee. (>@ PfP: Secretariats—Embedded, Inhouse Secretariats—Benefits)

Trustee—too trust-like? An international trustee is not meant to be a statutory or common law trustee, so you can go more generic with *administrator, financial intermediary, fiduciary, fiscal agent*, in part depending on the scope of responsibilities.

(>@ BfB: Key Terms)

HIGH-LEVEL FRAMING

EXPLANATIONS

Some partnership programs like to frame their engagement by listing out basic principles, fundamental tenets, strategic priorities, or shared intentions that apply across the board. This can give the initiative visible contours by *expanding the common foundation* upon which the participants decide to convene or *shaping the overarching umbrella* that connects all partners, depending on your choice of up-or-down image. It can send signals both internally and externally as to who participants strive to be and what they strive to do. This is about the *how* and *why*, more than the *what* that comes next.

Principles, pillars, parameters, strategic objectives, codes of conduct—whatever the label, these are baselines for engagement. They can set expectations and limits, with more or less operative effect, depending on what they regulate and how they are positioned. Positioning is a matter of wording. For example:

- *Aspirational.* The Partnership Program's guiding principles are …..
- *Ambitious.* The Partnership Program seeks to promote ….
- *Suggestive.* Partners endeavor to ….
- *Normative.* Partners are expected to …
- *Mandatory.* Partners commit to ….

(>@ PfP: Decision Making—Consensus)

CONSIDERATIONS

Why articulate a framework? It is easier to write long than short. Getting consensus on a crisp list of the things that matter most can be a challenge, but is usually worthwhile. For new partnerships, it can be a good exercise for confirming enough common ground to establish a solid foundation. For mature partnerships, the strategic view may have gelled enough, through experience and lessons learned, perhaps even a midterm review, to lend itself to articulation. This type of framing can happen at any time, whether part of the original charter, introduced later through a charter amendment, or approved in additional documents along the way as part of the governing body's regular, ongoing business. (>@ BfB: A Taxonomy of Trust Fund Agreements—Complementary Documents)

Are these requirements or just guideposts? This kind of overall framing can come with a light or heavy touch. (>@ BfB: Balance—Managing Trade-Offs) A light touch positions intentions and ambitions, without imposing strict standards or obligations. This can inform decision making without dictating results. A heavy touch positions criteria or requirements that are actively applied with tighter ringfencing of outcomes. High-level descriptions tend toward a light touch, if only because they are often vague enough to be more inclusive, while granular descriptions can exert a more exacting toll. Partners will want to decide how posturing or prescriptive to be. (>@ PfP: Decision Making—Consensus)

Are participants tying their hands? That is an important question. In the zeal of partnering, it is possible to overarticulate. Established parameters should not be so precise or inflexible that the partnership program cannot readily adjust to circumstances or be opportunistic over time. This may be the difference between defining and describing—either using heavy stakes to plant fence posts or simply setting a few buoys to lightly mark the shoals. A lot of this is in the wording. Principles and objectives are by nature aspirational. To be directional without dictating, the opening line can make clear this is about "seeking" results or "guiding" approaches, rather than hammering obligations with must-haves and gotta-dos. (>@ BfB: Deft Drafting—The Art of Writing—Weasel Words)

VARIATIONS

Example: The Partnership Program has the following overarching objectives:
   a) Increasing and stabilizing funding through harmonized approaches;
   b) Managing for results in accordance with the Partnership Programs results framework;
   c) Providing effective governance and efficient operations for the use of resources; and
   d) Collaborating among funders, implementers, other Partnership Program participants, and external partners.

Example: The Partnership Program's strategic objectives are:
   a) Food for People—Create and accelerate sustainable increases in the productivity and production of healthy food by and for the poor;
   b) Environment for People—Conserve, enhance, and sustainably use natural resources and biodiversity to improve livelihoods of the poor; and
   c) Policy for People—Promote policy and institutional change that will stimulate agricultural growth and equity to benefit the poor.

Example: The Partnership Program's guiding principles are:
   a) Country ownership
   b) Lower transaction costs
   c) Transparency
   d) Adaptability
   e) Support linked to performance

Example: To achieve its mission, the Partnership Program seeks to promote:
   a) Sustained increases in development aid
   b) Adequate and sustainable domestic financing
   c) Sound sector policies
   d) Increased accountability for sector results
   e) Mutual learning on what works
   f) Broad participation by countries and civil society

Example: The Partnership Program's operational framework rests on these pillars:
   a) Identification—Improving access to information and capacity to create, manage, and use this information
   b) Reduction—Improving planning, practices, policies, and investments to manage and reduce risks
   c) Preparedness—Strengthening the effectiveness of early warning, forecasting, contingency planning, and emergency responses
   d) Financial protection—Developing financing strategies and insurance markets to improve financial response capacity
   e) Resilience—Enhancing capacity for assessments and planning to improve the quality and timeliness or recovery and reconstruction

Example: The Partnership Program seeks to fill the "four gaps": policy, data, capacity, and finance.

Example: Developing countries that wish to be part of the Partnership Program are expected to:
   a) Develop National Plans that are comprehensive, realistic and prioritized, consistent with good practice, with participatory and inclusive processes;
   b) Allocate resources and carry out administrative reforms required for proper implementation of the National Plans;
   c) Take the lead in coordinating donor and government support within overall aid coordination frameworks beyond the Partnership Program; and
   d) Measure improvements using clear results frameworks with well-defined output and outcome indicators.

Donors and other partners that wish to be part of the Partnership Program are expected to:
   a) Respect country leadership and help build country capacity;
   b) Support activities that are part of National Plans and mobilize additional resources for implementation; and
   c) Deliver capacity-building programs in a harmonized and coordinated manner, utilizing program-based approaches and country systems wherever possible;

PROGRAM-LEVEL FRAMING

Part II. Scope

4.   *Program Objectives.* [provide description]

EXPLANATIONS

Scope. The charter can frame overarching intentions and ambitions, or strategic objectives (Part I), and it can also frame activities and funding, or program objectives (Part II). Moving from the introduction in Part I to the scope in Part II means moving deeper into implementation. The scope part of the charter dives into specific activities and funding vehicles by scoping out what the partnership program does and how it funds. "Scope" thus describes the box around the downstream content and funding streams under the partnership program brand. You don't have to use that word, but you get the idea.

Scope is generally about activities in relation to funds, or more specifically, partnership-branded activities supported by partnership-encompassed funding streams:

- In some cases, the scope is simply a matter of stating what the relevant trust fund can fund. This relegates the partnership scope to the trust fund scope, as defined in the first instance by the donors. This is particularly the case when the partnership program is supported by, and essentially revolves around, a single, dedicated trust fund (or multiple trust funds).

- In other cases, partnership program support may come from multiple funding vehicles, perhaps a combination of trust funds, parallel funding, and in-kind contributions. (>@ BfB: Annotated Charter—Funding) In these cases, it is especially important to be clear on scope. Which activities count as part of the partnership program and which do not should sit comfortably with all the participants. Do they all want to be associated with an activity that one of them is doing separately? Are they all agreed that it be done in the name of the partnership program? Or do individually implemented downstream activities stay outside the scope of the partnership program, as with a platform that is limited to convening and coordinating activities? (>@PfP: Typology—Trust-Funded Partnership Programs—Coordination Partnerships) There is no right answer per se, but something to be decided.

Objectives. Partners may prefer only high-level, strategic objectives (Part I) or downstream, programmatic objectives (Part II), or both, or neither, in their charter. They may see much or little value in describing the overall program or spelling out specific components in their common, baseline document. There is certainly leeway in whether and where framing elements are described. In general, however, giving partnership-wide definition to program content not only provides the usual benefit of establishing and confirming common ground among partners, but also helps keep the partnership's focus over time. In this way, the scope also shapes the brand, something that affects everyone coming together. (>@ PfP: International Partnership Programs—One Brand)

By way of comparison, *strategic objectives* that apply to the partnership program overall, and usually appear in the opening section of the charter, are higher level than *programmatic objectives* that apply to activities and funds. The former refers more broadly to what the partnership program is about, the latter to what the partnership program does. Programmatic objectives and program descriptions can give meaningful content to the partnership program's raison d'etre, particularly if focused on results. They can frame specific types of activities within a set of priorities.

VARIATIONS

Example: [country-specific trust fund] The Partnership Program supports activities designed to:

a) Increase coherence and coordination of international financing;
b) Promote effective and efficient delivery of assistance;
c) Fill key financing gaps by addressing underfinanced country priorities and urgent needs;
d) Complement national investments, lending, and private sector development; and
e) Support analytical products on critical thematic issues and cross-cutting areas.

Example: The Partnership Program is organized under the following program structure:

a) Country Operations: Activities that promote the mainstreaming of country development strategies and country investment programs.
b) Thematic Programs: Technical assistance, capacity building, and knowledge development in specialized areas.
c) Special Programs: Dedicated programs supported separately by one or several donors that target specific areas, countries, or beneficiaries.

Example: As one of the principal aims of the Partnership Program, the Trust Fund will contribute to mainstreaming disaster reduction in national strategies within the overall objective of supporting national capacity building to deal with the risks of natural disasters and enhance the speed and efficiency of international assistance for disaster recovery operations, while also catalyzing global and regional partnerships toward meeting international targets.

CONSIDERATIONS

How much framing is needed? Scope articulations—like programmatic objectives and program descriptions—are usually framing devices in the positive by saying what is included. They can also be in the negative, itemizing aspects that are excluded. (>@ BfB: Deft Drafting—The Art of Writing—Stating the Negative) They can be short or long, comprehensive or indicative, catchy or dry. In the end, there is no rule on how much threshold definition to give a partnership program, whether through the charter or otherwise. But there is a rule of thumb: The more partners define upfront, the less they may feel the need to be part of the more granular, activity-level decision making later.

What do participants want to stand for? Not to make too much of having a brand, but it can be a major factor for partnership programs that need to mobilize resources in a competitive donor landscape or that want to message for advocacy. As with the vision, mission, and goals, adding objectives at the activity level—succinctly framing the brand around products—can let the charter establish real bedrock for the partnership program. For donors that base their funding decisions on what they finance, and for all other partners, activity-level objectives can become part of a powerful message.

PARTICIPATION FRAMING

5.   [optional] *[Eligibility] [Participation Requirements].* [specify terms]

EXPLANATIONS

Another way to provide a framework for partnership programs is to focus on the participants. (>@ PfP: Partners and People) By defining eligibility, partners can draw lines for who is in and who is out—for example, who can apply for funding or who can act as a fiduciary. Partners can also be put on notice as to what is expected of them if they participate. A set of high-level principles for the partners themselves can reflect concrete attributes or contributions designed to make the partnership program deliver on its intentions.

International partnership programs tend to rely on good will, good relations, shared expectations, and consensus to get the participation and cooperation they need—or if not forthcoming, they may need to ask themselves if they have a sustainable venture. In this context, articulating minimum standards of behavior is more demonstrative than enforceable. But even in setting the tone, partners can establish who they are or aspire to be, and recall those words as needed.

CONSIDERATIONS

How stringent should requirements be? For sure, they don't need to be requirements at all. Any of the partnership program framing, whether strategic, operational, or personal, can be lighter or heavier. Objectives are usually more aspirational, criteria are usually more concrete, but both can be presented as guidelines or requirements. Partners may consider certain aspects to be imperative (for example, existence of a prevention plan before any funding flows), or they may instead wish to be more open-ended and opportunistic in receiving what comes in the door. In addition, the framing can be more objective (for example, numerical) or subjective (attributes based on judgment calls). Is the threshold fixed (at least 50% matching funds) or fuzzy (staff with sufficient technical expertise)? Partners can also decide whether all of the standards apply equally (the list ends with "and"), whether they are weighted in some way, or whether a single item met is enough (the list ends with "or"). It is usually good to leave some verbal wiggle room, so the defined scope does not become a straitjacket. (>@ BfB: Deft Drafting—The Art of Writing—Weasel Words)

VARIATIONS

Example: [eligibility criteria] Eligibility for participation in the Partnership Program is determined as follows:

a) **Donors:** Any country, including through one of its ministries or agencies, or an intergovernmental entity or private foundation, becomes a Member of the Governing Body upon committing a minimum of US$5 million to the Trust Fund by entering into a contribution agreement with the Trustee based on the form of contribution agreement approved by the Governing Body.

b) **Recipient Countries:** Upon request to the Secretariat by a Member, Recipient Countries may be agreed on a consensus basis by the Governing Body, with consent of the Trustee, subject to meeting the following criteria at the time of decision (as determined by each Member): (i) the country's total financing needs and existing financing support; (ii) the country's debt sustainability; and (iii) the socioeconomic impact of [nature of the issue].

c) **Downstream Fiduciaries:** The following entities are eligible to become Implementation Support Agencies upon entering into a transfer agreement with the Trustee based on the form of transfer agreement approved by the Governing Body: [provide list]. Upon request to the Secretariat by a Member, additional Implementation Support Agencies may be agreed on a consensus basis by the Governing Body, subject to an accreditation process acceptable to the Members and the Trustee, designed to assess the entity's record and capacity to manage funds entrusted to it, including guarding against the misuse or ineffective use of funds, in line with high international standards related to safeguards, procurement, financial management, and other critical areas.

Example: [participant contributions] To the extent applicable, participants agree to:

a) In the interest of shared knowledge, provide expert staff and resources to support Partnership Program working groups and task forces as needed;

b) In the interest of monitoring and transparency, provide data in accordance with the recommendations issued by the Partnership Program; and

c) In the interest of lessons learned, develop, share, and implement best practices for operating, monitoring, and reporting in support of the Partnership Program's objectives.

A Little Wiggle Room

To avoid making things too prescriptive or defining things too narrowly, here are some drafting points to keep in mind (>@ BfB: Deft Drafting):

- Use of the word "including" at the end of the header phrase opens the door to other things. What could have been a finite list becomes an indicative list. For example, "The objectives of the Partnership Program include: ...."

- "Normally," "usually," "expected to," and "seeks to"—these are all softeners that can take a definitive statement or prescriptive list and leave the door a bit ajar. For example, "Partners are expected *[but not obligated]* to align their own activities with those of the Partnership Program."

- Finishing a list with "and" or "or" can make a big difference. In the case of requirements or criteria, it is the difference between applicability of the entire list or any single item. Or applicability could be framed as "one or more" or some other subset. Some lists leave out the conjunction and modifiers altogether, and then "and" is typically presumed—but it is better to be precise than to presume.

ACTIVITIES

6.   *Activities.* The Partnership Program focuses on the following activities: _____.

EXPLANATIONS

By now, it is probably clear that a charter is a customized document. Nothing in the sections presented so far is boilerplate. Everything is specific to the context and what the partners are gathering to do. With the description of activities, the charter moves to its greatest degree of program granularity, from the big picture to operational detail.

Even so, as a framework, the charter does not spell out specific activities to be implemented, but rather describes activities as types, categories, or components. For trust-funded partnership programs, this has a lot to do with how typical multi-donor trust funds work, where multiple donors agree to provide funds for certain, pre-agreed activity areas. This approach is effective when funds are accumulated over time from multiple donors because broad activity descriptions leave room for more funds, more allocations, and more implementation. This is also known as two-phase or program-based governance, where the scope is defined upfront and specific fund allocations follow. (>@ BfB: Context—International Trust Funds)

There is no shortage of ways to describe activities in a charter, but they are usually grouped into buckets as part of a list. This gives some specificity, while also leaving some breadth. Here are some common approaches:

- Thematic grouping, based on types of projects or kinds of components
- Partner engagement, grouped in relation to which partners are involved
- Funding streams or vehicles, with descriptions divided by trust fund or source of contribution
- Applicable criteria, requirements, or allocation procedures may affect different subsets
- Implementation responsibility, whether with the trustee, downstream fiduciaries, or recipients

Some of these groupings are trust fund-centric, but that can help align the charter with the contribution agreements. An aligned description in the charter is more easily cross-referenced in the contribution agreements, one size fits all.

VARIATIONS

Example: The Partnership Program [engages in] [focuses on] the following types of activities, subject to the availability of resources:
   a) Global Activities, such as adoption and implementation of standards and practices, and development of recommendations on regulatory and operational best practices
   b) Country Activities, such as assistance to governments to meet Partnership Program Objectives, and pilot or demonstrate projects
   c) Knowledge Activities, such as organization of workshops for knowledge transfer, lessons learned, or best practice dissemination; high-level international conferences; stakeholder events; publication of reports; website; communications, and media outreach

Example: The activities to be financed by the Trust Fund are:
   a) Trustee-executed activities, for which the Trustee has implementation responsibility:

   _____ [insert Trustee-executed components/activities].

   b) Recipient-executed activities, for which recipients of Trust Fund funds have implementation responsibility:

   _____ [insert Recipient-executed components/activities].

VARIATIONS

Example: In general, the Partnership Program offers support to meet its Objectives, including the following types of activities:

  a Country Programs – long-term programmatic support at a multiple city, province, or national scale
  b) Catalytic Projects – shorter-term activities designed to catalyze change or partnerships
  c) Knowledge Activities – activities designed to fill knowledge gaps and build capacity at local, national, regional, and global levels
  d) Communications support and advocacy – activities designed to improve awareness of relevant policies and activities, and influence policies and behavior, at local, national, regional, and global levels

Example: The Partnership Program's activities include:

  a) Supporting peacebuilding, recovery, and reconstruction, including through a participatory approach with local and community-based consultations that reflect country priorities;
  b) Fostering socioeconomic recovery and stabilization by analyzing key constraints to economic development, identifying potential drivers of growth to generate employment and public support, and supporting building blocks of large public investment programs;
  c) Implementing a monitoring system to provide regular and reliable data on socioeconomic impacts of conflict and displacement and to track impacts of the Partnership Program;
  d) Building citizen trust by supporting national outreach and communications to promote national reconciliation, transparency, and information sharing; and
  e) Building capacity of national and local government institutions for sustainable recovery efforts based on strong ownership among national and local stakeholders.

Example: [selection criteria] Activities are chosen on the basis of the following selection criteria:

  a) Demonstrated track record of organizational capacity and resources to deliver on commitments
  b) Emphasis on strong outcomes with evidence-based results, including country capacity building
  c) Alignment with national priorities and strategies, as well as existing regional and global efforts
  d) Potential to be catalytic, have large spillover effects, and promote best practice learning

CONSIDERATIONS

How prescriptive should the activities description be? Donors may again prefer a more definitive list of activities, while trustees and implementing entities, trusting themselves and their downstream decision making, may be fine with more permissive terms. Much depends on the introductory phrasing, the short opening that precedes the list. Just a few words can position a whole spectrum of possibilities from flexible to fixed. Note the different levels of precision in these examples of how to broaden or narrow the scope:

• The Partnership Program focuses on the following activities: ….

• The Partnership Program engages in the following types of activities, subject to the availability of resources: ….

• In general, the Partnership Program offers support to meet its Objectives, including the following types of activities: ….

• Partnership Program activities include: ….

• Activities to be financed by the Trust Fund are: ….

Activities in the Charter; Cross-References in the Contribution Agreements

The activities description in the charter—which sits at the overall level of the partnership program—needs to be broad enough to cover the scope of all funding streams, including trust funds, that provide dedicated support to, or are otherwise encompassed by, the partnership program. This is where the partnership program can easily trip up.

- On the one hand, contribution agreements for trust funds invariably include descriptions of activities the trust fund may finance. Donors do not provide blank checks; they will always specify what the money is for before providing it.

- On the other hand, the charter is incomplete without a description of the activities that the partnership program conducts. All partners together agree on the scope and nature of activities with which they—through the partnership program—are associated. If those partners extend beyond the trustee and donors, then the written basis that collects and represents *all* of those views is not the contribution agreements, but rather the charter. (>@ BfB: Constitutive Documents)

This potentially makes for two activities descriptions, side by side, and that is a problem:

- *What should not happen* is that the contribution agreements present one recitation of allowable activities, and the charter presents another. This could lead to confusion or even conflicting wording, something the trustee sitting in the middle cannot afford. Trustees should not operate in parallel universes, bound to two different sets of terms that directly overlap and potentially conflict. (>@ ibid.—What to Watch For)

- *What should happen* is that the activity description should reside in one place, and one place only, to the extent possible. To get all participants on board, that place should be the more inclusively-approved document, which is normally the charter. The contribution agreements can then cross-reference the charter, which remains the living, breathing, operative document, fully applicable to and contractualized by each contribution agreement. (>@ BfB: Agile Alignment—Step-by-Step Alignment for Trust-Funded Partnership Programs, #6)

At the end of the day, the goal is first, to avoid repetition and overlap, and second, to put the partnership program's activity description in the more broadly agreed, more partner-owned document, the charter.

CONSIDERATIONS

How granular should the activities description be? From trustee and implementing entity perspectives, the answer is probably less is more—that leaves more latitude for them to proceed with fund use. From a donor perspective, with concerns about proper fund use, the answer is probably the reverse; more specificity, more comfort. In the end, as negotiated, the degree of detail will likely fall somewhere in between. This also meets a couple more objectives. First is to avoid feeling hamstrung when opportunities arise and circumstances change. Although amendments to expand or change the charter-defined scope can be agreed by the governing body (with carry-over effect to the contribution agreements; >@ ibid., #7), the original detail should ideally be enough to keep some flexibility. Second, the description of activities impacts marketing, advocacy, and resource mobilization for the partnership program. Covering enough bases to attract enough donors—in other words, with enough detail to reflect their interests—is one way to gauge how much to add.

Framing for Efficiency

The description of activities can be a key part of giving implementing entities (both fiduciaries and their recipients) significant discretion to decide specific activities and determine fund allocations. Rather than exert case-by-case micromanagement, other partners can use a high-level description to defer to implementing entities, while still giving donors the assurance that activities will be undertaken within prescribed bounds. This lets implementing entities do what they are good at—it leverages their operations—and usually ups the efficiency factor. Setting up this kind of implementation framework on a partnership basis is a good reason to adopt a charter.

To stay efficient, however, this type of activity-defining framework should not serve as an added policy layer that burdens implementation. It is one thing to define scope thematically or geographically, or to describe activities by buckets or lists. It is another, however, if that definition overlaps with the responsible fiduciary's existing operating framework. The point is to give fiduciary entities greater discretion to select activities using their own rules within the prescribed framework, not to undercut or conflict with the fiduciary's robust operating frameworks. (>@BfB: The Annotated Charter—Governing Body Roles and Responsibilities)

Examples in the Spectrum of Specificity When Describing Fundable Activities

Activity descriptions can be loaded with details, but should not be encumbered by policy prescriptions.

In broad terms	With detail	With policy overlay
Provide grants to selected recipients to support the objectives of the Trust Fund	Provide grants to selected recipients to support the objectives of the Trust Fund that involve forest strategies, land-use plans, investment plans, and related needs	Provide grants to select recipients drawn from donor recommendations to support the objectives of the Trust Fund
Programming to promote employment for conflict-affected populations	Programming to promote employment for conflict-affected populations, including labor market access, job creation, value chain improvement, and training	Programming to promote employment for conflict-affected populations, provided support can be suspended at any time as instructed by one or more donors
Provision of technical assistance to government institutions	Provision of technical assistance to government institutions for national outreach and communications to promoted confidence building, transparency, and information sharing	Provision of technical assistance to government institutions from consultants chosen from donor countries

CONSIDERATIONS

Why add selection criteria? The finite resource is usually funds, not proposals. Almost always, partnership programs have to selectively apply their funding, with far more need than can be met. That means partners have to agree on fund allocation processes, either by being part of the decisions themselves or by trusting in the delegated deciders, perhaps the trustee or secretariat. An in-between avenue, as with any of these framing exercises, is to set up criteria by which decisions are to be made. These can position requirements, present guidelines, establish standards, or signal priorities. Once in place, they can be applied directly for decision making or, equally useful, they can provide a framework by which, for example, the secretariat or technical advisory committee can pre-screen proposals before they reach the governing body for approval.

FUNDING

EXPLANATIONS

Charters may or may not dwell on funding sources. Funding may be so obvious that it is not spelled out—everything revolves around a central trust fund—but the more varied the funding streams, the more worthwhile the attention. No partnership program can operate without at least some financial support, so there is always at least some funding and likely some variety. This is rarely a non-topic, even if the charter is mum about it.

In a partnership program, both the partnership and the program need to be funded. Partners can pay their own way and finance their own activities, but those are still costs to be covered. (>@ PfP: Typology—Trust-Funded Partnership Programs—Coordination Partnerships) More often, partners share or transfer at least some funds within the partnership. If partners value visibility and branding, then funding for communications, publicity, outreach, and a website needs to come from somewhere. Any generation of content or implementation of activities needs resourcing on top of that. Financial resources do more to shape the contours of a partnership program than anything else.

If we take funding as a given for partnership programs, and governing as inherent to partnering, then funding and governance go hand in hand. This coupling of funding vehicles with governance structures is at the heart of partnership programs that combine collectivized funding and collectivized decision making. Then again, pooled funding can, ironically, be such a central feature that it crowds out shared governance. This is particularly true for one-stop-shops (>@ PfP: Typology—Introducing Two Mighty Oaks), which put the critical mass of activity in the supporting entity that provides the trustee, secretariat, chair of the governing body, and perhaps other functions. This allows the trust fund to be front and center, virtually defining the identity of the partnership program through its funding source. Such one-to-one cases are so straightforward that, with a weakened governing body, a separate section on funding sources may not be included in the charter—if those cases have a charter at all.

Not so for more complex constellations. The array of funding sources can be varied enough to constitute a design feature, in which case a section in the charter is recommended. This can be a single governing body across multiple funding vehicles (for example, a country-specific partnership convening around an international compact and multiple implementing channels), or there may be layers of governance with separate bodies for each funding vehicle under an overarching umbrella body. The point is to identify which funding sources feed into and fund the partnership program's portfolio (the program element) and to describe the relationships between each of those sources and the partnership program's governance, trustee functions, and secretariat support (the partnership elements). (>@ PfP: Structure—Whiteboarding)

Dedicated Funding

What is "dedicated" funding? A funding stream or funds in a funding vehicle are dedicated if they are exclusively given to or provided for a particular partnership program. We might think that such funding "belongs" to the partnership program, but only nominally because the partnership program is not a legal entity per se. Instead, the picture is somewhat more complex:

If the funds are in a trust fund, the legal ownership of those funds is with the trustee, although they are specifically for the partnership program, with donors retaining beneficial interests in the funds.

If the funds are granted to the secretariat to pay for core support, the grant is to the supporting entity, although, as specified in the grant agreement, for the purposes of the partnership program.

If the partnership program has a governing body, that body may well have direct purview over the funds to the extent it has decision making over their allocation and use (or indirectly, by approving a results framework).

If the funding becomes associated with the partnership program brand, it may or may not be dedicated, depending on whether it is also associated with someone else's portfolio.

It may not matter all too much if funding is dedicated or simply attributed, as long as it flows. However, partners may take comfort from knowing specific funding sources are dedicated to their partnership program. They may want to treat specific funding streams or vehicles as part of the partnership program's structure. One way to do so is to lay claim to those sources in the charter.

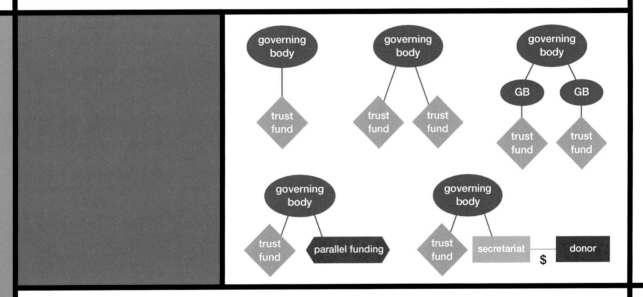

Accretive Funding

The one-to-one version—one governing body plus one trust fund equals one partnership program—is widespread and keeps things simple. However, partnership programs often end up with multiple funding sources even if they did not start that way. Original funding may be supplemented with opportunistic add-ons by creative program managers to keep the agenda going. This accretive tendency is not always fully transparent to the partnership program participants, especially if the trustee/secretariat has a strong implementation role. And yet, all partners have an interest in what supports their brand. It is good to give visibility to all dedicated and complementary funding channels in the charter or elsewhere, including as they change over time, while also identifying the respective governing and implementing relationships that go with each of them. (>@ BfB: Dualities—Connections and Delineations) Whether viewed from a structural perspective (potentially in the charter) or an operational perspective (potentially in an annual work plan or annual report), funding that feeds into the partnership program and becomes part of the brand is part of the collective.

VARIATIONS

The Partnership Program is supported by <u>one or more dedicated trust funds (collectively, the Trust Fund)</u>.

> *As a drafting sleight of hand, defining "one or more trust funds" as "the Trust Fund" is a simplified way of bringing in trust funds as they may emerge without having to amend the charter each time. (>@ BfB: Deft Drafting— The Art of Writing—Defined Terms) This placeholder is especially useful when new trust funds are opened by the trustee for accounting reasons, like allowing financial tracking in response to donor requirements, but still within the same programmatic context.*

One or More Trust Funds

Often a partnership program revolves around a single trust fund, in which case the identities of the partnership program and the trust fund are intertwined. But partnership programs can also have multiple funding sources, including more than one trust fund. More or less intertwined, this naturally creates more complexity. Roles and responsibilities, including particularly governing and implementing relationships, need to be spelled out carefully vis-à-vis each funding vehicle.

The Partnership Program is supported by one or more dedicated trust funds (collectively, the Trust Fund), <u>in addition to other parallel and in-kind support provided by the participants. All funding sources are approved by the Governing Body through an annual work plan [and budget] that identifies which funding sources or funded activities are considered part of the Partnership Program.</u>

> *Partnership programs that claim parallel-funded activities, thereby relying on funding sources that are not entirely dedicated to those partnership programs, must find a way to bring these activities under the partnership program umbrella, into the brand. Here an annual work plan can play that role, usually through a determination by the governing body. It can be high level with broad descriptions, with or without budget numbers, or it can be more detailed with specific line items and budgeted amounts, depending as always on what is agreed. It can also be updated, with activities added over the course of the year. It is important that someone has purview over this designation, that someone or some (governing) body deliberately decides what is part of the brand.*

An entity must receive Governing Body approval to become a donor to the Trust Fund.

> *Beyond eligibility requirements that partners may impose on new donors (>@ BfB: The Annotated Charter—Eligibility; Participation Requirements), they can require explicit approval. The usual approach is donor self-selection—you can join if you're willing to pay—which assumes a comfortable degree of like-mindedness. (>@ PfP: Partners and People—Choosing Partners) But there are cases where donor interest in joining may not dovetail with the original partners' desires. For example, a private foundation linked to a for-profit company with a questionable track record may be looking for a whitewash, while the existing partners may be wary of the association. The stakes are heightened in partnership programs where donor status automatically grants governing body membership. Existing donors may want more control over who has decision-making prerogative with them. And this is prudent when that prerogative includes a veto right through consensus decision making. (>@ PfP: Decision Making) So if threshold criteria are not enough and self-selection poses risks, approval—often routed through the secretariat for due diligence purposes—keeps the partners in control. Note that a separate right of consent by the trustee can be added if the trustee entity is not already part of the decision making.*

CONSIDERATIONS

What funding sources are under collective purview? To think about this, let's break partnership program funding down into three broad categories:

- *Dedicated funds.* There is no question that dedicated funding is under partnership purview; that is inherent in making the funding dedicated—even in the nuanced ways explained earlier.

- *Parallel funds.* Parallel funding can be brought into the partnership fold. As in-kind contributions, partners use their own funding directly to develop content or do projects and then associate it with the partnership program brand. The rest of the partners have to be okay with that, but it can be win-win, especially if a bigger partnership program portfolio promotes visibility and advocacy. Without extra effort, however, these partnership programs may not end up as strategically or substantively coherent as those that generate their activity centrally with collectivized funding. Getting parallel funds under collective purview means deliberate positioning, rather than relying on dedicated positioning.

- *Other in-kind contributions.* Collective purview does not usually follow other kinds of in-kind contributions. That includes the costs of individual partner participation, which most participants self-finance. Getting their governing body representatives to meetings, internally reviewing meeting documents, and participating in working groups or other shared tasks are inputs for which no cost recovery or compensation is usually expected or given (with the notable exception of developing country participation), and no collective purview applies in return. Contributing seconded staff to the secretariat is another common one-way contribution. The supporting entity has to be okay with it, of course, but it is not clear that the partners weigh in—although perhaps they should.

The bottom line is that partners can factor in both individually financed and collectively financed activities as part of the partnership program if they care to make the link.

What are the relationships? Given the variety of funding sources, those sources also vary in how they relate to other parts of the partnership program. It is useful to map out the funding streams and their relationships to the governing body, secretariat, and trustee as core partnership functions. Normally the governing body gets some say on what is done and promoted in the partnership program's name. In cases where the governing body has decision-making purview over the funds (as with dedicated funding), this usually happens ex ante, when approving annual work plans or funding requests—a decision point at the proposal stage. In cases where the governing body casts the net wider (as with parallel funding), this can happen either ex ante or ex post, after the project is already planned or underway—a decision point after the fact. Either way, activities are often included in the scope of the partnership program by referring to the funding source that makes them happen.

FUNDING REQUIREMENTS

8.   [optional] *Funding Requirements.* [insert minimum contributions/waiver process/etc.]

EXPLANATIONS

In trust-funded partnership programs, how the donors stack up can be a key question. Donors like to be decision makers, and that has structural implications. With an eye toward efficient governance and sustainable operations, partnership programs watch the numbers, both in terms of how many participants are seated around the table and how many are paying to be there. Some partnership programs can rely on self-selection if not too many select themselves and overall costs are adequately covered. However, some partnership programs have to work to keep the numbers manageable (too many donors) or incentivize core support (too few). That can mean finding mechanisms to winnow or leverage the ranks.

One way to do both simultaneously is to set minimum funding requirements. Putting a price tag on participation requires partners to step up, with the added benefit of contributing to core support costs. Not every participant can afford to be a donor, however, so this can cut against inclusivity. A threshold question is whether to leave funding to the donors—those partners who were already willing to carry the financial load—or to broaden to a membership fee model where everyone has something to pay. (>@ PfP: Trust Funds—Donors)

Partnership programs have experimented with different ways to position minimum funding requirements, and a couple of approaches are paraphrased here. In general, partnership programs tend not to wield funding as a stick, but look mostly for the carrot. Rather than put energy into policing amounts paid (negative), they may choose to rely on one or more champion donors—if they can find them—to foot the bill (positive). Partnership programs that succeed in getting early funding can try to leverage demonstrative pilots with decisive results into more funding, ultimately building a virtuous cycle to sustainability.

Pay In to Stay In—Easy to Say, Harder to Do

Minimum funding requirements can be challenging. First, the spread of what is reasonable to ask can vary significantly from traditional donors that have deep aid pockets, to multilaterals that may prefer to manage partnership program money, to developing countries that are looking to receive not give, and others in between.

I have seen partnership programs stratify their membership contributions into five or ten pay-what-seems-fair categories, each with a different rate. That can feel arduous and arbitrary. It can also give the impression that everyone is valued primarily for their money. Across-the-board funding requirements also tend to slice and dice partnership programs into haves and have nots, with higher amounts applying to developed countries and lower (or no) amounts applying to developing countries. That can be unfortunate if the basic principle is partner parity. And it gets especially tricky if the partnership program is paying out to some of the ones paying in. (>@ PfP: Trust Funds—Donors—Beneficiary Donors)

Finally, what happens if a partner does not pay? That may not sit well. Waivers and exceptions can get quite subjective—hard to apply, open to scrutiny and second guessing. International partnership programs shy away from enforcement, and terminating membership for nonpayment can feel pretty draconian. (>@ PfP: Trade-Offs—The Horizontal Buy-In Spectrum—Workarounds)

VARIATIONS

Example: [fixed amount and waivers] A Member must commit to contribute a minimum of $_____ for the funding period from _____ to _____ [three years] to the Trust Fund through a contribution agreement entered into with the Trustee. A partial or full waiver of this funding requirement may be requested by (i) a developing country; (ii) a multilateral organization; (iii) an entity that becomes a Member partway through the funding period; and (iv) an entity offering to provide part of its funding requirement through an in-kind or parallel contribution. Requests for waivers are submitted to the Secretariat for consideration by the Governing Body.

Example: [varied amounts] Entities can apply to become Members, provided they (i) are sponsored by two existing Members; (ii) endorse the Charter; and (iii) undertake to meet their annual fee requirement for the Trust Fund as set forth in the attached Schedule of Annual Membership Fees [where fees are itemized; for example, for traditional sovereign donors, beneficiary countries, multilateral organizations, international nongovernmental organizations, private foundations, private sector companies, and academic entities]. Requests to be a Member are submitted to the Secretariat for consideration by the Governing Body. The Governing Body may, upon recommendation by the Secretariat, decide upon exceptions to the annual fee requirement, including for recognition of in-kind and parallel contributions. Members that fail to make their agreed contributions for two consecutive years are no longer Members, as notified by the Secretariat. Members are encouraged to contribute more than the annual membership fee.

CONSIDERATIONS

Would funding requirements be helpful? Requirements can spur or kill behavior, depending on how they are positioned. A minimum funding requirement may set a motivating threshold for some donors, but may also exclude otherwise ardent or pivotal supporters. In this way, although requirements have incentivizing potential, they can be blunt tools. And membership fees, while egalitarian on one level, draw attention to status differences that can feel like power differentials. More tailored approaches to donor recruitment take more work, but they may be more effective in galvanizing engagement. If requirements are nonetheless imposed, are they attainable? Partners should avoid making the rule the exception and getting stuck in a long string of waivers and passes. Maybe the answer is to back off the commitment language and use encouragement instead: "Members endeavor to . . ." or "Donors are encouraged to . . ." Or maybe the answer is not to exact minimum funding requirements at all.

How stringent should requirements be? Requirements that are hard to maintain are more trouble than they are worth. To help make sure funding minimums do not become overly restrictive, it is good to be clear on the purposes they are meant to serve. While also thinking about downsides that might arise, it is good to carefully match the purposes to the requirements, and the requirements to the reality. Will partners pay? Will the right partners pay? Will they pay gladly? Partners can get carried away with their neat and orderly boxes, even as the organic growth and evolution of a healthy partnership program needs some fluidity over time. As a drafting tip, the more demanding the requirement, the more valuable the little weasel words, like "generally" or "except as otherwise agreed." (>@ BfB: Deft Drafting—The Art of Writing) As an operational tip, every requirement can have an escape valve, like a waiver process, if the terms are clear, and the waiver stays the exception.

Why require when you can request?

GOVERNANCE OVERVIEW

Part III. Governance

9. *Governance Overview.* The governance of the Partnership Program is designed to [state objectives]. It consists of

(i) the [governing body];
(II) the [other bodies, if any];
(iii) the [secretariat]; and
(iv) the [trustee].

EXPLANATIONS

Part III on Governance goes to the heart of the matter. The governance part of the charter governs, as a matter of responsibility and accountability. The opening statement introduces the governance intention of the partnership program, if this is something partners want to articulate. More important, however, is to line up the salient structural elements for further articulation in subsequent sections. This sets the stage for being clear, clean, and modular. (>@ PfP: Ten Tried and True Tips)

Governance and structure are closely related in partnership programs. Structure creates the links and relationships, and while some of those track fund flows, most of them also constitute or affect decision flows—which is to say, governance. It makes sense to introduce governance aspects by first giving a structural perspective and presenting key structural components. In this way, the charter focuses on **shared governance**, the part where partners participate. Decisions made by the secretariat or trustee can also be considered governance, but are more commonly understood to be operations. From a supporting entity's perspective, its internal governance (operations) is its own responsibility, sufficiently summed up by referring to its "applicable policies and procedures." External (shared) governance is the part that needs to be defined.

Partners invariably start out wanting light and nimble shared governance, with less cost, less delay, and more results, as in "value for money" (>@ PfP: International Partnership Programs—Coordinated Activities)—until reality kicks in. They may want more influence or control to stay in their safe zone. They may want more inclusivity and diversity to get enough buy-in and expertise. They may quickly end up with more structure, people, rules, and processes. Partners can put themselves more or less in the mix, or defer more or less to others, like the secretariat, trustee, or implementing entities. As on so many fronts, this is about trade-offs to be negotiated and agreed. (>@ PfP: Trade-Offs)

> Governance is the crux of the charter.

The degree of shared governance is always a worthwhile discussion, not just at the beginning, but throughout. If all goes well, there may be room to streamline over time, especially if the partnership program is flexible enough to adjust as it goes. What started as governing body meetings twice a year may shift to once a year, with no-objections in between. What started as governing body approvals for every proposal may shift to approvals for anything over a specified threshold. As partners create their culture and become comfortable with each other, shared governance can lighten up.

VARIATIONS

The structure of the Partnership Program is designed to [*sample objectives* – *pick as applicable*]

- *enable efficient, results-oriented implementation*
- *create a platform for knowledge generation and sharing*
- *promote coordination and collaboration among participants*
- *support country-led priorities*
- *strengthen the capacity of* _____
- *align with* _____

Name of the Governing Body. The label can stay "governing body," but it is nicer to give it some personality. Usually the label follows function, which is either decision-making or advisory/consultative.

- Decision-making examples: *Steering Committee, Governing Council, Partnership Council.* Use of the term "Board" is discouraged in international partnership programs. (>@ PfP: Governing Bodies—Characteristics—Informal vs. Formal)
- Advisory/consultative examples: *Advisory Council, Consultative Group, Partnership Council.*

Name of the Secretariat. A partnership program may or may not separately identify the secretariat role as distinct from the trustee role. In the one-stop-shop model, for instance, these functions tend to meld together, since they are typically provided by one and the same entity. As a result, there may be some confusion about secretariat vs. trustee roles. The labels matter less, though, than fully articulating the responsibilities. (>@ PfP: Typology—Introducing Two Mighty Oaks—One-Stop-Shops) International platforms, by contrast, usually work best if the trustee is delineated and separated from the secretariat, with limitations spelled out for both functions. (>@ ibid.—International Platforms) As with the governing body, the secretariat can take many forms and names, often signaling whether the partnership program is light or heavy on shared governance functions.

- Alternatives include: *Coordination Unit, Administrative Unit, Focal Point, Support Center,* or subsumed in the trustee role.

Name of the Trustee. The trustee is relevant only for partnership programs that have trust funds. A partnership program without a dedicated trust fund normally would not name a trustee. Partnership programs where an overarching governing body has purview over more than one trust fund managed by different trustees would name multiple trustees. "Trustee" is a customary term that goes with "trust fund," but in international circles, neither takes conventional common law or statutory meanings. (>@ PfP: Trust Funds—Trustees) For this reason, other terms with less baggage may be preferred.

- Alternatives include: *Administrator, Fiscal Agent, Financial Manager.*

CONSIDERATIONS

What is the central governing thrust of the partnership? As an overall matter, how do partners expect it to be run and by whom? Where is the governing center of gravity—is it more in one entity (the supporting entity) or shared among entities (the governing body)? (>@ BfB: Balance—Creating Critical Mass) Are partners on a par with each other; do downstream recipients, for example, have a voice in governance? Is inclusivity, diversity, or balance important? What about transparency or efficiency? By giving these and other aspects visibility and emphasis, partners can articulate a grounding foundation for partnership engagement.

What role does the governing body want to play? Participants need to find that sweet spot between being so high level that they are strategy stratospheric and so low level that they are minutely micromanaging. A governing body at its best engages right where its collective value lies. That insertion point can take many forms, including ex ante input (like strategic guidance that speaks to country activities) and ex post feedback (like M&E assessments that speak to global strategies).

Is the organizational structure fit-for-purpose? The tug-of-war between standardized and customized structure has bedeviled many a partnership program. (>@ BfB: Dualities—Standardization and Customization) On the one side is typically the supporting entity, the main administrative entity housing the secretariat and trustee, with incentives to streamline its partnership engagement here and across its portfolio. On the other side are the donors and other partners, with individual expectations for their input and partnership output. Partners may appreciate the efficiencies of standard approaches, but still want their bells and whistles. There are significant transaction costs, both establishment and ongoing, to create anew every time, but a fully standardized approach will also fall short. Every partnership program is different, with different players, different ambitions, and different circumstances that need accommodating.

Fit-for-Purpose Incentives

Why does being fit-for purpose matter? Partnership programs are voluntary, partners need to want to stay engaged. Even if it takes some coordination, compromise, and customization, the structure of a sustained partnership program can try to meet the following tests over time:

- Will partners see plans and results that reflect their reasons for engaging?
- Will funders find motivation to stay engaged and keep funding?
- Will supporting entities be given enough deference to take up responsibility?
- Will beneficiaries feel like they are being heard and truly benefited?
- Will decision makers find consensus and further partnership-wide interests?
- Will the partnership garner enough buy-in to be effective and appreciated?

GOVERNING BODY

10.   *Governing Body Context.* The Partnership Program is governed by the Governing Body. [describe broad partnership role, plus relationships to other governance elements, as relevant]

In a structural setting, with lines and links, elements do not sit in isolation. They are positioned in relation to each other. When taking up individual structural elements, it is helpful to first locate each element within its broader setting. The governing body is important in its own right, but its real importance lies in its relative role—for example, the governing body in relation to the secretariat and trustee, to project proposals and results, to the partnership program overall. Is the governing body a central pillar carrying the weight of the partnership program, an overarching roof with a strategic span, or an observatory off to the side? The context description can reveal a functional role or a specific relationship, whatever gets to the essence of situating the governing body in the broader landscape.

EXPLANATIONS

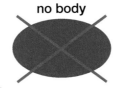

no body

advisory body

governing body

HANDOVER TO SUPPORTING ENTITY

- full delegation and deference by donors and other partners
- reliance on supporting entity for everything
- no shared governance

HYBRID IN BETWEEN

- where partner views count, but decision maker controls
- supporting entity is the decision maker (control matches responsibility)

GOVERNING BODY WITH DECISION MAKING

- insertion and intervention by donors and other partners
- supporting entity defers to governing body or stays in mix as member

Decision-Making vs. Advisory Bodies

Decision-Making Body. If shared governance involves a decision-making body, then certain things need that body's approval to proceed. Those things are itemized in the charter section on the governing body's roles and responsibilities. Decision points are teed up for consideration, often with the support of the secretariat and usually either at a meeting (consensus) or virtually (no objection). (>@ PfP: Decision Making) Decision points are not static, and deliberations can ensue if the governing body fails to approve something, like rejecting an annual work plan or declining a funding request. Sometimes modifications can be made in real time to salvage the proposal, but sometimes changes are substantial enough that they need another round of review, followed by a subsequent decision point, again either at a meeting or virtually.

Advisory Body. An advisory body can influence, but not determine, what proceeds. Strictly speaking, an advisory body is not really a "governing" body, but it creates enough of a shared governance dynamic to fit under the generic label. Even though an advisory body provides only advice, input, or feedback without having a final say, its views are generally not ignored. Much to the contrary, those views can carry a lot of weight to keep partners, especially donors, happy and engaged. Advisory shared governance usually leaves the decision making to other functions as part of their implementation roles, whether the secretariat, trustee, or implementing entities. Across a spectrum of possibilities, the balance of decision making may be a matter of negotiation. (>@ PfP: International Partnership Programs—Shared Decision Making) But even without explicit decision-making rights, partners on advisory bodies can carry their influence through the power of the purse, vocal interventions, and active engagement.

VARIATIONS

The governing body can be expressly positioned on the decision-making spectrum, including one of these three points:

1

The Governing Body is the shared decision-making body of the Partnership Program.

Shared decision making is where the governing body tends to go by default. That still leaves a big range of possibilities, from lots of decisions on lots of topics to something less. The more precise itemization of roles and responsibilities later in the charter should answer the question, decision making on what? For international partnership programs, where governing body participation is a part-time activity for the individual representatives, it is not feasible to make the governing body responsible for every decision. It is also natural to distinguish between oversight (high-level) and management (day-to-day) functions, as is the case for corporate boards. Unlike corporate boards, however, partnership programs in the international arena do not require any specific division of labor between oversight and management functions, beyond analogized notions of good practice. (>@ PfP: Partnering Internationally) And so, too, there is no first principle on whether the governing body is decision making at all. It is truly up to the partners to carve out the specific domain of the governing body.

2

The Governing Body is the oversight/strategic body of the Partnership Program.

Rather than positioning the governing body at the center of partnership program governance, it can be kept at a high level. This can mean giving the body a strategic, rather than hands-on, role. Partners that do not want activity-level involvement may prefer to sit at an elevated, broad-brush level, leaving proposal details and fund allocation decisions to others. This also gives governing board members less direct responsibility and exposure. Supporting and implementing entities may also prefer to keep partners at higher levels—weighing in strategically or only above certain thresholds—to avoid being micromanaged. High-level decision-making bodies are not quite advisory bodies, but they can come close, especially if they are spoon-fed strategies or work plans by strong secretariats. Having shared governance in the mix, but not in the minutiae, is sometimes the most conducive, mutually appreciated midway that maximizes the comparative advantages of the partners.

3

The Governing Body is an advisory/consultative body of the Partnership Program.

The governing body can also refrain from any decisive governing role. Some situations lend themselves to this more limited approach, where the body is an avenue for consultation and buy-in, but not essential to governing, and where deference is paid to the supporting entity and others to carry the load. This suits partners that do not want decision-making exposure. It also suits partners for whom the point of one-stop-shop engagement is offloading responsibility to a full trustee and secretariat. Those partners are happy with an advisory seat and nothing more. Similarly, supporting and implementing entities may reserve decision making for themselves as a precondition for undertaking their roles. From their perspective, if they are going to be made fully responsible, they should keep full decision making, so as to match responsibility with authority. (>@ PfP: Supporting Entities—Risk Profile)

CONSIDERATIONS

Who is making what partnership program decisions, and how does the governing body fit in? This is called mapping the decision making. (>@ PfP: Structure—Whiteboarding) On the funding side, you **follow the money**; on the decision side, you **follow the power**. (>@ BfB: Dualities—Connections and Delineations) All manner of things get decided in a partnership program, including this short list of usual suspects: who gets to partner, who sits on the governing body, what funding sources are counted, what those sources fund, how to route and review proposals, how to convene, how to decide, how to communicate internally, how to communicate externally, how to report, how to evaluate, and even how long to last. Many partnership programs place the critical mass of ongoing governance in the governing body, but many do not, across a spectrum of possibilities (>@ PfP: Typology—One-Stop-Shops vs. International Platforms) There is no rule about who decides what, except that the partners get to decide that.

Is the governing body (or the partnership program more broadly) operating in relation to other elements outside the partnership program? Some partnership programs are established in connection with broader initiatives. Especially if these elements are existential to the partnership program, they merit a by-line in the charter. For example:

- A country compact or needs assessment provides the backdrop for the partnership program and may have prompted its creation. For example: *The Governing Body operates within the framework of the [outside document], as the [outside document] may evolve over time.*

- An overarching framework, like an international treaty, political process, white paper, or call to action, undergirds and informs the partnership program's operations. For example: *The [outside element] provides the overarching framework for the Partnership Program. Or The Governing Body is not bound by the [terms of the outside document] [decisions of the outside body], but takes its [terms/determinations] into account in its own decision making.*

- The partnership program is operating in tandem with an international body with relevance in the field. For example: *The [external body] provides strategic and policy guidance on [describe initiative], including the Partnership Program. Or [Members of the Governing Body] participate in the [external body].*

- It is operating under a higher-level coordinating body. For example: *The Governing Body operates under the overarching guidance and strategic oversight of the [outside body] as part of the [name of larger initiative].*

Strategy-level shared governance is in the mix, not the minutiae.

Would no shared governance be better? To round out the options, some partnerships have no governing body, neither decision making, nor advisory, which is to say no ongoing shared governance. That means all shared decisions are made upfront, for example, as part of negotiated agreements for providing funds, after which the partnership materializes directly through the trust fund or other operations. All further decisions, particularly on what to do with those funds, are then made over time by the entity with those funds, consistent with the upfront agreed terms. (>@ PfP: Typology—The Even Broader Landscape of Structured Partnerships) This, then, is not in fact a partnership program as defined here, but may make the most sense for the partners.

MEMBERS

11. *Governing Body Decision-Making Members.* The Governing Body comprises the following decision-making members (Members): _____.

EXPLANATIONS

When it comes to designing the governing body of an international partnership program, there is lots to think about. Let's start by first seeing that the governing body is constituted at both the partner level (>@ PfP: Governing Bodies—Composition) and the representative level (>@ PfP: Governing Bodies—Participation), and the charter accordingly has a section for each. The governing body can also distinguish between members (decision makers) and observers (non-decision makers), so the charter also doubles up on these sections. Across all of this, the thing to understand is that international partners are always entities, and international partnership programs almost always convene either sovereigns, organizations created by sovereigns, or internationally active organizations.

It is true that the person sitting at the table is, of course, always an individual. However, for international partnership programs, that person is rarely sitting on an individual basis. Instead, she is representing an entity, usually her employer, rather than representing herself. In other words, that seat is filled in an organizational, not personal, capacity. For institutional participation, the member and the representative are two different things. For individual participation, which is not normally the case here, the member and the representative converge into one and the same; the individual represents (and is) herself.

Because institutional representation means that partnering is happening at the entity level, participation in international partnership programs does not normally depend on the individual. Indeed, the individual can be swapped out at any time, since the organization has control of the seat. If the individual leaves the organization, she is replaced, not retained, by the partnership. Governing body decisions are attributed to the organization, as does any visibility arising from them, whether the individual representative coordinates back or not. Credit for a job well done—or not—accrues to the participating entity.

Institutional, not Individual, Participation

Why do governing body participants from sovereign countries and international organizations engage as entities and not individuals? If you care about liability, one of the great advantages of sovereigns and international organizations is that they usually have immunities. (>@ BfB: The Annotated Charter—Privileges and Immunities) Privileges and immunities (P&I) attach to individuals in their status as employees—this is staff immunity. (>@ PfP: Supporting Entities—Privileges and Immunities) Government and international organization representatives either participate in governing bodies on behalf of their employers in a protected institutional capacity, or they bear the risk of exposure in their personal capacity. Neither the individuals nor their employers want this exposure. It is arguably the employer's responsibility—having asked the individual representative to participate—to make sure that representation is institutional and protected. Even when employees participate of their own volition, if the subject matter of that participation overlaps substantially with the employee's work program for the employer, the employer has an interest in treating the representation as institutionally aligned and P&I-protected. (>@ PfP: Governing Bodies—Characteristics—Applicable Duties)

Decision makers can be chosen or choose themselves. In the one case, partners can selectively invite decision makers to the table (and founding partners can effectively agree to invite each other). In the other case, partners can put forward a broad invitation based on specified requirements. Contribution to a trust fund is often the ticket, but other threshold terms can apply. Here are some variations on the theme:

VARIATIONS

Example: [by designation] The following entities participate in the Governing Body as decision-making members (Members): _____.]

Without needing to say more, this simply lists those who are in. The list is at the entity level, with institutional representation. It may be amended over time through the normal amendment process spelled out in the charter. More can be said to supplement the usual amendment process, like requiring membership proposals to go through the secretariat for organizing and vetting, or requiring prior consent by the trustee or other non-decision-making participants. Amendments can add new members, or delete ones that decide to leave.

Example: [by self-selection] An entity may participate in the Governing Body as a decision-making member (Member) upon meeting the Funding Requirements specified above.

If strategically deployed, minimum funding requirements can result in more money and fewer participants, which can be ideal for efficient implementation. However, in setting minimum funding requirements for governing body participation, it is best to apply the same thresholds to trust fund participation, keeping the two aspects aligned. This avoids two classes of donors, one that pays more and sits, and another that pays less and does not sit. (>@ PfP: Trade-Offs—The Horizontal Buy-In Spectrum—Workarounds) This also allows partnership programs to efficiently amend contribution agreements through the charter. (>@ PfP: Like Rock, Like Water) By combining donor minimums with other dedicated seats, partnership programs can engineer the level of balance, inclusion, diversity, resources, and efficiency that they want at the table.

Example: [by application, as an add-on]: Prospective members can apply to become Members if they (i) are sponsored by another Member; (ii) endorse this Charter; and (iii) meet their Funding Requirements. Applications are provided to the Secretariat for screening prior to submission to the Governing Body for decision.

Membership by self-selection and application differ in that the latter involves an explicit submission process. The submission process enables a degree of due diligence (by secretariat screening) and control (by governing body decision). The secretariat screening function can offer meaningful protection to all partners. (>@ PfP: Secretariats—Inhouse Secretariat Roles—Gatekeeping) Problem cases are rare, but secretariats are generally well-placed to manage reputational exposure to themselves, their supporting entities, and other partners. Any issues can then be raised to the governing body in conjunction with the decision on the proposed membership. On another note, charter endorsement can be an explicit item for new entrants, as shown here, or it can be indirect or implicit. For example, it occurs when a donor signs a contribution agreement that incorporates the charter by reference, or when a participant joins the governing body that is governed by the charter. If partners prefer to be explicit, however, charter endorsements can be part of the application process through a questionnaire, form letter, or online acknowledgment.

Participation by Constituency

When the numbers get too high, say twelve or twenty or more, constituency representation offers another way to keep the numbers in check. Whether a partnership program starts this way or makes the shift later, governing by constituency means a specific category of participants is identified (such as donors or developing countries) and then tagged with a fixed number of participants that can sit at the table on behalf of all the participants in that category. Each participant can still be considered a member, but not all members get a seat. As a result, not all members get a direct right to speak on the record or block a decision. The unseated members can do so only through their seated member, usually worked out beforehand, not in real time. And this constituency approach then applies to no-objection decisions as well. (>@ PfP: Decision Making) Constituencies can be hard work, but also useful to achieve balance among categories if parity matters (for example, three donor seats, three developing country seats, and three CSO seats). The key to constituency representation is that designated members recognize their obligations not only to their own organizations, but also to all members of their constituencies. This necessarily involves extra coordination and may justify longer time frames before meetings or during no-objection requests. (>@ PfP: Governing Bodies—Composition—Constituencies)

Typical Kinds of International Participants

In international partnership programs, where traditional participants are sovereign countries and international organizations, like United Nations agencies and multilateral development banks, participation is by the national sovereign or the international entity. For countries, whether donor or recipient countries, this usually means participation by or through a ministry or government agency as the legal entity. For international organizations, participation is by the multi-country sponsored institution, usually leveraging the full scope of the institution for the benefit of the partnership program. Multilateral organizations, like multilateral development banks, are especially interesting, since the same sovereign countries that are participating directly in the partnership program may also be participating indirectly as shareholders of those organizations. (>@ PfP: Synergistic Conflicts—Seeing and Seeking Synergies)

Participant Perspectives

The power to decide—especially when tantamount to a veto against consensus—is consequential. Partners rely on each other to be constructive decision makers. Different types of participants bring different interests and perspectives to their roles. With a bit of caricature:

- Sovereign donors make decisions based on what their governments and taxpayers expect to see.
- Private foundation (nonprofit) donors have their own purposes and tax requirements to meet.
- Private sector (for-profit) donors have business considerations in mind.
- Recipient countries look for a match with country strategies, priorities, and some politics.
- Supporting entities take a nuts-and-bolts perspective according to their rules.
- NGOs and CSOs bring their sector-specific focus and issue-specific agendas.
- Academia wants to know more and may in fact know more.

Every added perspective adds richness, but, admittedly, also complexity.

What is a comfortable, constructive size for the governing body? Partnership programs usually try to position membership in some finite, manageable way, although what that means in terms of numbers can vary. What is at stake?

- This is primarily a matter of logistics, to avoid cumbersome meeting dynamics and unwieldy decision making. If thirty members feel they each have to state their views on a particular proposal, they'll still be listening to each other an hour or two later. If twenty members need to agree on a complex, innovative, high-risk venture, it may take multiple forays to get everyone on board. (>@ PfP: Risk and Review—Risk Innovation) Two-tier governance can be used to allow more involvement (knowing two tiers can add logistics), if the division of responsibilities is clear and meaningful. (>@ PfP: Trade-Offs—The Vertical Continuity Spectrum)

- This is also a matter of commonality, to get enough common mindset around the table to reach consensus. (>@ PfP: Decision Making) A partnership program with a high-level strategic or advisory governing body—the lighter end of the spectrum—can more readily afford a larger group. A light-touch governing body may be a good choice precisely because it prioritizes inclusion. Even when governing body membership is limited, other complementary partnership elements can be more inclusive or open-ended, like having an annual stakeholder event. (>@ PfP: Structure—Broader Context)

CONSIDERATIONS

How about mixing institutional and individual representation? For partnership programs where institutional and individual representatives sit side by side, availability for meetings is one of the big differences. Institutions draw from a whole cast of characters, while individuals have no one but themselves. Coupling institutional and individual representation on the same body can lead to tensions if, for example, participation becomes too demanding or time-consuming for individuals, or if individuals do not respect and appreciate the multifaceted, bear-hugging engagement of a resource-rich institution.

> Simplicity has limitations, diversity has complications.

Is the governing body participation fit-for-purpose? The same kinds of considerations that arise for the partnership program's structure overall pertain to its decision-making core. In considering the long-term life of the partnership program, the following questions can be asked:

- Are all decision makers needed? Are any key decision makers missing?
- Is there enough experience and expertise around the table for well-informed decision making?
- Is there enough common mindset to reach consensus decisions?
- Are all decision makers ready to provide the resources to carry their load and do their part, including diligently prepping for and regularly attending meetings?

REPRESENTATIVES

12. *Governing Body Member Representation.* Each Member participates in the Governing Body through a standing representative. The names of current Member representatives are notified to the Secretariat at all times, including as names of record for no-objection decision purposes.

EXPLANATIONS

With representation, we are now at the individual, not institutional, level. The main trade-off with respect to governing body representation is balancing continuity with flexibility. Continuity of participation, at both institutional and individual levels, is crucial for smooth and informed proceedings. Partnership program business builds on itself over time. Informed and insightful decision making by participants improves with continuous participation. Successful partnership programs tend to turn continuity into their own culture.

At the same time, being part of the governing body is usually only a fraction of each representative's more than full and competing workload. Schedules easily conflict or overload, in which case institutional members benefit from their large cohorts of staff. A sizeable organization can send different individuals based on schedule availability and specific expertise—but at a cost. Swapping out participants can be disruptive, while continuity is an engine of consensus.

By and large, effective governing bodies seek stability and maximized partner input—hence, "standing" representatives (although they sit more than stand). It also helps to have an upfront sense of the appropriate level of representative participation—both in terms of seniority and time. The two are usually inversely proportional: the more seniority, the less time, and vice versa. Realistic expectations for governing body engagement can measure the anticipated workload in relation to secretariat support. This, too, is usually an inverse relationship: the more pre-cooking by the secretariat, the less prep time for the representatives.

Knowing who is in your cohort is especially important for no-objection procedures. Willy-nilly representation complicates decision making when the process requires that the message reach the right representatives. Even though the secretariat that handles no-objection requests can put the onus on the member to keep its contacts current, as in this clause, knowing who's who to a consistent certainty is always helpful. (>@ BfB: The Annotated Charter—Governing Body Decision Making)

CONSIDERATIONS

When it comes to no objection, silence is consent, provided that the email was well and truly sent.

Are there diversity or expertise factors that need adjusting? Partnership programs are increasingly mindful of the face of the partnership, including the faces around the table. When all the representatives show up, do they reflect the balance and variety that the partnership wants to portray? Some of this happens at the member (institutional) level—with Part 1/Part 2/UN/IFI/NGO/CSO and other categories of participants—but some of it happens at the representative level. Is there a good regional mix? Is there a good gender balance? Are the right types and levels of expertise weighing in? Stepping back to consider the canvas may be worth doing.

VARIATIONS

Sometimes the elements around individual representation are so implicit or understood that partners choose not to articulate them, potentially leaving this section out altogether. No problem here, if the terms are truly understood. Some partnership programs prefer to be more explicit for the good order. Depending on the specific dynamics or pitfalls, representation can be bolstered by the following:

Each Member participates in the Governing Body through a standing representative <u>or an occasional alternate at the representative's discretion</u>.

Intention: While Member representatives are expected to attend whenever possible for continuity's sake, they have the leeway to manage their participation.

Each Member has the right to be represented by [one representative] [two representatives] [up to two representatives for multiple ministries or agencies of a Member country].

Intention: Each Member entity has a limit to how many staff it may seat at the table. For sovereign partners, the rule goes a step further. Under this clause, membership is pitched at the country, not entity, level, with each country effectively treated as a constituency with a set number of participants, regardless of the number of government entities separately involved.

Members provide senior level representation on the Governing Body, supported by their technical staff as appropriate.

Intention: Members are expected to be sufficiently high level, but also sufficiently resourced.

Each Member representative seeks to assure continuity of representation on the Governing Body and to represent the interests of his or her [institution] [or constituency, as the case may be], while seeking to support the broader interests of the Partnership Program.

Intention: This poses an affirmative commitment to continuity of engagement and the goals and well-being of the partnership program. Note that the wording for this last point is still a far cry from the kind of personal fiduciary duty that corporate board members usually have to their incorporated entities.

CONSIDERATIONS

How much time and effort are member representatives expected to contribute? The engagement representatives need for a partnership program to succeed is a factor of the kinds of decisions to be made. For example, where a partnership program falls on the decision-making spectrum (>@ PfP: International Partnership Programs—Shared Decision Making) has a major effect on the amount of time and effort needed. If involvement is strategic, then senior level participants may engage based on what they know without much additional preparatory work. If the involvement calls for decisions on hundred-page proposals, then an informed decision takes more diligence in advance. If, however, the secretariat is tasked with digesting those hundred pages and providing one-page summaries with tabulated questions for discussion, then the burden becomes more manageable with the trade-off that member influence goes down, while supporting entity influence goes up. Taken as a whole, partners can carefully match up roles, contributions, and expectations in ways that are transparent, reasonable, and well-suited. This way, representatives can know what they are getting into before signing up for more than they are willing to take on.

OBSERVERS

13. Governing Body *Non-Decision-Making Observers*. The Governing Body includes the following [active] observers without decision-making participation (Observers): Secretariat Head, Trustee, and _____. Each Observer participates through a standing representative. The names of current Observer representatives are notified to the Secretariat at all times. At the invitation of the [Chair], additional non-decision-making participants may attend specific meetings for specific purposes.

EXPLANATIONS

There are various reasons to include non-decision-making observers on the governing body. The most obvious one is coordination. Whether a partner steps up to a decision-making role usually depends on what kinds of decisions are being made—for example, when donors get to decide about their money—but coordination goes beyond decision making. Governing bodies that do not just make decisions about money, but also convene to coordinate and collaborate, learn lessons and advocate, are prone to involving more participants.

Observers (capital O) that are named in the charter receive a fixed status with standing invitations—and standing expectations—to attend all meetings. The word "observer" may imply being seen and not heard, but that would be too limiting if the point is coordination and collaboration. For most international partnership programs, standing observers are expected to be active, not passive. (>@ PfP: Governing Bodies—Composition—Observers) They are encouraged to participate in discussions, provide information and expertise, make their views known, and help shape the outcomes. A standing seat (no pun intended) usually includes an invitation to engage. This applies to virtual, no-objection processes as well. Although observers are not deciders, they can be commenters. It is a good idea to copy all regular observers on no-objection requests, both to keep them in the loop on governing body business and to allow them to enrich the deliberations.

Pre-defined, standing observers are different from other non-decision-making participants that are invited on an ad hoc basis, usually for specific meetings and specific purposes. For example, prospective donors may be welcomed during a courtship phase. Or subject matter experts may be invited as resources for specific agenda items. The charter usually grants broad allowance to include such one-off (lower case "observer") participants, specifying not who can come, but who has the right to invite (typically the chair) and potentially how (for example, with governing body consultation).

What Do Observers Bring to the Table?

- *Secretariat and trustee.* The secretariat and trustee are clearly of value at the table, both in terms of giving and getting information. In most international partnership programs, the supporting entity providing these functions (typically the same entity) is also participating as a collaborating partner, not just relegated to a support function. As a result, these roles are likely to show up in at least some representative capacity. In one-stop-shops, one or more supporting entity representatives are likely to have decision-making status on behalf of its multiple roles. In international platforms, where trustee and secretariat roles are usually separate and delineated, separate representatives are likely to be present for each role, but "limited" to observer status. (>@ PfP: Governing Bodies—Composition—Supporting Entities)

- *Downstream recipients.* Funding recipients, especially country beneficiaries, may also be included as observers for developing country voice. Partners want to hear from those for whom the partnership program exists. Some partnership programs put supporting (donor) and benefiting (recipient) countries on a par, as equal decision makers. In other cases, partners may conclude that conflict of interest concerns should lead to a different result. Recipients may be considered too self-interested to decide funding allocations, in which case observer status could be a better fit. That said, there can also be ample room to see synergies rather than conflicts, allowing an upgrade to decision-making member status. (>@ PfP: Synergistic Conflicts—Seeing and Seeking Synergies—Upstream/Downstream Synergies)

- *Downstream fiduciaries.* Other downstream participants, particularly downstream fiduciaries, can be key collaborators at the table. Similar conflict of interest concerns, and a desire to keep a level playing field, can make observer status a good fit. (>@ BfB: Balance—Leveling the Field)

- *Multilateral organizations.* Then there are international or multilateral organizations that are recognized in their respective sectors, like United Nations agencies or treaty organizations with international mandates. Their presence can add depth to understanding and legitimacy to deliberations. They can be a bridge to the larger international community and send political signals of inclusion and cooperation. Members may not wish to give these organizations effective veto power, but can still integrate them through observer positions.

- *NGOs, CSOs, academia.* And finally, there may be NGOs, CSOs, academic institutions, and others, which are so central to the subject matter that their regular presence is welcome. Moreover, it can sometimes be savvier to have key voices chiming in on the inside than critiquing on the outside. (>@ PfP: Trade-Offs—The Horizontal Buy-In Spectrum—Inclusion vs. Efficiency) Observer status may be enough to achieve that.

VARIATIONS

The Chair may declare all or part of a Governing Body meeting to be closed for Members only.

In adding regular observers, it may be prudent to allow for members-only deliberations, if ever needed. This is usually limited to the rare case dealing with particularly sensitive material—confidential reports, unverified fraud allegations, human resources issues—as guarded space for off-the-record conversations. Most charters do not add this kind of clause, with the expectation that the chair can manage meetings as necessary. A skilled chair will know to manage participation as needed, including the ability to invoke the Chatham House rule, disinvite ad hoc participants, or other measures in support of productive business proceedings. Then again, a skilled chair might honor the valued role of observers and favor their inclusion.

CONSIDERATIONS

What observer positions can be most helpful to members in their decision making? The answer is usually a short list—members normally outnumber observers, especially if there is additional room to invite others on an ad hoc basis. Standing observers are ones where the two-way exchange of information and continuity of engagement is of benefit, where there is value in having members and observers stay on the same page. When observers engage as active participants in a consensus-based environment, the difference between members and observers need not feel obvious, as everyone contributes their part. Sometimes, observers are added more demonstratively than substantively, for reasons of inclusion, diversity, legitimacy, or straight-up politics. That is okay, too, if it works well for all partners.

Is the size of the governing body still manageable? Although not decision makers, observers take up space and may prolong discussions. As we saw with members, meetings should not become unwieldy with too many observers, but rather allow for comfortable deliberations with enough common mindset to promote consensus. (>@ BfB: Balance—Preserving Consensus) Then again, observers need not be active; they can be passive. A partnership program can add them on the understanding that they may listen in, but not contribute. Either way, partnership programs can be generous with observer seats if everyone understands why and how they are being included.

Members, Observers, What Else?

As far as formally defined categories in the charter, "Members" and "Observers" are usually enough. Some partnership programs like to create additional categories of participants—for example, "Partners" that explicitly associate with the partnership program, but need not be part of the governing body, or "Associate Members" that may be part of the governing body, but pay less or come from the private sector. However, before adding more categories, think twice. Extra layers of participation can be muddling. Who has what prerogatives when? Who gets access to information, who gets to provide input, particularly during reforms or other major initiatives and occurrences? Wider circles of engagement can create more partnership exposure. Different strata of engagements can create second class citizens, or leave them feeling neither in, nor out, or like appendages. Managing all this is bound to complicate the lives of the secretariat, chair, and other participants. Consider keeping it simple. (>@ PfP: Governing Bodies—Composition—Members)

CHAIR

14. *Governing Body Chair.* The Governing Body is chaired by [a senior representative of the supporting entity].

EXPLANATIONS

The chair is both a function and a person.
If functionality matters, personality matters.

The chair position is integral to international partnership programs and is usually drawn from the partners themselves. Its importance reflects the importance of the governing body. It tends to be a hands-on, shaping position, rather than a titular, prestige position. This is especially true if the chair doubles as a decision-making representative, which is usually the case. (>@ BfB: Balance—Securing Stability) In partnership programs where visibility is part of the agenda, the chair can also be the face of the partnership program.

In one-stop-shops, as per the sample clause here, the chair is likely to be drawn from senior management of the supporting entity. Bearing the load of the partnership program, the supporting entity may even make holding the chair position a precondition for its support. This serves efficiency. Linking the chair role to the trustee, secretariat, and other roles through the same entity enhances coherence and complementarity. This also manages exposure. Through the chair role, the supporting entity is better able to manage its risk profile by shaping and controlling governing body business. Other partners may see this as overreach, but it is in the nature of one-stop-shops. Keeping all these functions in one hand is perceived by many as an advantage. It also matches full responsibility with full authority and enables full support. (>@ PfP: Supporting Entities—Risk Profile)

For most partners, participating in the partnership program is but a fraction of what they do. They end up relying on the chair, together with the secretariat, to pull it all together and keep the momentum. From a cost perspective, the chair role is normally not remunerated or subject to cost recovery. That effectively makes the position an in-kind contribution, appropriate from a partnering (vs. service) perspective, although rarely articulated as such. With time and resources, the possibilities for the chair to have a major impact are great, both vis-à-vis the partnership and beyond.

- *Partnership-facing operational role.* Operationally, how active a chair needs to be for governing body business is inversely proportional to the strength and engagement of the secretariat. If the secretariat carries most of the load to set up meetings and decisions, the chair has less to do. Partnership programs that engage very high-level chairs should make sure the secretariat is amply staffed to do the legwork the chair cannot be expected to do. Even so, there are always moments when chair leadership is called for—like resource mobilization, strategic planning, performance reviews and restructuring—and ideally available.

- *Externally-facing visibility role.* Externally, how active a chair needs to be for partnership program business depends in part on how much visibility or activity partners want in other arenas. While the head of a strong secretariat can (also or instead) be the external face of the partnership program, the chair may enable a different and more political level of engagement. Expectations that the chair represent the partnership program in the wider international community are best discussed and confirmed in advance.

VARIATIONS

For partnership programs that are less supporting entity-centric than one-stop-shops, there are many other configurations, including a Member Chair, co-Chairs, a Chair plus Deputy Chair, rotating Chairs, and more:

Example: The Governing Body selects its Chair from among its Members for a [renewable/rotating] [one/three-year] term.

Example: The Governing Body is co-chaired by a Donor Member and a Recipient Member for [renewable/rotating/staggered] [one/two-year] terms. Each Co-chair is selected by [all] [its constituency] Members of the Governing Body. They allocate their responsibilities between themselves.

Example: The Governing Body is chaired by a senior representative of the [supporting entity] and selects a co-chair for each meeting. *[for example, as teed up by the secretariat, one member nominates and the governing body approves]*

Example: The Governing Body is chaired by the [beneficiary country/Ministry], as selected by the Government [and confirmed by the Governing Body]. *[for single country-focused platforms, especially if the country provides the secretariat]*

How active and influential a chair ends up being can be a combination of choice and culture. Governing body members can reserve the right to choose or approve their chair (either the partner institution or the individual). Governing body members can also indicate their pleasure or displeasure if a chair is motivating or overbearing. Partners can also set the stage with the charter by articulating their expectations in a list of key roles and responsibilities:

Example: [roles and responsibilities] The roles and responsibilities of the Chair include *[choose as relevant]*:

a) Ensuring that consensus decisions taken by the Governing Body are clearly stated and recorded in minutes of meetings that are confirmed by the Members;
b) Ensuring that no-objection decision processes organized by the Secretariat are clear, including providing responses to queries and pursuing ways to reach consensus in case of objections;
c) Facilitating coordination within and among constituencies;
d) Inviting ad hoc observers to individual meetings for specific purposes;
e) Leading ongoing resource mobilization, in coordination with all partners;
f) Ensuring periodic performance reviews, including of the Governing Body; and
g) Acting as international spokesperson for the Partnership Program.

CONSIDERATIONS

Does the chair position matter? The chair position can be a figurehead, or it can be a power center. If the latter, the chair puts its imprimatur on the meeting with great consequence. The chair navigates and may even cut off discussion, with significant substantive implications—welcome or not. The chair articulates consensus decisions for the record. If done well, she can manage tensions and differences—or if not, she may heighten concerns and feed undercurrents. Having the chair act as a gatekeeper for invited observers, a conduit to the secretariat, an impetus for reform, a face to the outside, even a visionary—these are all meaningful functions. Whom do partners trust with that power, if anyone? Are they better off with a strident leader or safe moderator, or something in between?

How much does the chair need to do? How much the chair does is relative to how much others do. In significant part, this depends on what the head of the secretariat, the other titular partnership program role, is set up (read: financed) to achieve. It also depends on the chair's comparative advantages, both the entity and the individual, and how that fits in addition to leading governing body meetings. For example, if the chair role skews to the visible and political, the secretariat can do the heavy lifting on content, while the chair addresses outside relations and advocacy. Whatever ends up on the chair's plate should be manageable. Too much reliance on a chair that fails to deliver is a recipe for stagnation or worse—or pushes the secretariat into rescue mode. (>@ PfP: Secretariats—Inhouse Secretariat Roles) Depending on the chair's bandwidth, energy level, and attention span, it may be best to keep the chair responsibilities narrow and let the secretariat, trustee, and other roles be in charge of the rest.

How much control should the chair have? This, too, tends to reflect the strength of other roles. The easy case is when the chair comes from the supporting entity (as in a typical one-stop-shop), in which case she carries the weight of the supporting entity's overall responsibilities into the room. That means lots of control, bolstered by a seamless relationship to the secretariat and trustee, who are direct colleagues. If, however, the chair is meant to be an active counterpoint to the supporting entity, the chair will likely come from another power center, like donors, possibly shared with another key stakeholder, like a beneficiary country. That can also mean lots of control, but not as inevitably as in the integrated one-stop-shop model. If the original vision is one of parity of partners, the chair or co-chairs will want to defer more than dominate, as long as everyone pitches in.

To what extent should the chair reflect diversity? Some partnership programs, especially ones with strong secretariats, appoint chairs that mirror their members. The chair position can, for example, reflect Part 1/Part 2 membership, or donor/recipient membership, in the form of co-chairs, or a chair plus a deputy chair. Rather than a long-term post, the chair position can be time-bound and rotate through the members, effectively adding leadership to the list of things being collectivized. (>@ PfP: International Partnership Programs—Collectivizing) Note, however, that this is a trade-off. More inclusion through sharing or rotating usually means less continuity and command. This lowers expectations for the role of the chair and puts more reliance on other functions, like the secretariat. Partnership programs that prefer to defer tend to centralize more than diversify. And with that, we are back to one-stop-shops, with the chair in the hands of the supporting entity.

GOVERNING BODY ROLES AND RESPONSIBILITIES

15. *Governing Body Roles and Responsibilities.* The primary roles and responsibilities of the Governing Body are as follows *[by way of example, pick and edit as relevant]:*

a) Providing strategic guidance for the Partnership Program;
a) Overseeing the Partnership Program;
a) Approving Partnership Program [strategies] [priorities];
a) Allocating envelopes of funding [to specified fiduciary recipients] for implementation in accordance with [agreed terms];
a) Approving annual work plans [and indicative budgets] for the Partnership Program, as prepared by the Secretariat, including fully-funded Secretariat and Trustee costs;
a) Approving funding allocations from the Trust Fund based on funding requests submitted to [and pre-screened by] the Secretariat;
a) Consider whether other proposed activities financed or undertaken by Members can be part of the Partnership Program based on requests submitted to the Secretariat.

[Pick one from a range of options, as described in the Variations.]

b) Approving a multi-year results framework for the Partnership Program;
c) Approving a risk management strategy for the Partnership Program;
d) Approving an annual work plan for the Partnership Program;
e) Reviewing financial reports prepared by the Trustee;
f) Reviewing progress reports [prepared] [compiled] by the Secretariat;
g) Agreeing on conflict of interest, confidentiality, and transparency [rules] [standards] for the Partnership Program;
h) Supporting resource mobilization efforts for the Partnership Program;
i) Approving the establishment of [working groups] [task forces] based on terms of reference prepared by the Secretariat;
j) Selecting the Chair of the Governing Body based on [recommendations by the Secretariat] [nominations from the Members];
k) Approving new Members and Observers;
l) Adopting and approving amendments to this Charter;
m) Reviewing and evaluating the overall performance of the Partnership Program, including the Governing Body;
n) Guiding monitoring and evaluation arrangements for the Partnership Program; and
o) Commissioning periodic independent evaluations of the Partnership Program.

Roles vs. Responsibilities

A role is a function; a responsibility is an obligation. But honestly, this is more about alliteration than distinction. The combination trips off the tongue as easily as rest and relaxation, or reading, writing, and 'rithmetic. Ultimately, the point is something you sign up to do—and allow others to rely upon.

EXPLANATIONS

Clarity is key. The itemization of governing body roles and responsibilities is important for setting shared expectations and confirming the willingness of members, individually and collectively, to accept those roles and responsibilities. As we follow the power (>@ PfP: Structure—Whiteboarding), partners may like being in the driver's seat, but should recall that great power brings great responsibility. Being in charge means they have to take the wheel and go for the long haul, in addition to paying for the gas. Sometimes that is a tall order for partners that have lots else going on. It is good to be judicious about the roles and responsibilities the governing body takes on. Follow-through takes effort and comes with consequences. (>@ PfP: Fund Use Responsibility—Collective Responsibility)

The list should also be considered in context by positioning the governing body relative to other partnership program components, like the secretariat, trustee, and other implementing entities, so the respective roles and responsibilities in the charter speak to each other. The spectrum for possible governing body operations is wide, and partners need to decide along a range of options from decision making to advisory functions, and high-level strategic to micromanaging functions. (>@ PfP: International Partnership Programs—Shared Decision Making)

For example, the scope of the governing body's responsibilities needs to align neatly with that of the trustee. Let's take fund allocation decisions. Either the trustee is responsible, the governing body is responsible, or they are both part of a multi-step process. Here are some examples:

- It is not uncommon for the governing body to approve a high-level work plan and then have the trustee approve allocations for specific projects under that plan.
- The governing body may get more into the weeds and approve a proposed project at the concept stage (pre-screening) and then let the trustee follow through to the final product.
- The governing body may instead defer more and agree to a funding envelope for some broadly defined set of activities, after which the recipient (like the secretariat or one or more grantees) arranges the specific projects.

Whatever the modality, the charter can lay out the respective, and related, roles and responsibilities, where partners can watch for gaps and overlaps. (>@ BfB: Agile Alignment—Step-by-Step Alignment for Trust-Funded Partnership Programs, #5)

The governing body's list of roles and responsibilities should also be formulated with contribution agreements and other legal documents in mind. (>@ BfB: Practical Packaging) As a package, these documents need to form a coherent whole that avoids overlapping, gapping, and conflicting provisions. It is usually better to cross-reference than repeat. (>@ BfB: Constitutive Documents—What to Watch For)

The list of roles and responsibilities in the charter is not meant to be exhaustive; that is why it says "including" at the top. Governing body business responds to context, events, member requests, lessons learned, and more over time. It is as hard to be all-encompassing as it is to predict the future. Generally, the list should be a solid baseline more than a straitjacket, projecting the key aspects owned by the governing body and other essentials for good governance. More items can be added over time through amendments. Or if the wording has some breadth to it, new roles and responsibilities can be interpreted within the spirit of the original ones.

VARIATIONS

From an overall perspective, governing body roles and responsibilities fall somewhere on the decision-making spectrum, with options ranging from high on the rooftop to deep in the kitchen, and points in between. We can focus on the opening line of the list to give a sense of the possibilities (in order from less to more governing body responsibility):

Example: [high-level, strategic advisory role with negligible responsibility]

> a) Providing strategic guidance for the Partnership Program;

This approach is particularly fitting for governing bodies that engage at the political level, more for visibility and advocacy than implementation. In these cases, the "strategic guidance" is likely to be in response to proposals from the secretariat or trustee, with the supporting entity in the kitchen. The goal is to coalesce around common positions that reflect partner buy-in and build program support. This model neatly refrains from putting responsibility on governing body members. Although they have some reputational risk from partnership program participation, real responsibility rests with those following through on partnership program operations.

Example: [oversight role with low responsibility]

> a) Overseeing the Partnership Program;

Oversight by the governing body can be a touchy issue, particularly if the secretariat/trustee is carrying the critical mass of partnership engagement and exposure. Even with this oversight, it is not clear that the supporting entity is subordinate to the governing body. Usually, the supporting entity prefers and expects to oversee itself. This may, however, be less of a gap than it seems, especially if the supporting entity is a multilateral organization, whose shared governance partners are also its shareholders and overseeing board members. (>@ PfP: Synergistic Conflicts—Seeing and Seeking Synergies) With that, the circle is closed, making this more of a tautology.

It also helps to understand that overseeing the partnership program is different from overseeing the trustee (operating in its own right) and the secretariat (operating on behalf of the partnership program). For these functions, support is provided through staff that are under the rules and management of the supporting entity, as they perform the work program of the supporting entity. (>@ PfP: Supporting Entities—Basic Elements) As such, they cannot be "overseen" by the governing body per se. Partnership program oversight also does not oversee the work program of any other partners that contribute to the partnership program. In effect, governing body "oversight" is limited to shared elements (like brand, strategic direction, priorities) for which operational responsibility is not lodged elsewhere. As a result, the level of actual responsibility accruing to governing body participants remains low.

Example: [strategic decision-making role with low responsibility]

> a) Approving Partnership Program [strategies] [priorities];

Anytime an explicit decision-making role appears (key word "approve"), the stakes increase. However, although the wording here translates to more reputational risk, it does not necessarily translate to more direct responsibility. Through their informal, collective nature, partnership program governing bodies tend to benefit from a Teflon effect, especially if the partnership program agreements and documents clearly direct responsibility elsewhere. (>@ PfP: Fund Use Responsibility—Collective Responsibility)

Example: [framework decision making with low responsibility]

> a) Allocating envelopes of funding [to specified fiduciary recipients] for implementation in accordance with [agreed terms];

An envelope funding approach defers specific implementation decisions to a specific entity, not as a blank check, but based on an agreed framework. This approach relies on a two-step process, where fund allocations occur at each step—first with an overall allocation by the governing body, and second with specific project allocations by the entity receiving the envelope. This modality is particularly appreciated by downstream fiduciaries whose projects are for smaller amounts or market-sensitive, or more generally where transaction costs of case-by-case governing body decision making outweighs the benefits of doing the projects.

Example: [framework decision-making role with medium responsibility]

> a) Approving annual work plans [and indicative budgets] for the Partnership Program, as prepared by the Secretariat, including fully-funded Secretariat and Trustee costs;

Annual work plans and budgets are also frameworks for implementation. Sometimes they come loaded with detail; sometimes they present outlines that reflect priorities rather than projects. Often it is the secretariat that determines, in the first instance, how detailed to be, although other partners will undoubtedly weigh in on the level of detail. Logically, deciding on more detail carries more governing body responsibility. However, governing body decision makers can still rest fairly easy. The real responsibility lies in the implementation, as delegated to other parts of the partnership program.

Example: [project-level decision making with high responsibility]

> a) Approving funding allocations from the Trust Fund based on funding requests submitted to [and pre-screened by] the Secretariat;

Relative to other options, this type of project-by-project decision making gives the governing body a very hands-on role—and arguably a handful of responsibility. In practice, however, that "responsibility" is more about reassuring than exposing donors. They exercise their decision making (hopefully responsibly) and then delegate implementation responsibility downstream. (>@ PfP: Fund Use Responsibility—Collective Responsibility) But downstream implementers are apt to resist this degree of shared decision making. It can feel like micromanaging and a drag on efficient delivery. Extending governing body decision making this far forces a lens on what it really means to rely on the trustee, secretariat, and other fiduciary entities to deliver on the partnership program's work plan.

Example: [project-branding decision making with high responsibility]

> a) Consider whether other proposed activities financed or undertaken by Members can be part of the Partnership Program based on requests submitted to the Secretariat;

Beyond dedicated funding sources, like trust funds established exclusively for their specific partnership programs, members may wish to include other parallel activities under their brand name. Usually this pertains to activities directly related to partners, with ready opportunities for collaboration. Including parallel activities may expose partners to more risk, but may also suit partners that are open to a larger umbrella for advocacy or other purposes. (>@ PfP: Typology—Trust-Funded Partnership Programs—Umbrella Arrangements) It is also possible to have a cross-cutting partnership program without attributing downstream activities to the brand or giving the governing body purview. (>@ibid.—Coordination Partnerships)

What roles and responsibilities are important to the members? The degree of governing body responsibility is often one of the most heavily negotiated points in international partnership programs, especially given the range of possibilities. These negotiations can turn on one word, whether the governing body gets to "approve" or "advise." This, in turn, reflects the partnership program's center of gravity: who shapes the brand, who has responsibility for operations, who bears the brunt of exposure. (>@ BfB: Balance—Creating Critical Mass) Negotiations also reflect trade-offs between operational efficiency and collective engagement. (>@ PfP: Trade-Offs—The Horizontal Buy-In Spectrum) The more the governing body engages, the more shared processing costs time and expense. Moreover, participants soon realize there are two sides to the coin: The more donors or other partners want to be in charge, the more they carry responsibility and risk. Often shifting that burden to the governing body is not feasible, if, for example, members are not prepared to devote their own time and staff to undertake the detailed work involved. On the other hand, even if they do, they may not feel the brunt of any responsibility, since they have delegated the real responsibility (of implementation) to others. Wherever this comes out, it is good to have these conversations upfront to avoid mismatches later. (>@ PfP: Like Rock, Like Water—Like Rock) Charter drafting, especially on sections like these, serves a valuable purpose in airing and converging partners' understandings, as part of a collective exercise. (>@ BfB: Deft Drafting—The Awesomeness of Articulating)

How much needs to be explicitly listed? The amount of detail in listing roles and responsibilities is partly a matter of preference, but ultimately a result of partners' cumulative needs and expectations. From a content perspective, a good litmus test is (1) whether the articulated list adequately clarifies the scope of the governing body's business for all members to appreciate what they are taking on; and (2) whether all other governing elements understand their roles in relation to the governing body. Partners should be able to read the governing body list in conjunction with other roles and responsibilities lists and see a totality that frames the division of labor and leadership. Against this backdrop, a sensitive chair and conscientious secretariat may have what they need to navigate over time.

What if the governing body wants to do something not on the list? The governing body's list of roles and responsibilities in the charter is not meant to be fully comprehensive; that is not feasible (accordingly "primary" roles and responsibilities). An item need not be listed for the governing body to take it up, as long as it is within the intended spirit, ideally accepted by all parties, and not directly infringing on someone else's functions. An overseeing governing body can, for example, decide to commission a strategic review of the partnership program even if not explicitly on the list, preferably as agreed with the secretariat and trustee (who will presumably hire and fund the consultant), and without infringing on their operations and institutional frameworks.

Should the governing body be a policy making body? For example, can it set up its own procurement rules and safeguards standards? How far can it go in defining selection criteria? Can it determine employment conditions for secretariat staff? Can it set audit requirements for the trustee? This topic has been a source of strife for many an international partnership program. Governing bodies often feel empowered to govern and inclined to populate their brand with specific standards and requirements. This works until it doesn't; that is, until it encroaches on existing policy environments of supporting or implementing partners. For example, if a partnership program includes fiduciary intermediaries, chances are they are being engaged because of their robust policies and procedures. Trying to replace or supplement those policies and procedures becomes a problem, even counterproductive. Supporting entities and fiduciary intermediaries are set up to follow their own policies and procedures, with staff and systems all geared accordingly. Deviating from them undercuts their robustness and increases risk and human error. Lots of exceptions are not scaleable. Although policy overlays may be well-intended, they pose a risk for everyone. Generally speaking, it is better to clarify upfront whose policy framework is meant to apply and prevail in what areas, and thereafter figure out where the governing body fits in. (>@ PfP: Typology—Introducing Two Mighty Oaks—International Platforms)

CONSIDERATIONS

What is the governing body's role in relation to funding allocations for activities? Having a two-step, programmatic approach (>@ PfP: Use of Funds—Expenditures and Results) does not pre-determine the degree of decision making by the governing body. Whether the secretariat or trustee (the supporting entity) takes all the decisions—both having the discretion and bearing the responsibility—about what activities occur under the name of the partnership program, or whether all the decisions are put in the hands of the governing body (which may include the supporting entity) with case-by-case approval rights, or something in between, needs to be decided and articulated as one of the partnership program basics. This is always a negotiating point in trust-fund partnership programs. The question is: Do partners handle or hand over fund allocation decisions?

light shared governance

negotiated framework with upfront parameters that let trustee, secretariat, and others specifically allocate and implement

heavy shared governance

governing body is used to position funds and activities under its collective purview for later implementation follow-up by others

Do partners handle or hand over fund allocation decisions?

Many Allocation/Attribution Decision-Making Options

Let's recap. The Charter sets the stage, but what actually gets funded and implemented as part of the partnership program—all the activities that belong to the brand—can come about in different ways. The governing body can be more or less hands off, and the funding can be dedicated, essentially coming from within the partnership program (let's call that "in-funded"), or can be brought in from outside (as in "out-funded"). Collective decisions on activities can play on various aspects like these:

- *Level of detail.* High level, conceptual review, like agreeing to an overall annual work plan and budget, including both in-funded and out-funded activities; or detail-oriented, micromanaging review, like approving specific in-funded activities or projects.
- *Timing.* Decision points before implementation, either pre-cooked at the early concept stage (with more shaping influence) or mostly cooked at the late appraisal stage (with less shaping influence).
- *Genesis.* Addressing activities generated directly for and by the partnership program, through dedicated funding sources; or bringing activities undertaken outside of the partnership program under the branded umbrella, as with the double-branding of so-called "parallel" activities.

Branding has a deliberate function in the context of directly funded or attributed activities. As noted here, you can brand activities that originate outside the partnership program as part of the partnership program. This kind of double counting is perfectly legitimate if it serves all parties—and the cause—and everyone agrees.

DECISION MAKING

16. *Governing Body Decision Making.* Decisions of the Governing Body may be made in person at meetings or electronically between meetings. Decisions at meetings are taken on a consensus basis by the Members present. Consensus means a decision is approved if no Member blocks the proposed decision. It need not reflect unanimity. A dissenting Member that does not wish to block a decision may state an objection to be recorded in the meeting minutes. Members may also abstain from a decision. The Chair articulates the consensus view to be recorded in the minutes. Decisions made electronically between meetings are taken on a no-objection basis by Members. No-objection decision processes are handled by the Secretariat.

EXPLANATIONS

Virtual decisions have their virtue: anywhere, anytime, anyhow.
Meeting decisions have their meat: all-in, all-on, all done.

It is worth distinguishing between "real" and "virtual" decision making. One refers to physical, in-person exchanges; the other refers to electronic, email exchanges. One is real time, in the same time and space; the other is over time, across multiple inputs and locations. For clarity, it makes sense to refer to only the first as a meeting. The second is a process.

There is a big difference between a decision taken through direct interaction, where the outcome reflects an interactive discussion and benefits from shared deliberations, vs. one reached through spaced out, drawn-out iterations. Both have their efficiencies. An in-person meeting decision has the virtue of being all-views-on-deck-and-done, but also means that decision-making members have to show up (usually physically in the room, but potentially also "present" via video or audio connection). By contrast, an electronic decision process lets members respond from wherever, whenever, and however (lounging in the sun on my cell phone, sand included, if I care to interrupt my beach weekend), or not at all. Meetings are high interaction but high cost, while emails are low interaction, low cost.

consensus = deliberative process + decision point

In addition to presenting these two decision modes, I am also vigorously pitching consensus in this sample clause. It is hands down the way to go for international partnership programs. (>@ BfB: Balance—Preserving Consensus) Consensus decision making is by definition collaborative. The goal is to reach consensus. It puts a premium on recognizing each partner and valuing each voice. It presumes a certain amount of common ground and willingness to work to make up the difference. It refuses to leave objecting views behind. In the spirit of cooperation, while also balancing the needs of individual partners, the most effective means of reaching consensus also allows for shades of gray. At the extreme, each member has an effective veto, if needed. However, each member also has the right to dissent on the record without vetoing, and the right to abstain on the record without deciding. A controversial decision point can be handled first through discussion to try to reach common ground, or if that fails, then through differing positions in the minutes for the record, before it results in a lack of consensus that blocks a decision. This gives the chair and the members a number of iterations and gradations to reach an outcome that can let the partnership proceed as a whole. It ensures sufficient buy-in, however assembled, before proceeding. In this way, consensus decision making is a deliberative process as much as a decision point. (>@ PfP: Decision Making—Consensus)

Electronic decision making is also a process. Like meeting decisions, this modality could be iteratively deliberative, back-and-forth, albeit in a drawn-out way. And yet, no-objection decision making is considered streamlined decision making. An email request goes out asking for any objections by a certain date, and hearing none, the matter is approved at the end of that date. In other words, silence is consent, no words wasted. Not coincidentally, this replicates consensus decision making at meetings—it only takes one to block the approval—since "no objection" is the standard. (>@ PfP: Decision Making—No Objection)

No objection is the Marie Kondo of decision making: decluttered and efficient enough to spark joy.

When Members Miss Meetings

Unless lack of a quorum precludes a meeting from taking place, missing a meeting means missing out. As a result, chairs usually try to schedule well in advance, and committed members try not to miss. Because members usually participate as institutions and have institutional representation, alternates can attend, as needed. This is usually allowed by governing bodies, out of practical necessity, even if it affects continuity. (>@ PfP: Governing Bodies—Characteristics) As for other arrangements, most are subpar. For example:

- *Proxies.* Decision making by proxy, where a member delegates its right to decide to another member, is not recommended. If the point is collaboration, meeting decisions are meant to leverage the collective views of participants, as informed by each other. Proxies, by contrast, interject individual, pre-formed decisions into the mix, disjointed from any deliberations, thus missing the point and potentially disrespecting other partners and their meeting contributions. Particularly for institutional partners that can send alternates, it is better to let other staff fill in.

- *Statements.* Absent members may want to provide statements in advance for the record, but that can raise the same spectre as proxies and is similarly discouraged, especially on controversial topics (and if not controversial, why go to the trouble?). A one-way, lobbed-in statement will be tone deaf to the meeting (and hallway) discourse and dynamics. As a courtesy to fellow partners, it is better to refrain from pre-cooked statements that swoop in out of context and undercut the governing body's deliberative process.

The goal is for institutional members to work toward attendance, including through the accepted use of alternates. And to be clear, if the decision making is by consensus, lack of attendance does not affect the right to approve, but rather the right to object. If an absent member has no objection, and no one else objects, consensus is not affected by that member's absence. No one is even counting. The only thing lost, which of course counts for something, is hearing and sharing the good commentary to support that consensus.

VARIATIONS

Decisions made electronically between meetings are taken on a no-objection basis by Members, <u>unless affirmative consent is required under the terms of this Charter</u>.

Because no-objection decisions equate silence with consent, partners may prefer that certain kinds of decisions—like ones that have legal consequences—be set to a higher bar. The charter can specify that specific types of decisions (for example, approving charter amendments) require express email confirmation from each member. Requiring this affirmative consent means a lack of objection (silence) is not enough. The point is to safeguard each member's interests and make sure an overlooked email does not result in an unintended approval. (>@ BfB: Annotated Charter—Representatives)

No-objection decision processes are handled by the Secretariat <u>based on a [reasonable] [two-week] review period</u>.

How long should a no-objection review period last? The secretariat can use its discretion, or the partners can prescribe a minimum duration. A "reasonable" review period is assumed, if not otherwise specified, but opinions may differ on what is reasonable. Members may prefer to be explicit, since pressures can easily conspire to shorten periods. Two weeks, or ten business days, or three weeks to facilitate constituencies (>@ PfP: Governing Bodies—Composition—Constituencies), are common. Adding a fixed time frame should not, however, become a cumbersome constraint. Having everything ready two weeks prior to a meeting may be no small feat for a secretariat, which typically relies on inputs from multiple sources. For urgent matters, a little leeway may be in order. Rather than cancel a meeting, a mandatory time frame can be waived by the governing body if circumstances merit. Technically, this waiver itself is subject to no objection—as in "this no-objection request will run [five days], if there is no objection to the shortened review period." A member could block a decision by objecting to the shortened period, but a tuned-in secretariat can usually tell when to ask for leeway.

The Governing Body may not [meet] [make decisions] unless a quorum of [number] Members is present.

Do governing body meetings need a quorum, meaning a minimum number of participants to take decisions? This depends on how formal and prescriptive partners want to be. A quorum requirement typically does not make it into the charter because:

- *A quorum is usually unnecessary if participation is fungible and representatives for partner institutions (not individuals) can show up as alternates.*
- *The chair or secretariat that schedules meetings is unlikely to proceed if not enough participants are able to attend.*
- *If participation by video or audio is allowed, more member exigencies can be accommodated.*
- *Quorums do not apply to no-objection decision making, for which all members are taken to be "present."*

If partners nonetheless want to add a quorum clause, it can specify a minimum portion of all members (like two-thirds) or split out minimums for certain categories (like two-thirds of all donors). Once set, however, those in attendance cannot very well waive a quorum requirement, since lack of a quorum precludes decisions, presumably including waivers. Not to mention that those absent are the ones who would likely object. In practice, if the partnership program is functioning well, cooperative partners usually know not to meet or make decisions unless there is enough participation to proceed, with or without a quorum.

If a decision item is not approved, it can be rescinded, modified, or repeated.

This is another it-goes-without-saying clause, but partnerships programs may like to say it anyhow. Either way, it is good to know that all options continue even after defeat. This is not a case where no means no way, no how.

> For partnership programs that convene to coordinate and collaborate, meetings are for more than decisions.

Should governing body decisions be by in-person meeting or by electronic email? While some decisions may lend themselves to one mode more than the other, there is no rule that dictates which one to use when. Partners usually decide to have both in-person and email modes available and then manage individual decisions as they best fit the circumstances. This includes the ability of even a single member to "object" to a no-objection request in order to push the topic to a meeting, so it can be more fully presented and discussed before decided (as in "we object for purposes of presenting the matter for decision at the next meeting"). Partners can alternatively decide that certain topics should always be decided at meetings (like funding allocations). They can even rely entirely on meetings to make their decisions, although that is a risky strategy in this day and age. The opposite is also possible. A partnership program with especially light governance can hold no meetings and handle all business electronically. Of course, what gets lost without meetings is the human factor. Decision points are often the culmination of sharing, learning, deliberation, and rumination—things partnership programs are especially good for.

CONSIDERATIONS

Should governing body decisions be by consensus or vote? Striving for consensus is usually worth the effort. Most international partnership programs seek to coordinate, collaborate, harmonize, and legitimize. Proceeding with the full approval of all decision-making members supports those goals in ways that fractional voting with minority dissents cannot. Even partnership programs that have formal voting mechanisms typically seek consensus before voting as a last resort. But if voting proves absolutely necessary, what does that say about the strength of the objection? If partners are partnership-minded, it should never be necessary to forcibly plow forward and leave dissenting voices on the stretch. That is bound to take a toll on harmony and stability, without which the program may not be partnering for long. (>@ PfP: Decision Making—Voting)

Where do observers fit into no-objection decision making? It is good collaborative practice to copy standing observers on no-objection decision requests. This keeps everyone on the same page for governing body business, especially if the decision has implications for the observer's operations or sets the stage for future deliberations. It also lets observers be part of the discourse. Once cc'ed, they can provide information or contribute opinions as part of the deliberative process, even if they do not determine outcomes. The idea is that the collaborative member-observer dynamics allowed in meetings can be replicated in electronic decision making.

If we "endorse" something, are we being a decision-making or advisory body? It is not uncommon to see this mismatch: an advisory body with endorsement roles. Unless the endorsement is purely discretionary, which is unlikely, these roles are more decision-making than advisory. Let's say a strategic plan is proposed for governing body consideration, on the agenda for endorsement. Does the plan need the endorsement to become operative? Can the governing body keep it from going into effect? If so, then the governing body is making a decision, not just advising. Advisory bodies may be given gratuitous endorsement roles, if they are just rubber stamps. However, endorsement of results frameworks, annual work plans, project proposals, and other operative content is usually taken to be meaningful. When asked to endorse, if partners can choose not to endorse, that would make an endorsing governing body a decision-making body.

MEETINGS

17. *Governing Body Meetings.* The Governing Body meets at least annually and may meet more frequently. Governing Body meeting locations, dates, and agendas are proposed by the Secretariat and determined by the Chair in consultation with the Members.

EXPLANATIONS

While potentially helpful for clarity, this section is not essential; you can do without it. Meetings can occur more organically, and scheduling specifics can be decided from meeting to meeting. The secretariat can cue the chair and members on what is needed, when, and how. That said, a governing body that prefers regularity and appreciates predictability can benefit from base expectations around meetings, whether they appear in the charter or elsewhere. (>@ BfB: A Taxonomy of Trust Fund Agreements—Complementary Documents)

In defining these basic rules of the road, partners can remember to balance clarity with flexibility. Whatever parameters are set, like lead times or deadlines, partners usually understand that they can be collectively waived as needed. Urgent situations arise, circumstances crowd in, and the last thing members want is to be held hostage to their own rules. A modicum of reasonableness can accompany any effort to conduct partnership business without undermining integrity.

One point of flexibility can be around agenda setting. Unless the secretariat and chair see a need to cap agenda items and control the clock, meetings can open with a request for "any other business" (AOB) that members want to raise, or such a request may have been communicated in the lead-up to the meeting. These AOB topics can then be handled under the chair's leadership at opportune times during the meeting. Does the topic lend itself to impromptu consideration? Would members have wanted more time to review and prepare? Is a decision point involved? Is it just a point of information, or a chance to tee something up for later consideration? Answers to these questions let the chair determine how to handle the additional item, knowing the AOB slot takes advantage of having everyone together and lets members feel more directly engaged and empowered.

A competent chair can encourage active engagement and manage agreed adjustments.

VARIATIONS

There are many variations on this theme, and each partnership program has a different sense of how to organize its meetings. (>@ PfP: Governing Bodies) By way of example, here are a few alternatives/additions to consider:

- The Governing Body meets at the invitation of the Chair with reasonable notice.
- Governing Body meeting locations and dates are determined at each meeting for the next meeting.
- The Governing Body is expected to meet semi-annually initially and may meet less frequently over time.
- Meeting participation is in person, including through video or audio connections.
- Members may request items to be put on the agenda by written notice to the Secretariat at least [three weeks] prior to the meeting.
- Meeting materials, including the agenda, are circulated at least [two weeks] prior to the meeting.

CONSIDERATIONS

How often does the governing body want to meet? The frequency of meetings is usually a direct reflection of the governing body's roles and responsibilities. Normally a governing body meets to conduct business, so if there is nothing to do, it need not incur the costs of meeting. If it can do things via email, it also need not convene. If it wants to keep a short leash on the secretariat, or if it wants to share experiences or generate lessons learned, it may want to come together more frequently. If things are starting out bit by bit, or partners are new to each other, that may justify more meetings in the beginning and fewer later.

Prepped partners make better decisions.

How much advance distribution of meeting materials should members get? Preparing for a meeting can be as important as the meeting itself. Members who carry decision-making responsibility can do so only if they know meeting times well enough in advance to block their calendars, and if they receive agenda and background information in enough time to do a diligent review. With institutional membership, diligent review often means a broad review within the organization, which can take time and extra coordination. Governing bodies with constituency representation also need lead times for coordination within each constituency. Setting minimum expectations for pre-meeting distributions in writing can help provide accountability and prevent slippage over time.

OTHER BODIES

18.   [optional] [*Other Bodies—name of body or element*]. [provide description]

EXPLANATIONS

One governing body is usually enough shared governance for an international partnership program. However, there may be good reasons to add components, like ones listed under the Variations, that complement the work of the primary decision-making body, including to:

- Enable greater inclusion and buy-in
- Create momentum and visibility
- Harness technical expertise
- Secure political and financial support
- Generate technical and issue-focused inputs
- Engage the private sector separately
- Share the governing body's workload
- Benefit from partners' comparative advantages

> **Added components add complexity and cost.**

To be sure, adding a component always adds complexity. (>@ PfP: Ten Tried and True Tips—Keep It Simple) At a minimum, it forces a line-drawing and relationship-defining exercise. For example, how does this component relate to the governing body, the secretariat, the trustee? What primary or secondary responsibilities does this component have? It is important that all structural elements of a partnership program be clearly positioned in relation to each other: first base, second base, coach, referee, support bench, and so on.

Added components also add cost. (>@ PfP: Trustee Types—Trustee Costs) In the case of added bodies that hold meetings, more convening results in costs for more participant travel and secretariat support, which is also the cost of being taken away from doing other things. Institutional partners may be leery of taking on bigger time commitments. Since time is money, however, partners also have to decide between providing more staff (for example, seconded to the supporting entity), other in-kind contributions (like meeting space), or simply more funding (perhaps to pay for expert consultants). It is not obvious that added components cost more than other kinds of support, but cost will likely always be a factor.

Whatever the added complexity and cost, the gains in broader participation, deeper knowledge, greater work span, increased activity, improved efficiency, and heightened visibility may nonetheless justify bringing more components into the mix.

VARIATIONS

Merely by way of example:

Example: [high-level stakeholder meeting] The Partnership Meeting is a high-level forum for mutual accountability to mobilize and sustain coordination, political momentum, and effective visibility. It enables a review of progress and challenges, generates lessons learned, and promotes consultation, collaboration, resource mobilization, and advocacy. The Partnership Meeting takes place every second year, or as otherwise decided by the Governing Body, usually in conjunction with Governing Body meetings. Participation in the Partnership Meeting is by invitation of the Chair of the Governing Body, with support of the Secretariat. The Chair of the Governing Body also chairs the Partnership Meeting. The Secretariat provides overall support and organization of the Partnership Meeting.

Example: [annual forum] The Partnership Forum is an annual platform open to all interested stakeholders to improve awareness of relevant policies, activities, and issues related to the Partnership Program's Mission and Objectives. The Partnership Forum promotes dialogue on key aspects of the Partnership Program strategy, policy, implementation, risks, and results. Participants may include country beneficiaries, multilateral organizations, academic and training institutions, nongovernmental organizations, civil society and community-based organizations, private foundations, and private sector companies. The Convener of the Partnership Forum is selected by the Governing Body and works closely with the Secretariat to organize the Partnership Forum, which is usually held in conjunction with a Governing Body meeting. Following the Partnership Forum, the Convener provides a report of the proceedings to the Governing Body and the Secretariat.

Example: [governing body committees] [working groups] [task forces] The Governing Body may establish standing or ad hoc committees (Committees) [or Working Groups/Task Forces] to facilitate the handling of its business. They are established through terms of reference (TOR) prepared by the Secretariat and approved by the Governing Body, which also approves the Chair [selected from among the Members]. Committees are not decision-making, but report to the Governing Body and may provide reports or recommendations consistent with their terms of reference. [Participants may be from the Partnership Program or from outside, consistent with the TOR.] The Secretariat provides administrative support to Committees.

Example: [technical advisory committee] The Technical Advisory Committee (TAC) promotes and coordinates technical aspects and activities of the Partnership Program. It supports the Governing Body, with administrative support from the Secretariat, and follows terms of reference prepared by the Secretariat and approved by the Governing Body. It consists of designated, expert representatives of Members and Observers that are accepted by the TAC Chair, who is selected by the Governing Body [from among its participants].

VARIATIONS

More examples:

Example: [private sector advisory council] The Private Sector Advisory Council (PSAC) is a consultative council that brings in private sector views to inform and enhance Partnership Program activities. It supports the Governing Body, with administrative support from the Secretariat, and follows terms of reference prepared by the Secretariat and approved by the Governing Body. It consists of private sector representatives convened by the PSAC Chair, who is selected by the Governing Body [from among its participants]. [Participation is based on a general principle of open access and avoidance of selective advantage among competitors. Private sector participants are expected to comply with a code of conduct adopted by the Governing Body.]

Example: [local coordination platforms] To promote engagement, inputs, and capacity building of affected communities, Local Consultative Committees (LCCs) that report to the Governing Body may be formed by local leaders on the basis of terms of reference prepared by the Secretariat and approved by the Governing Body. LCCs can support the Governing Body by (i) identifying local needs; (ii) consulting with affected communities; and (iii) providing advice to the Governing Body on relevant proposals. Meeting logistics, decision making, and other terms are determined by each LCC. [A representative of each LCC may participate in the Governing Body as an Observer.]

Example: [roster of experts] A roster of experts (RoE) provides expert advice for the selection of grant proposals. It supports the Governing Body's funding decisions and is managed by the Secretariat under terms of reference prepared by the Secretariat and approved by the Governing Body. The RoE is funded by the Trust Fund. [Information about the individuals selected to be part of the RoE is published on the Partnership Program website.]

CONSIDERATIONS

Does the partnership program need any of these extras? Partners may prefer streamlined and low-cost partnership structures. It may, however, be useful to keep an open mind about structural ways to bolster sustainability, efficiency, and impact, particularly if that means engaging a broader range of stakeholders. (>@ PfP: Structure—Broader Context) Although not all costs and benefits are easily calculated, proposed structural add-ons are best evaluated to make sure they are well-designed and worth having.

Do these extras need to be in the charter? Not necessarily. Partnership programs may want to keep things simple and flexible. Events, in particular, are often put on without being put in. A roster of experts can be readily set up without a charter reference, as can working groups and task forces that come and go. If, however, a structural add-on has an essential role, it is more transparent to mention it. That is especially true with structural elements that are fixed governance features, like a technical advisory committee on which the governing body relies for expertise and legitimacy, or elements that cover key relationships, like a private sector council that strikes a visible bridge to the corporate sector. If the feature responds to donor or stakeholder concerns, as with local platforms that allow greater direct input or a roster of experts that brings added credibility, that also speaks in favor of being mentioned in the charter. Ultimately, if the charter is treated as a living, breathing document (>@ PfP: Like Rock, Like Water), features can also be added or subtracted over time.

SECRETARIAT

19.   *Secretariat Context.* The Secretariat provides [overall] [administrative] support to the Partnership Program and the Governing Body [and other bodies].

EXPLANATIONS

In general, as with governing bodies, and in some ways as their foil, secretariats range across a spectrum of possibilities, from more to less hands-on, from broad to limited responsibility. If the secretariat is strong, the governing body can rely on it, even to the point of becoming a secondary (for example, advisory) appendage. If, however, the governing body is strong, drawing strength from its member engagement, it can keep the secretariat in a minimal support role. Then again, a strong governing body and a strong secretariat often go together. (>@ PfP: International Partnership Programs—Central Support—Strong Secretariats)

Not all partnership programs identify the secretariat role separately from other support roles like the trustee, in which case separate secretariat clauses would not be included. In fact, in those cases, there is a good chance there won't be a charter either. However, even in those cases, there are secretariat-type functions that support the governing body and other collective elements that need to be resourced and would be worth describing somewhere. (>@ PfP: Structure—Collectivizing)

The scope and strength of the secretariat directly correlates to the amount of funding and resources made available for its support. This is often referred to as "core support" because it operates at the core of the partnership program. Core support usually comes from unrestricted funding that is made generically available, instead of being restricted to specific downstream activities. (>@ PfP: Trade-Offs—The Central Harmonization Spectrum) In a successful partnership program, partners fund not only their pet projects and areas of special interest, but also foot the core support bill, whether through sufficient unrestricted contributions, membership fees, or other ways to contribute.

Like Trustee, Like Secretariat

Adding a trust fund to a partnership program tends to have a major impact on the position of the secretariat. The secretariat invariably gets defined as a factor of the trustee, either fully integrated (with the full trustee) or equally limited (with the limited trustee). (>@ PfP: Trustee Types) It should be the other way around, but unfortunately, it is all too common for partners to see the partnership program in the trust fund, rather than the trust fund in the partnership program. A secretariat that is integrated into a one-stop-shop trustee usually reflects the overall fee or cost structure of the trust fund. Its functions may simply show up as activities to be financed by the trust fund, rather than being a secretariat per se. By contrast, in international platforms, the secretariat is usually separated out and distinctly defined, like the trustee, with cost recovery through a separate secretariat budget or as part of approved partnership program work plans.

Contrasting the Secretariat Support of Our Two Mighty Oaks

The two mighty oaks of trust-funded partnership programs—one-stop-shops and international platforms (>@ PfP: Typology)—reflect different kinds of secretariat support as a study in contrasts.

In one-stop-shops, the supporting entity provides a full support package that normally includes an active and comprehensive secretariat function. In some cases, this function is so seamlessly wrapped into the trustee function that only the trustee is named. In other cases, especially when the partnership program seeks visibility, the secretariat tends to be a clear focal point, often with a well-positioned secretariat head, as an engine for shared governance, branding, advocacy, and other communications. Recognizing this kind of secretariat as a separate component in the charter, with ascribed roles and responsibilities, including in relation to the governing body, trustee, and other elements, makes sense.

In international platforms, a strong secretariat is often needed to manage major initiatives on the international stage. This usually comes in conjunction with a strong governing body and dispersed responsibilities to other partners. In this context, with so many strong and active players, it is even more important to carefully delineate the secretariat's place within the overall partnership program.

- Excessive secretariat influence can infringe—or be perceived as infringing—on *downstream fiduciaries*. Sensitivity to these dynamics is one of the main drivers for limiting the role of the international platform secretariat. By making it administrative rather than substantive, the secretariat can keep out of the messy middle, while keeping a level playing field across all downstream fiduciaries. (>@ PfP: Ten Tried and True Tips—Be Clean)

- An unleashed secretariat can encroach—or be perceived as encroaching—upon the primacy of the *governing body*. If the governing body expects to be in charge, the secretariat is expected to defer, taking rather than giving instructions. If the governing body is in the lead, the secretariat is asked to follow. This does not mean the secretariat is merely reactive. Even a dominant governing body can benefit from a proactive secretariat. But it does mean a supportive secretariat operates carefully within limits, without overstepping its bounds.

VARIATIONS

Here are some helpful additions for partnership programs that rely on secretariat support from a supporting entity partner (>@ PfP: Secretariats—Embedded, Inhouse Secretariats):

- The Secretariat is located in the [supporting entity].
- The Secretariat is headed by a [Program Manager] and consists of staff hired by the [supporting entity], as well as staff seconded to the [supporting entity] by other Partnership Program participants.
- Secretariat staff operate under [supporting entity] management in accordance with the [supporting entity's] applicable policies and procedures.
- Costs of the Secretariat are covered by the Trust Fund [as approved by the Governing Body].
- The Secretariat collaborates with the Trustee as needed for the Trustee to carry out its responsibilities.

> The secretariat reports managerially to management and informationally to partners.

CONSIDERATIONS

How much core support and dedicated staff are needed for the partnership program? Many partnership programs pride themselves on having a "lean" secretariat, preferring to put funds into downstream activities, rather than upstream and central support. But many partners also want a large presence on the international stage, which needs publicizing and nurturing; or they want active decision making, which means good prep work and project flow; or they want a diversified structure with more players and functions that need more coordinating. If partners want a strong brand, a visible profile, frequent governing body meetings, a mix of elements, and lots of collective outputs—if they consider that critical to reaching their goals and achieving impact—they will need a well-resourced and resourceful secretariat.

Is it better to have an empowered or limited secretariat? There is no one right answer; it always depends, including with respect to the one-stop-stop/international platform dichotomy described here. Beyond the specific scope the secretariat is given, it also helps to understand that the secretariat role tends to absorb whatever other roles are not doing. For example, if the governing body slacks off (maybe the chair has her attention elsewhere), the whole partnership program may end up in the doldrums unless the secretariat fills in what is missing—the secretariat in rescue mode. (>@ PfP: Ten Tried and True Tips—Be (A)ware) Similarly, if resources fall short, the secretariat's ability to rally interest through a vigorous publicity campaign or popular website may make the difference in donor interest—the secretariat in custodial mode. (>@ PfP: Custodial Effect) For better or worse, whether empowered or not, the secretariat tends to pick up where others don't.

How does the secretariat relate to other governance elements? Indeed, this is the main question. Is the secretariat in the lead, or the governing body? Is the secretariat distinct from or integral to the trustee? Is the secretariat head second string to the governing body chair or a figurehead in her own right? Will a strong secretariat add to or detract from strong branding? Who makes sure the partnership program is productive? Where the answers come out on such questions sets the tone and texture of how the secretariat is defined and developed.

SECRETARIAT ROLES AND RESPONSIBILITIES

20. *Secretariat Roles and Responsibilities.* The roles and responsibilities of the Secretariat include [by way of example, pick and edit as relevant]:

a) *[hands-on]* Providing overall support to the Partnership Program, including carrying out the Partnership Program's annual work plan, managing its day-to-day operations, supporting the Governing Body, and generally facilitating the work of the Partnership Program; [Any matters for decision by the Governing Body are initially directed through the Secretariat for review;]

a) *[hands-off]* Providing administrative and coordination support to the Partnership Program; [The Secretariat does not intend to encroach on the authority and prerogative of the Governing Body, which remains responsible for the substance of its decision making, nor does it intend to overlap with or act counter to the role of the Trustee;]

[Choose between the hands-on and hands-off versions, as described in the Variations.]

b) Arranging meetings of the Governing Body, including preparing the agenda and compiling supporting documentation;

c) Maintaining records of Governing Body business, including meeting minutes and no-objection decisions;

d) Participating in the Governing Body as an Observer [through the Secretariat Head or alternate];

e) Preparing annual Partnership Program work plans and indicative budgets for Governing Body review and [approval] [comment];

f) Pre-screening funding proposals for compliance with Partnership Program requirements;

g) Managing the roster of experts for feedback on funding proposals for Governing Body review;

h) Distributing funding proposals for Governing Body review and [decision] [comment];

i) Distributing financial reports for Governing Body review and comment;

j) [Preparing] [Compiling] and distributing progress reports for Governing Body review and comment;

k) [Coordinating implementation of] [Implementing] the annual work plan;

l) Preparing the Partnership Program's annual report [for Governing Body [approval] [review]];

m) Organizing the annual stakeholders forum in consultation with [the Chair of] the Governing Body;

n) Coordinating and supporting any [standing committees] [working groups] [task forces];

o) Managing the Partnership Program website;

p) [Managing] [Coordinating] relations and communications for the Partnership Program with national authorities, the media, stakeholders, and partner organizations;

q) Facilitating the sharing of data and development of lessons learned from Partnership Program activities;

r) Coordinating with the Trustee as needed to carry out their respective responsibilities;

s) Supporting resource mobilization efforts for the Partnership Program;

t) [Preparing] [Coordinating] background notes and other materials for Governing Body business;

u) Commissioning [periodic] [midterm] reviews and independent evaluations of the Partnership Program, including as requested by the Governing Body; and

v) Presenting to the Governing Body for review and decision any proposed amendments to this Charter.

It's a long list. As evident from this lineup, there is a lot the secretariat can do—and that's not even all. Not every secretariat will do all the things mentioned here, but most will do much more. The Charter list of roles and responsibilities is necessarily a fraction of what all will come the secretariat's way. (>@ PfP: Custodial Effect) It is particularly helpful to list items that the governing body or trustee expect to rely on or that the supporting entity wants to carve out for itself. It is also helpful to draft broadly without constraining the secretariat's support, but not so broadly as to give the governing body or anyone else a blank check on telling the secretariat what to do. The scope of the secretariat's responsibilities should rest comfortably within its overall role, the supporting entity's internal policies and procedures, and available resources—time, staff, expertise, and funding being the usual constraints.

As with the governing body, clarity is key. Here, too, itemizing secretariat roles and responsibilities sets shared expectations, including the willingness by partners to rely on and fund secretariat support. The two extensive "roles and responsibilities" lists in the charter, for the secretariat and the governing body, operate in tandem. Virtually every governing body role can be considered and articulated in relation to the secretariat. This interplay also relates to other governing components, such as the trustee. Each secretariat role should be positioned in the broader context.

CONSIDERATIONS

How much needs to be explicitly listed? As with the governing body list of roles and responsibilities, how much is spelled out depends in part on shared preferences and expectations. A useful gauge is whether the list adequately clarifies the degree to which the governing body plans to defer to and rely on the secretariat for partnership program business. An item need not be listed for the secretariat to take it up; indeed, it is impossible to list out everything the secretariat may be called upon to do. (>@ ibid.) However, the itemization should be sufficient to reflect a spirit or tendency as to how the relationships should play out. Read in conjunction with other lists and the Secretariat Context section, the secretariat list should frame the relative division of labor, influence, and control. The governing body chair and head of the secretariat can then navigate specific situations over time.

Are the secretariat's roles and responsibilities a good fit for the secretariat's supporting entity? The negotiated set of roles and responsibilities for the secretariat lies at the nexus between what governing body members want and what the supporting entity is willing to do. (>@ BfB: Constitutive Documents— What to Watch For—Embedded, Inhouse Secretariats) For an active, coherent, and sustained work program, partners will need the secretariat to pick up where the governing body leaves off. More than partners may realize, the secretariat is both glue and magnet, particularly when it serves as the legal entity undergirding the partnership program. As glue, the secretariat holds the partnership program together through its coordinating and recordkeeping functions. It is typically the only place with dedicated partnership program staff. As magnet, the secretariat attracts outside interest and input, usually intentionally. With the best overview and overall sense of the partnership program, it provides the impetus for branding and publicizing the partnership program. Its magnetic nature also makes it the first contact for queries, complaints and claims, typically addressed to the supporting entity with legal status and potentially deep pockets. If issues arise for the partnership program, the secretariat is bound to feel the fallout, and that translates directly to its supporting entity. All of which to say that embedded secretariats come part and parcel with their supporting entities, all in one. The supporting entity more than matters when defining secretariat roles and responsibilities.

Is the supporting entity managing its exposure? The risk profile of the supporting entity may call for preventive and protective measures. This includes having the secretariat act as a gatekeeper, having the last say or rights of consent, assuming drafting responsibility for partnership documents, and occupying the chair position. The secretariat may be a support function on the back bench, but carefully chosen features can strengthen the glue and fortify the magnet, while also providing safeguards.

VARIATIONS

There are a number of things to think about when itemizing secretariat roles and responsibilities, including:

Hands-on or hands-off?

Example: [one-stop-shop; comprehensive role and broad responsibility] Providing overall support to the Partnership Program, including carrying out the Partnership Program's annual work plan, managing its day-to-day operations, supporting the Governing Body, and generally facilitating the work of the Partnership Program; [Any matters for decision by the Governing Body are directed through the Secretariat for review and confirmation prior to consideration by the Governing Body.]

> *One-stop-shops are full support models, and the secretariat can be the embodiment of that. Here the first sentence sets up a custodial role on the part of the secretariat, as a major support function with default responsibilities across the board. In this approach, the secretariat can front the trustee role if both are supported by the same entity, making the secretariat an outward-facing, inward-operating hub of the partnership program.*

Example: [international platform; limited, coordinating responsibility] Providing administrative and coordination support to the Partnership Program; [The Secretariat does not intend to encroach on the authority and prerogative of the Governing Body, which remains responsible for the substance of its decision making, nor does it intend to overlap with or act counter to the role of the Trustee.]

> *The first sentence may be sufficient. The second sentence can be added for clarity and emphasis. It is especially valuable where expectations tend in the other direction. Sometimes saying the negative (what something is not) is as important as saying the positive (what something is). (>@ BfB: Deft Drafting—The Art of Writing—Stating the Negative) Inserting a principle as a guidepost for behavior also anticipates future situations where judgment calls may need to be made. A secretariat that thinks its role is being stretched uncomfortably far could legitimately push back on the basis of such a statement.*

Trustee or secretariat?

Trust-funded partnership programs can be pretty sloppy about articulating trustee vs. secretariat roles. Some refer only to the trustee, which then covers all partnership-facing coordination roles. Some refer primarily to the secretariat, which then subsumes implementation roles. Mostly this works out if both aspects are provided by the same supporting entity. In that case, the actual division of labor can be somewhat fluid. And more generally, there is room for leeway, depending on preferences. Should the trustee send its financial reports directly, or do partners prefer to get all partnership program materials straight from the secretariat, especially when multiple reports can be efficiently combined or compiled by the secretariat into one email or one report? (>@ BfB: The Annotated Charter—Trustee Roles and Responsibilities)

That said, the differences between the two roles are still worth appreciating. (>@ PfP: Secretariats—Lessons Learned) Accordingly, some discipline is still called for. Why does it matter? Because one role is more inward-looking, the other role is more outward-looking; one is a contracted principal, the other is an agent for the partnership. (>@ PfP: Supporting Entities—Baselines)

Preparing or compiling?

This is an example of the difference between substantive and administrative support, reflective of the difference between one-stop-shops and international platforms. A hands-on secretariat, as in a one-stop-shop, may have drafting or other content responsibility for background papers, action plans, strategies, progress reports, annual reports, and more. By contrast, a less hands-on secretariat, as in an international platform, may just compile content from others, especially if others are handling the downstream activities or if the assignment requires outside expertise. Limited secretariats (like those that go with limited trustees of international platforms) or more administrative secretariats are normally advised to be vigilant about keeping to a circumscribed compilation role and avoiding expectations that it will take care of content analysis, gap filling, or other substantive shortcomings. (>@ PfP: Supporting Entities—Duality and Balance)

Compliance checks?

Some governing bodies stay high level with framing decisions (for example, endorsing strategies, approving annual work plans, or setting criteria; >@ BfB: The Annotated Charter—Governing Body Roles and Responsibilities), while letting the secretariat (or trustee) make the project-level, case-by-case funding decisions. Other governing bodies like to decide what is to be funded, which can put them deep into the nitty gritty. To help with that, the secretariat can take up a "pre-screening" role.

This secretariat pre-screening is effectively a compliance role. The framework is prescribed by the partners (for example, through an agreed template or using selection criteria), and the secretariat's role is to apply those terms. Whether that application requires technical expertise depends on how the terms are presented. (For example, the difference between selecting projects that serve understaffed school systems vs. systems with student-teacher ratios above 20:1.) The responsibility placed on the secretariat in this role should be matched by the type of staff and amount of budget needed to meet the governing body's expectations. Even a limited secretariat can have a comfortably "limited" (non-substantive) role in making sure forms are filled out, process requirements are followed, packages are complete, and objective criteria have been met.

Results focus?

Donors and other partners are increasingly pressing for results, to both improve fund use and justify further funding. This emphasis on results emerges in performance criteria and results frameworks, at both program and project levels. It also affects the secretariat. First, if the secretariat has direct implementation responsibility (for example, implementing all or part of the work plan), it becomes directly responsible for results. However, this responsibility is not a performance guarantee, as with the trustee. (>@ PfP: Trust Funds—Contributions) There is no breach for failure to produce results, as long as the funds were properly used, and the effort was made. Second, if the secretariat has a coordination role for other partners' results, it may be tasked with compiling progress reports or other results information. This, too, is necessarily a limited responsibility. If the reports do not come in, the secretariat is only the messenger and cannot fabricate the other partners' results. These distinctions should be reflected in the secretariat's responsibilities, so they stay within the scope of what the secretariat can feasibly do.

TRUSTEE

21   [if relevant] *Trustee Context.* The [Trustee entity] acts as the trustee (Trustee) of the Trust Fund. Contributions to the Trust Fund are made under contribution agreements entered into by the Trustee with each donor. Trustee staff operate, and Trust Fund operations are conducted, under [Trustee entity] management in accordance with the [Trustee entity's] applicable policies and procedures.

Asking for your forbearance, this trustee discussion gets pretty technical. The trustee is engaged by the partners, but serves its own institution, which means we have to get into some nuances. Before diving into the technicalities, however, remember that only partnership programs directly supported by trust funds need to think about adding Trustee sections to their charters. If that is not your case, you can gleefully skip ahead.

EXPLANATIONS

When trust funds are involved, the trustee deserves a mention. Compared to the lengthy entries for the governing body and secretariat, however, the trustee gets but a cameo. Most of what governs the trustee relationship goes not into the charter, but into the contribution agreements under which funds flow to the trustee. This makes sense. Donors do not give funds in the absence of legally binding terms; the two go together. As a result, the charter is not really the place to elaborate on the trustee. Instead, the contribution agreement is where each donor wants to hold onto what the trustee is obligated to do. It is also where the trustee wants to be clear about what it agrees to do and no more. Trustee standard terms are usually considered non-negotiable and baked into standard agreements, unlike charters that offer some fluidity. (>@ PfP: Like Rock, Like Water) And because agreement terms carry liability (the trustee can end up in breach), they relate to operations that need system controls, predictability, and deliberate management—without lots of waivers, deviations, and exceptions. This is all in the four corners of the agreement. (>@ PfP: Use of Funds—Four Corners of the Agreement) As to the key point for our purposes here: What shows up in the contribution agreements is best not repeated in the charter. (>@ BfB: Agile Alignment—Step-by-Step Alignment for Trust-Funded Partnership Programs, #5)

So far, so good; all trustee- and trust fund–related terms appear in the fund flow agreements. Where this falls short, however, is where partnership program governance—shared governance—involves players beyond the parties to the fund flow agreements, in other words, beyond the trustee and the donors. These other participants, like recipients and beneficiaries, international organizations, NGOs, and CSOs, end up outside the scope of the agreed terms. Good news: The partners can fill this gap with a charter. The charter provides a common space where all relevant terms for all relevant parties can be agreed. (>@ BfB: Constitutive Documents—What's So Great About Charters)

What terms are relevant? Trustee relevance vis-à-vis charters turns broadly on governance and specifically on roles and responsibilities. Relevant elements are those in the nexus between the trustee and the partnership. This includes partnership program reliance on funding vehicles, trustee responsibilities to the governing body, processes around fund allocations (who decides on what terms), and fiduciary structures that affect the partnership program's risk profile. Some of this may appear in earlier Funding sections. And some is too detailed (better for the operations manual) or too donor-specific (better for bilateral agreements) to show up here.

Also relevant is the trustee's relationship to its own institution, whose operating environment applies. This institutional relationship is at least as important for the trustee as for the secretariat because the trustee is contracted with direct obligations, as a principal acting in its own right on its own behalf. Ultimately, the trustee needs a degree of operating independence—an arm's-length relationship (>@ PfP: Trustee Types—Trustee Entity)—as a fiduciary function that is qualitatively different from the secretariat as a support function.

As to scope of engagement, much like the governing body and the secretariat, the trustee can be positioned on a spectrum of possibilities, from more to less hands-on, from broad to limited responsibility. This range is played out in the Variations based on our two identifiable poles at either end of the spectrum: one-stop-shops and international platforms. (>@ PfP: Trustee Types)

VARIATIONS

Example: [one-stop-shop full trustee with integrated secretariat] The [Trustee entity] acts as the Trustee of the Trust Fund <u>and carries out the Partnership Program's annual work plan, manages its day-to-day operations, supports the Governing Body, and generally facilitates the work of the Partnership Program.</u>

> *Here we have an expanded first sentence that positions the trustee entity's comprehensive role in the one-stop-shop's full support package. These partnership programs may choose not to identify secretariat functions separately from the trustee (with no secretariat mention in the charter), instead wrapping them into the trustee description. The result is a kind of trustee-plus role that goes beyond financial management and fiduciary responsibilities to include shared governance, coordination, and implementation support as well. (BfB: Context—International Trust Funds)*

Example: [international platform with downstream fiduciaries] Contributions to the Trust Fund are made under contribution agreements entered into by the Trustee with each donor, <u>and transfers to [downstream fiduciaries] are made under transfer agreements entered into by the Trustee with each [downstream fiduciary]</u>.

> *Here we have an expanded second sentence that refers to both upstream and downstream trustee relationships to reflect the more modular fiduciary responsibilities characteristic of international platforms. International platforms are typically more customized and require more extensive establishment terms than presented in this charter, including introduction of the downstream fiduciaries as key players with major responsibilities, greater emphasis on governing body functions, and added details around relationships and procedures. This brief addition is but a start. (After the Primer for Partners and this Book for Builders, that would need to be book three . . .)*

Example: [commingled trust fund account] The contribution agreements include common provisions for all contributions to the Trust Fund.

> *This added sentence applies if funds are commingled. (>@ PfP: International Partnership Programs—Pooled Funding) It restates for everyone's edification how commingled funds work. While a clause of this sort is not needed in the charter, it would serve to underscore the importance of having all trust fund donors agree on terms that affect the use of funds and trustee operations. (>@ BfB: A Taxonomy of Trust Fund Agreements) Even if not added to the charter, this is how it should work in practice.*

Example: [cost recovery] Costs of the Trustee are covered by the Trust Fund [as approved by the Governing Body] [and subject to annual reconciliation].

Trustee costs are a subject of great interest to donors, who have to pay them, as well as trustees, who want them covered. Specific fees or cost recovery arrangements usually show up in the contribution agreements and therefore should not be repeated in the charter. However, partners may want to add a cost recovery principle as a benchmark if future expectations exceed the resources provided. The principle may also specify the governing body's role (having a say), along with automatic reconciliation (for trustee comfort). And even if not destined for the charter, mentioning it here may help make sure it gets into the contribution agreements.

Sample Contribution Agreement Clause for Cost Recovery

The Trustee and the Secretariat operate on the basis of full cost recovery. They each annually submit to the Governing Body a budget of anticipated expenses for the subsequent fiscal year. Upon approval by the Governing Body, the Trustee may transfer the respective amounts from the Trust Fund to itself and the Secretariat. Such amounts are then reconciled at the end of the fiscal year based on actual expenses incurred.

There's trust in trustee.

CONSIDERATIONS

Is fiduciary support in place from receipt of funds all the way to end use? Normally, fiduciary responsibility attaches to donor funds at the time of their receipt. Once attached, that responsibility can shift from one party to another, from the original trustee fiduciary to a subsequent downstream fiduciary, as long as the original terms flow through from one to the other, and the donors agree. This is the unbroken chain of fiduciary responsibility (>@ PfP: Use of Funds— Role of the Fiduciary), usually in one of three modes: (1) management of funds in the trust fund account; (2) fund use directly by a fiduciary entity; or (3) monitoring and supervision of fund use by others. These details do not belong in the charter. They are material terms of the contribution agreements. Donors may not insist on this much fiduciary support, but the terms should in any case be transparently agreed prior to the receipt of funds. (>@ BfB: Practical Packaging—The Package Approach to Establishment)

Is the fiduciary framework to be applied adequate for the partners? The short answer is that this depends on what the donors think. Each donor determines its own standards and then looks for fiduciaries that meet them, often relying on the same trustee and other downstream fiduciaries over and over again, as known quantities with proven track records. However, the long answer recognizes that all partners have a stake in how funds that support the partnership program are handled. All partners are joined in the venture, all have associational risk through common exposure under the umbrella brand. (>@ PfP: International Partnership Programs—One Brand) Because there are no universally agreed "international" fiduciary standards, it is not a given that all partners are looking for the same procurement rules, environmental and social safeguards, anti-corruption measures, anti-terrorism requirements, and disclosure practices. For established fiduciaries, like multilateral development banks, most partners are fine relying on their "applicable policies and procedures" to give robust fiduciary comfort. (>@ PfP: Trustee Types—International Platforms—Limited Trustees) However, for other scenarios, it is pertinent to seek a common understanding for all partners, not just donors.

TRUSTEE
ROLES AND RESPONSIBILITIES

22   [if relevant] *Trustee Roles and Responsibilities.* The roles and responsibilities of the Trustee are as defined in the contribution agreements entered into by the Trustee with each of the donors to the Trust Fund, consistent with the [Trustee entity's] applicable policies and procedures. The Trustee participates [as an Observer] in the Governing Body and coordinates with the Secretariat as needed to carry out their respective responsibilities.

EXPLANATIONS

Keep it neat; don't repeat.

As explained under Trustee Context, this is one place in the charter where less is more. In relation to the list of secretariat responsibilities, the trustee's list is notably short. In fact, it is not a list, but effectively a one-sentence cross-reference to the fund flow agreements between the trustee and each donor. The second sentence simply places the trustee in relation to other structural elements of the partnership program.

This brevity does not mean the trustee has fewer responsibilities. To the contrary, the trustee is often the only entity with directly contractualized obligations. This instead reflects the overall effect of the juxtaposed partnership program package of terms. Rather than repeat in the charter what is already covered in the contribution agreements—where trustee obligations are invariably covered—the charter points to those agreements. In part, this recognizes the primacy of contribution agreements over other agreed terms, a hierarchy that reflects the donor's view of the world. It also puts the priority on bilaterally committed funding terms, rather than broader partnership terms, a security that donors usually require. Accordingly, the terms of contribution agreements normally prevail over the terms of the charter, and, if the charter is incorporated by reference, the agreements normally say so. (>@ BfB: Agile Alignment—Step-by-Step Alignment for Trust-Funded Partnership Programs, #9)

In addition, deferring to the contribution agreements means avoiding overlap, confusion, and conflict. Unless the two sets of terms, the agreements and the charter, are absolutely identical, even small variances can give rise to different interpretations and contradictory meanings (as every lawyer knows). Verbatim recitations can be hard to do when the document context and format are as widely disparate as legal agreements and partnership charters tend to be. The one is typically given license to be in legalese, while the other is hopefully in plain English. (>@ PfP: Like Rock, Like Water—Like Rock) And even if the wording is verbatim, why amend text in two places if you can set it up to amend only once? The cleanest and safest route is to avoid repetition wherever possible and cross-refer whenever helpful.

Nota Bene: Remember, though, simply avoiding duplicated terms is not enough. The other part of the exercise is to put terms in the right place to begin with, deliberately choosing between signed agreements (more fixed) and adopted documents (more flexible). (>@ ibid.—Like Water) If, however, terms are placed in the charter to enable efficient amendability and then repeated in the contribution agreements, the need for an added signing exercise just undermined the intended efficiency.

Avoid repetition wherever possible; cross-refer whenever helpful.

As with all else, clarity is key. The fact that so much of what pertains to the trustee resides out of plain view and beyond the control of non-donor partners is a consideration. Since everyone in the partnership program is exposed to how dedicated funding vehicles are structured and what they allow, trustee and trust fund operations do matter across the board. If the partnership program includes more than just the trustee and donors as partners, that may be reason enough to allow one or the other descriptive clause to migrate from the contribution agreements to the charter, especially because those clauses are usually incorporated back into the contribution agreements from whence they came. It also underscores the importance of having the trustee at the table, as a visible conduit to the trust fund for all participants to see and hear.

VARIATIONS

Example: [specific roles and responsibilities] The Trustee compiles periodic updates of the financial status of the Trust Fund for the Governing Body, including all paid and unpaid contributions to the Trust Fund.

> *Although the first rule is no overlaps or repetition between the contribution agreements and the charter, there is discretion on where to put which roles and responsibilities, some in contribution agreements, some in the charter. Ones that affect all partners, not just the trustee and donors, may merit placement in a charter that is owned by all partners. For example, the statement here is a responsibility owed to all of the governing body, not just the donors. Donors may prefer to see this requirement in their signed agreements, but could also agree to a contractualized (incorporated by reference) charter that includes such a statement. Moreover, if partners expect some adjustments over time, high level language, like "periodic updates" instead of specific time frames, can keep terms somewhat open—for example, quarterly in the beginning and biannually after a couple of years. The exact timing can be as agreed with the trustee outside the scope of the charter and maybe memorialized in the minutes of a governing body meeting.*

Example: [pledges] The Trustee compiles periodic updates of the financial status of the Trust Fund for the Governing Body, including all paid and unpaid contributions to the Trust Fund, <u>as well as any additional pledges for the Trust Fund</u>.

> *Some partnership programs conduct replenishment cycles as part of their resource mobilization. This typically involves pledging sessions of a more or less formal nature, during which donors publicly indicate amounts they intend to contribute to the trust fund, with signed contribution agreements to follow. Pledges are not by themselves considered commitments, but have greater visibility and intentionality than more ad hoc funding indications. Pledging sessions, if donors are willing, can create excellent momentum for contributing.*

Example: [limited fiduciary responsibilities, as for international platforms] The Trustee's responsibilities arise with respect to funds deposited in the Trust Fund only during the time they are held by the Trustee, until their transfer from the Trust Fund. The Trustee has no responsibility for (i) the use of funds after they are transferred from the Trust Fund (Transferred Funds); (ii) implementing, monitoring, supervising, evaluating, or providing quality assurance for activities funded by Transferred Funds; (iii) providing financial, progress, results, or impact reporting for activities funded by Transferred Funds; or (iv) any misuse or misprocurement with respect to Transferred Funds.

> *Donors may expect the trustee to watch their funds from receipt to final use. But that is not how limited trustees work. (>@ PfP: Fund Use Responsibility—Transferred (No) Responsibility) To counter full-service expectations, limited trustee roles and responsibilities are best articulated in both the positive and the negative. (>@ BfB: Deft Drafting—The Art of Writing—Stating the Negative) This would be the negative.*

CONSIDERATIONS

Think charter for flexibility and amendability.
Think agreements for standardization and contractualization.

Are there things in the contribution agreements that should be in the charter? For various good reasons, not least donor prerogative, the lion's share of what pertains to the trustee and the trust fund is put in the contribution agreements. But there are also good reasons for putting trustee- and trust fund–related clauses in the charter. Keeping in mind that it should be either/or, charter or agreements, a good rule of thumb is that flexibility and amendability favor the charter, while standardization and contractualization favor the contribution agreements. (>@ PfP: Ten Tried and True Tips—Be Contextual) Another gauge is what pertains to donors and the trustee vs. what pertains to all. If it belongs to the partners as a whole, it should preferably be under the purview of the partners as a whole. That means making it part of the charter and then cross-referencing the charter in the contribution agreements.

Are there activities of the trustee that should belong to the secretariat? At the margin, some activities can belong either to the trustee or the secretariat, depending on who is better positioned. For example, the trustee may be tasked with providing financial reports and audits of the trust fund directly to the governing body, and may already do so for donors through an internet portal, or that distribution job could instead belong to the secretariat along with its other governing body distributions. Whether the trustee's responsibilities are specified in the contribution agreements or the charter, they should be read in tandem with the secretariat's list of responsibilities to watch for gaps and overlaps. (>@ BfB: The Annotated Charter—Secretariat Roles and Responsibilities)

Do the trustee's roles and responsibilities fit the larger partnership program context? Follow the power, follow the money often boils down to the power of the purse. Donors may dominate simply because most partnership programs need their funds. And yet, donor requirements may need tempering within the bigger picture. Are specific donor demands scalable to other donors? Are they absorbable under trustee entity policies and procedures? Are earmarked, restricted funds crowding out the core support needed to ensure a cohesive program? Are targeted results realistic in light of capacity constraints, externalities, politics, and country ownership? Do the implementation modalities leverage robust operating frameworks and safeguard investments? And so on. The negotiated set of roles and responsibilities of the trustee (and any downstream fiduciaries) lies at the nexus between what donors want and fiduciaries can do. For a fully functional trust fund, within a coherent partnership program, the trustee needs enough room to do its thing, donors need enough leeway to get their intended results, and the rest of the partnership program can be a powerful amplification of all that.

MONITORING & EVALUATION

23   *Monitoring and Evaluation Framework.* The Partnership Program's monitoring and evaluation (M&E) approach is designed to support successful execution of the Partnership Program's [annual work plans] [other plan or strategy] and translate the Partnership Program's [mission] [goals] into tangible results. Periodic evidence-based assessments are conducted on the extent to which Partnership Program activities, governance, and other aspects have achieved, or are likely to achieve, stated objectives. Donors are [expected] [encouraged] to manage their M&E needs with respect to the Trust Fund and other Partnership Program funding sources collectively through common processes.

EXPLANATIONS

Monitoring and evaluation is part of the ongoing life cycle of international partnership programs. Partners are accustomed to M&E at the project level (>@ PfP: Trust funds—Disbursements), but can also think of M&E in partnership and program terms. Are the collectives well-positioned? Is the program working? This kind of M&E looks across the structure and portfolio, everything under the brand name, and asks whether things are going well or could go better. (>@ PfP: Risk and Review)

A definitive tome on M&E for international partnership programs is still the detailed 2007 *Sourcebook* prepared by the World Bank's Independent Evaluation Group in connection with the OECD/DAC Network on Development Evaluation. It tells you that evaluations are for learning from experience, providing an objective basis for assessing results, providing accountability in achieving objectives, identifying and disseminating lessons learned, and framing recommendations—all to enhance the relevance and effectiveness of partnership programs, be accountable to political authorities and the general public, and improve the use of resources.

The Achilles heel of M&E is the pressure to do good and do well. Especially when it comes to development aid, if there is no demonstrated global, regional, or local good coming out of the endeavor, or if it cannot be shown that things were done well, partners may not sustain the effort, learn lessons, and try again with improvements. Donors may lose interest, and funding may be diverted, end of story. This disheartening prospect can inspire slanted reporting, with a tendency to underrate negatives and overrate positives. That way partners feel good, reviewers get rehired, and funds continue to flow. And that can defeat the point of evaluating.

For honest M&E, partners have to be open to failure and learn how to leverage underperformance. There is more to international development than quitting projects that do not deliver. Partners can seek to manage, not eliminate, risks and attempt, not assure, improvements, while absorbing real lessons learned and pointed evaluation recommendations along the way. Partnership programs want and expect success, but all success all the time is not the real world. When partners engage in M&E exercises, it matters how they tee them up and what they make of them. A thoughtful, well-calibrated approach often benefits from the collective attention of a constructively-minded governing body.

Donors are expected to manage their M&E needs with respect to the Trust Fund and other Partnership Program funding sources collectively through common processes to avoid supplemental or duplicative evaluations, <u>except as may be required by their respective statutory, regulatory, or policy environments.</u>

Leveraging M&E as a collective is efficient for all involved. The effort toward harmonized processing, monitoring, evaluating, and reporting is particularly helpful to downstream recipients and supporting entities that otherwise bear the burden of multiple formats. By contrast, customized reporting for individual donors or other partners is a drag on implementation, diverting attention and resources from activities. However, even well-intentioned donors may find it hard to settle on a common reporting format if they have specific domestic requirements that need accommodating. The exception provided here is a ringfenced, second-level alternative if the collective approach falls short of domestic, partner-specific requirements. To be sure, this is not a blank check to go unilateral. It is meant to be a balanced approach that allows special treatment as a justified, last resort.

The Governing Body monitors the performance of the Partnership Program, including its own performance, with respect to (i) strategic impact; (ii) programmatic performance and impact; (iii) managerial and governance performance; and (iv) financial performance and resource mobilization.

A sentence along these lines can be added, whether here or as part of the governing body's listed roles and responsibilities. While fiduciary and implementing entities are tasked with regular activity-level reporting, the governing body (with secretariat support) is best positioned to consider the broader picture, especially when it has an oversight or strategic role. It may help partners to commit to self-review early on, before that intention is overtaken by events.

What is the difference between monitoring and evaluating? Do partnership programs need both? The two are typically said in one breath and used practically interchangeably, but there is a nuance. Monitoring is typically understood to be an internal activity, in that partners do their own review (or hire someone to do it) on an ongoing basis. For partnership programs, that means partners monitoring themselves together (for example, as a governing body) and each as to its own role (for example, as donor, governing body member, secretariat, trustee, implementer). Evaluation is often positioned as an external activity, in that outsiders look in for a more objective, arm's-length assessment, usually at intervals. Partners use "midterm reviews" and "independent evaluations," typically with periodicities of every three to five years, partly depending on the lifetime of the partnership program. The midterm review can be self-administered or outsourced. The independent evaluation has to be from the outside to be considered "independent." Ultimately, though, the label is less important than the nature of the exercise, including by whom, with what scope, and on what evidence. This can be defined in terms of reference that are prepared by the secretariat and approved by the governing body for an external evaluator to follow.

What should M&E assessments of partnership programs cover? Partners may want to think about a multi-faceted approach, by which they have ongoing mechanisms to monitor partnership program performance, punctuated by a midterm review, that may or may not be independent, for course corrections, followed after a certain period with an externally-sourced, independent evaluation. Partnership programs with more complex implementation through, for example, multiple funding sources and vehicles, or multiple fiduciary and implementing entities, especially merit partnership-wide, rather than project-specific, M&E assessments. Key words to consider are relevance, effectiveness, efficiency, sustainability, risk, impact, and exit. If goals and objectives specified in the charter, and indicators for the overarching results framework, address partnership program performance, they can all serve as baselines for partnership program M&E over time. Ideally, this results in healthy feedback loops for all partners.

PRIVILEGES & IMMUNITIES

Part IV. General

24. *Privileges and Immunities.* Nothing in this Charter is intended to impair or limit, or may be considered a waiver of, any privileges or immunities of any Partnership Program participant under its relevant governing documents or any applicable law, all of which are expressly reserved.

EXPLANATIONS

In traditional international partnership programs, most participants have some form of privileges and immunities (P&I). Either they are sovereign countries, and their individual representatives are acting as domestic civil servants employed by government ministries or agencies, or they are international (intergovernmental) organizations, which are created by sovereign countries and typically granted P&I, with their individual representatives acting as international civil servants employed by these international organizations. That is the case with the traditional multilateral development banks and other international financial institutions, as well as United Nations agencies, whose shareholders and member states are the same sovereign countries. In a few additional cases, there are protections for topic-specific, dedicated corporate entities that claim quasi-international status in their local jurisdictions (for example, under the Host Country Act in Switzerland) and as negotiated with other countries, or other one-off protections.

The point is that, whatever the source and degree of P&I, partnership program participants are better off stating clearly—for claimants, courts, and anyone else to see—that each of them retains this protection individually even as they convene collectively. (>@ PfP: Partnering Internationally) The relevant audience is not just internal, among partners, but also external vis-à-vis potential third-party claimants and others who might allege inappropriate or damaging behavior arising from the partnership program.

To be clear, P&I attaches to individual partners, not the partnership program as a whole. Partnership programs may asymmetrically combine partners that have P&I status with partners that do not have P&I status, like private foundations and companies, NGOs, CSOs, and academia. When some have P&I and some do not, that is a legally uneven playing field. However, since international partnership programs and their participants are (so far) rarely subject to claims and liability, and since reputational and other risk concerns engender at least some degree of care and caution by everyone, the practical upshot is practically nil, and the asymmetry may hardly be noticed. But stay tuned. The more that partnership programs mix international public sector actors with private sector actors, and the more they engage in innovative or risky activities, the more this could change. An erosion of P&I coupled with greater litigiousness by third parties could result in some disruptive scenarios. The *JAM v. International Finance Corporation* case decided by the United States Supreme Court in 2019 has affected the behavior of some multilateral development banks, curtailing their engagement in certain kinds of activities. This is a space to watch.

VARIATIONS

Nothing in this Charter is intended to impair or limit, or may be considered a waiver of, any privileges or immunities of any Partnership Program participant under its relevant governing documents, <u>including [name of multilateral development bank] under its [governing document]</u>, or under any applicable law, all of which are expressly reserved.

Specific documents can be added as specific references, particularly for Trustee or Secretariat entities with significant exposure. (>@ PfP: Custodial Effect)

This Charter constitutes an expression of mutual good faith and does not commit any of the partners to provide support for any specific activity or project.

Expressions of "mutual good faith" and the like may go without saying, but in adding such language, partners can emphasize that their engagement rests on amicable relations and retains an underlying informality. In other words, they are not setting up litigious relationships or creating legally enforceable commitments that would land them in court. This has particular significance when a charter is incorporated by reference into contribution or other agreements. Although incorporation by reference "contractualizes" the charter, a clause like this can moderate the contractualizing effect. It expresses the clear intent of the parties (partners) and registers the spirit in which they are partnering. However, since most international partners are not intent on litigating their contribution agreements anyhow, this kind of explicit softening is not customary. Then again, in partnership programs that include private sector and other partners beyond the traditional scope of sovereigns and their multilateral organizations, the calculus might be different.

Cooperation under this Charter, and the activities and programs implemented in connection with this Charter, are subject to each Partnership Program participant's respective mandates, governing documents, funding constraints, and policies and procedures.

For partners that are really concerned about setting limits, a sentence like this explicitly ringfences engagement around internal constraints. Different partners have different sensitivities around the nature of charters, but few need this much protective language. Most partners are in it to make it work, knowing everyone is constrained, but trusting that everyone will pitch in as best they can. A statement like this is mostly obvious.

P&I means privileges and immunities, which means protected institutions.

Fifty Shades of "Commitment"

Is a particular clause a commitment? Is it considered binding and enforceable? That is not always clear on its face. The degree of expected or intended "commitment," or just expectation or intention, represented by the charter may vary, both in the eyes of the beholder and the overall understanding of the partners. In general, charters—as adopted documents—may not be viewed as having the same degree of enforceability as signed agreements. Some are not even sent to legal departments for review. Most do not specify whether their terms are binding or non-binding. However, two broad caveats are in order:

First, as mentioned, many charters are incorporated by reference into signed agreements and thereby contractualized. (>@ BfB: Agile Alignment—Step-by-Step Alignment for Trust-Funded Partnership Programs, #4) The degree of commitment is then in the choice of wording, with different degrees attaching to different language. To wit, from most to least committed:

- *Commitment.* The Governing Body meets at least annually. The Secretariat provides administrative support. The [Trustee entity] acts as Trustee.

  This is straightforward language that establishes an obligation and legitimately engenders reliance on the part of the partners.

- *Best/reasonable effort.* Governing Body members make their best efforts to participate in all Governing Body meetings. Secretariat responsibilities include reasonable efforts to support resource mobilization.

  This clarifies that there is a limit to what needs to be done, perhaps even that the outcome is not assured. This is particularly relevant where constraints (time, budget) are known. These qualifiers are rarely included because they are basically understood.

- *Expectation.* Donors are expected to manage their M&E needs collectively through common processes. Governing body constituencies are expected to coordinate their views in advance of meetings and for no-objection decision requests.

  This phrasing speaks to actions and activities, as in hoped-for behavior. It signals aspiration, not assurance. Nonetheless, partners set the bar and signal their reliance on this behavior.

- *Intention.* The structure of the Partnership Program is designed to leverage synergies. The Partnership Program seeks to operate in a transparent manner.

  Also aspirational, this phrasing speaks to a frame of mind. While potentially ambitious, it articulates where partners want to be, what they hope to attain. Indeed, these terms can be more ambitious precisely because they are aspirational.

Second, in the international arena, where partnership engagements are rarely premised on enforceability and enforcement, the actual difference between commitment and expectation is usually negligible. The point is more that both characterizations engender reliance. The partners take their expressions of engagement seriously, and the partnership program works only if partners follow through as agreed. An entity that agreed to be the trustee better have a really good reason to pull out after partners have put in a lot of time, effort, and expense based on that premise. The more reliance is riding on the matter, the more staying the course matters.

Sometimes just knowing the partners are counting on you is enough to keep the engagement going. Sometimes knowing how upset you will make everyone if you don't, and realizing what kind of reputational risk is at stake, is enough to turn a raised expectation into a force of commitment.

CONSIDERATIONS

How protective do participants want charter language to be? Legal, associational, reputational, and other exposure arising from international partnership programs is usually, gratefully, not a problem from one participant to another. International partners who engage in shared governance—sovereigns and international organizations established or run by those same sovereigns—are not normally in the business of suing each other. (>@ PfP: Partnering Internationally—Applicable Law) However, branching out to include others outside of this cozy community, like adding private companies with business interests, or private foundations with tax and other regulatory requirements, shifts the risk profile. As we saw with the *JAM* case described earlier, challenges can come from third parties, including locals that feel harmed by a project, or NGOs that take up their cause. It is always good to highlight available privileges and immunities, and it may not hurt to refer to good faith and good intentions. These backdrops set the tone, even if they have—to date—rarely been directly contested.

How binding do participants want charter language to be? Partners can modulate the legal status of their charter terms in at least two ways, as mentioned before:

- Clause-by-clause, they can vary the phrasing to capture the exact degree of engagement they collectively want to pin down. There is no prescribed approach for charter terms; it depends on what the partners want to make of it. The only constraint, at least in a consensus environment (>@ PfP: Decision Making—Consensus), is that everyone be on board for the wording. For example, if participants want to commit to attending all governing body meetings, but one has some hesitation, the statement may drop to a "reasonable efforts" or "as feasible" standard. Or if all partners seek to agree on a high-level objective, but instead end up with half a page of softer intentions, they can say as much or as little as they can all agree on. Often it is the lawyer who helps navigate this rich range of expression between binding and non-binding, as partners together choose what to say and how far to go.

- The charter as a whole may be non-binding (or at least, as is the norm, refrain from saying that it is binding), but can become incorporated into and made an integral part of a binding agreement. This lets partners operate at different speeds depending on their own needs. Non-donor participants may be fine with a looser arrangement. Donors with large sums at stake may need more legal certainty. And yet, sovereign donors have an almost surprising variety of preferences, usually driven by domestic parameters, including the avoidance of treaty procedures. (>@ BfB: A Taxonomy of Trust Fund Agreements—Upstream Agreements—Contribution Agreements for Multi-Donor Trust Funds) Some need to know that fund flow terms are fully committed, breachable obligations. Others insist that nothing in the document be considered binding and formally agreed. Good thing that a stand-alone charter, which itself need not be explicitly binding, can be framed in a binding, bilateral fund flow agreement in just the way the particular donor needs.

DISCLOSURE

25. *Disclosure.* The Partnership Program seeks to operate in a transparent manner, which includes public disclosure of this Charter. The Secretariat [and Trustee] may disclose Partnership Program [and Trust Fund] information in accordance with [its] [their] policies and procedures on access to information.

EXPLANATIONS

International partnership programs are under pressure to be more transparent about their activities. Information is power, most of the funding is public, and interested outsiders and stakeholders—like NGOs, CSOs, academics, and prospective beneficiaries—want to know.

Of course, partners control their own internal information and normally cannot be compelled to share something they consider confidential. However, when it comes to partnership program information—information partners collectively generate or that pertains to partnership program activities or funding vehicles—whether to disclose is a question for the collective. It can affect all partners and is presumably something for them to decide as a whole. Beyond that, however, partners should be comfortable with the access to information policies of their supporting entities, since those come with the package, as noted in the sample clause. (>@ PfP: Supporting Entities—Basic Elements) In practice, however, supporting entity policies tend to be pretty silent on how they apply to partnership programs and their collectives.

On the one hand, many partnership programs consider it good practice to post all signed agreements, adopted documents, approved minutes, annual reports, and other fundamental business documents directly on their websites, in plain view with direct access. On the other hand, there is always room for deliberation and, as needed, confidentiality, so partnership programs have to decide what is disclosable and what is not. For example, some prefer to treat preparatory meeting documents, like agendas and background information, as deliberative works in progress, thereby keeping them private among governing body participants. Others, however, take a more open stance and post these documents on their websites for public view as part of the partnership program's official business. How participants approach this may depend on the sensitivity of the topics and the visibility of the initiative. Even with clear disclosure rules, there are still judgment calls to be made around specific "deliberative" and "confidential" information exceptions to the rule.

It would seem legitimate for partnership program participants to carve out space for a safe zone. To promote frank exchanges, participants can benefit from commenting off the public record, including, for example, meetings that go by the Chatham House rule (information may be used, but not attributed). Putting principles of transparency into practice is always a balancing act between openness and effectiveness. An open approach may seem unassailable, but forcing it so wide open that it curtails constructive sharing and stymies sound decision making is not helpful.

As noted, the baseline for partnership program behavior around information usually stems from the policies for disclosure (information given out) and access to information (information taken out) of the trustee and secretariat. Their "applicable policies and procedures" are in turn those of the respective (or same) entities in which they are housed. (>@ BfB: The Annotated Charter—Secretariat Context; ibid.—Trustee Context) Trustee and secretariat supporting entities, like multilateral development banks or UN agencies, have well-developed frameworks for their own operations, resulting from extensive deliberations among management, board members, and other partners. By affecting trustee and secretariat operations for the partnership program, they end up affecting the partnership program overall.

Let's consider this from three perspectives:

- *Secretariat information.* A secretariat may be bound by the applicable policies and procedures of its institution to disclose everything in its possession, unless it meets a valid exception, as in the case of documents that are deliberative or confidential. If, for example, secretariat staff become aware of fraud or corruption allegations that the institution still considers confidential, this staff may have an obligation to inform their managers, but not (yet) be at liberty to inform other partners. Although this can be a point of tension, especially with donors, an internal management sphere for supporting entities is arguably indispensable for sound operations. Many of these donors rely on and benefit from the same deliberative and confidentiality exceptions in their board business as shareholders of the same institution.

- *Partner information.* That same secretariat may receive information from a partner for partnership purposes that the secretariat is required to publicly disclose under its applicable policies and procedures, unless a confidentiality or other exception applies. Partnership program participants would want to be aware that anything they give the secretariat or trustee could be disclosed, at a minimum to supporting entity management, but potentially more broadly. They would also want to be aware of available exceptions. In most cases, institutional policies allow information received from the outside to be labeled as "confidential" by the provider, and then staff are expected to follow that label.

- *Partnership information.* What about documents or information produced by the partnership program? Who decides about their disclosure? This can get murky because the partnership program, being informal, is not a legal entity with direct ownership or retention rights vested in the partnership per se. Moreover, material produced by the secretariat can legitimately be considered part of the secretariat's work program, even if undertaken for and financed by the partnership program. (>@ PfP: Supporting Entities—Privileges and Immunities) To avoid issues, partners should agree on how the supporting entity's policies affect material from or in the name of the partnership program. Ideally, a mature partnering environment recognizes that the secretariat and supporting entity can take collective partnership views into account when deciding what partnership program materials to disclose.

What is common among these three examples is that supporting entity policies and procedures prevail. It is normally not possible for a partnership program to position itself at odds with its supporting entity, which cannot contravene its own rules, nor should it be making lots of piecemeal exceptions. (>@ PfP: Secretariats—Inhouse Secretariat Roles) Here we can again see why it is so important for participants to understand from the start that trustee and secretariat rules apply. That is why it helps to make their Context sections in the charter so explicit. (>@ PfP: Custodial Effect—Eyes Wide Open)

In the end, the approach taken by a partnership program should sit well with the partners as a whole, as a collective understanding. For one, the supporting entity is there for support, not unilateral action. For another, a single partner that goes public prematurely can ruin it for all the others. It takes only one to disclose it for everyone. As is always the case in a collective, all partners should be mindful of all other partners, including of supporting entities.

Allegations of Fund Misuse

Allegations of fraud or corruption are trouble. When allegations of fund misuse arise, partners need to first confirm that the allegations are credible. Allegations by themselves are not enough, even as they pose reputational risks to the partnership program. This requires careful managing in the early stages for everyone's sake, including the intended beneficiaries. Donors can get jittery and move away, even if it later appears that allegations were politically motivated, or the facts were more nuanced or complex under the circumstances. This also requires careful navigating of different partner temperatures. Some may push for immediate and assertive audits and refunds, while others may prefer to tread more carefully to limit the fall-out and salvage what they can in view of the greater good.

Questionable fund use in connection with trust funds requires collective approaches commensurate with the collectivized funding. No single donor in a multi-donor trust fund has the full prerogative to direct the fate of a commingled pool. Partner demands may also take some coordinating to avoid multiple different investigations and audits that become a major cumulative burden. (>@ PfP: Fund Use Responsibility—Transferred (No) Responsibility—Managing the Accountability Gap) Whether this is a trustee, secretariat, or governing body role, or some combination thereof, allegations of fund misuse that affect the partnership program deserve substantiation and careful coordination before running roughshod over the whole venture.

It takes only one to disclose it for everyone.

Taking Disclosure Too Far

True case: A partner claims under its statutory requirements that it has to publicly disclose *all* information received from the partnership program, even confidential information. While we can have sympathy for a partner that wants to follow its own laws, it will not do for one partner to insist on publicly disclosing information from someone else that was legitimately labeled "confidential." Allowing such unilateral behavior to trump collective interest results in an untenable partnership environment. It undercuts the sharing; it undermines the trust. Simply shrugging shoulders and citing domestic legal requirements is a cop out. The burden is on the outlier partner to find an internal solution—or not "receive" the information to begin with—rather than burden all other partners with this kind of disruptive behavior.

VARIATIONS

Information may be disclosed by each Partnership Program participant consistent with its respective policies, procedures, and, in the case of countries, applicable legislation, except with respect to information that has been presented or marked in writing as confidential, which may be disclosed only with the presenting party's prior written consent. If any recipient party is required to disclose such confidential information upon receipt, it will refrain from receiving the information unless prior written consent has been obtained from the presenting party.

> *This can be added if partners want their respective policies to be acknowledged, alongside those of the secretariat and supporting entity. In so doing, however, the collective well-being needs to be preserved. It should, for example, be understood that information legitimately labeled "confidential" may not be disclosed, even if a recipient partner has competing domestic legal requirements. The onus is on every recipient partner to respect the presenting partner's request—to handle confidential information with care and, as necessary, manage any conflicting domestic requirements. Sustainable partnership programs cannot easily tolerate spoiler partners.*

CONSIDERATIONS

Is the standard of openness that partnership program participants want consistent with the disclosure policies of the secretariat and trustee? Too open or not open enough? Partners should expect the secretariat and trustee—generally any supporting entity function—to follow their own internal rules, which likely cover conduct related to disclosure of and access to information. This is consequential, since partners can also expect that much, if not most, of the partnership program's information and materials will be generated by or pass through the hands of the secretariat and trustee. These rules are likely to involve some discretion about what is deliberative and what merits confidential treatment, two categories that are usually treated as exceptions to full public disclosure. Conversations around this topic may help partners come to a common understanding of what is expected to be disclosed among partners within the partnership program, and what can be disclosed more broadly to the public. With a heads-up: The greater the number of partners, naturally the greater the chances that any disclosure within the partnership program also ends up as disclosure beyond the partnership program.

Is there any tension between the partnership program's ability to manage its public disclosures and the specific requirements of any of its partners? As noted under the Variations, this matters, especially when it comes to confidential information. To manage partnership dynamics, such tensions should be dealt with openly and directly until a reconciling position can be found for the partnership program as a whole. In the best case, this does not tee up as a bilateral issue between a partner and the supporting entity, but is instead treated as something that affects the collective and belongs to everyone.

AMENDMENTS

26.   *Amendments.* This Charter becomes effective upon adoption, and thereafter may be amended, by a consensus or no-objection decision of the Governing Body. Amendments may be proposed to the Secretariat for Governing Body consideration and approval by consensus or no objection. The Secretariat maintains and distributes the records of any such amendments. Amendments to this Charter are expected to apply directly to the Trust Fund's contribution agreements, as stated therein, without further need to amend such contribution agreements; provided that the amendments are consistent with (i) such contribution agreements and (ii) the [Trustee entity's] applicable policies and procedures, both of which prevail over this Charter in case of conflict.

EXPLANATIONS

A word to the wise: Anticipate change.

When the charter is finally ready, adoption and amendments may seem like footnotes, the subject of a minor legal clause tucked away at the back. But this location is deceiving. This clause is not mere legalese; it is the lifeblood of a healthy, sustainable partnership program.

The charter is best conceived as a living, breathing document, capable of adjustment: to go where the partnership goes, to follow the program as it grows, as it matures, learns, and adapts. As precise as the charter should be for clarity, it should also be flexible for longevity. When partners convene in the beginning, they are embarking on a collective journey, whose collective promise to achieve something has to remain attuned to circumstances and each other—how much money flows, what pilots and projects work, what lessons are learned, how the context evolves, who else seeks to collaborate, and more. Whether the shifts are big or small—like a second or third phase with a strategic overhaul and new funding requirements or just an additional member of the governing body—the ability to adjust the charter should be easy and immediate. To put it another way, the partnership program should define the charter, not the other way around.

It is usually the governing body that does the defining, and that is the beauty of it. By positioning the governing body to launch the charter through its adoption, it can also "own" amendments over time. All it takes is one decision point, representing agreement of the members to move ahead, and the change is done and effective. (>@ PfP: Like Rock, Like Water) And if trust funds are in play, adding the carry-over effect completes it all. (>@ BfB: Agile Alignment—Step-by-Step Alignment for Trust-Funded Partnership Programs, #7)

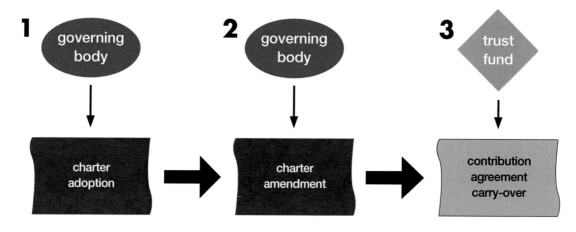

VARIATIONS

This Charter becomes effective upon adoption, and thereafter may be amended, by a consensus decision at a meeting <u>or electronically on the basis of an affirmative acceptance from each Member</u>.

Rather than allow silence to equal consent in electronic decision making, the added requirement of affirmative acceptance raises the "no-objection" approval bar. Because charter amendments are fundamental to the partnership program and can have legal consequences, partners may be wary that mere silence could reflect an oversight instead of acceptance. Requiring affirmative acceptances means every partner has to write back with an explicit "yes, okay" before the amendment takes effect. Not even consensus in a meeting requires this kind of affirmation, but that is, of course, different. In meeting settings, silence only arises as a deliberate decision not to raise an objection that blocks the approval (as in the real-time "speak now or forever hold your peace").

This Charter is expected to [be incorporated by reference into] [apply to] the Trust Fund's contribution agreements.

This can be added to the charter for clarity or visibility, but is not needed for the charter to become operative. Adoption makes the charter effective regardless of what happens with the contribution agreements. If contribution agreement terms conflict with the charter, the charter still takes effect on its terms. If a conflicting contribution agreement prevails over the charter (<@ BfB: Agile Alignment—Step-by-Step Alignment for Trust-Funded Partnership Programs, #10), that override affects only the donor and trustee that signed the contribution agreement. All other partners still follow the charter. That is why it is best not to have conflicting terms that all end up being operative at the same time. (>@ BfB: Constitutive Documents—What to Watch For—Document Alignment) As to the difference between "incorporating by reference" and "applying," that is more nuanced than practical. (>@ BfB: Agile Alignment—Step-by-Step Alignment for Trust-Funded Partnership Programs, #4)

Amendments to this Charter are expected to apply directly to the Trust Fund's contribution agreements, as stated therein, without further need to amend such contribution agreements; <u>subject to prior consent by the [Trustee] [Secretariat]</u>.

If the trustee and secretariat (or their supporting entity) are decision-making members of the governing body (as is usually the case for one-stop-shops), a right of consent is not needed, since they have the right to decide—and a right to block a decision. However, if the trustee and secretariat have only observer positions (typical of international platforms), or no position at all, a right of consent may be justified, particularly for amendments that could affect the trust fund, trustee/secretariat operations, or the supporting entity's risk profile. For contribution agreement amendments, the trustee entity already has a say as one of the signatories. However, for charter amendments, which have no controlling signatures, this has to be added, either through direct decision making (veto power) in the governing body or through something like this special right of consent. The trustee and secretariat could also go without such a safeguard, and sometimes do, but that leaves them vulnerable to changes they do not like, but cannot stop.

Amendments to this Charter are expected to apply directly to the Trust Fund's contribution agreements, as stated therein, without further need to amend such contribution agreements; <u>provided the amendments are subject to prior review by the [Trustee] [Secretariat] for consistency with (i) such contribution agreements and (ii) the [Trustee's] [Secretariat's] applicable policies and procedures, both of which prevail over this Charter in case of conflict.</u>

As explained above, charter amendments should not conflict with contribution agreement terms or the trustee's and secretariat's applicable policies and procedures. Because the trustee and secretariat are best positioned to interpret their own policies, it makes sense for governing body members to let them make those judgment calls. This clause puts the trustee or secretariat in a gatekeeping role to ensure charter amendments are well-positioned within the operative landscape, a role that is a natural for these functions. (>@ PfP: Secretariats—Inhouse Secretariat Roles—Gatekeeping)

Plan Ahead for Trust Funds

Adding trust funds to partnership programs is always a complicating factor. That is as true for charter amendments as anything else. In taking the recommendation to plan ahead, two things are key:

- First is a *sufficiently representative governing body*, and that includes all donors whose contribution agreements rely on the charter. This may not be the case if it takes more money to be on the governing body than to contribute. Different minimum amounts for contributions and governance can result in two classes of donors, one seated and one not. (>@ PfP: Trade-Offs—The Horizontal Buy-In Spectrum—Workarounds) However, those not on the governing body are not going to simply give up their rights and let others make changes to their agreements. Instead, to make governing body amendability work, all donors have to be represented, either directly or indirectly through a constituency. (>@ PfP: Governing Bodies—Composition—Constituencies)

- Second is what I call the *carry-over effect*. (>@ BfB: Agile Alignment—Step-by-Step Alignment for Trust-Funded Partnership Programs, #8) In trust-funded partnership programs, the charter and contribution agreements should point reciprocally to each other. The charter and the contribution agreements should parrot each other in saying that charter amendments take effect vis-à-vis contribution agreements without needing additional donor or trustee signatures. (>@ ibid., #7, including sample clauses) This way amendments to the charter immediately become amendments to the contribution agreements, and the changes apply across the board. (>@PfP: Like Rock, Like Water)

CONSIDERATIONS

What approval standard for charters do governing body members want? Members may be fine applying the same decision standards to charter adoption and amendments that they apply to everything else: consensus in person and no objection by email. (>@ PfP: Decision Making) However, some members, especially donors whose funds flow under separate agreements, may prefer a higher standard for electronic decision making. Instead of allowing approval through silence in response to an email distribution, they may require approval in writing with affirmative email responses, what is called affirmative acceptance or affirmative consent. This higher standard can also be attached to other types of decisions, like funding allocations above a certain threshold or other categories where there are sensitivities that make consent through silence too risky. In practice, any decisions to be made by the governing body are preferably also flagged enough in advance to catch no one unawares.

Do donors have enough governing body representation for charter amendments to also amend contribution agreements? If charter amendments are to carry over to contribution agreements, with automatic applicability that does not require additional signed amendments, the governing body members that approve the charter amendments need to include all who contribute to the trust fund. As previously explained, donors do not normally give up their rights to decide what terms apply to their funds. Each donor will want either a seat or a signature. The answer for easy amending is full representation, either directly or indirectly.

CONSIDERATIONS

Should the secretariat or trustee get a separate right of consent for charter amendments? Amendments to the charter are likely to affect the secretariat and trustee, as central partnership program functions, even if only by association. Not surprisingly, they (and their supporting entities) usually want to have a say about charter changes, at least through consultation if not control. There are at least four obvious ways for the support functions to have an influential hand in charter amendments (the latter two are picked up in the Variations):

- *Directly as a decision-making member of the governing body.* If the support function (secretariat or trustee) or its supporting entity (often the same for both) is a decision-making part of the governing body, and decision making is by consensus, this amounts to veto power—held by each member of the decision-making body—over charter amendments. They have what they need to determine outcomes, including blocking a decision, if necessary.

- *In a consultative manner as an observer on the governing body.* If the support function or supporting entity participates as an observer, this amounts to influence, but not control. There may be reasons why the supporting roles do not step up as partner equivalents from a governance perspective, but they may nonetheless seek other ways to amplify their influence over the direction of the partnership program. Partners may also have so much respect for the support functions—and reality check: so much dependence on them as well—that even advisory status garners conclusive control.

- *Indirectly through a gatekeeping role.* Active at the operational center, secretariats and trustees can exert their influence as clearing houses and gatekeepers. Even if the role is limited to compliance and non-conflict checks, it can still be an important safeguard from institutional and reputational perspectives. (>@ PfP: Secretariats—Inhouse Secretariat Roles—Gatekeeping) Other partners may also welcome this custodial input, as a form of due diligence and risk management that can benefit everyone. (>@ PfP: Custodial Effect) Gatekeeping discretion can range from more objective to more subjective, thereby giving more or less ex ante influence. With this approach, only items that get through pre-screening—for example, charter amendments that are deemed not to conflict with supporting entity policies and procedures and donor contribution agreements—make it to the governing body, which gives the supporting entity some control.

- *Separately through a right of consent.* If none of the above applies, or the support role prefers to reserve a separate, one-off control factor, it can ask for a right of consent. A right of consent usually attaches to specific decisions to be made (for example, addition of a new donor) or areas to be addressed (for example, anything that affects the supporting entity's operations). It takes a targeted approach to enable a last say (control) only where needed, without becoming an integral part of governing (as a governing body member) or taking an additional role (as a gatekeeper). While the secretariat or trustee may be reluctant to set itself apart with a special right, especially if everyone else is okay where it is not, it may still be the most elegant way to narrowly safeguard its interests where needed. A targeted right of consent can exert a limited scope of authority, without taking on greater responsibility.

Doing International Documents

In this Part Three, we study words, documents, and deliberations from a practitioner's perspective: being dexterous while holding the pen, bringing coherence and comfort through careful alignment, and creating closure by making it all come together—plus a closing shout-out to those who make it happen.

IT'S ALL IN
THE
BUILD

Chapter 1: Deft Drafting

Whether a lawyer or someone else is putting the partnership program to paper, a sense of articulation as architecture, along with some sly ways to work with words, can make for a steady hand.

Chapter 2: Agile Alignment

Part of the art lies in aligning adopted documents and signed agreements. This chapter presents a step-by-step guide on how to mesh the charter with contribution agreements.

Chapter 3: Practical Packaging

Moving from words to documents to negotiations, we build a holistic approach to establishment documents, treating them as a package.

Chapter 4: A Taxonomy of Trust Fund Agreements

Recognizing the importance of international trust funds as drivers and definers of partnership programs, we delve into fund flow agreements from upstream to downstream and beyond.

Coda: The Role of the Lawyer

Hail to the lawyers! We cannot leave the subject without recognizing the unsung heroes that orchestrate and integrate, from business plans to memorialized programs, from disparate views to common understandings, from concepts to closure, and thereafter for ongoing support.

1 DEFT DRAFTING

Partners, please note:

A thousand words can spare a thousand woes.

The written word is paramount for creating structured partnerships in the international arena. In the beginning was the word, and so it is with international partnership programs. You cannot be sure they exist until they are articulated and memorialized. Agreement may be a mirage without a confirmed written statement. The scope of agreed partnering is unknown without articulated parameters. This love of language is not just from lawyers enamored of their work product; it is for all partners. A picture may be worth a thousand words, but a thousand words in partnering can spare a thousand woes.

The Awesomeness of Articulating

By putting what they mean to be and do in writing, partners can:

1. be clear with each other, with clear expectations
2. confirm common ground for a solid partnership program foundation
3. define who's in, for what, and how
4. keep their house in order with explicit allocations of responsibility
5. develop rules to conduct partnership program business
6. signal their intentions externally, including for advocacy
7. anticipate issues and pre-agree processes to deal with them
8. anticipate change and built-in flexibility and amendability
9. refer back to agreed terms if anyone fails to act as agreed
10. reflect the views of all partners
11. establish the buy-in of all partners

Drafting upsides:
1. clarity
2. common ground
3. responsibility
4. order
5. predictability
6. signaling
7. anticipation
8. flexibility
9. accountability
10. voice
11. ownership

Partnership-agreed terms put a stake in the ground. They orient the partners to each other and their mission and modalities.

The value in memorializing lies not just in the end result, but also in the process. By exploring issues, testing formulations, agreeing on wording, and doing so iteratively and interactively, partners converge in their collaboration. (>@ BfB: Practical Packaging—The Package from a Legal Perspective) Allowing the process to unfold through multiple rounds of drafts and comments is a good thing, not to be feared or short-circuited. It engages partners and gives them voice, which can translate into greater ownership and involvement over time. Even if the process is messy, it is an important early test of compatibility, a check for like-minded participation. (>@ PfP: Partners and People—Choosing Partners) And if the process resists closure, that should give all partners pause, with a chance to reconsider whether the planned approach and prospective participants are right for each other. Putting it in writing is a fortifying way to establish true consensus among partners.

Words and agreed formulations can even be considered part of the partnership structure. You can pick your image: They are the ropes or sinews that strengthen the ties of one element to another. Constitutive documents are the foundation upon which partnership program operations rest. Fund flow agreements, starting with contribution agreements, are the channels along which funds flow. Minutes of governing body meetings are the touchstones that set the path. Plenty of images can underscore the ways in which articulation is architecture when it comes to building international partnership programs.

For partnership programs, articulation is architecture.

From a paper perspective, the roles and responsibilities of the respective partners in international partnership programs appear within the "four corners" of the documents—what you see is what you get. (>@ PfP: Use of Funds—Four Corners of the Agreement) What lies within these four corners gives partners a common understanding of their venture, as expressed in their baseline documents. These so-called "establishment" or "constitutive" documents establish and constitute the partnership program. Typically, this means a charter-type text, and, if trust funds are involved, accompanying trust fund contribution agreements. (>@ BfB: Constitutive Documents) Once these documents are effective—adopted or signed—they embody the identity of the partnership program. These common terms are put forth for partners to agree and for all to see.

The Art of Writing

If you are a lawyer, you probably like words. If you are an international partner, you can come to appreciate them, too, if you don't already. They can be your best friends not only when messaging, but also when building. After looking at the big picture in Part One and charter clauses in Part Two, we can now get granular and look at phrases and words. Here is my short list of things to keep in mind when doing some lawyerly drafting for international partnership programs, or virtually anything else:

1. CLARITY: Make it crisp and clear.

2. PLAINSPOKENNESS: Say what you mean.

3. PUNCTUATION: Pick and place your ":,;...?—!" well!

4. LEGAL STUTTERING: Four (4)-swear all extras, excesses, add-ons, and pile-ons.

5. WEASEL WORDS: Typically be indicative, except for what might otherwise arise.

6. WORD HIERARCHIES: Try this notwithstanding what it's subject to.

7. DEFINED TERMS: Give it a Name and give it meaning.

8. PRESENT TENSE: To be operative, rather than become.

9. STATING THE NEGATIVE: Don't miss out on the neither, nor, ne'er, and none.

10. FILLING IN PROCESS: Position how-to's in lieu of the what's.

11. SILENCE:

Being Clear

Putting things in writing is the only guarantee that things are and will be clear. And being clear is the only way to avoid misunderstandings and missed expectations in the life of an international partnership program. Even when partners are clear with each other in writing, they may still have different interpretations over time, but fewer and farther between. The more effort to clarify things upfront, the more hold that clarity will have going forward.

As long as everyone is relying on everyone else to do their part, operating from a core of clarity is like harboring a comfort zone. Partners know why they are joining and can hold others to account on priorities. Clarity about objectives can keep the focus on getting results. Clarity on roles and relationships can manage gaps and overlaps for getting things done. Clarity on who and what is in or out can protect everyone's, and the partnership program's, reputations. (>@ PfP: Typology—Trust-Funded Partnership Programs) It takes extra effort and engagement to be clear, but the written word can always be found at the crux of partnership program clarity.

Being Plainspoken

Putting things in writing is key, but not sufficient to make sure things are and will be clear. Wording should also be in plain English, or whatever language promotes clarity. That does not mean writing has to be boring. It can stay lively, but should not obfuscate. Of course, in an international setting, "obfuscate" might be considered an obfuscating word, instead of the perfect word for the exact meaning. Writing in plain English may thus be a trade-off between clarity and precision. My personal preference is not to dumb things down. An audience can step up to the meaning, as long as the formulation is direct, carefully chosen, and not overly adorned.

To be sure, it is harder to write a short piece than a long piece, because it is harder to be concise and to the point. However, less is more here, too, and meaningful brevity is worth the effort. A few pages that are owned and internalized by the partners can mean more than a lengthy compendium that explores every nuance and detail. Charters are the perfect place to capture the spirit and essence of the partnership program, certainly more accessible than fund flow or other legally loaded agreements. Plainspoken charters are crisp and clear documents that let partners ground their partnership programs in the essentials.

Powering Punctuation

Part of being clear is promoting punctuation. We play with punctuation all the time in our drafting, for good reason, for positioning and precision. Let's try it out—watch how the meanings change or stay the same:

- "…you can go, you can stay, or you can play subject to our requirements."
- "… (i) you can go, (ii) you can stay, or (iii) you can play, subject to our requirements."
- "… you can go, you can stay, or you can play, all subject to our requirements."
- "… you can (a) go, (b) stay, or (c) play; per our requirements."

Here we have four similar statements, but with different levels of clarity and formality and, as between the first and second pairs, somewhat different meanings. If you are holding the pen, it is in your hands to choose your style, to say exactly what you want to say and how.

Avoiding Legal Stuttering

Writing in plain English also means getting rid of legal stuttering. In an abundance of caution and overzealous clarification, lawyers have a tendency to double and triple their constructions. Rather than signal erudition, however, this is habitual overindulgence. Does it really help to write "three (3)," as if three did not sufficiently mean three? And what about "now therefore, for and in consideration of the mutual covenants and agreements contained herein, and for other good and valuable consideration, the receipt and sufficiency of which are hereby acknowledged" as a preamble closer, when the parties simply want to record that they agree? Which also applies to "the parties acknowledge and agree." Is there any way to agree without first acknowledging? Then there is "including, without limitation," as though including did not already mean open-endedly so. Have you ever heard anyone say "including, with limitation"? Of course not, that would make no sense—and that is the point.

Bravo (to you and not to me) if you spot legal stuttering in this book—it's ~~ever so~~ easy to do, but ~~ever so~~ unnecessary.

"We three (3) acknowledge and agree to include, without limitation, and in consideration of mutual covenants, agreements, and other good, valuable, received, and sufficient consideration, any and all matters that arise out of or result from any and every thing in connection with or relating to other matters."

Really?
Thou dost profess too much!

Chronic Stutterer

When it comes to liability, lawyers can really start stuttering, barely hiding their nervousness. Take a look at this for-real, single-sentence, virtually standardized clause that all commercial lawyers will have seen at least once if not a zillion times:

> The [first party] agrees to hold the [other party] harmless *from and against any and all claims, damages, losses, liabilities and expenses (including all fees and charges of internal or external counsel with whom the [other party] may consult and all expenses of litigation and preparation therefor)*, which may be asserted by *any person, entity, or governmental authority (including any person or entity claiming derivatively on behalf of the [other party])*, in connection with, or arising out of or relating to, the matters referred to [here], and *arising out of or resulting from any suit, action, claim, proceeding, or governmental investigation, pending or threatened, whether based on statute, regulation or order, or tort, or contract or otherwise*, before any court or governmental authority . . .

This is out of control, not to mention a gratuitous invitation to quibble over language. But the good news is that charters of international partnership programs are not the place for indemnifications. (>@ PfP: Supporting Entities—Middle Ground?) With formulations like this, we should all be motivated to keep it that way.

Don't belabor it; just say it!

A nice thing about charters, especially when used for international partnership programs, is that there are no statutory prescriptions, civil code requirements, or common law quirks in terms of content or format. They can be free of archaic formulations and arcane legalese. Partners can take full advantage of this freedom by leapfrogging into modern, keep-it-simple, to-the-point formulations and formatting. It's like those shoes that say "just do it." Don't belabor it, just say it!

Leveraging Weasel Words

"Weasel words" have a bad name, which not only slanders the weasel, but also gives them an undeserved bad rap. Weasel words do what weasels do: they slip into small spaces and find crafty solutions. These little words can be really useful, especially when you need the text to be expansive or open to change. Any good lawyer will have an arsenal of these one-word inserts at the ready.

Words like "including" or "usually" have just enough daylight in them that they do not fully limit or preclude. Instead, they give meaningful examples without closing the door to other possibilities—including scenarios we can't even imagine right now. Phrases like "are expected" give some breathing room, unlike "will" and "shall" that fit like corsets and lock the partners in. "Target" or "indicative" play the same role by positioning without obligating and framing without fixing. Weasel words are like little wedges that open a crack for other possibilities, future scenarios, and efforts over obligations.

Truth be told, this book is a wealth of weasel words. It is almost impossible to describe the universe of international partnership programs without them. I am the first to acknowledge that for every description I give, there is an exception, for every conclusory statement, a counterexample. In my goal to lay out the landscape, I have had to make some broad strokes, and surely painted over some details. The word "usually" alone is used over two hundred times in this book, averaging about once a page. Of course, writing a book is not the same as drafting and negotiating an agreement, with a charter somewhere in between, but the point is the same. You can use weasel words to create that bit of leeway, whether to paint some ideas more visibly or let your partnership program live and breathe more comfortably.

Understanding Word Hierarchies

It also helps to know the hierarchy of words. Take "notwithstanding," one of the most powerful words in the English language. Introducing a sentence with "notwithstanding all else herein" overrides everything else in the document in one fell swoop. Its converse, "subject to," does just the opposite. Adding "subject to [some other text]" suborns the text that follows this phrase to the other text, another powerful maneuver. Expressions like these are shortcuts that link or delink different parts of documents, creating paths and layers with quick and efficient strokes—like the Bob Ross of writing.

These kinds of stratifications can be used in different ways. They are, for example, good for dealing with one-offs. You may have standardized or harmonized terms that apply across the board, but in a specific case, or for a specific scenario, you need different terms. "Notwithstanding the minimum contribution requirement, a donor that joins midway through the three-year membership period may pay a prorated amount agreed with the Secretariat."

It can be a light tweak or like the Red Sea parting when you wield "notwithstanding." There is an art as to when to invoke this power, and it should not be overused or cause confusion. Here is an example I like because it is more normative than prescriptive. By positioning overarching principles as guideposts alongside itemized lists in the charter, you can allow the spirit to be as important as any specifics:

> *Notwithstanding the roles and responsibilities described herein:*
>
> *(i) The partners do not expect the [limited] Secretariat, acting as a support function, to encroach on the authority and prerogatives that the Governing Body sets for itself. The Governing Body remains responsible and accountable for the substance and results of its decision making.*
>
> *(ii) The partners support the limited fiduciary role of the [limited] Trustee, as described in the Contribution Agreements. Secretariat support is not expected to augment or act counter to this fiduciary role.*

Another useful stratifier is to put "provided that" after a semi-colon and add a qualifier. With a flick of the wrist, it takes whatever came before and conditions it wholesale. You may have all sorts of rights, or all sorts of obligations, but tack on a proviso, and you suddenly have an on-switch to control the start or an off-switch to invoke the end.

Provisos tend to show up in agreements where parties are laying out relative positions. Rights and obligations may not be absolute. They may depend on other things being in place or prior events happening. The condition may be consequential, the sequence may be chronological, or the caveat may be prophylactic. A good example is the wording around contribution agreement amendments for multi-donor trust funds. (>@ BfB: The Annotated Charter—Amendments) These amendments typically (there's that weasel word) take effect *provided that* all other donors have also signed the amendment (prior condition); and *provided further that* the amendment does not conflict with the trustee's policies and procedures (prophylactic). You cannot predict what amendments will come down the pike and what specific issues they might raise, but you can anticipate them and cover your bases.

notwithstanding

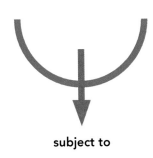

subject to

We'll be on our way; *provided* that I say go; *provided further* that we're all good to go; *provided, however,* that we go only until I say stop.

Positioning Defined Terms

Speaking of shortcuts, that is also the beauty of defined terms. Defined terms are characterized by initial capitals inside parentheses, with or without quotation marks. By describing something you want to reference and then inserting a ("Defined Term"), you can create a handle to be used over and over again that still means the original, more detailed thing that you first described. Defined terms let you package a whole lot of detail and nuance and then carry that heft into every use of the capitalized version.

One of my favorites, pitch perfect for the theme of this book, is:

> . . . the charter approved by the governing body, as may be amended by its terms from time to time (the "Charter").

See what happens? With very little effort, the Charter has suddenly become a living, breathing document. Wherever the word Charter appears, it now means the Charter as it stands at that particular point in time, not the one attached to the document (if it is), not the one originally adopted, not the one existing at the time of one signature or the other, but only the version at any particular time that the term becomes relevant.

Two more examples provide useful drafting shortcuts for trust-funded partnership programs, ones that go well in both the charter and contribution agreements:

- **"Trust Fund"** can be defined to mean one or more trust funds administered by the Trustee. A partnership program might, for example, begin with one trust fund, and then add others over time to accommodate specific donor requirements. No matter how many, the defined term can cover them all, without having to amend the documents over time. For drafting purposes, it does not really matter that a non-plural word represents a set of plural trust funds, as long as the defined term is set up that way.

  Example: *The [Trustee entity] acts as Trustee of one or more Trustee-administered trust funds (the "Trust Fund").*

- **"Contribution Agreements"** can be defined to mean both contribution agreements and contribution arrangements, which includes cases where donors prefer arrangement-type language. (>@ BfB: A Taxonomy of Trust Fund Agreements—Upstream Agreements) It is, of course, possible to refer explicitly to both variants every time, but for concise drafting, the definitional shorthand may be welcome. Donors will individually know which kind they have, while also knowing they are covered and all terms apply equally to both kinds.

  Example: *Contributions to the Trust Fund are made under contribution agreements or contribution arrangements, as the case may be, entered into by the Trustee with each donor (collectively, "Contribution Agreements").*

Applicable Policies and Procedures

It is useful to note that certain phrases, if used consistently with clear meaning, can also have the effect of defined terms without the conventional capitalization. One such example is the use of *applicable policies and procedures* as a way to bring in the entirety of a trustee's or other fiduciary's operating framework. It beats listing out the whole compendium of procurement, safeguards, anticorruption, antiterrorism, disclosure, human resources, treasury operations, and other rules that apply. It is also a way to be modular (each fiduciary's own applicable policies and procedures), keep up-to-date (the then-current policies and procedures), and stay comprehensive (all of the policies and procedures), all at the same time. This can give the donors comfort that they are leveraging and obligating the full panoply of protections afforded by their chosen fiduciaries. It can also give each fiduciary comfort that it is agreeing to its institutional set-up as is, without additional requirements or someone else's expectations or interpretations. (>@ PfP: Use of Funds—Four Corners of the Agreement—Applicable Policies and Procedures) For the charter, contribution agreements, or other operative documents, that little mantra, repeated with almost religious devotion, can do all that.

For Information Only

Partners often like to attach or annex documents, like the results framework or strategic plan, to the charter as part of the adoption, so all relevant documents visibly come together. Donors similarly like to attach documents referred to in the contribution agreement, including the charter, so all effective terms are in one place. That has its merit, but if these attached or annexed documents are modified subsequently, then the original documents need amending as well—and all the signatures that entails. (>@ PfP: Like Rock, Like Water—Like Water)

A better approach, especially for documents that are expected to change over time, is to treat them as stand-alone documents that are attached *for informational purposes only*. This operative cues the reader that the document is appended as a convenience at the time of adoption or signature, with the active version existing elsewhere.

If you do end up attaching documents with a limited shelf life, like a charter to a contribution agreement, first make sure the document includes a defined term that refers to the then-current charter, as described here, rather than tying the definition to the attachment. Second, insert something like this sentence at the top of the attachment:

The Charter attached here is subject to change in accordance with its terms and provided for informational purposes only.

Defined terms can be aggregated in a glossary upfront or at the back, which is also often where the acronyms go (international actors love those acronyms), but that can give the document an overly formal, legalistic quality. The use of defined terms in Charters can just as readily go with the flow. Peppering paragraphs with defined terms as and when they are used means dropping in the parentheticals immediately after the first descriptive phrase (as in the Charter defined term example below). This can be a comfortable way to bring the reader along. Granted, the first page may be full of parenthetical bursts, but each capitalized term enters the scene right as the meaning is made clear—in context, or *in situ* to use a scientific term. This also signals to the reader: This is important, it will be mentioned again, please pay attention. Such a dispersed, context-driven approach is especially useful for shorter documents and plain English texts, which charters are meant to be.

Replete with Defined Terms: Sample Charter Introductory Sections

The New Partnership Program Charter, adopted on _____.

1. The New Development Bank (the NDB) and the United Nations Agency (the UNA, and together with the NDB, the Founders), along with all donors (the Donors) to one or more trust funds administered by the NDB (collectively, the Trust Fund) for the New Partnership Program (the NPP), constitute the partners of the NPP (the Partners) and have adopted the present charter of the NPP (the Charter). New Partners may be added under the terms of this Charter.

2. The NPP is a collaborative arrangement among the Partners to provide technical assistance (TA) to low- and middle-income countries (LMICs). The following basic principles guide the NPP (the Principles): _____.

3. The NPP's objectives for the Trust Fund (the Objectives) are: _____. To qualify for Trust Fund support, proposals must meet the requirements set forth in Schedule A (the Project Selection Criteria), which are assessed by the Program Coordination Unit (the PCU) as part of its review of proposals submitted in response to its periodic calls for proposals (CfPs).

4. The NPP has a governing council (the Council), which provides strategic guidances to the NPP, as further described in this Charter. The Council comprises one representative of each of the Main Donors (as defined below), one representative of each of the Founders, and one representative chosen by the Donor Constituency (as defined below), in addition to other potential representatives from entities the Council decides to add as new Partners (collectively, the Council Members). "Main Donors" are Donors who have contributed at least US$ _____ to the Trust Fund. The "Donor Constituency" comprises all other Donors.

Using Present Tense

Continuing with the theme of living, breathing documents, international partnership programs are as organic as their constitutive documents are meant to be operative. (>@ BfB: Dynamics— It's Organic) Launching a partnership program is not a once-and-done, but approve-and-move. The approved charter and signed agreements are the basis upon which partners are expected to operate—and grow and mature and modify. Constitutive documents have a continuing life, and their meaning should stay relevant, including as amended over time.

In this sense, the documents will always be living in real time. That is different from the pre-establishment phase, when lawyers are memorializing for the future and partners are looking ahead. When preparing and negotiating drafts, it is instinctive to write in the future tense, as in "the governing body will comprise [list of members]" or "the roles and responsibilities of the secretariat will include [list of items]." And yet, as soon as the charter is adopted, those "wills" become obsolete. Now it should be "the governing body comprises . . ." and "the roles and responsibilities include. . . ." These statements are in effect; they are actually the case. To emphasize the active nature of the partnership program, and to anticipate its operative quality, it makes sense to write the charter in an active voice, the present tense.

Use of the present tense in adopted documents is different from agreements, like contribution agreements. Agreements memorialize obligations at a specific point in time to be followed over time. That continuous effect is reflected in agreements that are effective "as of" a particular date (rather than "on" that date). It is also captured in the use of "shall" as a future tense that carries legal obligations for future behavior (relative to the date of commitment), usually with binding, enforceable effect. At the risk of oversimplifying, signed agreements are obligatory, while unsigned charters, operations manuals, and the like are operative.

In the spirit of making charters operative and real-time reflections of the partners, it is wholly fitting to avoid "will" and "shall" and use the present tense instead.

Filling In Process

Here is a general maxim for partnership program design: When content is unknown, process can fill in. No one can predict how and when fund misuse might arise, or whether a consequential breach of commitment will need redress; indeed, everyone hopes neither will happen. However, even without knowing the specifics, it is possible—even advisable—to spell out the process by which any mishaps would be addressed within the partnership, *as a partnership matter*.

This is especially useful in environments where rights and obligations are spelled out bilaterally, as in contribution agreements for trust funds. If, for example, the partnership program is faced with allegations of fraud, each donor may seek to take its own steps under its own contribution agreement vis-à-vis the offending party.

- Donor A asks for all audited statements and other documents to embark on a significant desk review.
- Donor B gathers a team and invites itself onto the recipient's premises for interrogations.
- Donor C claims it needs to engage a third-party auditor to investigate.
- Donor D says it has to publicize the matter under domestic sunshine laws.
- Donor E prefers to keep it all under wraps, so as not to jeopardize the project until the evidence is more conclusive.

What a mess!

Charters reflect the partners.

Use process to fill in for content.

Not all of that can be avoided, but just imagine the partners had developed a set of collective recourse steps in advance. Step one, convene as a governing body, flesh out the facts so everyone is on the same page, share what each partner wants or needs to do, and consider if there is a possible collective approach. Step two, if and only if a particular partner has a particular reason that it has to act unilaterally, it can do so, but hopefully in consultation with others and mindful of their views and any collateral effects.

When we think of collectives, we do not necessarily think of collective remedies, but does it not follow? If the funds are pooled, all interests are pooled, and every donor has a stake in what happens if something serious comes up. At the end of the day, if the issue is fraud or corruption, it may turn out that the allegations are not substantiated; maybe it was a bad case of office politics (which has happened). But in the meantime, the pre-agreed process carries the partners. Partners know what comes next, have pre-agreed buy-in on joint steps to take, can avoid confusion and conflicting steps, and hopefully do not wreak havoc on what could continue to be a productive partnership program.

Stating the Negative

Where we state things in the positive, we can also state them in the negative. In drafting, we are mostly aiming to describe what is or will be, rather than what isn't and won't be. However, the negative can be a good complement to the positive, especially when terms are loaded with baggage that does not pertain or that you want to avoid. If, for example, a partnership program positions a *trustee* for a *trust fund*—common parlance for international partnership programs—but the lawyer knows these are just international terms of art and does not want to include all sorts of statutory or common law baggage about "trustees" or "trusts," a bit of negative verbiage can clarify the point (>@ PfP: Custodial Effect—Mutual Respect):

> *The Trustee shall be responsible only for performing those functions specifically set forth in this Contribution Agreement and shall not be subject to any other duties or responsibilities to the Donors, including those that might otherwise apply to a trustee or fiduciary under general or national principles of trust or fiduciary law.*

In the same vein, if a partnership program positions a *limited trustee* (>@ PfP: Trustee Types—International Platforms, Limited Trustees), and the lawyer knows full well that partners are used to having a *full trustee* (>@ PfP: ibid.—One-Stop-Shops, Full Trustees), it behooves the lawyer to state the negative. In an abundance of clarity, the lawyer can add a whole slew of negatives:

> *Upon the transfer of funds from the Trust Fund to a recipient, the [limited] Trustee shall have no responsibility, fiduciary or otherwise, for the use of the funds or activities carried out therewith, including no responsibility for (i) confirming the use of the funds; (ii) implementing, monitoring, supervising, evaluating, or providing quality assurance for activities financed by the funds; (iii) providing donors with financial, progress, results, or impact reporting for activities financed by the funds [other than compiling and distributing reports as a facilitating activity]; (iv) any misuse or misprocurement with respect to the funds; or (v) pursuing any donor interests or undertakings with respect to the funds.*

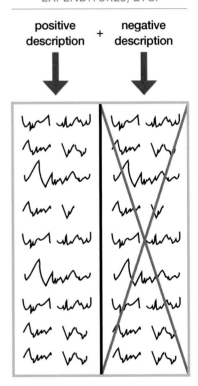

SCOPE OF THE TRUST FUND, TRUSTEE, INELIGIBLE EXPENDITURES, ETC.

positive description + negative description

Trust funds give us yet another example. Fund use is typically defined in terms of expenditures. (>@ PfP: Use of Funds) Usually this is framed in the positive as eligible expenditures—describing what funds can be used for—with the implication that anything else is ineligible (improper) fund use. However, this can also be framed to include explicit negatives with itemized ineligible expenditures, as carve-outs that are expressly off limits. In both cases, what appears is a list of categories, like goods, services, consultants, equipment vs. nuclear material, arms, and contraband, with the negative narrowing the positive.

It is telling that all three examples revolve around funds and funding vehicles. Fund flow agreements, being agreements, may exact more rigor—partly a consequence of more legal scrutiny and certainly a reflection of legal obligations—than many adopted documents. But the principle is the same for all constitutive documents and returns us to the concept that started our list: clarity.

Build clarity through both positive and negative descriptions.

Staying Silent

In the yin and yang of things, as with positives and negatives, it is useful to think of the other. While I am happy to promote more words for more clarity, there is also something to be said for silence. This is not like music, where rests are meaningful, and silence fills out the song. This is more like strategic silence, another tool in the drafter's toolbox.

On most topics, partners will want to test their expectations, resolve differences, align views, and substantiate their common ground. However, every once in a while, irreconcilable differences are better left unstated, leaving each party to its own perspective without forcing a compromise or exacerbating a conflict. The question is whether dueling perspectives can rest in silence side-by-side without disrupting the partnership basis. In other words, are these differences essential or tangential to the collective?

Not surprisingly, the most common sounds of silence fall in the legal category. There is little partner nostalgia if these clauses go missing. For example, international partners are used to having no governing law clause in their partnership program documents. They also do not much insist on being explicitly binding or non-binding. Look at most contribution agreements and charters; they are typically silent on both counts. Both examples exemplify difficult-to-reconcile topics that are resolved by being ignored. In the one case, an international collective avoids being put into a national box. In the other case, different partners have different preferences for binding or non-binding status of their agreements. Maybe we can manage without them, the thinking goes—and mostly, that is what happens.

These silences largely go unnoticed precisely because they are silent. International partners do not realize what they are missing, and what they are missing seems not to matter to the collective. International partnership programs do fine—in fact, they thrive—outside of national jurisdictions, and international partners rarely end up in litigious straits. As a result, they are not beset by lawyers trying to fill in these legal blanks. And in the end, on topics that are not crucial in the context, silence serves its purpose and lets the partnership program comfortably proceed.

Conclusion

The thought of silence is perhaps a good place to end this chapter. In drafting, it is also important to know when to stop. If you have stuck with me to this point, hopefully these tips on deft drafting will serve you well.

A few final words before I close:

Partners and their lawyers know this can be a pressurized environment, where transactions happen at the speed of light (or of your service provider, depending on how your messages transmit). That is especially true after the months, if not years, it took for a proposal to navigate the institutional bureaucracies and finally land on the lawyer's desk, hours from the deadline. Deft drafting too often also means accelerated writing. To this end, practice certainly helps make perfect, but those around you should also understand that what you, the lawyer, are practicing is an art. You are not just applying forms or formulas (there's that negative). Shortcuts can help, including the ones shared here, but so does a steady hand, with time and space to craft and create.

Writing like a lawyer:

It's not a form or formula; it's an art.

2 AGILE ALIGNMENT

After a chapter on structuring words, we can now move on to structuring documents.

Constituting Trust-Funded Partnership Programs

structural | contractual
adopted | signed
informal | formal
partners | signatories

The most common type of international partnership program is the one where the governing body, together with its supporting entity's secretariat, adds on the trustee, with one or more trust funds. This can be a one-stop-shop or an international platform (>@ PfP: Typology—Introducing Two Mighty Oaks), it can be an umbrella arrangement, or some other variation or combination in between (>@ ibid.—Trust-Funded Partnership Programs). There is tremendous variety in what international partners collectivizing in the international arena can do, and that, of course, is part of the attraction. And yet, these trust-funded partnership programs typically have a few things in common from a structural point of view:

- They intertwine structural and contractual elements.
- They position adopted and signed documents side-by-side.
- They combine informal expectations and formal commitments.
- They join entities as partners and some as signatories.

These four features all arise from the same source: the hybrid nature of international partnership programs. They are hybrid in combining an existing legal entity (leaving room for signed agreements) with a new informal governing body (leaving room for adopted partnership documents). (>@ ibid.—The Even Broader Landscape of Structured Partnerships) To maximize efficiency and effectiveness, partners can leverage the dualities that arise from this juxtaposition. (>@ BfB: Dualities)

It is in adding trust funds that these dualities come into full relief, when the good-practice set of establishment documents includes a charter-type document adopted by the governing body and bilateral contribution agreements signed by donors with the trustee. (>@ PfP: Like Rock, Like Water) The main interplay, and focus of this chapter, is accordingly between:

1. a multi-partner, adopted charter or equivalent stand-alone constitutive document, and
2. a series of signed bilateral contribution agreements or equivalent fund flow documents.

This may not sound like much, but the differences tend to be significant. Here is a run-down:

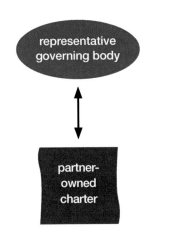

In Comparison: Charters and Contribution Agreements

CHARTERS	CONTRIBUTION AGREEMENTS
about partnership	about money
define decision flows	define fund flows
adopted	signed
belong to decision makers	belong to signatories
multilateral	bilateral
partners	donor/trustee
cover roles and responsibilities	cover rights and obligations
set expectations/reliance	set commitments
breach causes reputational damage	breach causes liability
voluntary participation	contractual participation
in plain English	in legalese
amended by single decision point	amended by multiple signatures

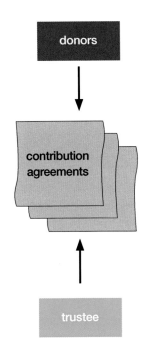

What these differences mean and how this relationship works is perhaps of interest to all partners, but of greatest relevance to the lawyers. They are tasked with getting from A to B, from business concept to legal closure. Even the best lawyers may not intuit the pitfalls or potential that this juxtaposition entails. What can be a boon for partners can just as easily become a bane, depending on how the documents are structured and handled. I believe this kind of structuring and handling is a practice area for lawyers to learn, one where experience and expertise can make a difference.

Truth be told, negotiating and navigating documents for trust-funded partnership programs may not be for the faint of heart. These structures often represent a convergence of many different competing and conflicting elements and interests, and ultimately rely on trade-offs and compromises. But whether the job is especially hard or somewhat straightforward depends on a clear understanding of the overall context and a systematic approach. The lawyers on the scene should be able to help manage who says what and what goes where, until a complete, structured package establishes the partnership program and accompanying trust fund(s). (>@ BfB: Practical Packaging—The Package Approach to Establishment)

For the principal documents, three maxims can help set the stage:

1. *Get everyone on the same page.* This means establishing converged expectations.
2. *Get enough on the page.* This means articulating clear and comprehensive terms.
3. *Get it all on a page.* This means aligning across a coherent set of documents.

There are step-by-step ways to achieve these objectives. The eleven steps presented here put the focus on partnership elements to help avoid results that favor trust fund elements at the cost of partnering. Keeping in mind that no rules are universally applicable, and each case merits individual attention and assessment, these steps present a general outline for how to proceed when aligning a charter with contribution agreements.

•

Eleven Steps to Align the Charter and Contribution Agreements

1. In defining the trust fund, signed agreements for the receipt of donor contributions should specify all essential elements relating to fund use and trustee functions.

2. In defining the partnership program, shared governance and other partnership elements are often best described in a separate constitutive document, like an adopted charter.

3. The timing on adoption and signatures may be tricky, but can be managed.

4. For the purposes of combining contribution agreements and charters, the contribution agreements bring in the terms of the charter.

5. Overlaps and gaps are best avoided when juxtaposing charters alongside contribution agreements.

6. For strengthened alignment, the charter and the contribution agreements should speak the same language.

7. For legal support, the charter and the contribution agreements should cross-refer to each other.

8. For efficient amendability, charter amendments should apply automatically to the contribution agreements (the "carry-over effect").

9. Amendments to the charter should not occur without the trustee/supporting entity's consent.

10. Charter amendments should be given agreement status and agreement-type review.

11. In the event of conflict between the charter and the contribution agreements, it should be clear which terms prevail.

•

Step-by-Step Alignment for Trust-Funded Partnership Programs

1. *In defining the trust fund, signed agreements for the receipt of donor contributions should specify all essential elements relating to fund use and trustee functions.*

This statement is fairly obvious for matters having to do with donor-driven specifications of what the funds can finance, like the scope of activities and the categories of expenditure. It is also clear that this includes the trustee's operating procedures, like how the trustee handles investment income or what happens when the trust fund winds down. Less clear, but no less important, is that this should include partnership elements when the trust fund is part of a partnership program. This usually includes:

- a description of the governing body, or any other shared governance or partner input pertaining to the trust fund, like advising on strategic direction (high level) or deciding on funding allocations (activity level); and
- a description of the secretariat, or any other supporting entity role, in addition to support as the trustee.

These and potentially other relevant partnership aspects are among the essential elements that should be transparently described and clearly agreed *before* funds are received and activities are implemented. They can be specified directly in the contribution agreements or, when governance is best described in a separate document like a charter, they can be incorporated into the contribution agreements by reference to a charter. This brings us to step #2.

2. *In defining the partnership program, shared governance and other partnership elements are often best described in a separate constitutive document, like an adopted charter.*

The primary trigger for moving partnership terms out of the contribution agreements and into a stand-alone document is when the main upstream participants, like participants in the governing body, go beyond the donors and the trustee. Contribution agreements involve only the donors and trustee as the signatories. That leaves non-signatories out of the loop. But how can that be when they, as participants in the governing body, are partners, too, and when shared governance terms apply to them as well? This kind of engagement calls for a more widely shared document that can involve everyone. A separate charter represents a collective, more inclusive approach.

Separating governance terms into a charter serves the full partnership. Granted, introducing a charter adds the need to synchronize documents side-by-side, but that is manageable, made worthwhile by all the benefits. As explained in these pages:

Charter virtues:

voice
ownership
peer partners
plain English
flexibility

- It can reflect the spectrum of partner voices. (>@ BfB: Constitutive Documents—Why Have a Charter)
- It can be "owned" by the governing body as a shared expression of intention. (>@ ibid.—Who Owns the Charter)
- It represents horizontal partner-to-partner relationships, rather than being caught in fund flow verticals. (>@ BfB: Dualities—Verticals and Horizontals)
- It is freed from legalese and can be written in plain English. (>@ BfB: Deft Drafting—The Art of Writing—Being Plainspoken)
- It opens the door to flexibility through efficient amendment processes. (>@ BfB: Constitutive Documents—What's So Great About Charters)

Some of these advantages are so great that even when the governing body is limited to donors and the trustee, it may still be worth having a separate charter document. Partners are more likely to converge around a plain English, concise articulation of who they are than the usual contribution agreements loaded with standard trustee terms and supporting entity boilerplate. (>@ PfP: Like Water, Like Rock) The key factor is the creation of a governing body, which opens the door to a charter. As its first item of business, when the governing body first convenes, the donors and trustee, and any other decision-making partners, can collectively adopt their stand-alone, partnership-agreed charter for inclusion in the contribution agreements.

———————————————————— ● ————————————————————

Umbrella Arrangements Love Charters

While inclusivity is relevant for individual trust funds, this ability to be inclusive through charters is especially evident in umbrella arrangements. (>@ PfP: Typology—Trust-Funded Partnership Programs) When a partnership program has multiple trust funds, or other funding sources, especially if they involve different trustees and different sets of donors, the charter can provide an overarching governance framework that brings them all together, under its "umbrella." Umbrella governance functions the same way for multi-trust-fund programs as shared governance functions for one-trust-fund programs, only with greater reach. Instead of tying into one set of contribution agreements with identical trust fund terms for commingled funds, umbrella charters tie into different sets of contribution agreements. And yet, in both cases, there is one overarching partnership program governing body with a designated supporting secretariat. In addition to this overarching governance, each trust fund can also have its own governance layer, provided its relationship to the overarching layer is clear. There is no prescribed limit to the number of funding sources and vehicles that can be under the purview of one and the same governing body operating on the basis of one and the same charter.

———————————————————— ● ————————————————————

3. *The timing on adoption and signature may be tricky, but can be managed.*

Like the proverbial chicken and egg, adoption of the charter and signature of the contribution agreements go hand in hand. On the one hand, membership in the governing body that adopts the charter is commonly conferred by signature of the contribution agreement; donor status grants membership. On the other hand, donors are usually not ready to sign on the dotted line until governance terms are clear and agreed.

In practice, one of the two steps ends up going first, since it is unnecessarily challenging to orchestrate adoption and signatures all at the same time. That gives us two choices: either adoption first and signatures later, or signatures first and adoption later. It goes like this:

- *Adoption first.* You can hold the first governing body meeting with prospective donors based on formal or informal pledges, at which the charter is formally adopted. Adoption means the charter becomes effective on the basis of one decision point, usually by consensus (or a virtual no-objection procedure). (>@ PfP: Decision Making) After the charter is adopted, the donors can sign their contribution agreements with reference to an adopted, effective charter.

- *Signature first.* In the alternative, you can engage key partners in an informal process—like a working group or some self-acknowledged founders—to confirm the terms of a draft charter. This version is then used, by common understanding, as the basis upon which donors sign contribution agreements. Once they (or enough of them) have their formal donor status, these partners can then meet for a first governing body meeting to formally adopt the informally confirmed charter (subject to any last refinements they might all agree on). The contribution agreements are signed with reference to the charter to be adopted.

A key factor that can help all of this stay in synch is having one central drafting locus for all the establishment documents. The best situation is to have one (possibly overworked) individual who holds the pen—the keeper of the live drafts. Drafts in and out, points negotiated and aligned, iterations rippling through. It is no surprise that this central individual is most effectively based in the supporting entity, the custodial seat of the partnership program that will have the lead oar in running the partnership program as agreed.

Legal Orchestration

As a legal matter, how do you get adopted documents and signed agreements to mesh with each other? Since you basically need both parts—the charter and the contribution agreements—to be in effect for trust-funded partnership program operations to begin, it may be important to accommodate time lags. That can mean holding one part in abeyance while letting the other catch up, all of which can be done with some deft drafting. Here are some alternatives:

- *Agreements are effective, but no disbursements until charter adoption.* Contribution agreements can specify that no funds will be disbursed (or even received) by the trustee until the charter is adopted. This approach essentially treats contribution agreements as holding agreements pending completion (>@ BfB: A Taxonomy of Trust Fund Agreements—Upstream Agreements). The governing body then meets, adopts the charter, and the trustee can start disbursing (or receiving) funds.
- *Agreements are signed, but not effective until adoption.* Adoption of the charter can be a condition of effectiveness for the contribution agreements. They can be signed as in the first example, but effectiveness is put on hold until the charter is adopted, at which point everything goes into effect at the same time. Whether alternative one or two fits best may depend on the donor's budget rules. If the point is recognizing a committed contribution in the relevant fiscal year, is a committing signature enough, or is effectiveness needed to show commitment?
- *The charter is informally agreed prior to signatures.* This is the "signature first" variant above. This approach relies on enough charter finality despite an informal process to proceed with signatures, as well as partners refraining from renegotiations after signatures have begun—or everything unravels.

---

4. *For the purposes of combining contribution agreements and charters, the contribution agreements bring in the terms of the charter.*

Contractually this can be done in at least two ways: either by legal "incorporation by reference" or, one step short of legal incorporation, by having the charter "apply." Donors may prefer one or the other approach for internal reasons, but the same approach should be used across all donors to the same trust fund for consistency across commingled terms. The practical difference is negligible.

- *Incorporating by reference.* This first way is the most common, whereby the "incorporated" charter becomes part and parcel ("an integral part") of the contribution agreement. The charter gets added into the donor/trustee agreed terms—it is contractualized vis-à-vis each donor and the trustee—while it continues to be a standalone, adopted document, subject to its own terms. The signature that makes the contribution agreement effective essentially carries over to include the charter. However, as a separate, stand-alone document, the charter can be independently amended over time.

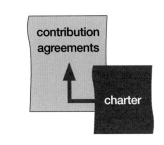

  Sample clause in the contribution agreements: *The Contribution shall be administered by the Trustee on behalf of the Donor in accordance with the terms and conditions specified in this Contribution Agreement, including the annexes, as well as the Partnership Program Charter, as may be amended from time to time, which is hereby incorporated by reference, all of which constitute an integral part of this Contribution Agreement. [The version of the Partnership Program Charter as of signature is attached hereto as Annex X for informational purposes only.]*

- *Applying.* The second way reflects a lighter touch than full legal incorporation. Nevertheless, when charters are made to merely "apply" to contribution agreements (without being incorporated by reference), partnership program participants, including donors, are still relying on those terms. Even when those terms are just applied and not fully contractualized, charters can still be considered to have practical, if not technical, agreement status. At the end of the day, the trustee still knows what to do, and donors still expect the trustee to do it, whether the charter is integrally incorporated or operationally applied.

TO APPLY

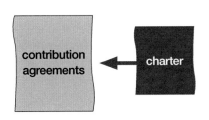

  Sample clause in the contribution agreements: *The Contribution shall be administered by the Trustee on behalf of the Donor in accordance with the terms and conditions specified in this Contribution Agreement, including the annexes, which constitute an integral part of this Contribution Agreement, and in accordance with the Partnership Program Charter, as may be amended from time to time, whose terms shall also apply hereto. [The version of the Partnership Program Charter as of signature is attached hereto as Annex X for informational purposes only.]*

5. Overlaps and gaps are best avoided when juxtaposing charters alongside contribution agreements.

A thorough and diligent lawyer may think it is good practice to make sure each document is complete, and all documents say everything that needs to be said. She may work hard to be as comprehensive as possible, leaving nothing out. That instinct is a good one, except that the execution may need some tempering. Yes, everything that is relevant should be included—that goes with the "four corners" principle (>@ PfP: Use of Funds—Four Corners of the Agreement)—but some parts are best included directly, while other parts can be included indirectly. The goal is "no gaps, no overlaps," where documents are structured, layered, and aligned. In much the same way that partnership elements can be modular, so, too, can the documents. Taking the same kind of comparative advantage analysis we apply to roles and responsibilities, we can be deliberate in thinking about what text goes where and how it connects. This is about layering and interrelating efficiently in a smooth and seamless manner that aligns the documents.

Alignment is an art.

Alignment is an art. The first step is recognizing multiple documents as part of a package (>@ BfB: Practical Packaging)—appreciating that signed, adopted, and operational documents can each have their place as part of the whole. From an establishment perspective, the foundational layer should be woven together, as interlocking, rather than overlapping, documents. As the documents sit side-by-side, they should not be duplicative; they should neither repeat, nor conflict. Why is that?

- When saying the same thing in two different documents, especially heavily negotiated documents, it can be very hard to ensure not a single difference in wording. Documents are structured differently; they may or may not use defined terms, enumerations, and other style elements that can have substantive effects. Even minor wording and placement differences can lead to confusion, if not conflict. A seasoned lawyer knows the interpretation of a clause can turn on a single word, the placement of a single comma, or the use of introductory phrasing. (>@ BfB: Deft Drafting—The Art of Writing)

- If only one partnership-agreed articulation of key terms is included, then only one place needs amending. The same clause in two documents would need double amending, which has two collateral effects. First, if we want to leverage the governing body for efficient amendability (>@ PfP: Like Rock, Like Water—Like Rock), adding an inefficient signing mode moots the advantage. Second, it easily happens that one is amended, but not the other, which then creates a direct conflict. In all likelihood, this discrepancy is not trivial, since the amendment was important enough to make. Partners may not remember to update the second document, or even if they do remember, there is a lag time and extra effort before the second amendment is effective, before the will of the partners is fully in place. Partners expect the new, approved language to apply, but in fact, it does not fully, at least not for a while. In the meantime, the trustee, secretariat, and other partners have to operate in parallel universes, bound to perform under two documents that say different things.

Every case is different, but this is usually a good approach:

- include partnership-level descriptions, like descriptions of activities by component or subject area and descriptions of shared governance by elements and roles and responsibilities, directly in the charter and then indirectly in the contribution agreements by cross-referencing to the charter (either by incorporating or applying);
- include a general reference to the trustee and trust fund in the charter as well, with a broad cross-reference to the contribution agreements for details;
- include trust fund–specific descriptions, like the descriptions of detailed fund use requirements, categories of expenditure, and specific trustee obligations and donor rights, in the contribution agreements without needing a cross-reference in the charter; and
- when unsure about what to put where, err on the side of a more comprehensive charter for partnership aspects, so as to emphasize the collective and facilitate amendability.

Parsing this way can avoid conflicts and overlaps, with the added benefit of avoiding double hops to amend—if the carry-over clause is added. That brings us to step #6.

DOCUMENT DIVISION OF LABOR

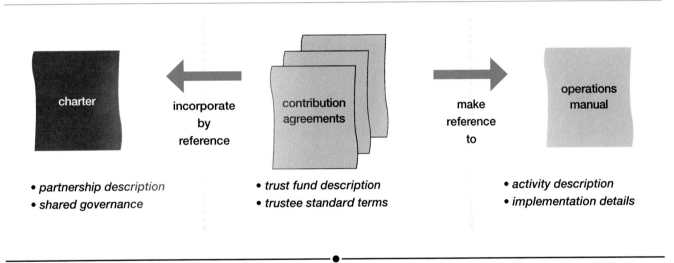

- *partnership description*
- *shared governance*

- *trust fund description*
- *trustee standard terms*

- *activity description*
- *implementation details*

The Trickiness of Multi-Step Amendment Processes

Doing multi-step amendments across multiple documents usually inserts some inconvenient lag time. Partners think they are done, but they are not. That can raise tricky operational questions. For example:

- A charter amendment approved by the governing body adds a partner as a decision-making member, but contribution agreements still contain the old membership list. How does the secretariat handle a new no-objection request? Does it get sent to the new partner? What if the new partner objects, does that count and block the decision? No, probably not—the contribution agreements need amending—but it is awkward.
- The selection criteria for grant recipients is amended in the charter to add new requirements, but contribution agreements still include the old list. How does the trustee decide on new recipients? Does it hold off with the new criteria until all contribution agreements are amended? What if the contribution agreement list had been "for information only," while deferring to the charter for the operative list— would that have helped? Yes, it would have.

6. *For strengthened alignment, the charter and the contribution agreements should speak the same language.*

The handshake between charter and contribution agreements is a critical bridge that holds the trust-funded partnership program package together. (>@ BfB: Practical Packaging) From a drafting perspective, this bridge can be fortified by common terminology that acts as girders across the span. We are not talking about filling documents with sanctioned legal labels, but rather trying to accurately reflect, and perhaps even guide, the common parlance of the partners. If partners refer to the Coordination Unit instead of the Secretariat, then the same, commonly used label should show up in both the charter and the contribution agreements.

Alignment between all establishment documents, as well as other operative documents like the operations manual, should flow coherently from the voice of the partners directly into the defined terms of the documents. However, a carefully attuned lawyer will not only write the words that she hears partners using, but will also write words that help the partners find their language, with labels that are accurate and meaningful. For example, if partners are referring to "implementing entities," but the lawyer understands that they are actually supervising entities, a tweak toward "Implementation Support Entities" might be in order. Or if, in the interest of transparency, the partners want closed sessions of the governing body to be rarely if ever used, the lawyer can employ the defined term "Exceptional Closed Sessions" when introducing the concept in the rules of procedure. Sometimes a lawyer knows what needs identifying and labeling better than the partners themselves.

By amplifying the careful and consistent use of shared terminology, drafters and negotiators can increase both the practical relevance of partnership documents and the clarity of shared terms that more directly communicate expectations and understandings.

> ### The Charter-Contribution Agreement Handshake:
> ### When I amend, you amend. We always stay aligned.

7. *For legal support, the charter and the contribution agreements should cross-refer to each other.*

Along with common language that spans the operative documents, the bridge between the charter and contribution agreements deserves extra fortifying with mirror abutments at each end, one clause in the charter and one clause in the contribution agreements. It is not only the polite thing to do, to acknowledge the other one individual in the room, but it is also useful. Cross-referring particularly in the context of amendability—the main theme of this chapter on alignment—introduces the "carry-over" concept discussed more fully in step #8. Here are complementary examples of how this can work:

- **Sample Charter Carry-Over Clause.** *This Charter may be amended by a Governing Body decision [e.g., consensus as stated elsewhere in the Charter]. Any amendments to this Charter will become applicable to the Contribution Agreements as such amendments take effect without further need to amend the Contribution Agreements; provided that such amendments do not conflict with other terms of the Contribution Agreements and are consistent with the Trustee's applicable policies and procedures, as determined by the Trustee. The Secretariat maintains and distributes clear records of any such amendments.*

- **Sample Contribution Agreement Carry-Over Clause.** *This Contribution Agreement may be amended by written agreement between the Trustee and the Donor; provided that (i) the common annexes attached hereto may be amended only by written agreement between the Trustee and all donors contributing to the Trust Fund, and (ii) the Charter may be amended by the Governing Body according to its terms with such amendments becoming directly applicable to this Contribution Agreement as and when such amendments become effective without the need for further written or signed agreement between the Trustee and the Donor; and provided further that, with respect to both (i) and (ii), any such amendments do not conflict with other terms of the contribution agreements for the Trust Fund and are consistent with the Trustee's applicable policies and procedures, as determined by the Trustee.*

8. For efficient amendability, charter amendments should apply automatically to the contribution agreements (the "carry-over effect").

If so stated in the documents—as per the sample buttressing clauses presented in step #7—amendments to the charter can apply directly to the contribution agreements without need for further amendment. When you are dealing with a dozen or more donors, or even just a few, that can be huge. A relief for all partners, this is particularly true for supporting entities that, either as trustee or secretariat, bear the burden of corralling all those amendments.

The amendment may be a simple, non-controversial addition of a member to the governing body, and yet, it still takes all the drafting, legal review on both sides, internal clearances, signature formalities up the chain, senior management signatures, and transmission—and that times the number of donors—to get the amendment in place. With so many touches, the process is extenuated, and the ripple effect of delays is multiplied. A supporting entity must also realize that every time it goes to a donor with a request for a bilaterally signed amendment, that opens the door to other requests for amendments (while we're at it . . .), a tweak here, a requirement there, and before you know it, agreement negotiations may burst into full bloom, and then a bouquet. There is a time for amendments, and that can be embraced, but multi-party engagements are best channeled through more compact and controlled processes. With single decision points in a governing body, you get ducks in a row, while trust fund agreement amendments leave you herding cats.

When coupling a charter and contribution agreements, the charter invariably contains material terms for donor contributions. A donor would not be making its contribution without these terms. As explained in step #4, the contribution agreements should bring in the charter, making it part of the incorporated or applicable terms for the particular trust fund. This in turn embeds the trust fund in the partnership program. And here is the point: In the same breath that the charter is brought into the contribution agreements, those agreements should also be made amendable by the charter. Legitimately from a package perspective, as and when charter amendments take effect, they will also change the contribution agreements. This makes sense, since the charter has become an extension of the contribution agreements.

It is all part of the handshake between the two documents. The charter says its amendments are expected to apply to the contribution agreements without needing signed donor amendments, and then the contribution agreements in turn say the same, deferring to the governing body for those amendments. Amending becomes a partnership act, not a bilateral act. Bilateral relations are subsumed into partnership relations.

---●---

Key Ingredients for the Carry-Over Effect

To put it all together, we can sum up a few elements that make the carry-over effect work smoothly, all of which can benefit from a lawyer's vigilance:

1. First and foremost, this approach takes a partnership perspective, as reflected in a governing body that has a meaningful role in approving revisions to foundational charter terms.
2. All donors contributing to the trust fund pool need to be represented, either directly or indirectly, with a decision-making voice on the governing body, to correspond to all contribution agreements.
3. As the other signatory to the contribution agreements, the trustee entity needs to have a decision-making voice on the governing body, as the trustee will normally want a last say in matters pertaining to its responsibility.
4. Careful consideration needs to be given to what goes into the charter vs. the contribution agreements (>@ PfP: Like Rock, Like Water—Like Water), so "easy" amendability does not exceed appropriate bounds.
5. Well-planned drafting needs to pre-position cross-amendability by linking the charter and contribution agreements through built-in mirror clauses (the abutment examples in step #6).
6. Due care, and relevant due diligence, needs to be applied in recognition that charter amendments take on a more legal, agreement quality by virtue of simultaneously amending contribution agreements.

If all this is in place, the partnership program can stay current. Members can take fate into their own hands and make changes as needed, with the necessary consensus. With this kind of strong alignment, the trust fund can keep up with the partnership for a more balanced and sustainable partnership program.

---●---

The Downsides of No Charter and No Carry-Over

It may be that the lawyer working on the contribution agreements is focused on them because they are prescribed and required. It may be that this lawyer is perfectly content to bring everything into the contribution agreements, staying focused on the trust fund, rather than the partnership program of which it is a part. A charter may not even be a consideration, not part of this lawyer's repertoire. It may also be that the lawyer prefers to avoid the extra work of aligning two documents, especially if the timing is tight, and contributions are ready to pour in, with or without a charter. There always seems to be ample reason not to bring in a charter in addition to the contribution agreements, so let's review the implications:

> Leveraging a charter and the carry-over effect can avoid multiple headaches when a partnership program involves multiple donors. It enables a one-and-done decision point across all documents. Lack of the carry-over effect means that charter amendments require separate and additional amendments to each and every contribution agreement for the same pooled fund, requiring extra effort and delay.

> This extra effort and delay causes dissonance within the partnership program. When all partners think they have agreed on a change, intending and assuming immediate effect, the change is not complete until every last donor signs an amendment.

> This extra effort and delay can also cause trustee schizophrenia. While the trustee stays bound to outdated contribution agreements, it of course wants to respect the will of the partners vis-à-vis the current charter.

> This time lag can become chronic if any donors have since disappeared from view, even though they are technically still donors with funds in the pool. At some point comes the awkward decision about whether their lack of input can simply be ignored. (It won't do to let a single, inactive donor hold everyone hostage.) (>@ PfP: Partners and People—Being a Good Partner)

> Trustee schizophrenia can also become chronic. The trustee may not even be aware that its binding obligations are out of synch, if there is lack of transparency and accountability in the process.

It may be tempting to dismiss all of this as unnecessary housekeeping, with a little sloppiness here and there, of no consequence if business views stay aligned. And that is often how it goes. But letting documents and partnership practice get out of synch can also get messy and out of balance. Especially for the supporting entity, who has the general (custodial) role of keeping things in order (>@ PfP: Custodial Effect), the ability to keep abreast of changing circumstances is a marker of partnership program health and sustainability.

To put a point on it, this is about far more than housekeeping. The question is as fundamental as deciding whether and to what extent collective decisions rule. Is the multilateral charter or the bilateral contribution agreement the driving factor for donor relations? Remember that the trust fund is only part of the partnership program, not the other way around. In a partnership program setting, it makes sense to go with the partnership.

9. *Amendments to the charter should not occur without the trustee/supporting entity's consent.*

This may be stating the obvious, but to the extent charter terms affect trustee or secretariat operations—basically always—any changes to these terms need to have the supporting entity on board. This often occurs structurally and naturally when the supporting entity is part of the governing body that approves the charter amendments, perhaps even as its chair. (>@ PfP: Governing Bodies—Composition—Supporting Entities) As long as decisions are on a consensus basis, this gives the supporting entity an effective right of consent (or veto power in the negative), one of the virtues of consensus decision making. (>@ PfP: Decision Making)

Engaging the supporting entity also means respecting the supporting entity.

An artful technique is for charter amendments to reach the governing body only through the secretariat. This puts the secretariat in clearing house and compliance roles that ensure the supporting entity is on board. (>@ PfP: Secretariats—Inhouse Secretariat Roles—Gatekeeping Support) Any amendment proposal would be forwarded by the secretariat to the governing body only after appropriate internal vetting. Even in cases where the supporting entity is not one of the governing body decision makers, such a clearing house role can help the supporting entity manage decision points upfront and avoid tension points over time.

Ideally this prior review works not just for the benefit of the supporting entity, but of all partners, with the interests of the whole partnership program in mind. No one is better positioned to understand what all is at stake and at play than the supporting entity. This is part of what it means to be the custodian of the partnership program. (>@ PfP: Custodial Effect)

In all cases, any amendment to the charter or the contribution agreements has to be consistent with relevant policies and procedures of the supporting entity, meaning not in conflict or violation. This may or may not prove restrictive, depending on the nature of the supporting entity's applicable policies and procedures and any terms that were otherwise negotiated for the partnership program. Accepting the support of a supporting entity has to mean accepting the institutional context in which that support is provided. Partners hopefully step into that context with eyes wide open. (>@ ibid.—Eyes Wide Open) As we have seen in some of the sample clauses, good practice would add language for this kind of consistency/compliance with applicable policies and procedures in the relevant documents.

Some combination of the following can be specified in the documents:

- amendments cannot be considered unless tabled by the supporting entity (as chair or secretariat);
- amendments require consensus for approval (including the supporting entity as a decision maker); and
- amendments must be consistent with applicable (or negotiated) trustee/supporting entity policies and procedures.

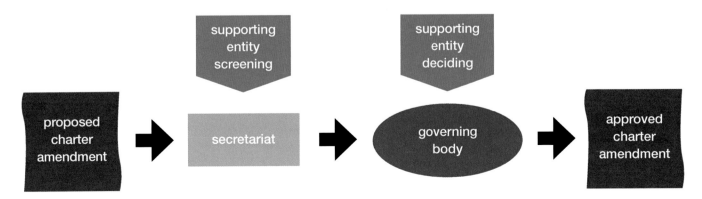

10. *Charter amendments should be given agreement status with agreement-type review.*

Even though charters are adopted documents, usually not directly endowed with the legally binding effect of signed agreements, they can become binding, or in any case, contractualized. (>@ BfB: Constitutive Documents—What to Watch For—Legal Status) Once they are incorporated by reference, and even if they are only made to apply, they acquire at least some degree of agreement status. When charters have agreement status, actually or effectively, charter amendments should also be accorded agreement status, including giving them the same type of internal review and clearance as would be given to a contribution agreement amendment.

This stepped-up approach is especially true for the trustee/supporting entity and the donors, the contribution agreement signatories, who have leaned on the charter for their contribution agreement content. When they act as governing body members, instead of signatories, they are still representing their respective institutions in ways that have legal effect. When considering charter amendments, they should remain mindful of their internal vetting processes prior to agreeing to those amendments. They should also recognize that the charter and the contribution agreements have been bridged and packaged, to be seen as one.

Bottom line, the status of charters as stand-alone documents, "owned" for amendment purposes by their governing bodies, are not stand-alone from a legal perspective if they are brought into contribution agreements. In these cases, the decision points for charter amendments are also decision points for contribution agreements. They should be considered subject to each governing body member's commensurate, agreement-like standard of internal review.

Watch when charter amendments acquire agreement status.

11. *In the event of conflict between the charter and the contribution agreements, it should be clear which terms prevail.*

In the first instance, care should be taken to draft the various constitutive documents to minimize the potential for conflict. As already indicated in step #5, a rule of thumb is to avoid overlapping text on the same subject matter. It may, nonetheless, be hard to predict where conflicts could arise, so it is always prudent to add a prevalence clause. Here we have one of two choices:

> *In the event of conflict, the terms of the Contribution Agreements shall prevail over the Charter.*

> *In the event of conflict, the terms of the Charter shall prevail over the Contribution Agreements.*

So which should prevail, the charter or the contribution agreements? That is a negotiated choice. There is no inherent requirement that it has to be one or the other. However, as the practice usually goes, the right to dominate is usually given to the contribution agreements, for at least two reasons:

1. Agreements are apt to get more internal attention, more legal review, more formal clearances, and more visibility rising up to a ranking signature. Charters often do not get the same kind of attention because, as adopted documents, they may bypass standard internal procedures for signed documents. Given this asymmetry, the ability to add a charter may depend on having the contribution agreement prevail.

2. Fund flow hierarchies put contributions at the top. Donors who initiate the funding chain like to see everything flow downwards from their agreed terms, if only because they are internally bound to use their funds for specific purposes under specific conditions. Other terms and interpretations are not meant to override their carefully crafted contribution terms.

Prevalence clauses are important, but they only traffic in conflicts. Whatever is not conflicted in either the charter or the contribution agreements applies in full on its stated terms. If documents are carefully drafted, including avoiding overlaps, the question of conflict should rarely, if ever, arise.

Conclusion

So many steps could leave a reader breathless, or you may discover they are but a walk—or waltz—in the park. These guidelines appear in detail to provide context and anticipate issues, but ultimately increase agility. You can reach out for a do-si-do, twirl your partner. You can also reach out across documents and twirl them into alignment.

This interplay of partnership program documents reflects the dance of the governing body and the fiduciary, each respecting the other, each relying on a clear understanding of their respective roles. One is governed by its own charter, resting on partnership structure, and the other is governed by its own agreements, resting on contracted obligations. The charter document leverages the partnership through the governing body. The fund flow agreements leverage the funded program through the fiduciary.

This structure and contract duality, between governing body and trustee, between decision making and fund flows, meets its match when it comes to the documents. Certainly by then, a lawyer realizes they have to relate to each other and create a uniform whole. In positioning the package, as we will see in the next chapter, aligning the documents fastens the nuts and bolts to undergird the overall arrangement.

A key starting point is the open floor of the international arena, and a key element is a desire to be contextual, inclusive, responsive, and flexible among partners. Debating whether partnership program documents should enable such flexibility is a red herring. International partnership programs have to be flexible to stay attuned to changing circumstances, voluntary participation, transitioning partners, and lessons learned. Flexibility is not an optional feature; it is integral. And depending on how you stage the dance, it can be more or less efficient, more or less agile on two or twenty feet.

This alignment ten-plus-one-step may not be the rousing Texas two-step, but you can swing your partners joyfully all the same.

Step together, do-si-do.

3 PRACTICAL PACKAGING

We have considered how to position words. We have considered how to position documents. Now let's consider how to position negotiations for partnership program establishment. As with the alignment of charters and contribution agreements, we can continue to focus on the combination of shared governance and pooled funding, as a multi-dimensional case to think through.

The Package Approach to Establishment

Particularly when creating trust-funded partnership programs, it is useful to think of the establishment (or constitutive) documents as a package. Adopted charters and signed contribution agreements—a common combination—address different aspects and serve different purposes (>@ BfB: Dualities—Harmonization and Individuation), but they relate to each other and should talk to one another. In an ideal situation, these documents should not only cross-refer to each other, but, as much as possible, be drafted and negotiated at the same time, with both in mind. That is how the step-to-step alignment in the prior chapter works. (>@ BfB: Agile Alignment—Step-by-Step Alignment for Trust-Funded Partnership Programs)

When dealing with multiple downstream fiduciaries (as with international platforms), this package approach is especially important. Then it is valuable to add downstream transfer agreements to the mix, so everyone can see everyone's involvement—from upstream contributions, to central administration, to downstream implementation, all in a flow and a loop. Because donors have privity (are signatory to) only to upstream agreements, not downstream ones, they have assured visibility of contribution agreements, but not necessarily transfer agreements. And yet, downstream fiduciary terms are relevant to their contributions. In fact, everyone benefits from negotiating the transfer agreements at the same time as the contribution agreements, along with the charter or other key governance terms as well.

By treating all these documents as a package—usually at least threefold: (1) form of contribution agreement, (2) charter, and (3) form of transfer agreement—the trustee and secretariat pre-position a coherent, interlocking set of terms where everyone sees everything, and no one has surprises or upsets later down the road. The alternative, which is all too common, is to negotiate in a cascade, starting at the top of the fund flows hierarchy and finishing that off before continuing with the bottom. There are plenty of bruised lawyers who can attest to the challenge. If contribution agreements are all signed up, then any changes arising from subsequently negotiated transfer agreements can upend the initially negotiated contribution agreements. Even small changes, if required, can result in painfully circular signing exercises.

International partnership programs are not widgets that come off an assembly line. Experience shows that the way to avoid negotiating whiplash, where changes reverberate up and down the chain, is to put everything on the table at the same time. With donor visibility of the downstream, and implementer visibility of the upstream, you negotiate everything at once and fit the pieces together. As they say, you're not done until you're done—but then, once you're done, you're really done.

> Share downstream agreements with upstream donors, and upstream agreements with downstream recipients.

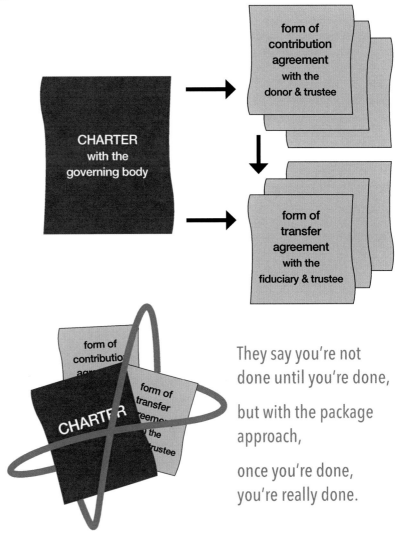

> They say you're not done until you're done,
>
> but with the package approach,
>
> once you're done, you're really done.

Partnership-oriented package negotiating starts with a partnership vision. That may be counterintuitive if the attention is on securing funds or driving implementation, which in either case puts the focus on the trustee and its bilateral agreements (contribution agreements upstream and transfer or grant agreements downstream). A partnership program that focuses too much on fund flows and pushes contribution agreements into place before establishing the partnership elements may forever find itself caught in the fund account paradigm. To become a sustainable partnership platform over time, partners are better off articulating their funding aspects within their partnership program scope, not the other way around.

It may also be that the trustee/supporting entity has been given (or has taken) enough responsibility and control that documentation is simply produced, rather than negotiated. That no longer looks like much of a partnership.

For sure, it takes extra effort and discipline to prioritize the partnership perspective when trust funds are involved. But it is the partnership dimension that will bring sustainability. It is the partnership platform that will leverage efficiencies and synergies and ultimately enable better results.

THE SPECTRUM OF HOW PARTNERSHIP TERMS COME ABOUT

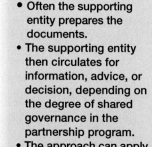

- Often the supporting entity prepares the documents.
- The supporting entity then circulates for information, advice, or decision, depending on the degree of shared governance in the partnership program.
- The approach can apply to the whole package or vary document-by-document.

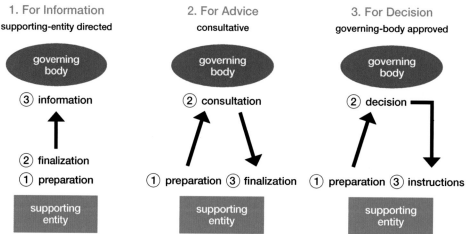

It's Iterative . . . That's Normal

By the time you are on your twelfth draft, you may be cursing your stars, but go with it. My file folders are full of annotated versions and line-edit mark-ups, replete with composite track changes upon track changes until they could no longer be parsed, and then we started anew with clean. It's not just normal, it's healthy. One of the best harbingers of sustained commitment is early engagement. You want partners to step up and dig in, to own their partnership, to make it collectively theirs.

So when you get that long list of questions and comments from the tenth donor, and face the prospect of another long night, know what it is good for. Be grateful that partners are pitching in. Be patient with requests and requirements while they can be still be addressed, rather than when it is too late. Not every partner needs to pick up the pen, and no one should go crazy, but you do want a critical mass of key participants—hopefully a few lawyers among them—to weigh in. That added weight is extra ballast for a stronger foundation going forward.

If you are the lawyer, your drafts are the terrain upon which partnership building takes place. It is worth indulging the process. Ask your business colleagues to indulge it as well. Give partners enough time to review and comment. Give them your full attention in response. Understand their issues, state your reasons, and work it out.

An early iterative process can make better partners and better partnerships. Encourage and embrace it.

The Package from a Legal Perspective

To add to the many perspectives, it is also useful to consider partnership program documents from a legal perspective, especially since lawyers are running point on the documents. When we do that contextually, we can see that the legal traits are reflections of the partners' relationships. Whether documents are signed or adopted, whether they deal with rights and obligations vs. operations, whether they are owned by the parties or the partners, these kinds of questions are for lawyers, but they are also about partnership engagements and business choices. Lawyers who have a good grasp of the partnership/business context can use their informed understandings of possible constructs to develop and document a solid partnership program structure. They can recognize that partnership program documents are modular, stackable, and come as a package.

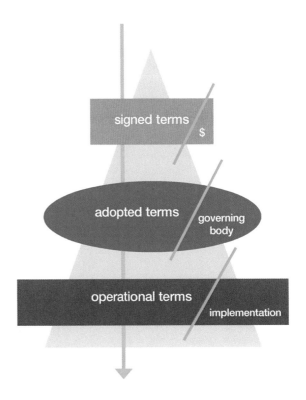

To that end, architecting international partnership programs, especially ones with trust funds, can be like baking a triple-decker document cake. We can think of three layers for lawyers to bake and balance, while also summarizing some of what we have explored in this book:

- **Signed terms.** Think primarily of *contribution agreements* and *transfer/grant agreements* for trust funds. They need signatures because they deal with fund flows (>@ PfP: Structure—Connecting Fund Flows and Decision Flows), which makes them more formal and rigid, harder to change. Naturally, this is where you put terms that are less susceptible to change, or where one or the other party wants to deter change. Standard, non-negotiable operating terms of the trustee fit into that category, perfectly placed in a non-negotiable, standard form annex of the contribution agreement, a very modular, secure place to be.

- **Adopted terms.** Think primarily of *charters* for partnership programs. They can be adopted because they belong to governing bodies, which makes them living, breathing, and open to change. This, then, is where you put terms that are likely to change, or where the partners want the flexibility to adjust over time. Membership, roles and responsibilities, even mission, objectives, and the scope of activities, all can be responsive to single decision points to stay fit-for-purpose. (>@ BfB: Dualities— Informal and Formal) Neatly plugged into the contribution agreements by cross-references (>@ BfB: Agile Alignment—Step-by-Step Alignment for Trust-Funded Partnership Programs, #4), these adopted terms are stand-alone enough to be another modular, flexible piece of the puzzle.

- **Operational terms.** Think primarily of the *operations or "ops" manuals.* Sometimes endorsed (approved) by the governing body, but just as often simply developed by and for the entities that use them, they get into the operational weeds and deal with the downstream details. These are practical documents, emerging from and responsive to actual implementation. They can be tedious in their clarity and comprehensiveness, dwelling on criteria, processes, requirements, restrictions, and erring on the side of more, even a hundred and some pages later. They are usually highly specific to the partnership program and trust fund at hand, fleshing out the foundational understandings with policy and practical applications. While not normally considered part of the establishment documents, they round out the modular package.

Packaging Trust-Funded Partnership Programs

When it comes to establishing partnership programs that include trust funds, what does the actual practice of the package approach look like?

1. **Documents.** The key here is that **all establishment documents are part of the collective**. The centerpiece, from a partnership perspective, is the multilateral charter, which is prepared and reviewed as a shared, to-be-adopted document. Flanking the charter are the fund flow agreements, which also need collective attention, even though they are bilateral, to-be-signed documents. To make this work, these agreements—primarily the contribution agreements—are drafted, negotiated, and accepted as "forms of agreement" among all prospective signatories before they are individually signed. The "form of contribution agreement" is basically all the common annexes (on fund use and trustee operations) attached to a cover agreement that has plug-and-play blanks for donor-specific information (like contribution amounts, payment schedules; >@ BfB: A Taxonomy of Trust Fund Agreements—Upstream Agreements). This allows common terms to settle, leaving only donor contribution details to be added, before anyone starts signing.

   A Word to the Wise: The alternative can get pretty ugly. Donor A signs, donor B renegotiates a term and signs subject to A amending, A amends, meanwhile donor C signs with another revised term subject to A and B amending, B amends, A does not like C's amendment and reopens negotiations, negotiations conclude, and A, B, and C amend with the revised agreed text, donor D wants to sign but also has an issue. . . . It is truly a shame, when donors are deterred by uphill processes, contributions are delayed or even derailed, and operations are postponed. With forms of agreement, you can **ban the whiplash**.

2. **Negotiations.** The key here is a **speak-now-or-forever-hold-your-peace attitude**. All partners are on notice that now is the time. Anyone who wants direct involvement at some point—for example, as a signatory of a fund flow agreement or a member of the governing body—is expected to engage now, together in a package approach: all establishment drafts *on* the table and all prospective partners *at* the table. The upstream sees what the downstream is planning, and the downstream can react to what the upstream is requiring. The process needs ample time for all individual partners to review and comment, enough space for all voices to be heard. Perhaps this process can be done virtually (although have pity on the lawyer tracking all the iterations), whether everyone sees everyone's comments for transparency or closure is reached bilaterally bit-by-bit. Or it can be done physically in a meeting, where anyone who wants to can pipe up until agreement has been reached.

   A Word to the Wise: Kudos to the partners who are willing to join all together in a conference room flipping pages, going point-for-point until all the open issues are addressed. I have seen it done in all-day sessions with forty and more. "Page 14, any points? . . . No, then on to page 15. Section D.3 has proposed rewording, and the section after that has conflicting views. The floor is open for comments. . . ." And on to the last page. That is called closure! Then if a partner comes back some time later and says "I need to change this" or "I can't do that," the answer is, "Sorry, your time to comment has come and gone, please get on board." It can work. With large, multiparty negotiations, sometimes it is the only way. You can **ban the churn**.

The package approach:

all establishment drafts on the table;

all prospective partners at the table.

3. *Approval.* The key here is *getting the critical mass to move forward.* Partners first need to self-identify and then think about who else is essential to the mission. In trust-funded contexts, the temptation is for donors and the trustee to stay insulated, but there is room to think about who else matters. Who else can help leverage success? Establishment documents are partnership documents because they establish the partnership. It is circular, but partnership documents need approval by all partners, however that is defined by the partnership. (>@ BfB: Constitutive Documents—How the Charter Happens) New partners can join over time, but the foundation comes from core partners signing off on core elements of the partnership program. In this way, the critical mass pertains to both participants and content. Starting with essential players and essential points at the table is predictive of partnership program success over time.

A Word to the Wise: This is not just about inclusion and openness, but rather a more deliberate and discerning view of who and what matters for partners to proceed. Not everyone will agree with first principles; not everyone will be ready at the same time. However, assessments of "critical mass" can take the long view. Do we have the most important and sufficiently like-minded actors on board; do we have the basic understandings confirmed among us to ensure a strong foundation? Answering yes is like signing up to a no-surprises insurance policy. Partners need to think about the baseline of who and what they need to succeed. You can *ban the blind spots.*

Ban the whiplash.

Ban the churn.

Ban the blind spots.

1. DRAFTS	2. DISCUSSIONS	3. DECISIONS

ZERO VERSIONS: WORKING DRAFTS

- electronic distribution to governing body plus group presentation
- email comments/mark-ups to central lawyer
- bilateral follow-up as needed

REVISED VERSIONS: CONSOLIDATED COMMENTS

- comment matrix: who/issue/response
- composite mark-up with annotated margins
- plenary page-turning session for real-time resolution

FINAL VERSIONS: CONSENSUS VIEW

- package to be confirmed
- email approval or no objection (silence approves)
- official email confirmation
- media launch and post on website

Getting Consensus Around the "Form of Agreement"

The way to take bilateral agreements and make them multilateral in content, while keeping their bilateral form, is to have all signatories agree on a *form of agreement*. For example, all donors to a multi-donor trust fund agree on one version that includes all the common (multilateral) terms and leaves blanks for the individual (bilateral) terms. This is a "form," and the opening paragraph of such a contribution agreement could look like this:

> The [Trustee entity] (the Trustee) acknowledges that the _____ [full name of donor] (the Donor) agrees to provide the sum of _____ [currency and amount of total contribution] (the Contribution) for the [name of the trust fund], [number of the trust fund account] (the Trust Fund) for the [name of the partnership program] (the Partnership Program) in accordance with the terms of this Contribution Agreement. Other donors are also expected to contribute to the Trust Fund. The Donor shall provide the Contribution in accordance with the following schedule into the bank account designated by the Trustee:
>
> (1) Promptly following countersignature, _____ [currency and amount of tranche];
> (2) By _____ [date], _____ [currency and amount of tranche]; and
> (3) By _____[date], _____ [currency and amount of tranche].

Note that the blank lines to be filled in are limited to information specific to each individual donor. All the rest stays the same, donor to donor. By getting baseline agreement from all donors plus the trustee on the *form of agreement*, the only variability upon signature will be on points, like names, dates, and amounts, that are intended to differ.

Note also that the blanks are minimized to the extent possible. This is *plug-and-play*. Finalizing the form of agreement should be clear and easy, almost mindless, since all the substantive points have already been resolved and captured in the rest of the text.

Two more points to note:

- First, this plug-and-play format is one step away from a *term sheet* approach. When doing deals, a term sheet is the concise document that itemizes the major deal points. It helps the parties zero in on the points to be negotiated, but also reflects the specific points of agreement between the parties. If all the fill-in-the-blank information for the example here were instead listed on an annex—Annex 1 with all the donor-specific terms—that would be an even clearer, more modular way to complete the contribution agreement. As a bonus, the trustee back office would have an exceptionally easy time of lifting Annex 1 data points into their master data set for a good portfolio overview.

- Second, this is also not far from *automation*. A form that is a simple plug-and-play version can be populated in a web portal instead of prepared by hand. There is so little room for error, and so little need for further drafting, that no lawyer is needed. Plug and play into the portal, and let the computer spit out the finished product, ready for signature—or at least a first draft, ready for further work. In practice, there are usually more variables, alternate scenarios, and possible exceptions to consider, and full reliance on a computer portal can get fairly complex. Automation of fund flow agreements may not be a slam dunk. But the plug-and-play philosophy is the first step to getting you there.

To make the point more clearly, the traditional, embedded fill-in-the-blank approach is not necessarily the most efficient and arguably not the most technologically up-to-date way to go. However, for partnership purposes, the point is to agree on the content in the form of an agreement, whatever form that takes.

Conclusion

When my daughter is doing her algebra, she works hard at deciphering and structuring relationships, maneuvering variables amidst coefficients, and managing all the pieces while keeping the equations balanced. How can I not be reminded of partnership programs? Of course, as we have seen over and over again, these international constructs are more organic than automatic, but they require similar skills sets.

Math educators who go beyond numbers on a page have come up with a wonderful description of their larger goal of *mathematical proficiency* (*Adding It Up: Helping Children Learn Mathematics*, National Research Council, 2001). Next time you are faced with the task of establishing an international partnership program, puzzling together all the pieces, think about the five strands they consider necessary for success:

- *conceptual understanding*—comprehension of concepts, operations, and relations
- *procedural fluency*—skill in carrying out procedures flexibly, accurately, efficiently, and appropriately
- *strategic competence*—ability to formulate, represent, and solve problems
- *adaptive reasoning*—capacity for logical thought, reflection, explanation, and justification
- *productive disposition*—habitual inclination to see the subject as sensible, useful, and worthwhile, coupled with a belief in diligence and one's own efficacy.

Take heart; if you are perusing these pages, **partnership program proficiency** is within reach. Some basic understanding and room to explore and create can put you on the path to letting all partners go beyond math and make the whole larger than the sum of the parts.

4 A TAXONOMY OF TRUST FUND AGREEMENTS

This book was written mainly to highlight charters, since they tend to be neglected stepchildren when it comes to trust-funded partnership programs. However, given the importance of fund flow agreements in many international partnership contexts, it is worth taking a deeper dive into them before we conclude. No matter how standardized the trust fund business may be, fund flow agreements are developed within specific contexts and have to respond to various scenarios. Different agreement types can be briefly catalogued to help lawyers and partners think about what fits best where.

Upstream Agreements

In international partnership programs, it is common to give fund flows a vertical pitch—from donor down to the trustee and further down to the recipient/beneficiary. (>@ BfB: Dualities—Verticals and Horizontals) This translates into an upstream/downstream view of the partnership program. (>@ PfP: Structure—Bridging Action and Results—Upstream/Downstream) The trustee is in the middle, receiving from above and then pivoting to transmit down below. Because this perspective also follows the nature of the fund flow agreements—the trustee looking upstream to receive and then looking downstream to disburse—we can use it as a way to break down this taxonomy.

When cash flows into trust funds, each donor can provide its money to a separate single-donor account, or multiple donors can collectively provide their money to a single multi-donor account. There are plenty of single-donor trust funds that support international partnership programs, but because we are most interested in the dynamics of collectives (>@ PfP: International Partnership Programs), we will focus on multi-donor trust funds. Recall that the point of multi-donor trust funds is to commingle funds in a common pool that allows donors to be strategic, scale up, reduce costs, enhance visibility, and other multiplier effects that come from collectivizing their resources. Let's see how that commingling affects the incoming fund flow agreements.

Contribution Agreements for Multi-Donor Trust Funds

The dynamics of multi-donor trust funds have major implications for donor contributions. In a commingled pool, all funds become one and are treated equally as part of an indistinguishable whole. (>@ ibid.—Pooled Funding) When donors decide to commingle their funds, they sign up to common terms, often positioned as one or more common annexes to their contribution agreements. (>@ BfB: Practical Packaging—Packaging Trust-Funded Partnership Programs) In this way, verbatim, one-and-the-same annex wording applies across all contribution agreements for the single, commingled trust fund.

Sometimes it is easy to come up with a scope of fund use, broad enough to satisfy everyone, but not so broad as to transgress anyone's zone of acceptability. But sometimes it is not. A major test of compatibility for trust-funded partnership programs is whether donors can rally around a common description of fund use, an aspect that is always partnership program-specific and custom-negotiated.

After initial donors establish the common fund use parameters and memorialize them, subsequent donors can either agree to the defined scope or decline to contribute. As explained previously, some or all of that memorializing can be in a stand-alone, cross-referenced charter. (>@ BfB: Constitutive Documents) Once operations have begun, and disbursements and implementation are underway, it can be impractical, if not impossible, to narrow the trust fund scope without jeopardizing ongoing operations and operational consistency. Moreover, any revision to the scope, whether narrowing or broadening, can go into effect only after all existing donors have agreed to the revision, since everyone is affected. (>@ PfP: Like Rock, Like Water—Like Water)

Upstream agreements:
1. multi-donor contribution agreements
2. holding agreements
3. framework agreements
4. contribution agreement amendments

Downstream agreements:
1. grant agreements
2. transfer agreements

Plus:
1. operations manuals
2. rules of procedure
3. codes of conduct
4. side letters

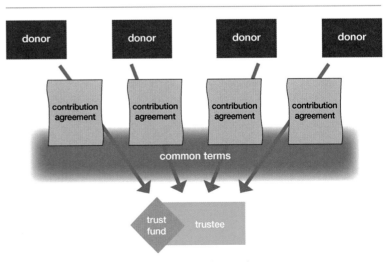

BETWEEN DONORS AND THE TRUSTEE

Drafting Contribution Agreements: Common vs. Custom

Since they keep coming up, we can take a closer look at how to structure contribution agreements.

First, most contribution agreements are bilateral between the donor and trustee, even for multi-donor trust funds. (>@ BfB: Dualities—Multilateral and Bilateral) Second, all contribution agreements for multi-donor trust funds contain both common and customized terms. The pool of funds is common (commingled), but the contribution is individual, and both sets of common and customized terms come together in each contribution agreement. Separating between custom terms and common terms, reflecting both bilateral and multilateral elements, is a great way to organize the agreement.

An oft-used approach for bilateral contribution agreements is to position a cover agreement that contains mostly donor-specific terms with basic boilerplate, and then attach the common annexes. In general:

- The cover agreement follows a standard approach while containing customized, donor-specific details, like the contribution amount and currency, payment schedule, the donor entity's legal name and contact information, any soft preferencing (>@ BfB: Dualities—Harmonization and Individuation), the nature of the agreement (administrative, non-treaty, >@ PfP: Partnering Internationally—Applicable Law), and other terms that do not affect the commingled pool, along with references to the annexes, amendment procedures, prevalence terms, and a few other basics. These cover agreement clauses constitute the main body appearing above the signature lines. This typically makes for a pretty short and sweet cover agreement.

- The common annexes attach to the cover agreement as appendages and contain trust fund details, both trust fund–specific and trustee-standard terms, that are usually separated into two annexes: (1) an annex for trust fund–specific terms (scope of fund use); and (2) an annex for generic, standardized trustee terms (trustee operations). In cases where shared governance is not set out in a stand-alone charter, or donors want to include other common documents (>@ BfB: Deft Drafting—The Art of Writing—Defined Terms), those governance or other terms may appear in additional annexes.

The convention of splitting out common terms into structured annexes provides a helpful organizational tool:

- In the first instance, it organizes the parts that need to track across all donors contributing to a commingled fund. The terms that appear in distinct annexes can be readily replicated—verbatim—from one contribution agreement to the next.

- In the second instance, many of these donor-wide terms are also ones that flow down as the funds flow, into grant agreements and transfer agreements, particularly those defining the use of funds, like scope of activities, categories of expenditure, financial and progress reporting, and targeted results.

The effect is also visual. By segregating these areas into separate annexes, the commonly agreed terms become clearly visible, as non-variable fixtures for every contribution. While donors have a chance to negotiate terms with the trustee before the trust fund is established, once funds are deposited into the trust fund, all other funds have to adhere to the common terms, effectively making the terms non-negotiable after a certain point. Donors coming in on the ground floor have an ability to shape the trust fund in a way that later donors usually do not (although, of course, money has heft if the price is right).

main body		common annexes		
Cover Agreement		**Annex 1**	**Annex 2**	**Annex 3**
• legal name • amount/currency • payment schedule • soft preferencing	• agreement status • donor-trustee signatures	• objectives • activities/components • expenditure categories • selection criteria	• trustee operations • investment income • fiduciary obligations • disbursements	• governing body • other bodies • secretariat support • fund allocation process

Not a Treaty

International donors and trustees usually agree they do not want to end up in the United Nations Treaty Collection. This means avoiding getting caught under Article 102 of the Charter of the United Nations: "Every treaty and every international agreement entered into by any Member of the United Nations . . . shall as soon as possible be registered with the Secretariat and published by it." If something is not an "international agreement," in the sense of this clause, presumably it need not be registered. As described below, to be absolutely sure Article 102 does not apply to their contributions, some donors make it a point to enter into an "arrangement" and avoid agreement language altogether.

"Agreements" vs. "Arrangements"

In drafting contribution agreements for multi-donor trust funds, one specific aspect—whether the parties are signing an "agreement" or an "arrangement"—can vary from the usual verbatim rule for the common annexes. Normally, donors enter into contribution agreements without having to dilute the agreement nature of the document. However, some donors prefer to tone it down by entering into contribution "arrangements," or even "administrative arrangements." In particular, they fear that too much binding language could imply treaty obligations, which could in turn trigger parliamentary or other procedural steps that no one wants to take for routine trust fund contributions. Each country is different in what makes treaties effective—some require parliamentary approval, some require legislative consent—but no donor wants to unnecessarily complicate its ability to provide development funds.

Treaty-sensitive donors that err on the side of caution may request special terminology. In this case, from a drafting perspective, that is easy enough to accommodate without undermining the uniformity of common terminology. The difference can be considered cosmetic, not substantive. We are talking about swapping out terms like these:

- *arrangement* for agreement
- *participants* for parties
- *accept* for agree
- *will* for shall
- *terms* for obligations
- *modification* for amendment

Making these changes would not seem to matter so much, but apparently it does. For some donors, it works like magic. Plug in these softer alternatives, and voilà, the document is treaty-proof. Despite the usual imperative for verbatim terms that affect the pool of funds and trustee operations, there is just enough tolerance in the construction to allow for this difference. The plain meaning of these alternate terms is effectively the same as the originals, and any discrepancy from one contribution agreement to another is not worth the worry. This should not become a universal approach to drafting, but on this one point, customary practice tends to say it is okay.

To strengthen the non-treaty notion further, donors also like to add a clause to the main body of the agreement—where custom clauses can be tolerated anyhow—along these lines:

> It is understood that this Contribution Arrangement, including any annexes, is not an international treaty and is not eligible for registration as a treaty under Article 102 of the United Nations Charter, nor is it, in the Donor's understanding, any other form of international agreement. It is an administrative arrangement between the Trustee and the Donor.

Holding Agreements

If trust fund establishment is still a work in progress, but a donor is under pressure to deposit funds, usually for budget reasons, the timing is out of whack. Partners may lose the donor's funds if there is no way to bridge the gap. But there is a way. It is called a holding agreement, a kind of halfway house pending completion.

Under a holding agreement, the trustee agrees to "hold" the funds outside of the actual trust fund, pending its establishment, while terms are being worked out. Holding agreements can usually fit onto a single page; the essence can fit into a text box (below). From a legal perspective, the hold entails a donor's commitment to pay (a stated amount) for a specific purpose (the upcoming trust fund). That can be enough under some donor budget rules for the funds to be considered spent and secured (committed), especially if coupled with an actual transfer to the trustee. Typically, the disbursed funds are parked in an account held by the trustee on the donor's behalf, potentially a standing administrative account set up for other processing purposes, like getting pro rata distributions from closing trust funds. In this way, the holding agreement allows the donor to offload the funds, while at the same time allowing the trustee to take up the funds, even as the trust fund terms are still being negotiated, and internal clearances are still being chased.

> A holding agreement is a halfway house pending a trust fund home.

Usually this happens only when the parties, donor and trustee, are pretty sure the trust fund will come to pass. There should be enough convergence of terms to inspire confidence in the initiative and justify the extra effort and transfer of funds. But for many partners who say rather safe than sorry, it can be better to secure the funds provisionally than let them slip back into the donor's general budget forever.

Nonetheless, holding agreements usually contain time limits, like six months. If the trust fund is not completed within the agreed time frame, the funds are returned by the trustee to the donor, and the commitment is unwound. Of course, if six months are not enough, that end date can be extended—as long as the donor's budget rules allow, the trustee is willing, and closure still looks promising. Then, if all works well, once the new trust fund is in place, the holding agreement funds are transferred by the trustee, with ease, from one internal account to another.

Sample Holding Agreement Terms

The Trustee and the Donor acknowledge the Donor's intention to make available to the Trustee US$ ____ (the "Contribution") to be held by the Trustee in the [account] (the "Donor Account") pending completion of negotiations between the Donor and the Trustee for the signing of a new contribution agreement (the "New Contribution Agreement") for a new trust fund for [name of partnership program] (the "New Trust Fund"). Upon signature of the New Contribution Agreement, the Trustee shall transfer the Contribution from the Donor Account to the New Trust Fund. . . . Any accrued investment income shall [remain in the Donor Account] [be transferred to the New Trust Fund]. . . . If the Donor and the Trustee have not signed the New Contribution Agreement by [date six months later], the Trustee shall [allocate the Contribution Amount from the Donor Account to another specified, existing, Trustee-administered trust fund] [return the Contribution amount to the Donor by deposit in a specified Donor-owned account].

Framework Agreements

Some relationships between trustees and specific donors are so well-established and yet so particular that they may merit special treatment. Ideally all donors fit like square pegs into the trustee's square hole—they accept the trustee's standardized, system-supported approaches—but that does not always work. The occasional donor may have specific requirements that go beyond the standard set-up, which the trustee may be willing to accept if three things apply: (1) the special requirements do not skew the use of common terms for commingled pools; (2) the donor's contributions are sizeable enough to justify the special treatment; and (3) the special treatment is ringfence-able enough to avoid setting a precedent for other donors to demand the same. This assumes the trustee does not want to mainstream the one-off customized approach, which would, of course, moot the exercise. While such donor-specific aberrations produce inefficiencies, they can be somewhat reduced by framework agreements.

In the context of fund flows, a framework agreement establishes key terms that apply to ensuing contribution agreements. Certain clauses that are stated once in the framework need not be repeated in each contribution agreement thereafter. It is a way of collecting broadly applicable terms and then applying them by cross-reference. For example, the framework agreement spells out the contact information, specifies that nothing amounts to an international treaty, and sets up an annual consultation about the overall donor-financed portfolio. Then each subsequent contribution agreement starts by saying "under the terms of the framework agreement incorporated by reference herein," while also specifying which agreement prevails in case of conflict.

But let's consider the upshot: As customized, donor-specific approaches, framework agreements are the antithesis of standardization. This particularly affects trustee operations, which may not easily tolerate more and more exceptions. The merits of framework agreements come into play only after a decision to deviate from the norm has already been made, as a way to soften the full impact of deviating. Framework agreements are usually second-best solutions to first-order concessions.

In multi-donor contexts, the use of framework agreements should be limited to terms that are greenlit for donor-specific treatment. That means keeping the special terms outside of actual fund use or trustee operations, which are affected by commingling. (>@ PfP: Trust Funds—Contributions) Customizable examples could include the treatment of investment income and institution-specific arrangements in case of dispute. Most terms, however, are not fair game for special treatment in a commingled context. Donors, to be expected, talk among themselves and word spreads. As a matter of fairness, channeling investment income to a separate account or committing to arbitration could be viewed by some donors as preferential treatment. (>@ BfB: Balance—Leveling the Field)

Because of the need to keep the same terms across commingled funds, special treatment donors may not be suitable for multi-donor trust funds. This means the framework agreement would be available for only single-donor trust funds. However, resorting to single-donor, rather than multi-donor, trust funds is also a second-best solution. (>@ BfB: Context—International Trust Funds)

Bottom line: While framework agreements may seem attractive at first, they are apt to become less so when the rubber hits the road. Donor-specific framework agreements directly contradict multi-donor approaches. They tend to give license to bilateral negotiations that, once started, may be hard to control. And they create asymmetries that other donors may either question or seek to replicate for themselves. Trustees should tread carefully.

> Framework agreements are second-best solutions for first-order concessions.

Contribution Agreement Amendments

Contribution agreements are framework agreements for supplemental contributions.

Having just disparaged framework agreements, I should hasten to point out that contribution agreements are, in fact, a form of framework agreement—in this case, in a good way. Donors already have the benefit of "framing" their relationships with the trustee through their regular contribution agreements. It is common practice for the initially signed contribution agreement to be used repeatedly as a platform for subsequent contributions. The first contribution may be for twenty million dollars (which can include contributions receivable over time). Six months later the donor is ready to give more and enters into an amendment to that same contribution agreement for another ten million dollars. And that can go on indefinitely, as long as the original contribution agreement terms are considered current.

These contribution agreement amendments for supplemental contributions are very short documents. They need to specify only what is new, since all of the original agreement still applies. When the point of the amendment is to add funds, then only replenishment language is needed: the amount, currency, and payment schedule. All the other terms stay effective for the new money.

Other amendments can be added, like new contact information or an extension to the trust fund end date. (NB: Trust funds should always have end dates.) However, and this is an important caveat, amendments that affect the commingled pool of funds or donor-wide trustee operations should not become effective until all other donors have agreed to the same amendment. Contact information is donor-specific, but a new end date is something all donors need to amend. (>@ BfB: Dualities—Harmonization and Individuation)

This, again, is where the use of annexes can be helpful. If the common terms—the ones that affect the funds or trustee operations—are separated into annexes, those annexes can be made subject to agreement on the part of all existing donors. That would involve a sentence in the cover agreement that looks something like this:

> *All annexes hereto constitute an integral part of this Contribution Agreement, whose terms taken together constitute the entire agreement between the Donor and the Trustee. This Contribution Agreement may be amended only by written amendment between the Trustee and the Donor; provided, however, that any annexes to this Contribution Agreement may be amended only by written amendment of all donors contributing to the Trust Fund.*

———————————————— ● ————————————————

Additional Contributions by Automation

The customary amendment approach to trust fund replenishment described here is, in the opinion of your author, more cumbersome than necessary. It works well enough, but is labor intensive and legal overkill. The day has come, perhaps long passed, when supplemental contributions can happen without signed amendments. Once the original contribution agreement has been signed and the terms agreed—in other words, once the framework is in place—there is no legal necessity to add signatures by both donor and trustee to add more funds under the same terms. Instead, the original terms can be written to automatically—anticipatorily—cover any new funds. Once those terms are "on the shelf," they can be brought down every time new money comes in, and the rest is then mechanics. The contribution agreement has to spell out a specific process, but there is no magic to setting up an electronic portal that confirms the fund transfer at both ends. Kudos to those trustees who have already figured out a way to make this work.

———————————————— ● ————————————————

What this means in practice is chasing down signatures from all donors. If the number of donors to a multi-donor trust fund is high, that can become a major exercise. Every single donor needs to deliver a signed amendment extending the trust fund end date, or whatever common term is being amended. Every legal department may need to give its clearance. Every senior manager with signing authority needs to be informed and organized to sign on the dotted line. To say this can take a long time is sometimes optimistic. I have seen signing exercises like these take a year or more because one or two signatures remained outstanding. And meanwhile, all other donors had signed off, thinking the amendment was effective—or were left wondering why not. I have even seen cases where early donors went AWOL, never to be heard from again, And yet, they were still existing donors, their funds part of the commingled pool (even if long ago disbursed downstream), whose terms could not simply be changed by fiat.

What to do? Trustees may be forced to assess the business risk of going ahead without an affirmative signature. The last missive may be a notice statement, indicating that the amendment will go into effect by a certain date (maybe thirty days later), unless the so-far-silent donor objects. And then on the 30th day, the amendment is declared effective if no peep is heard. That is not the ideal scenario, but if the donor has truly taken a hike, and the amendment is less than controversial, that may be the best way to close the loop and move on.

Maybe by now it is even clearer why charters can be a blessing. It really helps to put decisions in the hands of an active governing body that represents the donors and can make a change in a single decision point. No extenuated signing exercises. No dormant donors. No delay. No disruption. Simply do it and done.

Document Hierarchies

In the hierarchy of fund flows, incoming funds are at the top and travel down. (>@ PfP: Structure – Upstream/ Downstream) This has implications for the documents, specifically how the flow of terms follows the flow of funds. When juxtaposing terms, on the other hand, parties can create a hierarchy of documents to reconcile "conflicting" terms. In the first case, terms flow vertically. In the second case, terms are horizontal, but can be made vertical. Let's tease this apart.

We can look at this in terms of the parties. The issue of consistent flow-down arises when the parties switch off. First, the donor signs with the trustee and conditions fund use on specific requirements. Then the trustee turns around and signs with the grant recipient on the basis of the same requirements. The requirements are supposed to flow with the funds. The onus of making this happen lies with the trustee, the party in common. The onus does not lie with the grant recipient, which only has to follow its own grant agreement and has no obligation toward, and often no visibility of, the donor's originating contribution agreement.

For example, if the contribution agreement does not allow for equipment purchases (either because they are specifically excluded or the relevant category of expenditure is not included), the grant agreement should reflect that. If it does, then purchasing a jeep with the donor's funds would be a grantee breach (vis-à-vis the trustee). However, if it does not, that purchase would be a trustee breach (vis-à-vis the donor).

This is not a case of "conflict" that could be cured by a prevalence clause. The contribution agreement/grant agreement terms are misaligned, but not directly "conflicting" between the same parties. Prevalence clauses work for different documents agreed by the same parties. If a donor and trustee sign a contribution agreement and bring in a separately adopted charter (whether applied or incorporated by reference), they can also agree on the hierarchy of those documents for themselves.

For example, a charter may envision a co-chair of the governing body, but the contribution agreement refers only to a chair. If the contribution agreement is said to prevail, this could be considered a direct conflict, and only a chair would be selected. But careful here. "Conflicts" do not arise with respect to supplemental terms, so one might instead argue that the co-chair is a legitimately agreed addition to the original chair, not a violation of the contribution agreement. Both positions may have merit.

So this is to say that drafting should not occur in a vacuum. It is also a plug for the package approach. (>@ BfB: Practical Packaging) Tricky as it can get, staying mindful of related documents, their potential gaps and overlaps, and the relative positions of the parties/partners can help.

Eleven Tips for Upstream Fund Flow Agreements

1   Think of contribution agreements as framework agreements.

2   Put all essential terms for trust fund operations in the four corners.

3   Use common annexes to cover fund use and trustee operations.

4   Don't let donor differences create common term discrepancies.

5   Sometimes silence is the best drafting tool for common terms.

6   Whether agreement or arrangement, it doesn't much matter.

7   You can cross-refer and contractualize adopted documents, like charters.

8   Watch for gaps and overlaps when aligning documents.

9   Avoid major signing exercises by amending through charters and governing bodies.

10   Hold on to funds with holding agreements before the trust fund is ready.

11   Let the partnership frame the trust fund, not the other way around.

Downstream Agreements

When looking downstream, funds can leave the trust fund after the trustee and a recipient agree on terms that are consistent with the upstream terms. A grant agreement or transfer agreement is signed by both parties and becomes effective upon countersignature or when preconditions are met. Just as no money flows into the trust fund without agreed terms, no money flows out of the trust fund without agreed terms. And yet, the dynamics are quite different. Disbursements unmingle what donors commingled. For inflows (donor contributions), the key factor is horizontal alignment across donors. For outflows (recipient grants), the key factor is vertical alignment along the fund flows hierarchy. (>@ BfB: Dualities—Verticals and Horizontals)

Contributions commingle, disbursements de-mingle.

Grant Agreements and Transfer Agreements

While there may be some or even significant commonality across downstream grant or transfer agreements (especially if standard forms are used), the real pressure point is the need to conform disbursement terms to contribution terms—what is called *flow down*. Terms agreed by the trustee with the donors are flowed down by the trustee into terms agreed with the recipients. The trustee cannot afford any discrepancy between its obligations to the donors and those obligations as they pertain to recipients. In fact, one of the trustee's obligations is to stay within the original terms.

What is the difference between grant agreements and transfer agreements? It's not merely a matter of semantics. Having clear labels can help clarity overall. It is useful to distinguish between grant agreements to supervised recipients and transfer agreements to unsupervised recipients. The difference has to do with fiduciary status and who bears what downstream responsibilities.

- *Grant Agreements.* These are fund flow agreements between *full trustees* and supervised grantees. The grantee recipient does not have sufficient capacity and financial management systems to satisfy donor fiduciary requirements. This means a fiduciary stays active in between donors and downstream recipients.
- *Transfer Agreements.* These are fund flow agreements between *limited trustees* and fiduciary transferees. The transferee recipient is pre-vetted and deemed to have sufficient financial management controls and experience to have fiduciary status for donor purposes. This means it can take on the funds without needing a layer of supervision in between.

BETWEEN THE TRUSTEE AND RECIPIENTS

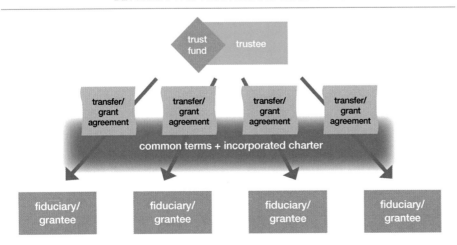

Full Trustees

For full trustees who retain fiduciary responsibility over the downstream grant recipient (as in one-stop-shops), matching upstream and downstream terms can be made easier if you keep two things in mind:

1. *With respect to the applicable operating framework.* If the trustee's receipt of donor funds is premised on the trustee's "applicable policies and procedures," which fully leverages the trustee's fiduciary framework, then it is a simple matter of agreeing to those four words both up- and downstream. (>@ BfB: Deft Drafting—The Art of Writing—Defined Terms). Donors will have confirmed, for example, that the trustee's procurement rules apply, and that grantees will be required to apply them. That is pretty straightforward. If the trustee agrees to any deviations from or additions to its applicable policies and procedures—the fewer, the better (>@ PfP: Risk and Review—Institutional Factors)—that can be clearly identified upstream with donors and specified as a customized provision downstream.

2. *With respect to the trust-fund specific terms.* Each trust fund has its own defining terms, like objectives, activities, eligible expenditures, fund allocation processes, and other governance terms. These can be neatly collected into separate annexes to the contribution agreements or appear in stand-alone charters. Once organized this way, like tabs in a binder or chapters in a book, they can more readily be channeled as discrete elements from upstream to downstream. Agreement text can be cut-and-pasted verbatim, and stand-alone charters can be incorporated by reference. Often the grant agreement is written to cover just a subset of activities relative to what the trust fund allows overall (>@ PfP: Use of Funds—Role of the Fiduciary), which works as long as the scope of the grant agreement is fully within the scope of the contribution agreement.

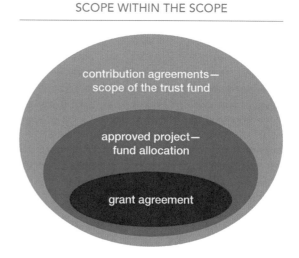

SCOPE WITHIN THE SCOPE

contribution agreements—
scope of the trust fund

approved project—
fund allocation

grant agreement

Limited Trustees

For limited trustees who pass fiduciary responsibility on to the downstream fiduciary (as in international platforms), the match between upstream and downstream terms pivots in a similar fashion:

1. *With respect to the applicable operating framework.* The relevant reference point is still "applicable policies and procedures," but with a twist. Downstream, the applicable policies and procedures are those of the downstream fiduciary, not the trustee. This is logical because the trustee relinquishes responsibility at the point of transfer, and the downstream fiduciary ends up with operating responsibility under its own rules. This modularity is one of the major benefits of limited trustee arrangements. Donors agree upfront that applicable policies and procedures apply, but transparently and comfortably allow different sets to apply at different times, since they have determined that every engaged fiduciary's applicable rules are pre-vetted and acceptable.

2. *With respect to trust-fund specific terms.* The defining upstream terms, like the scope of fund use, stay relevant as limiting parameters, even though the players and rules may change downstream. As a result, these limiting parameters need to take the downstream shifts in applicable policies and procedures into account. For example, the list of eligible expenditures is typically based on the fiduciary entity's system controls, which can vary from one fiduciary to another. (Although there may be common practices, there is no standard international list). The common upstream terms either need to be sufficiently broad to cover all the downstream operational variations, or they can broadly defer to "applicable policies and procedures" of the relevant fiduciaries to keep everything seamless and aligned. The latter approach is more modular, more deferential, and probably easier

Remedies for Misused Funds

Legally, under the two-tiered, upstream/downstream agreement construct, the donor loses privity of contract with the downstream recipient. The donor has privity with the trustee through the contribution agreement, but is not a party to the downstream agreement. When the donor and downstream recipient are not parties to the same agreement, they have no direct legal rights or obligations to each other. This lack of privity is a side effect of intentional distancing. By inserting the trustee, or other fiduciary intermediary, into the middle, donors are shielded from direct responsibility for fund use or any downstream behavior. In the contribution agreements, the donors get most of the rights (save obligations to pay), while the trustee/fiduciary gets most of the obligations (mainly making sure funds are used properly). This hands-off arrangement upstream lets the donors hand everything off downstream.

Sounds like a good deal, and it is. That is why donors invoke trustees and other fiduciaries time and again. (>@ PfP: Fund Use Responsibility—Delineating Responsibility) But back to the loss of privity. The one downside is that, without privity, donors have no direct recourse against downstream recipients when funds are misused. Instead, donors have to rely on the trustee, who has direct privity, to follow through on any remedies. Indeed, donors first have to rely on the trustee to include appropriate remedies in the downstream agreements. Typically, this is treated as an operational matter, with recourse rights wrapped into the trustee's obligation to apply its "applicable policies and procedures," including those regarding its pursuit of refunds or other remedies.

Usually this works well, even if international trustees agree only to pursue refunds for misused or missing funds, not guarantee them, and certainly not to pay out of their own pockets (unless for their own breach by being negligent in supervising). That is when the trustee is a full trustee, when it takes full fiduciary responsibility. At least then, the responsibility is with the party with whom the donor has privity. However, when the trustee is a limited trustee and passes off fiduciary responsibility, the legal nexus is even more attenuated. Then we have what is often called an "accountability gap"—and donors are left with privity to neither the responsible fiduciary, nor the recipient. A quick fix for that can be to add third-party beneficiary rights in the downstream agreement vis-à-vis the downstream fiduciary. Better yet is some form of collective remedies that benefit the whole partnership in a harmonized fashion. (>@ PfP: Fund Use Responsibility—Transferred (No) Responsibility—Managing the Accountability Gap) Clauses could look like this:

> **Contribution Agreement:** *Each Transfer Agreement will name the Donors as third-party beneficiaries with direct rights to seek recourse thereunder and will provide the Trustee with rights of novation and assignment, as needed, to enable each Donor to seek such recourse against the Transferee.*

> **Transfer Agreement:** *The Transferee accepts that each Donor is a third-party beneficiary with direct rights to seek recourse under this Transfer Agreement, for which the Trustee may exercise rights of novation and assignment, as needed, to enable such Donor to seek such recourse.*

> **Transfer Agreement with Collective Remedies:** *The Transferee accepts that each Donor is a third-party beneficiary with direct rights to seek recourse under this Transfer Agreement, for which the Trustee may exercise rights of novation and assignment, as needed, to enable such Donor to seek such recourse; provided that any effort to seek such recourse requires approval of the Governing Body and will be undertaken by a member specifically designated by the Governing Body to act on its behalf for this purpose (the "Remedies Representative Donor"); provided further that each Donor may seek direct recourse against the Transferee if Governing Body approval is not obtained and such Donor has a statutory, regulatory, or policy requirement to seek such recourse. The Transferee irrevocably consents to any novation and/or assignment by the Trustee to the Remedies Representative Donor, acting on behalf of all Donors. The Transferee accepts that the purpose of this clause is to enable the Donors to have recourse against the Transferee with respect to any unmet or breached obligations, including the intended use of the Funds, hereunder.*

Complementary Documents

As we have seen with charters, not everything needs to be a signed agreement for parties, or partners, to agree. Charters have a special constitutive role in defining a partnership program for establishment purposes (>@ BfB: Constitutive Documents), but other unsigned documents can be included as part of the baseline package. These flanking documents can be part of the mix at the beginning, to support the launch, or they can come on board over time, as they become relevant or as partners get to them.

The reasons for putting terms in unsigned documents vary, including the desire to avoid legalese and legal clearances. That may say more about the relationship to the legal department than about the documents. More substantively, the principal distinction is whether something is intended to be binding and enforceable (a signed agreement) vs. something more active and operational. But that difference is arguably more theoretical than practical for international partnership programs. Just because a document is unsigned does not relegate it to mere guidance or make it optional. Partners still expect follow-through and accountability. I tell the teams I support not to look for much daylight between these two modes, but rather to assume documents approved by the partnership rank the same as documents signed by partners as parties.

Operations Manuals

Operations manuals are usually not considered agreements, since they usually do not bear signatures. However, they can rise to the level of obligations, or at least engender reliance and expectations, especially when approved by governing bodies. It is therefore useful to put these in context as well.

Operations manuals are, by their nature, downstream in the operational weeds. They are like how-to guides for specific projects or activities—the instruction manual, as it were, for how to run the thing. (>@ BfB: Practical Packaging—The Package from a Legal Perspective) Although not agreements per se, they flow from agreement terms as more detailed articulations of applicable policies and procedures, along with more detailed contextual application. Most operations manuals are deep enough in the weeds that they do not make it to the lawyers, even though they are heavy on content. For this reason, to be on the safe side, operations manuals are always subordinate to the relevant agreements (the agreements "prevail") and should not contradict or conflict with these or other framing agreement terms.

As noted earlier in the charter discussion (>@ Constitutive Documents—What's in the Charter), a key question for partnership program architects is what goes into the charter vs. the operations manual. The broad distinction is between establishment (constitutive) terms vs. operational terms, although this line drawing can be fuzzy in practice. Another, more legal way to think about it is to distinguish between terms that should be contractualized (as when charters are incorporated by reference in contribution agreements, >@ BfB: Agile Alignment—Step-by-Step Alignment for Trust-Funded Partnership Programs, #4) vs. terms that simply need to be operationalized. Again, this has some fuzziness to it. Another litmus test is whether the subject matter goes to the partnership essence as opposed to operations. Is it a defining feature or an implementation detail? Okay, still somewhat fuzzy.

Perhaps the most useful gauge in practice is length. To be user-friendly, the charter should be short and sweet, while the operations manual can fill out the pages as needed. (>@ ibid., #2) If the charter is getting too long (say more than twenty pages), that may be a sign that details are crowding in beyond the essentials. Then again, some partnership programs prefer to meld the two into a bible version of the charter—everything you need to know in one handy place. Maybe a charter with multiple annexes, or one longer combo. This can be particularly helpful in international platforms, where more of the details are bespoke and decided by the partners. There it can be useful to include not just the essence, like objectives, structural components, and roles and responsibilities, but also eligibility criteria, process flow, templates for funding proposals, templates for reporting, agreed performance indicators for results frameworks, and more. So even length is not a perfect determinant. Ultimately, how charters and operations manuals divvy it up depends on what the partners prefer.

No need to let labels get in the way—make it functional, whatever you call it.

Rules of Procedure

While operations manuals help define downstream implementation, rules of procedure help define upstream governance. Classic rules of procedure are particular to governing body business. However, as with codes of conduct, more partnership programs could benefit from additional rules and processes on how to behave. Partnership programs with large governing bodies or a penchant for more formal, structured interactions could find such a document useful.

The charter usually contains the essential details for shared governance, potentially detailed enough that an additional set of rules proves superfluous. But partners can also decide to streamline the charter and load their governance details into a comprehensive document for internal governing body/secretariat purposes. Here is a sampling of topics these rules could cover:

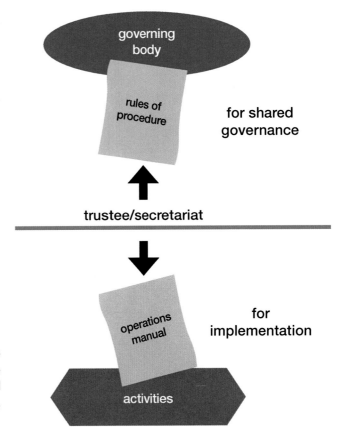

- advance notice for meeting materials
- finalization of meeting minutes
- no-objection decision process
- confidentiality
- executive sessions
- conflicts of interest
- chair nominations
- constituency management
- participation of alternates

For governing body participants and secretariats that like to keep the house in order, this and much more can be itemized in an approved set of rules of procedure designed to widen the collective understanding, anticipate issues, and pre-agree approaches.

Codes of Conduct

The scope and effect of codes of conduct can be both upstream and downstream. They are usually positioned partnership-wide. They address partner behavior, especially partners in relation to each other, to the partnership program, and to the branded activities. Typical examples include statements around conflicts of interest (>@ PfP: Synergistic Conflicts) or private sector precautions (>@ PfP: Partners and People—Engaging the Private Sector). The governing body is in a good position to approve a code of conduct, often prepared with help from the secretariat. It signals to all partners, and anyone outside the partnership program, what behavior is promoted or discouraged.

The best way to understand the potential for codes of conduct is to present some sample statements, which need not all appear together in the same document:

> • *Partners commit to avoiding potential, perceived, or real conflicts of interest or undue bias in their engagements. Partners are expected to demonstrate transparency, diligence, and fairness in their decision making.*

> • *Partners seek to safeguard the interests of society, public safety, and the environment in all Partnership Program activities. Partners seek to inform themselves about the norms and customs of individuals and communities affected by Partnership Program activities and avoid engaging in behaviors that could be construed as disrespectful, offensive, or inappropriate according to those communities' cultures, religions, and popular beliefs.*

> • *Partners are expected to provide information, data, and materials relevant to Partnership Program activities, including for the purpose of facilitating increased awareness, knowledge, and lessons learned.*

> • *Partners do not by their participation or otherwise endorse any specific product, technology, or service of any partners, particularly in the case of for-profit companies. No partner may use, display, or manipulate the name, logo, or other material under the control of another partner in public or private communications or any other manner without prior consent.*

> • *No partner may engage, directly or indirectly, in fraudulent behavior, corrupt practices, illegal actions, or any other activity that is incompatible with the values expressed in this Code of Conduct, the Charter, or otherwise relevant to the effective implementation of Partnership Program activities.*

> • *Partners commit to promptly disclosing to the [Governing Body Chair] [Head of the Secretariat] any potential, perceived, or actual breach of this Code of Conduct and may propose corrective measures, while also taking reasonable steps to assist in remedying the breach.*

All of this may go without saying and not need articulating. Plenty of partnership programs that do not have codes of conduct behave as well as, or better than, partnership programs that do. But in cases of particular sensitivity, or where partners want to flag their intentions, or flash their true colors, a code of conduct approved by the governing body and posted on the branded website can join the foundational documents. In so doing, it puts all partners on notice, and everyone else on notice as well.

Codes of Conduct can:

- protect decision making
- safeguard beneficiaries
- foster data sharing
- restrict endorsements
- respect logos
- preserve values
- encourage reactions
- and more

Side Letters

A final word on a pet peeve. The short answer is no.

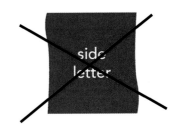

At least not if you can help it, not unless there is a very good reason. In the interest of clarity and transparency, donors, trustees, and other partners should look askance at side letters. The very nature of a "side" letter signals that it is an exception to what is normally acceptable, or it needed to be concealed, both of which should breed skepticism.

When dealing with international partnership programs and particularly international trust funds, the terms agreed by the partners are, as previously explained, within the four corners. (>@ BfB: Deft Drafting—The Awesomeness of Articulating) That is also an invitation for partners to put everything of importance into the four corners, not somewhere in a fifth corner, or under the rug. Good practice is for the relevant partnership program documents and fund flow agreements to be "the entire agreement and understanding," at least on essentials. Additional terms that supplement, or possibly even undermine or contradict, the original terms can muddy the water. They also pose operational or legal risks when they are not processed, cleared, or filed in the ordinary course. Considering that partnership programs are made of people (>@ BfB: Dynamics—It's Organic), and people come and go, stray side letters can easily get lost or overlooked. That is not helpful to anyone.

If the matter is important enough to be memorialized, it is important enough to be part of the visible, above-board documents and agreements. No side letters, please.

Conclusion

Upstream, downstream, and in between is the hierarchical view that follows the funds. That is how we have followed different kinds of trust fund agreements and complementary documents in this chapter. When trust funds are part of broader partnership programs, we have to work harder to take a more holistic view, with a partnership lens. From a partnership program perspective, we can see other ways to think of fund flow agreements in conjunction with other partnership documents, like multilateral vs. bilateral, informal vs. formal, structural vs. contractual. These documents collectively slot into many of the dualities we considered earlier. (>@ BfB: Dualities) With every duality, we can develop dynamics that help fortify international partnership programs. The more we work with these structural features, the more we can bring balance to the endeavor.

In this respect, our taxonomy of trust fund agreements works only if those agreements are positioned as part of the whole package. Trust-funded partnership programs derive their stability and flexibility from the way those agreements and other partnership documents connect and delineate vis-à-vis each other, and how they are positioned within the partnership program. This is where the chapters in this book have sought to guide and inspire you. To avoid half-baked solutions that collapse in on themselves, it is best to scan the options, mix and match, and keep it all in the balance.

CODA

The Role of the Lawyer

Lawyers can be heroes when it comes to international partnership programs. They are mostly unsung, but often relied upon to make things come together, reach closure, and work. Some lawyers are more equipped than others to handle partnership programs, especially trust-funded ones. This is not a practice they teach in law school; it is mostly not even considered a practice. Nor is it intuitive or always logical. It is no mean feat to pull together all the strands into one coherent whole that satisfies enough interests to close the deal.

As with other "essential workers," few lawyers are in it for the accolades, nor do they get the spotlight. They more likely rank as an afterthought, or even obstacle to be avoided, when, in fact, their job can require something more like superpowers. Although the reliance on lawyers may be required more than desired, if the assignment is an international partnership program, we can say thank goodness for the lawyers. When no one down the line brings experience and expertise to the task of structuring the partnership program—including *articulating, analyzing, drafting, and negotiating the documents*—the lawyer is left holding the pen, and somehow has to make it happen.

There are many ways to try to make it happen, including some shots in the dark. There are good shortcuts, and bad. Progress built by triage and band-aids. Trial and error that begets more error. Sometimes it means operating by analogy, often with questionable fit. Or starting with some other standard form that gets tweaked or overhauled to shapeshift into place. Business details may be murky, or at odds. Then add the opaqueness of a relegated desk assignment with hit-or-miss drafting in the abstract—knowing that unattuned advice can be as bad as it can be good. Timing, too, may be impossibly tight. After the team spent months if not years cooking up the initiative, the lawyer gets brought in at the last minute, with all the time left sucked out of the air. Those may sound like extreme scenarios, but they are common, especially when lawyers do not bring structuring expertise, and business teams do not appreciate how much experience it takes.

It might help everyone to understand the pivotal role lawyers can play when it comes to crafting international partnership programs. Let's take a closer look.

Articulating

Lawyers can be an international partnership program's best friend. The bespoke nature of each initiative is an act of creation, and the international arena is fertile ground for creativity. In this land of plenty, the importance of articulating as a means of reaching and confirming common ground is right up the legal lane. Lawyers excel at the precise use of terms and transparent detail, and this focus and precision can be a boon for participants. Admittedly, lawyers can also excel at obfuscation and sleight of hand, which may be needed at times, but usually does not ensure a solid foundation. Instead, coherence and consistency are natural watchwords for lawyers, who can play a key role in creating and affirming common understandings and expectations among partners.

International partners come together with a lot of languages in more ways than one. While English is usually one of their collectives (and can we note how impressively non-native speakers have that at their command!), there are still nuances of understanding and shades of interpretation that a lawyer must be alert to. At the point of articulating a common text, not just the words, but also the meanings need to converge. Lawyers who translate intentions into sentences can also anticipate tensions and prevent mixed messages. Articulating a partnership program is about seeking common words as well as common understandings.

Articulation can also be seen as a reflection of the partners' values. In addition to the actual words on a page, the amount of consensus behind them and the strength of the partners' buy-in add to their meaning. When supporting the creation of an international partnership program, a lawyer's trade is not only memorializing agreed terms, but also highlighting agreed themes. That can be jargonistic, and certainly reflects the trends of the times, but words like *evidence-based, inclusive, voice, results-oriented, priority, safeguards,* all bring layers of meaning and intent that a lawyer can appreciate and work with. What a pity, then, if articulation fails to go beyond the mere regurgitation of standard forms. While giving due respect to institutional formats and standards, a well-crafted set of establishment documents also gives ample room for specific partnership terms that drive the collaboration. Ultimately, articulation of partnership programs is meant to give voice to the partners. It puts pen to paper in that collective word and spirit.

Analyzing

Lawyers tend toward the analytical. In partnership programs, they naturally see things in structural terms, parsing roles and responsibilities, defining connections and delineations—basically taking a modular approach. Modularity rests on divisions of labor and reflects divisions of responsibility, a lawyer's bailiwick. Modularity also creates clarity and flexibility, both at inception and over the life of the partnership program. Similarly, the kinds of labels that pervade this book—like upstream/downstream, collectivizing, structure vs. contract—can come naturally to lawyers. Used as tools to visualize analytical underpinnings, they can be leveraged to give partnership programs structural strength. Used as tools to negotiate, they can coach understandings and frame deliberations for more solid partnership consensus and better partnership articulation.

A prime area of analysis when establishing and running partnership programs is on risks. This entails both risk assessments and risk mitigation, something lawyers can discern particularly well because they know the documents. Legal terms—or a lack of them—can be a source of risk, something a lawyer needs to study. Skilled lawyers will both study risk and seek to mitigate it by negotiating accordingly.

To leverage this legal skill set, it behooves everyone to empower the lawyer or legal team as central players, basically as part of the team. Effective lawyers are engaged lawyers. Their ability to contribute is directly proportional to their degree of engagement. It is not just that lawyers can help if they are enabled, but also that lawyers can do harm if they are not. Most lawyers are not on the front line, but instead positioned as support functions, doing their part from the trenches. That can be fine as long as information flows, but damaging if not. Whether lawyers engage from the back office or the business vanguard, leveraging what they do well works best if they are well-integrated.

This does not mean lawyers must be in lockstep with their business partners. To the contrary. The typical lawyer operating in these spheres wears two hats, one to serve the interests of their business colleagues and one to serve the interests of their institution. Most of the time, these interests converge, but there are times—often the critical times—when they diverge. For example, a business sponsor might push for closure before a looming deadline, but if readiness is lacking, institutional interests might call for getting things more fully in place first. Or money being offered by a dubious corporate entity might grease the financial skids and ensure payroll for secretariat staff, but also expose the institution to reputational risk.

It can be challenging for lawyers to manage both roles, to simultaneously stand up for the business team and the institution. Often, they are the only ones keeping an active eye on both. And even though business sponsors may be wary of their lawyers because of this dual role, they, too, perhaps improbably and against their own self-interest, should also be watching out for the institutional interest. For this reason, cues from senior management are critical to making sure everyone follows through with all relevant interests in mind—and with encouragement to escalate issues up the management chain, as needed.

Drafting

Drafting is more art than science when it comes to international partnership programs. The length of this book may indicate as much. You won't find the answer in a precise table of elements. In practice, when it comes to establishing structured partnerships, especially international platforms that engage multiple parties, funding sources, objectives, ambitions, and more, the difference between a seasoned lawyer with honed drafting skills and a novice becomes apparent. That is not a criticism of the novice lawyer, but an acknowledgment that building structured partnerships is a legal skill based on experience and expertise. Senior lawyers benefit from having been around the block, and junior lawyers benefit from being taken along. It is the classic master-apprentice view, but valid for an area that is a practice and takes practice.

Good drafting means being down in the weeds, while also scoping the big picture. It serves as a bridge between business aspects and legal terms. It is the physical act of connecting the dots from business intentions and expectations to legal understandings and obligations. When helping build partnership programs, lawyers act as interpreters and translators. Business teams say what they want, and lawyers write what they mean. Business teams say what they do not want, and lawyers write what that means. And then lawyers also write about the implications of what both of those mean. This reflects a chain of thought that travels through the document and across documents. A well-drafted document has integrity within itself and alignment with related documents, through the choice of words and the organization of contents and documents.

On the choice of words, not enough can be said about the marvel of defined terms. Only a legal word geek might say that, but there is no denying that the deft use of defined terms can hugely alleviate the drafting task. This is not about occluded or contorted meaning; that would mischaracterize the act. This is instead about fullness of explanation coupled with ease of presentation. Defined terms can take complex ideas, reduce them to appropriate, hopefully illuminating words or phrases, and carry the day, page by page. All it takes is a clear definition and initial capital letters—used consistently thereafter throughout the document—and the drafting is comprehensive and concise at the same time.

Defined terms are not just for lawyers. They can also help partners choose language for their own partnership. Vocabulary that is developed through defined terms in the documents can become functional labels for participants to use among themselves— the partnership program's own utilitarian jargon. The same way that acronyms are conducive for branding, defined terms are conducive for communicating. Defined terms can even send signals. Deliberate choices around capitalized words can emphasize certain aspects or make key distinctions between related terms. For example, the "Global Window" for contributions emphasizes its global scope and global (unrestricted) availability, as opposed to specific country windows. Or the "Council" and "Program Head" are more apropos than the statutorily-encumbered corporate board and CEO. Indeed, developing defined terms in partnership program documents is both a business and legal exercise, where lawyers can productively collaborate with their business counterparts.

On the organization of contents and documents, the flow of each document, and the flow from one document to the next, especially hierarchical fund flow agreements, should be smooth and seamless. For internal cohesion, lawyers want their documents to work from front to back, with a stepped logic and overall integrity. Individual clauses have their separate meanings, while also corresponding to other clauses affected by those meanings. When it comes to fund flows in particular, there should be no conflict or contradiction between relevant documents, as they cascade from donor to trustee to implementing entity to end user. And there is much room for connections among documents, as their terms carry over from the governing body to the trustee, from decision flows to fund flows. Connections and delineations pertain to partnership program documents as much as they pertain to partnership program roles.

Negotiating

It is tempting to analogize the creation of trust-funded partnership programs, especially the larger international platforms and more innovative varieties, to a three-ringed circus, but that would understate the complexity. Negotiating these orchestrations can be yeowoman's work. It is not just the challenge of articulating and confirming common ground, but doing so across multiple interests and requirements, in the context of trade-offs and inevitable time pressures. Sometimes it can feel like the roof is off and the bottom has dropped out, as prospective partners bring their checklists and itemize their must-haves, while donors leverage their funding levels. Meanwhile, the lawyer is left in the center trying to make all those disparate ends meet, two at a time, ten at a time, whiplash and backlash included. This is particularly symptomatic of the supporting entity lawyer, whether for the trustee or secretariat or both, who must also duly observe the institutional parameters of the home entity.

Indeed, it is the supporting entity lawyer who usually drafts the base documents— specifically the establishment documents, like the charter and the contribution agreements—and then becomes the primary negotiating lawyer, often the primary negotiator period, even across all partners. It is rare that anyone on the business team knows the oft-voluminous, always intricate details of the documents as well as the lawyer who drafts them. From what I have seen, no one else can hold a candle to the lawyer's ability to work the terms, inside and out, front to back, until everyone's questions, comments, and concerns are accounted for. That means tweaking language where possible, rejecting terms where necessary, and striking compromises, managing terminology, or conjuring other solutions to bring closure everywhere else. No one else is likely to have the perspective and wherewithal to integrate the business interests of all partners, including the not-to-be-neglected institutional interests of the supporting entity, and get them from principle to paper for all to confirm and agree. Superhero powers indeed.

That is not to say the supporting entity lawyer is everyone's lawyer or even the partnership program's lawyer. That would be a big misunderstanding. The supporting entity lawyer, central or omniscient as she may be, is still just the supporting entity's lawyer. With due attention to respective roles and responsibilities, and each entity responsible for itself, partners must remember that any "lead" lawyer on the scene is not their lawyer. Attending to everyone's interests, which this lawyer has to do for closure, is not the same thing as representing everyone's interests, which this lawyer cannot do. Each partner must decide for itself how much of its own lawyering to bring to the table and how much legal review to give the documents internally. The supporting entity lawyer is likely to welcome input from other partners' lawyers—it can be lonely in the legal trenches, and two pairs of eyes are better than one—but whatever choices partners make to engage their own respective lawyers is up to each of them.

It is a curious fact that many partners seeking to join partnership programs do their best to avoid their own lawyers, especially when taking comfort from an active supporting entity lawyer. While that can reduce the number of legal cooks in the kitchen, it may not help overall. Ultimately, if the partnership foundation is built by partners who fail to do the necessary review, legal or otherwise, only to later discover some major gap or misunderstanding, then over-reliance on others will not have done the partnership a favor. Instead, each participant's organization is better off nurturing and engaging business-friendly lawyers, ones that protect the organization, but also understand the practice of structuring partnerships and appreciate the opportunity to support the business.

Maintaining

Once the partnership program is established, that is not the end of the story. International partnership programs have life cycles; they grow, mature, adapt, and reform. Legal support stays relevant after the real work of partnership program operations and implementation begins. The intense lawyering of the inception phase may be over, but the partnership program still needs legal counsel for unanticipated matters, ongoing partner requests, interpretive questions, and general follow-through. This is true for each partner and its respective lawyers, but particularly true again for the supporting entity lawyer, who is close to the trustee and secretariat, and accordingly also close to legal entity functions and related legal issues for the partnership program as a whole.

Legal entity and custodial-type support, usually considered part of the secretariat role, are critical for partnership programs to operate smoothly. Ideally, the lawyer or legal team that helped with the establishment can continue in an ongoing escort role, being sensitized to the peculiarities that every partnership program uniquely has. There is just no substitute for legal support from someone who knows the documents, as well as the history of the negotiations, the quirks and preferences of the participants, the parameters of the supporting entity, and many other factors that shaped the outcome.

Supporting a partnership program is not rote, cookie-cutter lawyering. A partnership program lawyer who operates from an informed backdrop can bring integrated insights and solutions that likely no one else can provide. Partnership program managers are quick to hire communications experts, results experts, and procurement experts, but rarely think of legal experts. And yet, as validated by my own experience many times over, teams that nurture relationships with their "inside lawyer," effectively keeping the equivalent of dedicated inhouse counsel on tap, can give themselves a major advantage in dealing with partners and managing the partnership program business.

***

On a personal note, most of my partnership program experience comes from the legal department in an international supporting entity. As a lawyer helping build international partnership programs, I often wondered where the other lawyers were. Presumably every partner had interests to preserve and expectations to express, but my direct legal counterparts were nowhere to be found. I suppose some of those lawyers preferred to stay behind the scenes, letting their business teams front the positions. Or perhaps their business teams were keeping them out of the loop, believing less is best for success. But it is just as likely that our structuring exercise simply did not rank as a legal matter. No agreement to sign? Then it must not be legal—or let's just say it's not.

On one level, I did not mind. Fewer legal interventions and negotiations made my life easier. However, I was unsure what role the partners thought I was playing. Did they see me as their lawyer, too—much as they assumed other default support from the supporting entity? I may have simply come across as part of the package. On another level, I did mind. As all-encompassing as I sought to be, I was the supporting entity's lawyer. The only interests I could be certain to uphold were those to which I owed my sole duty of loyalty. Even so, I sought to craft partnership programs in the interests of everyone, believing that was also in the interest of the supporting entity.

Now I can make it official. This book is for everyone, for all partners, and especially all their lawyers and supporting architects and construction crew. I hope you embrace this practice area for yourself and for your partners, for more sustainable, efficient, and impactful partnership programs. Where some would let it hang in the balance, you can practice your craft, bring care and creativity, and stay in the balance.

CONCLUDING REMARKS

As I write from my home in our self-sequestered space, with the whole world in various forms of shutdown and lockdown, international collaboration is being tested. We have a renewed clarity about our borderless humanity and the need to work together. Do we also have the partnerships and platforms to do so? Are they sustainable, efficient, and impactful?

Perhaps the greater question is whether they reflect our values and purposes. Collective action needs structure, which needs to rest on shared intentions, agreed expectations, and common understanding. Coordination among partners is organic, and it needs room for context, changing circumstances, and business choices. People are at the center of international partnership programs, in the institutions they serve and the seats they take at the collective table. When we design and define partnership programs, we do that for us, not for the sake of being structured.

We have a collective responsibility to make the most of our coming together. In our ever-changing, ever-challenging world, stability and flexibility bring strength in the balance. It is that striving for balance, across every aspect of partnering, every duality, every trade-off, every dynamic, that marks a healthy and effective venture. We have the privilege to reach across institutions, across borders, across the world to connect and make a difference. We owe it to ourselves and the next generations to practice our partnerships through the art of articulation and alignment, as we architect our collective action.

Washington, D.C.
December 2020

INDEX

ABOUT THE AUTHOR

A true believer in the benefits of inclusive collaboration and the synergies of structured partnerships, Andrea Emily Stumpf is an experienced transactional lawyer who specializes in international partnership programs and trust funds. She supports international partnering initiatives through her business, Structured Partnerships, based in the Washington, DC, area. She provides advice on how to structure and design international partnership programs and their governing bodies, secretariats, and trust funds to a wide variety of clients, including donors, private foundations, non-governmental organizations, academic institutions, trade associations, and multilateral organizations.

Over the years, Andrea has worked with hundreds of partners on hundreds of partnership programs and trust funds across a great variety of initiatives. Her experience draws from more than thirty years in the international, public, and private sectors, including many years as Lead Counsel in the World Bank's Legal Department. She spent most of her time at the World Bank as a focal point for partnership matters, in addition to supporting country operations in Africa and the Middle East. Prior to joining the World Bank, Andrea worked as inhouse counsel for several major global telecommunications companies and before that in the Paris and New York offices of two prominent international law firms.

Andrea holds a JD from Yale Law School and a double major BA with honors in international studies and German from the University of North Carolina at Chapel Hill. Immediately following law school, she clerked for the late Honorable Frank M. Johnson, Jr., a renowned judge on the Eleventh Circuit Court of Appeals.

ABOUT THE ILLUSTRATOR

Still in school, the Illustrator has no shortage of creativity; it's time that is always in short supply. And yet, as she can tell you, the more streamlined the image, the more time it can take. Getting that just-right look, the most expression for the least lines, is the essence of Männlein art. You might not think it, but these little fellows are tricky to draw. And isn't that just like life: What was meant to be easy—and seems so simple—turns out to be especially hard.

Männlein are unique to the Illustrator, her own creation, and that is by design. No one can tell if they were properly drawn; there is no standard to which they need to conform. Instead, they are made to fit the context. That makes them perfect companions for this book.

Made in the USA
Monee, IL
22 March 2021